About This Book

Teach Yourself More Java in 21 Days is an answer to our readers who asked us, "Where do I go from here?" upon completion of the ever popular *Teach Yourself Java in 21 Days.* This book builds on the basic foundations of Java programming taught in its predecessor to include more in-depth coverage of many new and advanced topics including: the AWT, JDBC, JavaBeans, Java security, RMI, CORBA, and much more.

Who Should Read This Book

This book has been written for people who have a basic understanding of Java programming who want to learn more advanced and specialized topics of Java programming. This group includes the following people:

- [ ] People who have completed *Teach Yourself Java in 21 Days*
- [ ] People who have had some other basic introduction to Java programming
- [ ] Java programmers looking for a crash course in learning the newest Java technologies

Anyone who has Java programming experience should be able to find at least few new useful tidbits of information; if you have no Java programming experience at all, however, then you really should be looking at *Teach Yourself Java in 21 Days* or, for those of you who feel that they need a little extra help getting started, *Teach Yourself Java 1.1 Programming in 24 Hours.*

How This Book Is Structured

This book is intended to be read and absorbed over the course of three weeks. During each week, you'll read seven chapters that present concepts related to the Java language.

Conventions

NOTE

> A note box presents interesting information related to the surrounding discussion.

TIP

A tip box offers advice or teaches an easier way to do something.

WARNING

A caution box alerts you to a possible problem and gives you advice on how to avoid it.

NEW TERM

New terms are defined in new term boxes, with the term in italics.

Teach
Yourself
MORE JAVA™
in 21 Days

Teach Yourself
MORE JAVA™
in 21 Days

Michael Morrison
Jerry Ablan

201 West 103rd Street
Indianapolis, Indiana 46290

President Richard K. Swadley
Publisher Jordan Gold
Executive Editor Mark Taber
Indexing Manager Johnna L. VanHoose
Director of Marketing Kelli S. Spencer
Product Marketing Manager Wendy Gilbride
Marketing Coordinator Linda B. Beckwith

Acquisitions Editor
Beverly M. Eppink

Development Editor
Scott D. Meyers

Production Editor
Heather Stith

Copy Editor
Alice Martina Smith

Indexer
Cheryl A. Jackson

Technical Reviewer
Eric Wolfe

Editorial Coordinators
Mandie Rowell
Katie Wise

Technical Edit Coordinator
Lorraine E. Schaffer

Resource Coordinators
Deborah Frisby
Charlotte Clapp

Editorial Assistants
Carol Ackerman
Andi Richter
Rhonda Tinch-Mize
Karen Williams

Cover Designer
Aren Howell

Cover Illustrator
Eric Lindley

Book Designer
Gary Adair

Copy Writer
David Reichwein

Production Team Supervisors
Brad Chinn
Andrew Stone

Production
Elizabeth Deeter
Jennifer Dierdorff
Tim Osborn
Ian Smith

Overview

Foreword   xvii

Introduction   xxi

Week 1 at a Glance   1

Day 1   Applets and Applications: A Java 1.1 Refresher Course   3

2   Maximizing the Delegation Event Model   19

3   Creating Custom Components   41

4   Foundation Classes and Java Frameworks   71

5   Introduction to JavaBeans   105

6   Using JavaBeans Effectively   121

7   Networking with Java   145

Week 2 at a Glance   165

Day 8   Introduction to Database Programming with JDBC   167

9   Advanced Database Programming with JDBC   189

10   Internationalization: Parlez Vous Java?   213

11   Reflection: Looking Inside   239

12   Object Serialization   253

13   Remote Method Invocation   267

14   Java and CORBA   287

Week 3 at a Glance   319

Day 15   Introduction to the Java Web Server and Servlets   321

16   Programming with the Java Servlet Development Kit   339

17   Working with Java Archives   361

18   Introduction to Digital Security and the Java Security API   373

19   Creating Signed Java Objects   391

20   Things You Can't Do in Java: Using the Java Native Interface   407

21   Things to Come in Java 1.2   441

Index   453

Contents

Week 1 At a Glance   **1**

Day 1   Applets and Applications: A Java 1.1 Refresher Course   3

Bringing Applets and Applications Together 4
    The main() Method 5
    A Frame with a View 5
    A Safe Place to Execute 6
A Minimal Applet 7
    Controlling Applet Execution 7
    Embedding an Applet in a Web Page 8
    Testing the Minimal Applet 9
A Minimal Application 10
    Application Versus Applet Execution 12
    Testing the Minimal Application 12
A Minimal Appletcation 13
    Testing the Appletcation 15
    Pondering the Appletcation 16
Summary 17
Q&A 17

2   Maximizing the Delegation Event Model   19

Revisiting the Delegation Event Model 20
    Low-Level Events 21
    Semantic Events 25
    Event Delivery 27
    Event Adapters 30
Using Event Adapters and Inner Classes 31
Defining Custom Events 33
Summary 39
Q&A 40

3   Creating Custom Components   41

Types of 3-D Borders 42
    Lowered Borders 42
    Raised Borders 43
    Grooved Borders 43
    Ridged Borders 44
Creating a Custom Component 44
    The BorderStyle interface 45
    Adding Methods to Your Madness 45
Your Custom Component: BorderPanel 46
    Creating the BorderPanel Class 46
    Constructing a BorderPanel 49

Smoke and Mirrors: Creating the 3-D Border Illusion 49
    Drawing 3-D Borders 49
    Testing the BorderPanel 53
    The ImagePanel Class 54
    Testing ImagePanel 58
Creating the TabPanel Class 60
    Designing the TabPanel Class 61
    Managing the Panes 61
    Managing the Tabs 62
    Drawing the Tabs 63
    Putting Them All Together 66
    Testing TabPanel 67
Summary 69
Q&A 69

4   Foundation Classes and Java Frameworks   71

JFC : The Future of Java Class Libraries 72
    Lightweight Component Framework 74
    Delegation Event Model 75
    Printing 75
    Clipboard Data Transfer 75
    Desktop Colors 75
    Mouseless Operation 75
    Other Miscellaneous Goodies 76
The JFC to Come 76
    Pluggable Look and Feel 77
    Lightweight Component Suite 77
    Drag-and-drop 78
    Advanced 2-D Graphics 78
    Accessibility for the Physically Handicapped 78
Swinging with the JFC 79
    Pluggable Look and Feel 79
    The MVC Architecture 80
    The Swing Component Suite 81
    The SwingSet: A Swing Tour de Force 82
Netscape's IFC 86
    Views and Components 88
    Choosers 90
    Windows 91
    Drawing with the IFC 91
    An IFC Sample Applet 92
Microsoft's AFC 100
    Application Components 100
    Graphics Effects 102
    Win32 Resource Support 102
    CAB File Services 102
Summary 102
Q&A 103

5   Introduction to JavaBeans   105

The JavaBeans API Revisited 106

Property Management 106

Introspection 107

Event Handling 108

Persistence 108

Application Builder Tool Support.. 108

Usage Scenarios 109

Using Beans with an Application Builder Tool 109

Using Beans in Handwritten Code 110

Using Beans Through a Bridge 111

The Basic Structure of a Bean 111

What Constitutes a Bean? 113

Must Be Instantiable 113

Must Have a Default Constructor 113

Must Be Serializable 114

Must Follow JavaBeans Design Patterns 114

Must Use the Delegation Event Model 115

Standard AWT Components as Beans 115

Converting Your Own Components to Beans 115

Supporting Serialization 116

Packaging the Beans... 118

Summary 119

Q&A 119

6   Using JavaBeans Effectively   121

The JavaBeans Development Kit (BDK) 122

The BeanBox Test Container.. 122

Sample Beans and Source Code 123

API Source Code 123

JavaBeans Tutorial 123

Using Beans in the BeanBox Test Container 123

Working with Beans in the BeanBox 127

Wiring Beans Together with Events.. 129

Using Runtime Mode 130

Saving Your Work 130

Testing Your Own Beans in the BeanBox 131

Testing the `BorderPanel` Bean 131

Testing the `ImagePanel` Bean 133

Saving a Bean for Later 134

Using Beans the Old-Fashioned Way 134

Creating Beans Programmatically 135

Customizing Beans Programmatically 136

Connecting Beans Programmatically...................................... 137

Testing Your Own Beans the Old-Fashioned Way 137

Using Beans Through a Bridge 140
Bridging Properties 141
Bridging Methods 141
Bridging Events 142
Summary 142
Q&A 143

7 Networking with Java 145
E-mail and the Internet 146
MIME Encoding 146
Internet Text Messages 146
Reading Mail from a Server 147
Reading Mail with Java 148
Creating the POP3Reader class 149
Testing the POP3Reader Class 156
Sending Mail to a Server 157
Simple Mail Transfer Protocol 157
Sending Mail with Java 158
Creating the SMTPSender Class 158
Testing the SMTPSender Class 162
Summary 163
Q&A 163

Week 2 At a Glance 165

Day 8 Introduction to Database Programming with JDBC 167
What Is a Database? 168
Database Terminology 168
Database Locations 170
Local and Remote 170
Tiering 1-2-3 171
Database Access Methods 172
Native Drivers 173
ODBC 173
SQL 174
JDBC in Depth 178
The DriverManager Class 179
The Driver Class 179
The Connection Class 181
The Statement Class 183
The ResultSet Class 184
A JDBC Sample Program 185
The Future for JDBC 187
Summary 187
Q&A 187

9   **Advanced Database Programming with JDBC**   **189**
    Making JDBC Easier to Use 190
        The `Connector` Interface Methods 190
        The Connector Interface Code 192
    Creating New Classes 193
        The `DBConnector` Class 193
        The `ODBCConnector` Class 197
    A Simple JDBC Retrieval Program 198
        The Database 199
        The User Interface 199
        Initializing the Database 202
    Enhancing the Simple Application 205
        Providing a Placeholder 205
        Clearing the Screen 205
        Finding Data 206
        Saving Data 208
        Deleting Data 209
    Summary 210
    Q&A 211

10 **Internationalization: Parlez Vous Java?**   **213**
    Understanding Global Programming 214
    Internationalization and Localization 215
        Program Data 217
        User Data 217
        System Data 217
    Working with Locales 217
        The `Locale` Class 217
        Creating Locales 221
        Getting Information about a Locale 222
    Using Resource Bundles 223
    Handling and Formatting International Data 224
        Numbers 225
        Dates and Times 226
        Text Messages 227
        Text Collation 228
        Text Boundaries 228
    The `WorldExplorer` Sample Applet 229
        Developing the Main Applet Code 230
        Bundling the Locale-Sensitive Data 234
    Summary 237
    Q&A 237

11 **Reflection: Looking Inside**   **239**
    Reflection Basics 240
        Applications Requiring Public Member Access 240
        Applications Requiring Complete Member Access 241

The Significance of Reflection 241
    The Role of Reflection in JavaBeans 241
    The Role of Reflection in Java Serialization 242
The Reflection API 243
    The `Class` Class 244
    The `Member` Interface 245
    The `Field` Class 245
    The `Method` Class 246
    The `Constructor` Class 247
    The `Array` Class 247
    The `Modifier` Class 247
Reflection and Security 248
`ClassDissector` : A Complete Reflection Example 249
Summary 252
Q&A 252

12 Object Serialization   **253**

Introduction to Serialization 254
    Copies of Objects and Clones, Oh My! 254
    Persistence 255
    Input and Output Streams 256
    Object Streams 257
Serializing Your Own Classes 259
    The `Serializable` Interface 259
    The `Externalizable` Interface 261
Protecting Data from Serialization 262
    Making `transient` Data 262
    Making `static` Data 262
    Implementing the `Externalizable` Interface 262
    Not Implementing the `Serializable` Interface 262
Versioning Serialized Objects 263
    Generating Version Numbers 264
Summary 265
Q&A 265

13 Remote Method Invocation   **267**

Distributed Computing with Java 268
    RMI and CORBA 269
    A Network of Objects 269
Deep Inside RMI 272
    Remote Objects 272
    Stubs and Skeletons 274
    Generating Stubs and Skeletons 275
Passing and Returning Data 276
    Serialization Basics 277
Designing an RMI Application 277
    Minimizing Object Lookups 277
    Callbacks 279
    Security 279

A Simple RMI Application 280
Summary 285
Q&A 285

14   Java and CORBA   287

The World Wide Object Web 288
CORBA: A Whirlwind Tour 289
    The Object Management Group (OMG) 290
    CORBA Defined in One Long Paragraph 290
Why Use Java with CORBA? 297
Selecting a Java ORB 298
    Web Browser Support for CORBA 298
    An Evaluation of Java Object Request Brokers 299
A Basic Java/CORBA Application 303
    Building `CapitalQuery` Using VisiBroker 303
    Building `CapitalQuery` as a Java Applet 310
Comparing DCOM to CORBA 314
Comparing Java RMI to CORBA 315
Summary 316
Q&A 316

Week 3 At a Glance   319

Day 15   Introduction to the Java Web Server and Servlets   321

The Java Web Server 322
    Installing the Java Web Server 323
    Administering the Java Web Server 324
Isn't a Servlet a Napkin? 327
    Servlet Security 329
The Java Servlet API 330
    The Servlet API Classes 331
    The `Servlet` Interface 332
    Implementing the `Servlet` Interface 333
Summary 336
Q&A 337

16   Programming with the Java Servlet Development Kit   339

The Servlet Life Cycle 340
    Loading Servlets 340
    Running Servlets 341
    Servicing Requests 345
    Shutting Down 347
Servlet Types 347
    The `GenericServlet` Class 347
    The `HttpServlet` Class 347
Writing a Servlet 351
    Servlet Design 352
    Servlet Implementation 353
    An Alternative Servlet That Uses the `GET` Method 358

Summary 358
Q&A 358

17 Working with Java Archives **361**

Understanding Java Archive Basics 362
Fewer HTTP Transactions 362
Efficient File Storage 362
Security.. 362
Platform Independence 363
Backward Compatibility 363
High Extensibility 363
Understanding Manifest Files 363
Using the JAR Utility 365
Examining an Existing Archive 366
Creating a New Archive 368
Extracting Files from an Existing Archive 369
Using JAR Files 370
Understanding JAR Files and JavaBeans 371
Summary 372
Q&A 372

18 Introduction to Digital Security and the Java Security API **373**

Cryptography 101 374
Conventional Encryption... 375
Public-Key Encryption 375
Applet Authentication 379
Access Control Lists 380
The Java Security API 380
Providers 381
Keys 382
Digital Signatures 383
Certificates 386
Message Digests 386
Access Control Lists 388
Summary 388
Q&A 388

19 Creating Signed Java Objects **391**

Using the javakey Security Tool 392
Identities and Signers 392
Keys 394
Certificates 396
Options 398
Signing JAR Files with javakey 400
Becoming a Signer 400
Generating a Key Pair 401
Generating a Certificate 402
Signing a JAR File 403

Summary 405
Q&A 406

20   Things You Can't Do in Java: Using the Java Native Interface   407

JNI Basics 408
The When and Why of Native Code 409
    Reaching Beyond the Java Environment 410
    Improving Performance 410
    Interfacing to Legacy Code 411
The Cost of Native Code 411
    Platform Dependence 411
    Security Woes 411
    Method Call Overhead 412
Two Sides of the Fence 412
    The Java Side of the Fence 412
    The Native Side of the Fence 414
Generating Native Headers with `javah` 415
Mapping Java Data Types 419
Accessing Java Information from Native Code 420
    Identifying Java Information 420
    Accessing Java Fields 421
    Calling Java Object Methods 429
    Accessing Java Objects 431
Summary 438
Q&A 439

21   Things to Come in Java 1.2   441

The Future of Java 442
Java Core Enhancements 443
    Java Foundation Classes (JFC) 443
    Java Commerce 443
    Java Interface Description Language (IDL) 445
    JavaBeans Glasgow 446
Standard Java Extensions 447
    Java Naming and Directory Interface (JNDI) 447
    Java Media 447
    Java Management 449
Other Java Technologies 449
    PersonalJava 449
    EmbeddedJava 450
    JavaBeans Migration Tools 450
Summary 451
Q&A 452

Index   453

Foreword

I envy writers who can write about subjects that don't change, or at least, that don't change very much. Writing about traveling Europe on $5 a month, I'd have to revise my books only once a year or so. If I wrote about, say, physics or chemistry, I might need an extra chapter every 10 years to bring the book current. And if I were Martha Stewart, I could write about making a croquembouche and not have to worry in the slightest that croquembouche 2.0 will come out and make all my work obsolete.

That's the life.

But I write computer books, and computer books, with few exceptions, change a lot. Take, for example, a popular little book called *Teach Yourself Java in 21 Days* that Charles L. Perkins and I wrote in late 1995. At the time, Java was the new hot topic, and *Teach Yourself Java* was one of the first books out on the market about it. Java, in 1995, was a fairly small system, limited primarily to simple programs that could be embedded in Web pages. Covering most of it in 500 pages and 21 chapters was not overly difficult, even if we assumed that our readers didn't have a lot of experience in programming.

But times change, and they change especially much when the Internet is involved. These days Java has grown to be a much larger, much more complex system as the months have passed. With the growth of the core Java system as well as the appearance of a number of other class libraries developed by different organizations, there's little you cannot do with Java these days.

Teach Yourself Java in 21 Days has gone through numerous revisions as Java has changed and, despite the huge number of competing Java books, continues to be one of the more popular ones for beginning Java programmers. But what has become apparent to us (the original authors and those that have helped with revisions) is that Java itself has grown so much that 21 days is no longer enough time to cover it all, at least, not if we want to start at the beginning.

We could turn *Teach Yourself Java* into a much longer book (*Teach Yourself Java in 243 Days?*). We could abandon its focus on beginners and compress all the beginner stuff into a couple of pages. But we think a better idea is to leave *Teach Yourself Java* for the simpler, more basic topics and to create a companion book for the advanced topics that more experienced programmers need.

Teach Yourself More Java in 21 Days picks up where *Teach Yourself Java in 21 Days* left off. The authors, Michael Morrison and Jerry Ablan, are both experienced Java programmers themselves. If you need to do more with Java than just applets, if you want to know more than the syntax of a for loop, if you've got to integrate huge amounts of Java code into an enterprise system using distributed databases or CORBA—you need this book. Even if you haven't read *Teach Yourself Java in 21 Days*, you'll find something of use in this book.

Enjoy!

Laura Lemay

September 1997

Dedication

To Mahsheed, who I never thought I would be so lucky to find.

—Michael Morrison

To Cassandra, my little wookie bear.

—Jerry Ablan

Acknowledgments

I would like to thank Beverly Eppink immensely for rolling with the punches as I consistently missed every deadline. I'm all out of excuses for the next project!

I would also like to thank everyone who made our first home such a wonderful reality: Reese L. Smith III and Steve Smith for giving us such a generous deal, Keith Nash for his steady hand, Derrick Hooie for his size 13 stomping finesse, Mehrdad Gamshad for his parquet wrecking abilities, Safoura Moainipour for her wallpaper stripping expertise, Amiri Gamshad for his green thumb, and last but most definitely not least, my mom and dad for all the love, sweat, and guidance.

—Michael Morrison

I'd like to thank the people at Sams, Beverly Eppink most importantly. She has been my friend and confidant for two years now. If it weren't for her, I wouldn't be writing. Thanks Beverly for getting me involved in this project. I'd also like to thank Scott Meyers for his excellent development of the material and Heather Stith for her diligent grammatical strictness. A special thanks goes out to Kim Hannel. And thanks to the rest of the Sams.net team who make these books possible.

I'd like to thank the people at MindBuilder, LLC for their support and encouragement through the arduous writing period. Thanks to Mark Challenger, Jim Vitiello, and Tony Karwatowicz. I'd also like to thank my close friends. Because I was writing, I couldn't socialize too much. So thanks to Tom and Karen, George and Alex, Tom and Nancy (and Sean!), and Jim Burke.

Finally, and as usual, I'd like to thank my wife and daughter. I promised them that I would not write any more. I broke my promise, and they didn't kill me. Kathryn helped me and supported me. Thanks to both of you, I love you this much (arms spread wide)!

—Jerry Ablan

About the Authors

Lead Authors

Michael Morrison (www.thetribe.com) is a writer and skateboarder living in Nashville, Tennessee. Michael is the author of various Java and Internet technology books, along with a few magazine articles and a Web-based JavaBeans course (www.digitalthink.com). Michael is currently busy constructing a koi pond in his backyard so he will have company while his wife is busy working a real job. The things you do for love! Michael wrote Chapters 1, 2, 4, 5, 6, 10, 11, 17, 18, 19, 20, and 21.

Jerry Ablan (munster@mcs.net) is the Director of Technology for MindBuilder, LLC (http://www.mindbuilder.com). It is a leader in the interactive multimedia training management area. Jerry lives near Chicago with his wife Kathryn, daughter Cassandra, their dog (Flatus the Great), three cats (Uncle Pat, T.C., and Kato), and a tank full of fish. Jerry is an avid gamer and can be found playing almost any real-time strategy online war game, but probably Ultima Online.

Jerry is the author of *Developing Intranet Applications with Java* from Sams.net and is the co-author of the *Web Site Administrator's Survival Guide* from Sams.net. He also was a contributing author to: *Special Edition: Using Java* (Que), *Platinum Edition Using CGI, HTML, and Java* (Que); and *Java 1.1 Unleashed* (Sams.net). Jerry wrote the Introduction and Chapters 3, 7, 8, 9, 12, 15, and 16.

Contributing Authors

Bryan Morgan is a software developer with TASC, Inc. in Fort Walton Beach, FL. He has experience in both traditional client/server programming and Web applications development using Java and CORBA. He was the lead author of *Visual J++ Unleashed* and co-author of several other books for Sams Publishing, including *Java Developer's Reference* and *Teach Yourself SQL in 14 Days*. He holds a bachelor's degree in electrical engineering from Clemson University. Bryan wrote Chapter 14.

George Reese (borg@imaginary.com) holds a degree in philosophy from Bates College in Lewiston, Maine. He currently works as a lead systems analyst for Carlson Marketing Group's Internet and intranet development team. In addition, he does consulting through Caribou Lake Software where he markets a Java persistence library. His Java writing has appeared in several Sams titles as well as in articles for the *Java Developer's Journal*. He was the creator of the first JDBC driver, the mSQL-JDBC driver for the MiniSQL database engine. George lives in Bloomington, MN with his two cats Gypsy and Misty. George wrote Chapter 13.

Tell Us What You Think!

As a reader, you are the most important critic and commentator of our books. We value your opinion and want to know what we're doing right, what we could do better, what areas you'd like to see us publish in, and any other words of wisdom you're willing to pass our way. You can help us make strong books that meet your needs and give you the computer guidance you require.

Do you have access to the World Wide Web? Then check out our site at http://www.mcp.com.

NOTE
> If you have a technical question about this book, call the technical support line at 317-581-3833 or send e-mail to support@mcp.com.

As the team leader of the group that created this book, I welcome your comments. You can fax, e-mail, or write me directly to let me know what you did or didn't like about this book—as well as what we can do to make our books stronger. Here's the information:

Fax: 317-581-4669

E-mail: newtech_mgr@sams.mcp.com

Mail: Mark Taber
          Comments Department
          Sams Publishing
          201 W. 103rd Street
          Indianapolis, IN 46290

Introduction

by Jerry Ablan

The Java revolution has been a wild and bumpy ride for many of us. Back in the old days, around 1996, Java was just another name for coffee, but Sun Microsystems slapped the programming world in the face. They introduced a programming language called Java, named after that steamy island in the Pacific. Java is, as Sun claims, a simple, object-oriented, network-savvy, interpreted, robust, secure, architecture-neutral, portable, high-performance, multithreaded, dynamic language. What a mouthful!

What Java really is is a very cool language. It has all the benefits of C++ without the language features that make it hard to learn and debug, such as pointers and multiple inheritance. Java also forces you to write programs in an object-oriented manner.

Java took the world by storm. Everyone was jumping on the Java bandwagon. It was then that Laura Lemay and Charles Perkins wrote *Teach Yourself Java in 21 Days*, a book that will live in infamy. This best-selling book introduced the world to Java programming. If you wanted to learn how to program in Java, it was the book to buy.

But Java has evolved in the last year. The latest release, as of this writing, is 1.1, and many things are different. *Teach Yourself Java in 21 Days* has been updated, but it only takes you to a certain point. That's where this book comes in. *Teach Yourself More Java in 21 Days* picks up where *Teach Yourself Java in 21 Days* leaves off. You'll learn about the advanced features of the Java language in the same easy-to-read style as the first book.

How This Book Is Organized

Teach Yourself More Java in 21 Days covers the advanced features of the Java language that were not included in *Teach Yourself Java in 21 Days*. The material is separated into three separate weeks, each week covering a general topic area. As you progress through the book, each day's topic is more advanced than the last.

In the first week, you'll focus on user interface and the Java Abstract Windowing Toolkit:

- ☐ Day 1 is a refresher course. It discusses Java 1.1 and the differences between it and Java 1.0.
- ☐ On Day 2, you'll learn how to take advantage of Java 1.1's delegation event model.
- ☐ On Day 3, you'll discover how to create custom user interface components.
- ☐ On Day 4, you'll learn all about Java application frameworks like the Internet Foundation Classes.
- ☐ Day 5 is a key day. You'll learn all about JavaBeans.
- ☐ With your new knowledge of JavaBeans, you'll learn how to maximize that knowledge and create awesome reusable components on Day 6.

☐ On Day 7, you'll learn some advanced networking concepts with Java. In particular, you'll create some classes that send and receive e-mail.

Week 2 centers on JDBC, reflection, internationalization, and serialization:

☐ Day 8 serves as an introduction to the Java Database Connectivity, or JDBC, API. With JDBC, you can make your applets and applications read and write data from almost any database.

☐ On Day 9, you'll build on your JDBC knowledge and create a fully functional data entry application.

☐ On Day 10, you'll learn how to make your Java programs speak foreign languages. This day is dedicated to internationalization.

☐ Day 11 introduces reflection. Reflection allows your Java programs to interrogate other classes and find out what's inside of them.

☐ Day 12 focuses on object serialization, which is the process of reading and writing objects to a data stream. That stream can be a disk file, a database, or even another computer over a network.

☐ On Day 13, you'll learn all about Remote Method Invocation or RMI. RMI allows your objects to invoke classes and methods on other machines.

☐ On Day 14, you'll learn all about Java and CORBA. CORBA is a standard used to invoke classes and methods on other machines.

Week 3 includes several advanced topics that are very interesting:

☐ Day 15 introduces you to the world of the Java Web Server and Java servlets. Servlets are server-side applets that provide services for the calling Web browser.

☐ Day 16 builds on the coverage from Day 15 and teaches you how to program servlets with the Java Servlet Development Kit.

☐ Day 17 introduces you to the JAR file format. A JAR file is a special archive that contains a set of classes. Archiving enables you to send classes over a network in one shot instead of sending each class individually.

☐ Day 18 introduces you to digital security and the Java Security API. This API allows you to create secure applets and applications.

☐ Day 19 builds on the Day 18 discussions and teaches you how to create signed objects. Signed objects are considered secure and enable your applets and applications to be trusted.

☐ Day 20 delves deep into the Java Native Interface. When you can't do something in Java, you have to use another language. To interface with Java, however, you use the Java Native Interface.

☐ On Day 21, you'll learn about some of the things to come in Java 1.2.

WEEK
1

1
2
3
4
5
6
7

At a Glance

☐ Applets and Applications: A Java 1.1 Refresher Course
  Bringing applets and applications together
  Creating a minimal applet
  Creating a minimal application
  Creating a minimal *appletcation*
☐ Maximizing the Delegation Event Model
  The basic concepts critical to understanding the delegation
  event model
  Using event adapters with inner classes to clean up event
  processing
  Defining custom event types

☐ Creating Custom Components

The basics of creating custom components

Creating a simple component that provides a three-dimensional appearance

Creating a tabbed folder component

☐ Foundation Classes and Java Frameworks

JavaSoft's JFC

Netscape's IFC

Microsoft's AFC

☐ Introduction to JavaBeans

The JavaBeans API

The basic structure of a Bean

Standard AWT components as Beans

Converting your own components to Beans

☐ Using JavaBeans Effectively

Using the JavaBeans Development Kit, or BDK

Testing Beans in the BeanBox

Using Beans through the ActiveX Bridge

☐ Networking with Java

The finer points of Java network programming

How to implement a POP3 e-mail reading class

How to implement an SMTP e-mail sending class

Day **1**

Applets and Applications: A Java 1.1 Refresher Course

by Michael Morrison

The first lesson in this book begins with the two fundamental pursuits of Java programming: applets and applications. Because you are expected to already have some knowledge of Java applets and applications, this lesson sets the tone for the remainder of the book by showing you how to seamlessly develop applets and applications from one set of source code. You learn in this lesson that you don't need to worry much about whether you are developing an applet to be executed in a Web browser or an application to be executed by itself. The lesson covers the following topics:

- ☐ Bringing applets and applications together
- ☐ Creating a minimal applet

☐ Creating a minimal application

☐ Creating a minimal *appletcation*

This lesson is designed to give you a jump start and demonstrate that using Java is more than just creating classes and reading API documentation. This lesson is also a good refresher course just in case you are a little rusty with your Java 1.1 programming skills.

Bringing Applets and Applications Together

Most introductory Java books begin by showing how to create a skeletal Java applet or application, which is an applet or application that contains a minimal amount of overhead to execute properly. This lesson starts the same way, but with a different goal in mind. The goal here is to show how you can merge applet and application code to create a single Java bytecode executable, an *appletcation* if you will, that is capable of running as an applet or an application, depending on the context it is executing in. In other words, if you place the executable in a browser, it will run as an applet, but if the class is executed in a stand-alone Java interpreter, it will run as a graphical application. The interesting thing is that both the applet and the application rely on the exact same code to perform basic functions such as drawing themselves.

You may be wondering how this can be possible, considering the fact that a big distinction is always made between applets and applications. Although the two certainly are different in some ways, they both accomplish roughly the same thing.

Keep in mind that I'm referring to graphical applications when I make comparisons to applets. Command-line applications are a different animal altogether because they have no graphical user interface. For this reason, the discussion here focuses on graphical applications as they relate to inherently graphical applets.

To fully understand how you can treat applets and applications as one, you must be sure of their differences:

☐ An application requires a `main()` method; an applet does not.

☐ An application must create its own frame window; an applet gets its window from its parent Web browser.

☐ An application has few security restrictions, but an unsigned Java applet has very strict restrictions, such as not being able to write files.

NOTE

> Unsigned Java applets are those that have no digital security signature; digital signatures are used as a security measure to indicate that an applet hasn't been tampered with and is therefore safe to use. Signed Java applets can circumvent the stringent security constraints imposed by the applet security model. You learn about applet security and how to digitally sign applets in Week 3.

The following sections examine each of the differences between an applet and an application in a little more detail to clarify what you can accomplish by bridging the two.

The `main()` Method

Like C or C++ applications, all Java applications require a `main()` method to get things going. The `main()` method in a Java application is the first method called for the application; it creates an instance of the application class. How can the `main()` method, which is a member of the application class, be executed before an instance of the class is created? The reason is that the `main()` method is static, which means that it has class scope; in other words, the `main()` method is specifically designed to be used to construct an object of the class in which it resides. The Java interpreter automatically calls the `main()` method, which results in the creation of an application object. From that point, the application object takes over.

Unlike applications, applets don't require a `main()` method. Why is that? The Web browser in which the applet is embedded provides much of the overhead for an applet, including the start-up overhead that the `main()` method provides in applications. More specifically, Web browsers provide a frame window for an applet to display itself in. As a result, the applet only needs to provide an `Applet`-derived class, which is very much like a normal AWT component. The frame window itself is another difference between applets and applications, but it also helps illustrate why an applet doesn't need a `main()` method.

The bottom line with applets is that they have the luxury of a parent Web browser that gives them a certain level of support that applications must provide on their own. The `main()` method is an example of such support; it provides a place for an application to create its graphical user interface and get up and running. An applet, on the other hand, is started automatically by its parent Web browser.

A Frame with a View

You have learned that an application requires a *frame window* to house its graphical user interface, and an applet has a frame window provided by its parent Web browser. This difference is the second major distinction between applets and applications because an application must handle the task of explicitly providing a frame window. Granted, providing a frame window is not exactly a complicated task, but it is a task that applets don't have to be concerned with.

> **NEW TERM** *frame window:* A platform-specific window with a title, menu bar, close boxes, resize handles, and other window features.

Application classes typically are derived from the Frame class, which means that the main application window is itself a frame window, much like the Web browser framing an applet. The primary difference between the two frame windows is that an applet must share window space with other Web page elements, but an application has complete control over its frame window space. This control gives applications the capability to create and manage their own menus, along with being able to resize and move the frame window. In this way, applications have somewhat of an advantage over applets in terms of window management and screen real estate.

Even though frame windows are closely linked to graphical applications, applications don't automatically know to quit executing when their frame window is closed. For this reason, applications require some additional code to tell them to exit properly when their frame window is closed. Again, applets don't require this type of code because a parent Web browser manages their frame window.

A Safe Place to Execute

The last difference between applets and applications is security; applets are required by default to conform to a very stringent security model that limits them in a variety of ways, but applications have no security limitations. Up until Java 1.1, this distinction between applets and applications was very significant because applets had no way to dodge the security limitations. However, Java 1.1 ushered in digital security signatures, which allow applets to be digitally signed and therefore deemed safe. Digitally signed applets are also referred to as *trusted applets.* The stringent applet security model is not applied to digitally signed applets, so these applets can do things that applets of the past could not do. For example, a digitally signed applet can write files.

> **NEW TERM** *trusted applet:* An applet that has been digitally signed for security authentication purposes.

Now that you have a solid understanding of the differences between applets and applications, you're ready to review how each is implemented.

A Minimal Applet

Very little code is needed to create an applet with a minimal level of functionality. By dissecting such an applet, you can clearly see the small amount of code required to get an applet up and running. Listing 1.1 contains the source code for a very minimal applet. You can find the complete source code and executable for the minimal applet on the companion Web site at http://www.mcp.com/info/1-57521/1-57521-347-8.

Listing 1.1. The MinApplet class source code.

```
 1: import java.applet.*;
 2:
 3: public class MinApplet extends Applet {
 4:   public void init() {
 5:     System.out.println("Applet initialized.");
 6:   }
 7:
 8:   public void start() {
 9:     System.out.println("Applet started.");
10:   }
11:
12:   public void stop() {
13:     System.out.println("Applet stopped.");
14:   }
15:
16:   public void destroy() {
17:     System.out.println("Applet destroyed.");
18:   }
19: }
```

The MinApplet class extends the Applet class (Line 3), which is a strict requirement for all applets. The Applet class makes it possible for applets to integrate with a parent Web browser. Beyond extending the Applet class, an applet need not do anything else if you don't want it to. In this example, I went ahead and implemented four methods that play an important role in the execution of applets: init(), start(), stop(), and destroy(). All of these methods are called automatically and are a useful place to put applet start-up and clean-up code.

Controlling Applet Execution

The init() method is called to initialize an applet whenever the Web page containing an applet is loaded. Likewise, the start() method is called whenever the Web page containing an applet is opened. Notice that I'm making a distinction here between loading a Web page and opening a Web page. This distinction is important in terms of applets because an applet's init() method is only called the first time a containing Web page is loaded, but the applet's start() method is called any time the page is opened. In other words, the first time a Web page containing an applet is visited, both the init() and start() methods are called;

subsequent visits to the Web page in the same browser session result in only the start() method being called.

The destroy() and stop() methods play a complementary role to the init() and start() methods. The stop() method is called whenever a user leaves the Web page containing the applet, and the destroy() method is called when the Web browser removes the Web page from memory. The stop() method acts to pause an applet, but the destroy() method releases an applet's resources and completely gets rid of an applet from memory.

You might be thinking that it seems redundant to have both destroy() and stop() methods, or init() and start() methods for that matter. The significance of these methods has to do with the fact that an applet is controlled by the Web browser it is executing within. Because an applet doesn't know what's going on with its frame window, the Web browser, the browser must let the applet know when the applet can be initialized and executed. The Web browser does this by making a call to the init() method, followed by a call to the start() method.

Just as an applet doesn't know when it can be initialized and executed, it doesn't know when it is supposed to quit running and let go of its resources. Again the Web browser steps in and tells the applet what to do by making a call to the stop() method, followed by a call to the destroy() method. If the user leaves a Web page containing an applet, the Web browser tells an applet to pause by calling the stop() method without calling the destroy() method. If the user returns to the page, the browser tells the applet to continue by calling start(). This process can continue until the browser decides to clean up the page containing the applet, in which case it calls the destroy() method.

Embedding an Applet in a Web Page

Because you're going to be testing the applet in Listing 1.1, this section quickly covers the technique used to embed an applet in a Web page. Applets are embedded in Web pages by using the <APPLET> tag, which is an HTML tag specifically designed for Java applets. You must provide three attributes with the <APPLET> tag: CODE, WIDTH, and HEIGHT. The CODE attribute indicates the name of the applet class file. The WIDTH and HEIGHT attributes indicate the size of the window that contains the applet; this information is important because applets have to spatially coexist with other Web page elements such as text and graphics. Listing 1.2 contains the HTML code for a very simple Web page containing the MinApplet applet.

Listing 1.2. The HTML source code for the Minimal Applet Web page.

```
<TITLE>Minimum Applet</TITLE>
<HR>
<APPLET CODE="MinApplet.class" WIDTH=200 HEIGHT=200>
</APPLET>
```

Testing the Minimal Applet

To test the minimal applet, you can use the appletviewer utility that ships with the Java Development Kit or a Java-enabled Web browser. I suggest using the appletviewer utility so that you can watch the messages generated by the `init()`, `start()`, `stop()`, and `destroy()` methods. Type the following command to execute the applet in the appletviewer:

```
appletviewer MinApplet.html
```

NOTE

Because the minimal applet presented here doesn't rely on any Java 1.1-specific features, it will execute fine on any Java-enabled Web browser, even though it was compiled using the JDK 1.1 compiler. Unfortunately, the same can't be said of the minimal application you learn about in the next section. Because the application uses the Java 1.1 AWT event handling approach, you'll have to use the Java 1.1 interpreter to execute it.

As the applet is loaded and started (see Figure 1.1), the following messages appear in the command-line window:

```
Applet initialized.
Applet started.
```

NOTE

If you are using a Java 1.1-enabled Web browser instead of the JDK appletviewer utility, you'll need to display the Java console window. For example, in Netscape Communicator, you would select Java Console from the Communicator menu.

Figure 1.1.

The minimal Java applet executing in the appletviewer.

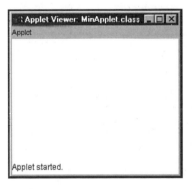

NOTE

> You may be wondering why an applet can run in the appletviewer, when I've spent the better part of this lesson telling you that an applet requires overhead provided by a Web browser. This operation is possible because the appletviewer functions as a minimal Web browser of sorts. It provides the same overhead applets require of Web browsers, but it doesn't display other HTML elements such as text and images.

When you close the appletviewer session and terminate the applet, the following messages appear in the command-line window:

```
Applet stopped.
Applet destroyed.
```

The appletviewer utility includes commands under the Applet menu for testing the stopping and starting of an applet, among other things. Try out some of these commands and notice the messages generated by the applet in response to each.

A Minimal Application

If the applet discussion was a little too much review for you, then bear with me just a little longer because you still need to learn about some application nuances. If you've never written a graphical Java application, you may be surprised to find out that it requires a little more work than an applet. You might think an applet would be more trouble because it is executing within a Web browser, but the Web browser's support is what makes applets easier to develop. Even a minimal application requires a fair amount of code.

Check out Listing 1.3, which contains the source code for a minimal graphical application. You can find the complete source code and executable for the minimal graphical application on the companion Web site for this book.

Listing 1.3. The MinApplication class.

```
 1: import java.awt.*;
 2: import java.awt.event.*;
 3:
 4: public class MinApplication extends Frame {
 5:   public static void main(String[] args) {
 6:     System.out.println("Calling main() method.");
 7:     MinApplication app = new MinApplication("Minimum Application");
 8:     app.setSize(200, 200);
 9:     app.show();
10:   }
11:
12:   public MinApplication(String name) {
13:     super(name);
```

```
14:      System.out.println("Creating application object.");
15:      addWindowListener(new MyWindowAdapter());
16:   }
17:
18:   class MyWindowAdapter extends WindowAdapter {
19:     public void windowClosing(WindowEvent e) {
20:       System.out.println("Frame window closing.");
21:       System.exit(0);
22:     }
23:   }
24: }
```

The MinApplication class extends the Frame class (Line 4), because, as you learned earlier in the lesson, applications are required to provide their own frame window. Next comes the static main() method that was discussed earlier, which is where execution begins in the application. The main() method creates a MinApplication object (Line 7), and then sets the size of the frame window with a call to setSize() (Line 8). The call to the show() method (Line 9) is necessary to make the frame window visible.

The constructor for MinApplication first calls its parent class constructor, super(), and passes the frame window name as the only argument (Line 13). It then makes a call to the addWindowListener() method (Line 15), which is where things get interesting. If you are familiar with the new Java 1.1 delegation event model, this line of code probably makes perfect sense. If you aren't familiar with the new approach to handling Java events, then you're probably pretty curious as to what's going on. I'll spare you the gory details of how the Java 1.1 delegation event model works for now, but suffice it to say that an application must listen for a special event to know when it should exit. This event is the window closing event, which is sent when the user closes the application's frame window.

NOTE   Although you may already be familiar with the Java 1.1 delegation event model, you learn about some of its finer points in the next lesson, "Maximizing the Delegation Event Model."

To be able to listen for the window closing event, the application must register itself as an event listener by calling the addWindowListener() method. However, you may notice that the code on Line 15 is registering an object of type MyWindowAdapter rather than the application object itself. The MyWindowAdapter object is responsible for receiving window closing events for the application. For reasons you learn about in the next lesson, using special classes called *adapter classes* makes it easier to handle events under the new Java 1.1 delegation event model.

The `MyWindowAdapter` class implements a single method, `windowClosing()`, which is the method called whenever a window closing event is sent to the adapter class (Line 19). When this method is called, the application must exit because the user is closing the frame window (Line 21).

Application Versus Applet Execution

The flow of execution for an application is handled very differently than that of an applet. First of all, applications don't use `init()`, `start()`, `stop()`, or `destroy()` methods. The reason is that the concept of pausing as applets do with the `start()` and `stop()` methods is nonexistent in applications. However, applications do have rough equivalents for the `init()` and `destroy()` methods. An application's initialization code is placed in the application class's constructor; this code is very similar in function to the `init()` method in applets. Similarly, clean-up code for an application is placed in the `windowClosing()` event handler method; this method has a function similar to the `destroy()` method.

The point is that although applets and applications execute in different ways, they also have some similarities. These similarities are what you will use to build a hybrid program that can function either as an applet or an application, depending on the way in which it is executed. Before you do that, take the minimal application for a test drive.

Testing the Minimal Application

To test the minimal application, you must use a Java 1.1-compatible interpreter because the application uses the Java 1.1 delegation event model. I suggest using the Java interpreter that ships with the JDK 1.1. Type the following command to execute the application in the JDK 1.1 interpreter:

```
java MinApplication
```

As the application is being executed (see Figure 1.2), the following messages appear in the command-line window:

```
Calling main() method.
Creating application object.
```

When you terminate the application by closing its frame window, the following message appears in the command-line window:

```
Frame window closing.
```

As you can see from the messages output by the application, the flow of execution for an application does follow closely with that of an applet, even though the specific methods involved differ.

Figure 1.2.
The minimal Java application executing in the Java interpreter.

A Minimal Appletcation

You now understand the relationship between applets and applications well enough to attempt a functional merger of the two. The goal is to combine the minimal overhead for each into a single program that can execute either as an applet or an application, depending on the environment in which it is executed. For example, if the program is embedded in a Web page that is opened in a Web browser, it will execute as an applet. Likewise, if it is launched from within a stand-alone Java interpreter, it will execute as an application. I call this new hybrid program an *appletcation* to signify the fact that it is part applet and part application.

Listing 1.4 contains the source code for a minimal appletcation. You can find the complete source code and executable for the minimal appletcation on the companion Web site at http://www.mcp.com/info/1-57521/1-57521-347-8.

Listing 1.4. The MinAppletcation class.

```
 1: import java.applet.*;
 2: import java.awt.*;
 3: import java.awt.event.*;
 4:
 5: public class MinAppletcation extends Applet {
 6:   public static void main(String[] args) {
 7:     System.out.println("Calling main() method.");
 8:     MinAppletcationFrame app = new MinAppletcationFrame("Minimum
        ➥Application");
 9:     app.setSize(200, 200);
10:     app.show();
11:   }
12:
13:   public void init() {
14:     System.out.println("Applet initialized.");
15:   }
16:
17:   public void start() {
18:     System.out.println("Applet started.");
```

continues

Listing 1.4. continued

```
19:    }
20:
21:    public void stop() {
22:      System.out.println("Applet stopped.");
23:    }
24:
25:    public void destroy() {
26:      System.out.println("Applet destroyed.");
27:    }
28: }
29:
30: class MinAppletcationFrame extends Frame {
31:    private MinAppletcation applet;
32:
33:    public MinAppletcationFrame(String name) {
34:      super(name);
35:      System.out.println("Creating application object.");
36:      addWindowListener(new MyWindowAdapter());
37:      applet = new MinAppletcation();
38:      applet.init();
39:      applet.start();
40:      add("Center", applet);
41:    }
42:
43:    class MyWindowAdapter extends WindowAdapter {
44:      public void windowClosing(WindowEvent e) {
45:        System.out.println("Frame window closing.");
46:        applet.stop();
47:        applet.destroy();
48:        System.exit(0);
49:      }
50:    }
51: }
```

The MinAppletcation class is derived from the Applet class (Line 5), which may lead you to believe that this implementation is biased toward applets. However, moving down one line of code is all it takes to see that this program truly is a merger of all you've learned in the lesson thus far. The MinAppletcation class implements a static main() method (Line 6), which is called whenever the program is executed as an application. The main() method creates a MinAppletcationFrame object, which represents the frame window when the program is executing as an application. This code is very similar to that of a normal application, except that the main() method was implemented directly in the frame window class in a normal application. This won't work in the appletcation because the MinAppletcation class must be derived from Applet.

Why must the MinAppletcation class be derived from Applet? Because a Web browser assumes this class is an Applet-derived class whenever the class name is embedded in a Web page via the <APPLET> tag. In other words, there's no way to fake a Web browser into running an application as an applet. However, the reverse isn't necessarily true. The appletcation basically is an embedded applet executing within an application; the application is providing the overhead typically provided by a Web browser in the form of the application frame window.

Getting back to the code, other than the main() method, the MinAppletcation class is identical to the MinApplet class. This fact should make it clear how the program functions as an applet. Keep in mind that a Web browser knows nothing about the main() method, so that method is just ignored when the program is running as an applet. In fact, all of the code for the minimal appletcation is ignored when the program is running as an applet.

When the program is executed as an application, however, the main() method is called and a MinAppletcationFrame object is created. The MinAppletcationFrame class is where things really get interesting. This class contains a private member variable of type MinAppletcation, which is the applet object that is embedded in the application frame window.

The constructor for MinAppletcationFrame starts off just like the constructor for the minimal application you saw earlier in the lesson (Lines 34-36). However, after the event registration is completed, things take a different course; a MinAppletcation object is created (Line 37). Then, the init() and start() methods are called on the newly created applet object (Lines 38-39). By calling these two methods, the application is imitating the flow of execution a Web browser imposes on an applet. From the applet's perspective, the init() and start() methods may just as well be getting called from a Web browser. After calling the init() and start() methods, the constructor adds the applet to the frame window and makes sure it is centered with a call to add() (Line 40).

The windowClosing() method implemented in the MyWindowAdapter class was used in the minimal application to exit the application. The method serves the same purpose here, but it also takes care of calling the stop() and destroy() methods on the applet object to allow the applet to clean itself up (Lines 46-47). This step completes the life cycle for the applet and allows the application part of the appletcation to exit.

Testing the Appletcation

To test the appletcation, just try it out in the same environments you used for the minimal applet and application developed earlier in the lesson. To test the appletcation in applet mode, issue the following command:

```
appletviewer MinAppletcation.html
```

You should notice no difference between the execution of the appletcation in the appletviewer and the execution of the minimal applet you tested earlier in the lesson. The reason is that the main appletcation class is in fact an applet class.

The trickiness of the appletcation comes into play when you execute it as an application:

```
java MinAppletcation
```

Upon executing the appletcation as an application, the following messages are displayed:

```
Calling main() method.
Creating application object.
Applet initialized.
Applet started.
```

The first two messages are the same ones displayed by the minimal application from earlier in the lesson, and the second two messages are the same ones displayed by the minimal applet. These messages show how an application is being created to house an applet. When the appletcation is terminated by closing the main frame window, the following messages are displayed:

```
Frame window closing.
Applet stopped.
Applet destroyed.
```

Again, these messages directly correspond with those for the minimal application and applet combined. Clearly, the closing of the frame window signals the end of the application as well as the cleanup of the embedded applet.

Pondering the Appletcation

The appletcation class is very skeletal and provides just enough overhead to support the execution of the class as an applet or application. To add real substance and create a fully functioning appletcation, you typically will add code to the applet class because the frame window class is provided merely as a shell for the applet to execute in. The primary drawback of the appletcation is that it ultimately is an applet at its core, although it certainly is a neat trick and does provide a means of creating a single program that can execute as an applet or an application.

The appletcation eliminates two of the three differences between applets and applications outlined at the beginning of the lesson. First, the appletcation provides both a main() method and a frame window, which applets aren't responsible for worrying about. The only remaining difference in the appletcation is the security constraints imposed on untrusted applets, which seemingly could be troublesome when the appletcation executes as an application. However, the security model for an application executing in a Java interpreter is completely different than that for an applet, even though this particular application uses an applet internally. So, whenever the applet part of the appletcation is executing in application mode, the typical applet security constraints aren't imposed.

NOTE

> Prior to Java 1.1, the security differences between applets and applications were a major issue. However, Java 1.1 ushers in support for trusted applets, which are applets with digital signatures. A digital signature provides a means of verifying the source of an applet, which can be a basis for relieving applet security constraints. You learn much more about Java security and trusted applets on Day 18, "Introduction to Digital Security and the Java Security API," and Day 19, "Creating Signed Java Objects."

Summary

This lesson used Java applets and applications as the basis for a Java 1.1 refresher course. Unlike most refresher courses, however, this lesson covered the details of applets and applications in the context of an interesting sample program. The sample program is called an appletcation, and it is a merger of an applet and an application into a single entity that can behave differently depending on the environment it is being executed in.

You began the lesson with a presentation of the plan to build a hybrid program that could function both as an applet and an application. You then reviewed the differences between applets and applications to get an idea of what needed to be addressed in the hybrid program. From there, you took a few steps back and developed a minimal applet and a minimal application to get a feel for the code required to make things work. You then finished up the chapter by putting everything together to create a hybrid appletcation capable of executing as either an applet or an application.

Q&A

Q **What happens if I don't implement the init(), start(), stop(), and destroy() methods in an applet?**

A Nothing in particular. These methods are provided as a means for you to place your own applet-specific code and aren't responsible for doing anything else. In other words, if you don't have any code to put in these methods, then you don't need to implement them. Keep in mind, though, that practically any applet that uses threads needs to implement the start() and stop() methods, because threads aren't automatically halted when an applet is stopped.

Q **What happens if I don't implement the `main()` method in an application?**

A The Java interpreter will exit with an error because it won't be able to find the `main()` method, which it must call to get the application started.

Q **Is it really necessary to implement the `windowClosing()` method and handle the window closing event in an application?**

A Yes, because the closing of the frame window is the signal for an application to exit. If you didn't implement this method and handle the event appropriately, an application would be unable to exit.

Q **The hybrid appletcation functions as an application by embedding an applet in an application frame window behind the scenes. Is it possible to do the reverse and design a hybrid program that embeds an application in an applet?**

A No, because there is no way for an application to execute within a Web browser when the program is functioning as an applet. Likewise, applets always require a frame window, which can only be provided by an application when the program is functioning as an application.

Day 2

Maximizing the Delegation Event Model

by Michael Morrison

Events play such a critical role in the structure of Java that they have seen a great deal of change over the past few years. The delegation event model new to Java 1.1 is the third event model adopted by Java and is the first to provide an event architecture extensible enough to allow Java to grow as a technology. The book *Teach Yourself Java in 21 Days* (published by Sams.net) covered the basics of using the delegation event model along with how it differs from the Java 1.0 event model. The aim of this lesson is to pick up where that book left off and dig into the delegation event model in more detail.

This lesson covers the following topics:

☐ The basic concepts critical to understanding the delegation event model
☐ Using event adapters with inner classes to clean up event processing
☐ Defining custom event types

By the end of this lesson, you will have a few new tricks up your sleeve when it comes to working with the delegation event model and a better understanding of how it all works.

Revisiting the Delegation Event Model

One of the main premises behind the design of the delegation event model is the division between event-handling code and the core application code. It became apparent in the Java 1.0 event model that event handling was too closely linked with core application code, resulting in an often complex blend of user interface code and back-end application code. For large applications, it is favorable to have user interface code as isolated as possible from back-end application code. Beyond just being favorable, the isolation of event-handling code is an absolute necessity when it comes to developing component-based software using JavaBeans. JavaBeans is, in fact, responsible for the creation of the delegation event model.

NEW TERM   *event:* Something that happens within a component that an application or other component might want to know about and possibly react to.

The delegation event model establishes the concept of event types, where each type of event is given a unique class type derived from a common event class. Event objects of a given event type, also called *event state objects*, are passed between event sources and listeners to constitute an event notification. *Event sources* can generate events; *event listeners* are designed to respond to events. An event is propagated from an event source to an event listener when the event source invokes a method on the listener and passes an object of the given event type.

NEW TERM   *event state object:* An object used to store information associated with a particular event.

event listener: An application or component capable of responding to events.

event source: A component capable of generating events.

Event listeners are connected to event sources through a registration mechanism that requires a listener to call a registration method on a source. When the registration method is called, the source is told to send event notifications to the listener. Registered listeners can also be unregistered, or removed as listeners, from a source. Event sources are required to support the addition and removal of listeners through a pair of public event registration methods.

When an event occurs in an event source, the source sends an event notification to any listeners that have been registered. The event notification is sent with a method call on each registered listener. Listeners are required to implement an event listener interface, which contains a list of methods that can be called by an event source in response to an event. These methods are known as *event response methods* because listeners implement them to provide code that responds to an event.

New Term

> *event response method:* A method defined in an event listener and used to respond to event notifications sent by an event source.

The Java 1.1 API supports a variety of event types and associated event listener interfaces. These event types are conceptually divided into two different types: low-level events and semantic events. *Low-level events* are events used to convey information about a low-level input or graphical user interface interaction such as a mouse move, key press, or focus change. *Semantic events*, on the other hand, are events used to convey information about a high-level graphical user interface interaction that has meaning within the context of a certain component. For example, an item event is fired whenever a menu item changes. Several low-level events (such as key presses) are fired to arrive at the menu change, which results in a single semantic event.

New Term

> *low-level event:* An event fired in response to a low-level input or graphical user interface interaction.
>
> *semantic event:* An event fired when an action occurs based on the semantics of a particular component.

Low-Level Events

Low-level events are fired in response to a low-level input or graphical user interface interaction such as a key press or component focus change. The Java API defines a set of event classes that represent the different types of low-level events. These classes are used to generate event state objects that are passed between a source and listener when an event occurs.

Following are the low-level event classes supported by the Java 1.1 API:

ComponentEvent

ContainerEvent

FocusEvent

KeyEvent

MouseEvent

WindowEvent

NOTE

All event classes (low-level and semantic) are derived from the AWTEvent class, which encapsulates general characteristics shared by all events. The AWTEvent class is so generic that you typically never interact with it directly. This is evident because no event listener interface is defined for AWTEvent.

Figure 2.1 shows the inheritance tree for the low-level event classes. The next few sections describe these event classes in more detail and give you an idea about when they are fired. You also get a glimpse at the event listener interface associated with each event type. Forgive me if the next few sections look like a reference; I just want to give you a quick idea about how the Java API manages events.

Figure 2.1.

The inheritance tree for the low-level event classes.

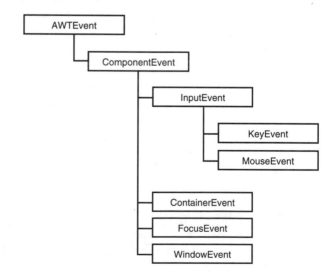

The ComponentEvent **Class**

The ComponentEvent class encapsulates component-level events such as resizes, moves, and visibility changes. For example, when a component is resized, a ComponentEvent event is fired. The listener interface for ComponentEvent is ComponentListener, which supports the following event response methods:

Method	Description
componentMoved()	Called when a component is moved
componentResized()	Called when a component is resized
componentHidden()	Called when a component is hidden
componentShown()	Called when a component is shown

The ContainerEvent **Class**

The ContainerEvent class encapsulates container-level events including the addition and removal of components. When a component is added to or removed from a container, a ContainerEvent event is fired. The listener interface for ContainerEvent is ContainerListener, which supports the following event response methods:

Method	Description
componentAdded()	Called when a component is added to a container
componentRemoved()	Called when a component is removed from a container

The FocusEvent **Class**

The FocusEvent class is used to convey focus changes within components. Two types of focus changes are supported by the FocusEvent class: permanent and temporary. A *permanent focus change* occurs when the focus directly changes from one component to another. An example of a permanent focus change is the user moving from one component to another using the Tab key. A *temporary focus change* occurs when a component loses or gains focus indirectly based on some other operation such as a dialog box being displayed. The difference between the two types of focus changes is that temporary focus changes are eventually restored. Both types of focus changes are represented by the FocusEvent class; to distinguish between the two, you can call the isTemporary() method.

The listener interface for FocusEvent is FocusListener, which supports the following event response methods:

Method	Description
focusGained()	Called when a component gains focus
focusLost()	Called when a component loses focus

The KeyEvent Class

The KeyEvent class encapsulates component-level keyboard events such as key presses and releases. For example, when a component has focus and a key is pressed or released, a KeyEvent event is fired. As you saw in Figure 2.1, the KeyEvent class is derived from InputEvent, which is an organizational class used to group input event types. Input events are delivered to listeners before being processed by their sources, which gives listeners an opportunity to consume the events. The listener interface for KeyEvent is KeyListener, which supports the following event response methods:

Method	Description
keyPressed()	Called when a key is pressed
keyReleased()	Called when a key is released
keyTyped()	Called when a key is *typed* (which consists of a key press/release combination

The MouseEvent Class

The MouseEvent class represents component-level mouse events such as mouse moves and button clicks. For example, a MouseEvent event is fired whenever the mouse is moved or clicked over a component. Additionally, events correspond to the mouse entering and leaving a component's surface area. Like KeyEvent, the MouseEvent class is derived from InputEvent because it represents mouse input events.

Two listener interfaces are used with the MouseEvent class: MouseListener and MouseMotionListener. Following are the event response methods defined in the MouseListener interface:

Method	Description
mousePressed()	Called when the mouse button is pressed
mouseReleased()	Called when the mouse button is released
mouseClicked()	Called when the mouse button is *clicked* (which consists of a button press/release combination)
mouseEntered()	Called when the mouse pointer enters a component's surface area
mouseExited()	Called when the mouse pointer exits a component's surface area

The MouseMotionListener interface is designed specifically to handle mouse movement events; it supports the following event response methods:

Method	Description
mouseMoved()	Called when the mouse pointer is moved over a component
mouseDragged()	Called when the mouse pointer is moved over a component with the mouse button held down

The WindowEvent Class

The WindowEvent class encapsulates window-level events such as a window being activated or closed. For example, a WindowEvent event is generated whenever a window is opened or closed. The listener interface for WindowEvent is WindowListener, which supports the following event response methods:

Method	Description
windowActivated()	Called when a window is activated
windowDeactivated()	Called when a window is deactivated
windowOpened()	Called when a window is opened
windowClosed()	Called when a window is closed
windowClosing()	Called when a window is in the process of being closed, but hasn't yet closed
windowIconified()	Called when a window is minimized to iconic form
windowDeiconified()	Called when a window is restored from iconic form, or deiconified

Semantic Events

Semantic events are fired in response to high-level graphical user interface interactions that have meaning within the context of a certain component. For example, selecting an item from a list results in an ItemEvent event being generated; the event fired in this case is specific to the list's functionality. The Java API defines a set of event classes that represent the different types of semantic events. Following are the semantic event classes supported by the Java 1.1 API:

```
ActionEvent
AdjustmentEvent
ItemEvent
TextEvent
```

Figure 2.2 shows the inheritance tree for the semantic event classes. The next few sections describe these event classes in more detail and give you an idea about when and why they are fired.

Figure 2.2.

The inheritance tree for the semantic event classes.

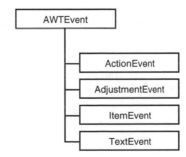

The ActionEvent **Class**

The ActionEvent class encapsulates component-specific actions such as clicking a button component or menu item. Following are the AWT objects capable of firing ActionEvent events, along with why they fire them:

Object	Description
Button	Fires an action event when clicked
List	Fires an action event when an item is double-clicked
MenuItem	Fires an action event when an item is clicked
TextField	Fires an action event when the Enter key is pressed

The event listener interface for ActionEvent is ActionListener, which only defines one event response method:

Method	Description
actionPerformed()	Called when a component-specific action occurs

The AdjustmentEvent **Class**

The AdjustmentEvent class encapsulates component-specific value changes, such as the value of a scrollbar being changed. Scrollbars are actually the only AWT components that fire AdjustmentEvent events. The event listener interface for AdjustmentEvent is AdjustmentListener, which defines only one event response method:

Method	Description
adjustmentValueChanged()	Called when a component-specific value adjustment occurs

The ItemEvent **Class**

The ItemEvent class encapsulates component-specific item changes, such as selecting an item from a list. Following are the AWT objects capable of firing ItemEvent events, along with why they fire them:

Object	Description
Choice	Fires an item event when a choice item is selected
List	Fires an item event when a list item is selected
Checkbox	Fires an item event when a checkbox is checked or unchecked
CheckboxMenuItem	Fires an item event when a checkbox menu item is checked or unchecked

2

The event listener interface for `ItemEvent` is `ItemListener`, which defines only one event response method:

Method	Description
itemStateChanged()	Called when a component-specific item change occurs

The `TextEvent` Class

The `TextEvent` class models events fired in response to a change in the text of a text component. Following are the text components capable of firing `TextEvent` events, along with why they fire them:

Component	Description
TextArea	Fires a text event when the text changes
TextField	Fires a text event when the text changes

The event listener interface for `TextEvent` is `TextListener`, which defines only one event response method:

Method	Description
textValueChanged()	Called when the text changes in a text component

Event Delivery

To effectively process and manage events, you must thoroughly understand the event delivery process. The event delivery process involves three objects: an event source, an event listener, and an event state object. The process begins when an event listener notifies a source that it wants to listen to a particular type of event. It does this by calling an event listener registration method provided by the source. Once the listener is registered, the source is ready to deliver events to it. Whenever a change occurs in the source that generates an event, the source creates an event state object describing the event and sends it out to the listener. The source does this by calling one of the event response methods defined in the listener's event listener interface and passing along the event state object.

Event delivery is completely synchronous, meaning that an event is guaranteed complete delivery without interruption. However, there are no rules regarding the order in which events are delivered to a group of listeners. Speaking of groups of listeners, this brings us to the two main types of event delivery: unicast and multicast.

Unicast and Multicast Delivery

All the standard AWT components support multiple event listeners, which means that multiple event listeners can be registered with and receive events from a single event source. This type of event delivery is known as *multicast event delivery* because an event is broadcast to multiple event listeners simultaneously. With multicast event delivery, event listeners can be added and removed at will using event listener registration methods; the event source is responsible for keeping track of the listeners and dispatching events to each. Figure 2.3 shows an example of multicast event delivery.

NEW TERM   *multicast event source:* An event source capable of generating events for retrieval by any number of listeners.

Figure 2.3.
Multicast delivery of an event to multiple listeners.

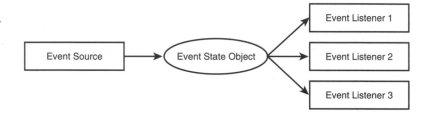

Although multicast event delivery is the most popular and versatile type of event delivery, the delegation event model also supports *unicast event delivery,* in which only one listener can listen to a source at a time. Unicast event sources can have only one registered listener at any given time. Event listener registration methods for unicast sources are designed to throw an exception if an attempt is made to register more than one listener. Figure 2.4 shows an example of unicast event delivery.

NEW TERM   *unicast event source:* An event source capable of generating events for retrieval by only one listener.

Figure 2.4.
Unicast delivery of an event to a single listener.

Unicast event delivery is a more limited form of delivery and should be used only when absolutely necessary. The fact that all standard AWT components are multicast event sources should give you an idea about how JavaSoft feels about unicast event delivery. Fortunately, unicast event delivery is such a rare form of delivery that you are unlikely to ever need it. It is so rare that I can't even think of a situation that would require its use. Should you ever run into such a rare situation, however, keep in mind that unicast delivery is available.

Unicast event sources are distinguished from multicast sources in that their event listener registration methods can throw the TooManyListeners exception. This exception is often the only clue you may have about the type of event delivery supported by a component. For example, the following event listener registration method supports multicast delivery:

```
public void addCrunchListener(CrunchEvent e);
```

In this example, the CrunchEvent event can be fired to multiple listeners that have been registered with the addCrunchListener() registration method. If a CrunchEvent event source is unicast, it supplies the following addCrunchListener() method:

```
public void addCrunchListener(CrunchEvent e) throws TooManyListeners;
```

The only difference between the two addCrunchListener() methods is the addition of the throws clause to the latter method. If more than one event listener is registered with this method, a TooManyListeners exception is thrown.

Delivery Concerns

Although event delivery under the delegation event model is typically a very smooth process, there are a few concerns worth mentioning. One potential problem arises when an event listener throws exceptions back to an event source. The problem relates to how an event source should react to such an exception. Unfortunately, there are no rules governing what should happen in such a situation. Java 1.1 stipulates that the manner in which an event source deals with listener-generated exceptions is entirely implementation dependent, meaning that you must consult the documentation for a particular source to find out how it handles this exception.

Another problem associated with event delivery occurs when the group of event listeners registered with a multicast source is updated during the delivery of an event. In this situation, it is technically possible for a listener to be removed from the source before its event has been delivered. When this happens, it is possible for an event to be delivered to a listener that is no longer registered, which certainly seems like a problem. Again, there are no strict rules governing how event sources are to deal with this problem, so you should consult the documentation of an event source if you are worried about this situation. Fortunately, this problem isn't likely to cause trouble in most Java programs because event listeners are typically thrown away once they are unregistered.

Event Adapters

I didn't really explain earlier in the lesson why event listeners are provided in the Java API as interfaces instead of as classes. The reason is that event listeners are used as a way for Java programs to provide application-specific code that responds to event notifications. This means that no default behavior is ever associated with event response methods. Because event listener interfaces are comprised entirely of event response methods, there is no reason to provide a specific implementation. Classes that want to respond to events must implement an event listener interface and provide implementations for all the event response methods defined in the interface.

One problem with this event listener approach is that it requires a class to implement all the event response methods defined in a listener interface. Without implementing all the methods, the class would remain abstract and could not be instantiated and used. This isn't an issue for situations in which most or all of the event response methods defined in an interface are going to be used by a class. However, what about the situation in which you want to implement only a single event response method and the interface provides a variety of them? Because you are required to provide implementations for all the methods in the interface, you would have to add empty do-nothing methods for all the methods you aren't interested in. This solution clearly is annoying because you would have to add unnecessary code.

Fortunately, there is a better solution to this problem. The Java API provides a set of *event adapters*, which are "convenience classes" used to make the process of implementing event listener interfaces cleaner. Event adapters enable you to implement only the event response methods you need, freeing you from the hassle of writing a bunch of useless empty methods. Event adapters are classes, not interfaces, so you must derive from them rather than implement them. Because they are classes, you can selectively provide event response methods.

 NEW TERM

> *event adapter:* A "convenience class" used to make the handling of events much cleaner.

An event adapter class is associated with each low-level event listener interface. Each event adapter implements all the methods defined in its corresponding event listener interface. You may be wondering why there are no event adapters for semantic event listener interfaces. If you recall from earlier in this lesson, the semantic event listener interfaces each define only one event response method. Because there is only one method to be implemented, there is no "convenience" to be gained by using an adapter class.

Event adapters are simple classes. Just so that you believe me, take a quick look at the code for the KeyAdapter event adapter class, taken straight from the Java API source:

```
public abstract class KeyAdapter implements KeyListener {
  public void keyTyped(KeyEvent e) {}
  public void keyPressed(KeyEvent e) {}
  public void keyReleased(KeyEvent e) {}
}
```

It doesn't get much simpler than that! As you can see, the KeyAdapter class just implements the KeyListener interface and provides do-nothing methods for all the event response methods defined in the interface.

Using Event Adapters and Inner Classes

As you just learned, event adapters are used to help clean up the process of responding to events. However, using an event adapter class isn't always as simple as just deriving from the appropriate class and implementing some methods. A common problem is the situation in which you want to use an event adapter class directly with an applet or application class. The problem is that applets and applications already have a parent class and therefore can't be derived from an adapter class. This is clearly a pesky problem because there is no way to circumvent Java's single-inheritance design.

One possible solution is to create a separate event handler class that derives from the adapter class, but the event handler is likely to need access to private and protected members of the application class. Because Java has no facility like the C++ friend classes, it's not really possible to give the event handler class access to the members of the application class. What to do?

A new feature to Java 1.1 called *inner classes* provides just the mechanism necessary to solve this problem: You implement an adapter class as a member of an application class. The adapter class definition is completely contained within the application class and is derived from a suitable AWT event adapter class. This arrangement allows you to implement only the specific methods you need; in addition, you can access private and protected members of the application.

NEW TERM | *inner class:* A class defined within the scope of another class.

Listing 2.1 contains the source code for the ClickMe applet, which demonstrates the difference between using an event adapter inner class and implementing an event listener interface directly.

Listing 2.1. The source code for the `ClickMe` applet.

```
 1: public class ClickMe extends Applet implements ActionListener {
 2:    private Button     button;
 3:    private AudioClip clickClip, thanksClip;
 4:
 5:    public void init() {
 6:       // Load the audio clips
 7:       clickClip = getAudioClip(getCodeBase(), "ClickMe.au");
 8:       thanksClip = getAudioClip(getCodeBase(), "ThankYou.au");
 9:
10:       // Create and add the button
11:       button = new Button("Click me!");
12:       add(button);
13:
14:       // Register the applet with the button as a listener
15:       button.addActionListener(this);
16:       button.addMouseListener(new ClickMeAdapter());
17:    }
18:
19:    public void actionPerformed(ActionEvent e) {
20:       // Play thanks clip in response to button action events
21:       thanksClip.play();
22:    }
23:
24:    class ClickMeAdapter extends MouseAdapter {
25:       // Play click clip in response to button mouse entry events
26:       public void mouseEntered(MouseEvent e) {
27:          clickClip.play();
28:       }
29:    }
30: }
```

The `ClickMe` applet contains a button that plays an audio clip when it is clicked (see Figure 2.5). A button click results in an `ActionEvent` event being fired, which is responded to directly by the `ClickMe` applet class. This is apparent because the applet class implements the `ActionListener` interface (Line 1) and also registers the applet as an action event listener (Line 15). The action event response method, `actionPerformed()`, is directly implemented in the `ClickMe` applet class and is responsible for playing a *thank you* audio clip.

Figure 2.5.

The `ClickMe` *applet.*

Until now, the ClickMe applet has seemed to be no different than any other delegation event handling applet that directly implements an event listener interface. However, the ClickMe applet also uses an adapter inner class to respond to mouse-movement events. The adapter inner class is named ClickMeAdapter and is defined within the scope of the ClickMe applet class (Lines 24 through 29). The ClickMeAdapter class is purely a helper class used within the context of the ClickMe applet class; it overrides the mouseEntered() method to play a *click me* audio clip whenever the mouse pointer enters the button's surface area. An instance of the ClickMeAdapter class is created and used as the argument to the addMouseListener() registration method in the init() method. That's all it takes to create and register an adapter inner class.

The end result of the event response methods in the ClickMe applet is that, when the mouse pointer enters the button's surface area, a *click me* audio clip is played to encourage the user to click the button. When the user clicks the button, a *thank you* audio clip is played.

Defining Custom Events

In tomorrow's lesson, "Creating Custom Components," you learn how to create custom AWT components from scratch. Some custom components require their own event types, just as the various AWT components use different event types. What do you do if you need an event type that isn't included in the AWT? You create your own, of course! The rest of this lesson demonstrates how to create and use a custom event type in the context of a reusable component.

The component in need of a custom event type is called Timer and acts as a general-purpose timer. The timer component fires timer events at regular intervals that can easily be changed for application-specific timing purposes. You're going to create a custom event type for the timer events fired by the timer component. Before you get to that, however, review the implementation of the Timer class. Listing 2.2 contains the source code for the Timer class.

Listing 2.2. The source code for the Timer class.

```
 1: public class Timer implements Runnable {
 2:    private transient Thread          timerThread;
 3:    private transient TimerListener   timerListener = null;
 4:    private int                       period; // in milliseconds
 5:    private boolean                   oneShot;
 6:
 7:    // Constructors
 8:    public Timer() {
 9:      this(1000, false);
10:    }
11:
12:    public Timer(int p, boolean os) {
13:      // Allow the superclass constructor to do its thing
```

continues

Listing 2.2. continued

```
14:      super();
15:
16:      // Set properties
17:      period = p;
18:      oneShot = os;
19:
20:      // Create the clock thread
21:      timerThread = new Thread(this, "Timer");
22:      timerThread.start();
23:    }
24:
25:    // Accessor methods
26:    public int getPeriod() {
27:      return period;
28:    }
29:
30:    public void setPeriod(int p) {
31:      period = p;
32:      if (timerThread != null)
33:        timerThread.interrupt();
34:    }
35:
36:    public boolean isOneShot() {
37:      return oneShot;
38:    }
39:
40:    public void setOneShot(boolean os) {
41:      oneShot = os;
42:    }
43:
44:    // Other public methods
45:    public void run() {
46:      while (timerThread != null) {
47:        // Sleep for the period
48:        try {
49:          timerThread.sleep(period);
50:        } catch (InterruptedException e) {
51:          // Restart the loop
52:          continue;
53:        }
54:
55:        // Fire a timer event
56:        fireTimerEvent();
57:
58:        if (oneShot)
59:          break;
60:      }
61:    }
62:
63:    // Event processing methods
64:    public synchronized void addTimerListener(TimerListener l) {
65:      timerListener = TimerEventMulticaster.add(timerListener, l);
66:    }
67:
```

```
68:    public synchronized void removeTimerListener(TimerListener l) {
69:      timerListener = TimerEventMulticaster.remove(timerListener, l);
70:    }
71:
72:    protected void processTimerEvent(TimerEvent e) {
73:      // Deliver the event to all registered timer event listeners
74:      if (timerListener != null)
75:        timerListener.timerTriggered(e);
76:    }
77:
78:    // Private support methods
79:    private void fireTimerEvent() {
80:      processTimerEvent(new TimerEvent(this));
81:    }
82: }
```

The Timer class defines a few member variables for managing its operation (Lines 2 through 5). For the purposes of this discussion, the main member variable of interest is timerListener, which is of type TimerListener (Line 3). The TimerListener interface is an event listener interface for the TimerEvent event class. The Timer class uses the timerListener member to manage the addition and removal of listeners. You learn more about how this works in a moment.

The Timer class defines two constructors (Lines 8 through 23) and a couple pairs of accessor methods for providing access to its public properties (Lines 26 through 42). There is also a run() method that keeps up with the timing for the component and determines when to fire timing events (Lines 45 through 61). The run() method calls the fireTimerEvent() method to actually fire a timer event (Line 56). You learn about the fireTimerEvent() method in just a moment.

The addTimerListener() and removeTimerListener() methods are used to add and remove event listeners, respectively (Lines 64 through 70). Because the Timer class is a multicast event source, it uses the TimerEventMulticaster class to manage multiple event listeners. You learn how the TimerEventMulticaster class pulls this off a little later in the lesson. The processTimerEvent() method is responsible for delivering timer events to registered timer event listeners (Lines 72 through 76). It simply checks to make sure that the timerListener member is valid and then calls the timerTriggered() event response method (Lines 74 and 75).

The last method defined in the Timer class is fireTimerEvent(), which is a private helper method used to fire timer events (Lines 79 through 81). The fireTimerEvent() method creates a TimerEvent object and passes it to processTimerEvent() (Line 80). You may be wondering why the fireTimerEvent() method is even necessary. If you recall, the fireTimerEvent() method is called in the run() method to fire timer events. Rather than directly placing a call to processTimerEvent() in the run() method, the code is cleaner and easier to follow by defining the fireTimerEvent() method and calling it instead.

With the `Timer` class taken care of, let's move on to the specific event management code. Listing 2.3 contains the source code for the `TimerEvent` class, which models a timer event.

Listing 2.3. The source code for the `TimerEvent` class.

```
1: public class TimerEvent extends AWTEvent {
2:   public static final int TIMER_FIRST = AWTEvent.RESERVED_ID_MAX + 1;
3:   public static final int TIMER_LAST = TIMER_FIRST;
4:   public static final int TIMER_TRIGGERED = TIMER_FIRST;
5:
6:   public TimerEvent(Object source) {
7:     super(source, TIMER_TRIGGERED);
8:   }
9: }
```

As you can see, `TimerEvent` is a pretty simple class; it defines three constant members and a single constructor. The constants are necessary to maintain consistency with the organization of the AWT event model (Lines 2 through 4); every event subtype is given a unique identifier used to determine which event response method is called. In the case of `TimerEvent`, there is only one event subtype, `TIMER_TRIGGERED`, and therefore only one event identifier (Line 4). The `TIMER_FIRST` and `TIMER_LAST` identifiers are used to establish the limits of the timer event identifiers should any be added later (Lines 2 and 3). It's very important that these limits be based on `AWTEvent.RESERVED_ID_MAX` to avoid clashes in event types.

The constructor provided by `TimerEvent` is used to create a timer event state object that can be passed from an event source to an event listener (Lines 6 through 8). This constructor calls the parent `AWTEvent` constructor and passes along the event source and the identifier of the event subtype, `TIMER_TRIGGERED` (Line 7). That wraps up the `TimerEvent` class!

Next on the agenda is the `TimerListener` interface, which defines the event response method used to respond to timer events. The source code for the `TimerListener` interface follows:

```
public interface TimerListener extends EventListener {
  public void timerTriggered(TimerEvent e);
}
```

This source code is so simple that it didn't even warrant a formal listing! All the `TimerListener` interface does is define a single event response method, `timerTriggered()`, that is called on a listener whenever a timer event is fired.

The last support class required to make the `TimerEvent` event class functional is `TimerEventMulticaster`, which is responsible for managing multiple registered listeners. Listing 2.4 shows the source code for the `TimerEventMulticaster` class.

Listing 2.4. The source code for the `TimerEventMulticaster` **class.**

```
 1: public class TimerEventMulticaster extends AWTEventMulticaster implements
    ➡TimerListener {
 2:   protected TimerEventMulticaster(EventListener a, EventListener b) {
 3:     super(a, b);
 4:   }
 5:
 6:   public static TimerListener add(TimerListener a, TimerListener b) {
 7:     return (TimerListener) addInternal(a, b);
 8:   }
 9:
10:   public static TimerListener remove(TimerListener l, TimerListener oldl) {
11:     return (TimerListener) removeInternal(l, oldl);
12:   }
13:
14:   protected static EventListener addInternal(EventListener a,
      ➡EventListener b) {
15:     if (a == null)
16:       return b;
17:     if (b == null)
18:       return a;
19:     return new TimerEventMulticaster(a, b);
20:   }
21:
22:   protected EventListener remove(EventListener oldl) {
23:     if (oldl == a)
24:       return b;
25:     if (oldl == b)
26:       return a;
27:     EventListener a2 = removeInternal(a, oldl);
28:     EventListener b2 = removeInternal(b, oldl);
29:     if (a2 == a && b2 == b)
30:       return this;
31:     return addInternal(a2, b2);
32:   }
33:
34:   public void timerTriggered(TimerEvent e) {
35:     if (a != null) ((TimerListener) a).timerTriggered(e);
36:     if (b != null) ((TimerListener) b).timerTriggered(e);
37:   }
38: }
```

The `TimerEventMulticaster` class is by far the most complex of the classes for the timer event because it has to handle the details of managing multiple event listeners. Before you jump into the code dissection, here's a little background on how multiple event listeners are supported by the Java API. The Java API provides a special class named `AWTEventMulticaster` to maintain a list of event listeners. A single `AWTEventMulticaster` object maintains references to two listener objects. Because the `AWTEventMulticaster` class is a listener itself, the two listener objects it manages can also be multicasters. This can effectively result in a linked list, or chain, of multicasters and listeners.

The AWTEventMulticaster class is used to manage multiple listeners for all standard AWT events. However, you can't just use the class as-is with new event classes because it performs operations based on specific types of events. You have to derive from AWTEventMulticaster if you want to provide multiple listener management for a custom event type. That's exactly what is done in the TimerEventMulticaster class.

The TimerEventMulticaster class provides a protected constructor (Lines 2 through 4), which means that it isn't possible to directly create instances of the class. Instead, you call the static add() method, which in turn calls the addInternal() method (Line 7). The addInternal() method adds an event listener to the listener chain (Lines 14 through 20). The remove() method uses the removeInternal() method to remove a listener from the listener chain (Lines 22 through 32). Finally, because the TimerEventMulticaster class implements the TimerListener interface, the class must provide an implementation of the timerTriggered() method. It does so by recursively calling the timerTriggered() method on every listener in the listener chain (Lines 35 and 36).

That wraps up all the code required to support a custom event and a component that uses it. Now you're ready to build an applet that tests out all these classes. Listing 2.5 contains the source code for the TimerTest applet, which uses a timer component to change a pair of counters every second.

Listing 2.5. The source code for the TimerTest applet.

```
 1: public class TimerTest extends Applet implements TimerListener {
 2:    private Timer  timer;
 3:    private Label labelUp, labelDown;
 4:    private int    countUp = 0, countDown = 100;
 5:
 6:    public void init() {
 7:      // Create the timer
 8:      timer = new Timer();
 9:
10:      // Create and add the labels
11:      labelUp = new Label("Ready...");
12:      labelDown = new Label("Ready...");
13:      labelUp.setFont(new Font("Helvetica", Font.BOLD, 36));
14:      labelDown.setFont(new Font("Helvetica", Font.BOLD, 36));
15:      add(labelUp);
16:      add(labelDown);
17:
18:      // Register the applet as a timer listener
19:      timer.addTimerListener(this);
20:    }
21:
22:    public void timerTriggered(TimerEvent e) {
23:      // Increment the count and update the label
24:      labelUp.setText(String.valueOf(countUp++));
25:      labelDown.setText(String.valueOf(countDown--));
26:    }
27: }
```

The TimerTest applet consists of two labels used to display two different counts (see Figure 2.6). One of the counts increases over time, and the other decreases. The TimerTest class includes a timer member variable that is an instance of the Timer class (Line 2). This member variable is initialized in the init() method (Line 8), along with the labels and counters (Lines 11 through 16). More importantly, the applet is registered with the timer as a timer event listener with a call to addTimerListener() (Line 19).

Figure 2.6.

The TimerTest *applet.*

The TimerTest applet class implements the TimerListener interface (Line 1) and therefore provides an implementation of the timerTriggered() method (Lines 22 through 26). This method increments the up counter, decrements the down counter, and updates both labels to reflect the new counter values. The timerTriggered() method is called once every second because one second is the default interval used by the Timer class.

Summary

This lesson took you inside the delegation event model and showed you how to do some interesting things. You started the lesson by revisiting many of the conceptual issues related to the delegation event model. Although some of these concepts were covered in *Teach Yourself Java in 21 Days*, this lesson dug deeper and gave you more perspective on how the delegation event model works. With a solid amount of theory under your belt, you moved on to learning about the event classes provided in the Java API and what types of events they represent.

The second part of the lesson focused more on practical issues, starting with an example that used adapter inner classes to facilitate a clean approach to event handling. From there, you moved on to learning how to define and build a custom event from scratch, including a component that uses the event. You also developed a test applet to try out the component and its related event support classes.

Q&A

Q **What is the significance of the name *delegation event model*?**

A The Java 1.1 event model is called the delegation event model because it allows you to delegate event handling authority to any object that implements the appropriate listener interface.

Q **Why are mouse events divided between two event listener interfaces, `MouseListener` and `MouseMotionListener`?**

A Because mouse motion events tend to occur rapidly and therefore require a fair amount of system overhead, it is more efficient to isolate them so that an application using only mouse button events, for example, isn't burdened by the heavier mouse motion events.

Q **Why was the AWT `PaintEvent` class not covered in this lesson?**

A Because the `PaintEvent` class is a special event class used internally by the AWT that isn't meant to be used with the event source/listener model.

Q **Can the `TimerEvent` event class be used with other components?**

A Absolutely. Event classes and their respective listeners have no allegiance to a particular component. This fact is evident in the AWT itself, in which event classes are shared among many different components.

Day **3**

Creating Custom Components

by Jerry Ablan

Now that you're (back) up to speed on Java, it's time to dig in. As you know, Java's Abstract Windowing Toolkit (AWT) package contains classes that you can use to interact with the user of your programs. These classes are more commonly known as *components*. The components that come with Java are basically the least common denominator across all Java-supported operating systems. If one operating system has a component and another doesn't, then Java doesn't support it. Therefore, Java's core set of components consists of only basic items such as buttons, text boxes, and list boxes.

What do you do if you need a specialized component, something really cool? You create it, of course! Creating custom components with Java can be fun and easy, as you'll discover by reading about the following topics:

☐ The basics of creating custom components
☐ Creating a simple component that provides a three-dimensional appearance
☐ Creating a tabbed folder component

Types of 3-D Borders

One of the first things you notice about any visually pleasing component is that it has a raised, or sunken, three-dimensional (3-D) appearance. 3-D components give a nice touch to any input screen and can transform a boring screen into one bubbling with personality. Most of Java's components exhibit this 3-D look, but sometimes you just need a custom component to do the job. The component may be a list box with a button connected to it or something more elaborate. Whatever the case, you'll need to draw a 3-D border around your component.

A 3-D border around a component is one of the easiest and most professional looking types to program. Drawing a 3-D border around any component requires two details: border style and border thickness. The first step is to decide which 3-D border style you want to draw. The classic styles are: lowered, raised, grooved, and ridged.

Lowered Borders

A lowered border is a border that looks sunken or lower than the area that contains it. With this type of border, the light seems to come from the upper-left of the component. Figure 3.1 illustrates the concept of a lowered border.

Figure 3.1.
A lowered border.

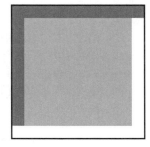

To make the object appear sunken, you need to create what appears to be a shadow. To do this, the upper and left sides of your component should be darker than the lower and right sides. In Figure 3.1, I started with a background of light gray. The upper and left sides are a darker gray. The bottom and right sides are white. This effect looks like a pushed-in button.

Raised Borders

A raised border is a border that makes the component it surrounds look like it is coming off of the screen. Buttons and other "clickable" objects commonly have this look. Figure 3.2 illustrates the concept of a raised border.

Figure 3.2.
A raised border.

To make the object appear raised, you need to create a shadow at the bottom of the object. To do this, the upper and left sides of your component should be lighter than the lower and right sides. In Figure 3.2, I again started with a light gray background. The upper and left sides are white, and the bottom and right sides are black. For a better effect, I added a dark gray line inside the bottom-right corner.

Grooved Borders

The grooved border looks like a tiny canyon on your screen. Commonly used to group components, this effect is easy to reproduce. Figure 3.3 illustrates the concept of a grooved border.

Figure 3.3.
A grooved border.

This effect is similar to the lowered border because the result is a sunken look. If you are familiar with the Microsoft Windows operating system, you will recognize this effect as a group box border.

To make the object appear grooved, you need to create a white shadow at the bottom of a dark rectangle. In Figure 3.3, I started with a white rectangle and drew a dark gray rectangle inside of it. I then filled it with a light gray and put a white highlight on the upper and right sides of the inside of the dark gray rectangle.

Ridged Borders

The ridged border is the exact opposite of the grooved border. Similar to the raised border, the ridged border is a raised effect. Figure 3.4 illustrates the method for creating a ridged border.

Figure 3.4.
A ridged border.

Making the object appear ridged is similar to the grooved procedure. The difference is that what was white in the grooved border is now dark gray and vice versa. In Figure 3.4, I started with a dark gray rectangle and drew a white rectangle inside of it. I then filled it with a light gray and put a dark gray highlight on the upper and right sides of the inside of the white rectangle.

Creating a Custom Component

Now that you have an idea of what is involved in creating a 3-D border style, this section explains how to create a custom component that displays itself with the 3-D border. You can use this component for many things, such as grouping components, grouping buttons, and displaying images. But before you start creating your component, you need to create an interface that defines your border styles.

An *interface*, as you'll recall, is a template or pattern to which a Java class must adhere. Using an interface in this instance allows you to reuse your border styles in other classes and will make the transition to JavaBeans easier. JavaBeans are covered completely on Day 5, "Introduction to JavaBeans," and Day 6, "Using JavaBeans Effectively." For now, just think of JavaBeans as custom components with special features.

The interface you'll create includes indicators for each of the border styles that the custom component can display. Table 3.1 shows the various border styles that the component will support.

Table 3.1. Component border styles.

Style	Description
None	No border
Flat	A flat, 2-D border
Lowered	A lowered, or sunken, border
Raised	A raised, 3-D border
Grooved	A grooved, chisel-like border
Ridged	A ridged border

The BorderStyle interface

You need to create a constant, or final variable, for each border style. You will then use these constants to indicate the style of the border in the component. Here's what the constants look like:

```
public interface
BorderStyle
{
    //    Constants
    public final static int      NONE = 0;
    public final static int      FLAT = 1;
    public final static int      LOWERED = 2;
    public final static int      RAISED = 3;
    public final static int      GROOVED = 4;
    public final static int      RIDGED = 5;
}
```

As you can see, the interface is named BorderStyle. Each of the styles previously mentioned are represented here by a constant. The values of these constants are irrelevant as long as they are all different.

Adding Methods to Your Madness

Interfaces are a good place to store constants for your classes. They are also an excellent way to enforce a standard behavior. You can add two methods to the BorderStyle interface to ensure that consumers of this interface adhere to your usage guidelines.

These two methods are usually called *accessor methods*. Accessor methods are used to access private or protected member variables within a class. By defining accessor methods in your interface, you are requiring any implementor to adhere to your accessor methods. The following is the listing for the accessor methods for BorderStyle:

```
public void setBorderStyle( int style );
public int getBorderStyle();
```

The first method, setBorderStyle(), is used to set a border style. The second, getBorderStyle(), returns the current border style. If you have programmed in Visual Basic, Delphi, or another object-oriented development environment, you may recognize that these methods are quite similar to properties. In fact, many new languages support the property paradigm. All properties really are, however, is masked accessor methods. Although you might not be calling an accessor method directly, the language is creating code behind the scenes for you.

One last note about accessor methods. When you convert your components to JavaBeans (on Day 5), these two methods become the property accessor methods. As you will see, no further coding will be necessary.

Your Custom Component: BorderPanel

Now that you've created an interface for border styles, you need to create the shell of your new component. You want your component to inherit some behaviors. You could create your component based on the Canvas class, but you would have to do a lot of component management work. Instead, you will base your new class on Java's Panel class. Using this class allows you to use the component as a container of other components as well as nesting it within other containers. Also, members of this class know how to use layout managers.

Creating the BorderPanel Class

Start off your new component as you would any other class:

```
import java.awt.Panel;

public class
BorderPanel
extends Panel
implements BorderStyle
```

Note that this code extends the Panel class and implements the BorderStyle interface. Implementing this interface requires you to add the two accessor methods (getBorderStyle() and setBorderStyle()) and makes all of the constants available to this new class.

Finish up the class by declaring a protected variable to hold the value of the panel's border style. Call this variable borderStyle. Next, add constructors and the two accessor methods as shown in Listing 3.1:

Listing 3.1. The BorderPanel class.

```
1: import java.awt.Color;
2: import java.awt.Dimension;
3: import java.awt.Graphics;
4: import java.awt.Panel;
5: import java.awt.Insets;
6:
```

3

```
 7: public class
 8: BorderPanel
 9: extends Panel
10: implements BorderStyle
11: {
12:     protected int borderStyle = NONE;
13:     protected boolean skipTop = false;
14:     protected boolean skipLeft = false;
15:     protected boolean skipBottom = false;
16:     protected boolean skipRight = false;
17:
18:     public
19:     BorderPanel()
20:     {
21:         this( NONE );
22:     }
23:
24:     public
25:     BorderPanel( int borderStyle )
26:     {
27:         this.borderStyle = borderStyle;
28:     }
29:
30:     public void
31:     setBorderStyle( int borderStyle )
32:     {
33:         this.borderStyle = borderStyle;
34:         repaint();
35:     }
36:
37:     public int
38:     getBorderStyle()
39:     {
40:         return( borderStyle );
41:     }
42:
43:     public void
44:     setSkipTop( boolean onOff )
45:     {
46:         skipTop = onOff;
47:     }
48:
49:     public boolean
50:     getSkipTop()
51:     {
52:         return( skipTop );
53:     }
54:
55:     public void
56:     setSkipBottom( boolean onOff )
57:     {
58:         skipBottom = onOff;
59:     }
60:
61:     public boolean
62:     getSkipBottom()
```

continues

Listing 3.1. continued

```
63:        {
64:              return( skipBottom );
65:        }
66:
67:        public void
68:        setSkipRight( boolean onOff )
69:        {
70:              skipRight = onOff;
71:        }
72:
73:        public boolean
74:        getSkipRight()
75:        {
76:              return( skipRight );
77:        }
78:
79:        public void
80:        setSkipLeft( boolean onOff )
81:        {
82:              skipLeft = onOff;
83:        }
84:
85:        public boolean
86:        getSkipLeft()
87:        {
88:              return( skipLeft );
89:        }
90:
91: }
```

NOTE

> Wait! Before you type in the code from that listing! The code in Listing
> 3.1 and in the rest of this chapter can be found on the companion Web
> site at http://www.mcp.com/info/1-57521/1-57521-347-8.

Line 12 defaults the borderStyle to NONE so the new class acts like a regular Panel if no style
is specified. Line 34 calls the repaint() method within setBorderStyle() so that the border
style can be changed on the fly. This code allows you, for example, to show a button being
clicked by lowering the border and then raising it again.

The skipTop, skipLeft, skipBottom, and skipRight variables allow you to not draw a
particular side of the border. When one of these variables is set to true, that side is not drawn.
You'll understand more about these variables when you draw the border. Note that the
repaint() method is not called when these variables are set. That means that if you call them
after your panel is displayed, you must call the repaint() method yourself in order to see the
changes. Most likely you'll set these variables before you display the panel.

Constructing a `BorderPanel`

You can construct a `BorderPanel` in two ways. You can use it as a regular Java `Panel` by creating it with no arguments:

```
BorderPanel myPanel = new BorderPanel();
```

Or you can create one that has a specific type of border:

```
BorderPanel myPanel = new BorderPanel( BorderStyle.RAISED );
```

Refer to Figures 3.1 through 3.4 for a gander at the different border styles available for a `BorderPanel`.

Smoke and Mirrors: Creating the 3-D Border Illusion

If you're at all like me, you are probably ready to look at some more in-depth source code. I'm sure you're wondering how to create those cool 3-D border effects. It doesn't take smoke and mirrors or a degree from a clown college. It's quite simple, and I'll show you how.

Drawing 3-D Borders

In order to draw the border around the panel, you need to augment the `paint()` method of the new class. You do this as follows:

```
public void
paint( Graphics g )
{
    if ( borderStyle != NONE )
        draw3DBorder( g );

    super.paint( g );
}
```

If the border style has been set to anything other than none, you call a new method called `draw3DBorder()`. This method draws the 3-D border around the panel. After the border is drawn, you call the superclass's `paint()` method, which allows ancestors of your class to act upon this event.

The `draw3Dborder()` method performs the following steps:

1. It retrieves the dimensions of itself (the panel).
2. It stores the current color of the panel.
3. It interrogates the currently set border style and draws it.
4. It restores the old current color that it stored.

NOTE

> Storing the old color of the Graphics canvas is more of a courtesy than a necessity. Others may depend on this color being there. If you don't do this step, subsequent drawing of other components may be colored incorrectly.

This procedure is fairly simple if you take it a step at a time. First, you declare the method and get the size of the panel:

```
public void
draw3DBorder( Graphics g )
{
    Dimension    bounds = size();
```

Next, you store the current color:

```
Color oldColor = g.getColor( );
```

You then switch on the current border style:

```
switch ( borderStyle )
{
```

If you need a flat border, set the color to dark gray and draw a rectangle:

```
case FLAT:
    //    Draw a plain rectangle
    g.setColor( new Color( 128, 128, 128 ) );

    //    Top
    if ( !skipTop )
       g.drawLine( 0, 0, bounds.width - 1, 0 );

    //    Left
    if ( !skipLeft )
       g.drawLine( 0, 0, 0, bounds.height - 1 );

    //    Bottom
    if ( !skipBottom )
       g.drawLine( 0, bounds.height - 1, bounds.width - 1, bounds.height - 1 );

    //    Right
    if ( !skipRight )
       g.drawLine( bounds.width - 1, 0, bounds.width - 1, bounds.height - 1 );
    break;
```

A lowered border is a bit more complex. You set the color to dark gray, and then draw the top and left lines:

```
case LOWERED:
    //    Top...
    g.setColor( new Color( 128, 128, 128 ) );
```

```
//    Top
if ( !skipTop )
    g.drawLine( 0, 0, bounds.width - 1, 0 );

//    Left
if ( !skipLeft )
    g.drawLine( 0, 0, 0, bounds.height - 1 );
```

Next, you set the color to white, draw the bottom line, and then draw the right side line:

```
g.setColor( Color.white );

//    Bottom
g.drawLine( 0, bounds.height - 1, bounds.width - 1, bounds.height - 1 );

//    Right...
g.drawLine( bounds.width - 1, 0, bounds.width - 1, bounds.height - 1 );
break;
```

The raised border is similar to the lowered, except the colors are different. Also, there is a dark gray inset line on the lower and right sides:

```
case RAISED:
    g.setColor( Color.white );

    //    Top
    if ( !skipTop )
        g.drawLine( 0, 0, bounds.width - 1, 0 );

    //    Left
    if ( !skipLeft )
        g.drawLine( 0, 0, 0, bounds.height - 1 );

    //    Bottom
    g.setColor( Color.black );
    g.drawLine( 0, bounds.height - 1, bounds.width - 1, bounds.height - 1 );

    //    Right...
    g.drawLine( bounds.width - 1, 0, bounds.width - 1, bounds.height - 1 );

    //    Inset
    g.setColor( new Color( 128, 128, 128 ) );
    g.drawLine( 1, bounds.height - 2, bounds.width - 2, bounds.height - 2 );
    g.drawLine( bounds.width - 2, 1, bounds.width - 2, bounds.height - 2 );
    break;
```

The ridged border is not as difficult as the raised border. Here you are simply drawing a dark gray rectangle that is two pixels wide on the left and bottom sides. Then, you draw a white rectangle right on top. The grooved border is the exact opposite of the ridged border in terms of color. In fact, you can use the same code:

```
case RIDGED:
case GROOVED:
    g.setColor( ( borderStyle == RIDGED ) ?
        new Color( 128, 128, 128 ) : Color.white );

    //    Top
    if ( !skipTop )
        g.drawLine( 0, 0, bounds.width - 1, 0 );

    //    Left
    if ( !skipLeft )
        g.drawLine( 0, 0, 0, bounds.height - 1 );

    //    Bottom
    if ( !skipBottom )
        g.drawLine( 0, bounds.height - 1, bounds.width - 1,
            bounds.height - 1 );

    //    Right
    if ( !skipRight )
        g.drawLine( bounds.width - 1, 0, bounds.width - 1,
            bounds.height - 1 );

            //    Second...
            g.drawLine( 1, 1, bounds.width - 2, 1 );
            g.drawLine( 1, 1, 1, bounds.height - 2 );

    //    Draw inset...
    g.setColor( ( borderStyle == RIDGED ) ?
        Color.white : new Color( 128, 128, 128 ) );

    //    Top
    if ( !skipTop )
        g.drawLine( 0, 0, bounds.width - 2, 0 );

    //    Left
    if ( !skipLeft )
        g.drawLine( 0, 0, 0, bounds.height - 2 );

    //    Bottom
    if ( !skipBottom )
        g.drawLine( 0, bounds.height - 2, bounds.width - 2,
            bounds.height - 2 );

    //    Right
    if ( !skipRight )
        g.drawLine( bounds.width - 2, 0, bounds.width - 2,
            bounds.height - 2 );
    break;
```

Lastly, you set the old color back:

```
g.setColor( oldColor );
```

You probably noticed that before you draw each line, you check to see whether a variable is set. These variables (skipTop, skipLeft, skipBottom, and skipRight) allow you to not draw a border on a particular side. Each of these variables has its own accessor method defined in the BorderPanel class. These variables are extremely useful when you build more complex components out of the BorderPanel class, such as the TabPanel you work on later today.

Testing the BorderPanel

To test BorderPanel, create an applet that draws each of the different types of borders in a separate panel by creating a blank applet and inserting a bunch of BorderPanels. Call this applet BorderTest. Listing 3.2 provides the code for this applet.

Listing 3.2. The BorderTest applet.

```
import java.awt.*;
import java.applet.*;

public class
BorderTest
extends Applet
{
    public
    BorderTest()
    {
        setFont( new Font( "Helvetica", Font.BOLD, 14 ) );
        setBackground( Color.lightGray );

        BorderPanel myPanel = new BorderPanel( BorderPanel.RAISED );
        myPanel.setLayout( new FlowLayout() );

        Panel p;

        myPanel.add( p = new BorderPanel( BorderPanel.FLAT ) );
        p.add( new Label( "Panel1" ) );
        p.add( new Label( "Panel1" ) );
        p.add( new Label( "Panel1" ) );
        myPanel.add( p = new BorderPanel( BorderPanel.RAISED ) );
        p.add( new Label( "Panel2" ) );
        p.add( new Label( "Panel2" ) );
        p.add( new Label( "Panel2" ) );
        myPanel.add( p = new BorderPanel( BorderPanel.LOWERED ) );
        p.add( new Label( "Panel3" ) );
        p.add( new Label( "Panel3" ) );
        p.add( new Label( "Panel3" ) );
        myPanel.add( p = new BorderPanel( BorderPanel.GROOVED ) );
        p.add( new Label( "Panel4" ) );
        p.add( new Label( "Panel4" ) );
        p.add( new Label( "Panel4" ) );
        myPanel.add( p = new BorderPanel( BorderPanel.RIDGED ) );
        p.add( new Label( "Panel5" ) );
        p.add( new Label( "Panel5" ) );
        p.add( new Label( "Panel5" ) );
```

continues

Listing 3.2. continued

```
        //    Add to the center...
        add( "Center", myPanel );
    }
}
```

This test is simple: You create five BorderPanels and place three labels inside each of them. It's not much, but it's nice to look at. Figure 3.5 shows the output of this applet.

Figure 3.5.

The output of the
BorderTest *applet.*

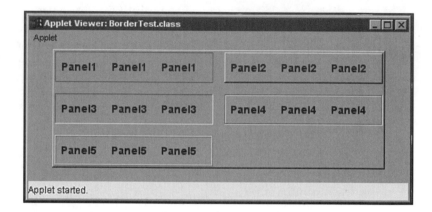

The ImagePanel Class

The ImagePanel class is an extension of the BorderPanel class that loads an image and resizes itself to the size of the image. This class is useful for many applications, such as displaying buttons or icons.

There are three ways to construct an ImagePanel. You can use a simple constructor that defaults to an offset of five pixels:

```
ImagePanel ip = new ImagePanel( "c:\\image.gif" );
```

Or you can use a constructor that allows you to set the offset:

```
ImagePanel ip = new ImagePanel( "c:\\image.gif", 15 );
```

Or you can specify an offset and a border for the image as well:

```
ImagePanel ip = new ImagePanel( "c:\\image.gif", 15, ImagePanel.RAISED );
```

TIP

Remember that you can set the border style with the getBorderStyle() and setBorderStyle() methods of the new ImagePanel class. That is because they are inherited from the base class BorderPanel.

Each constructor takes as the first argument the name of the graphic file to load. Whatever image types Java supports, the ImagePanel also supports. Currently, only GIF and JPEG image formats are supported. Listing 3.3 gives the code for the new class.

Listing 3.3. The ImagePanel **class.**

```
 1: /*
 2: * Class: ImagePanel.java
 3: */
 4:
 5: import                    BorderPanel;
 6: import                    java.io.File;
 7: import                    java.awt.Graphics;
 8: import                    java.awt.MediaTracker;
 9: import                    java.awt.Dimension;
10: import                    java.awt.Image;
11: import                    java.awt.image.ImageProducer;
12: import                    java.awt.Insets;
13: import                    java.net.URL;
14:
15: public class
16: ImagePanel
17: extends BorderPanel
18: {
19:     protected Image           myImage;
20:     protected int             offset;
21:     protected String          imageToUse;
22:
23:     /**
24:     * Construct and load an ImagePanel
25:     * @param imageToUse The image to display
26:     * @param offset The offset to display at
27:     * @param borderStyle The style of the border
28:     */
29:     public
30:     ImagePanel( String imageToUse, int offset, int borderStyle )
31:     {
32:         //    Construct a BorderPanel...
33:         super( borderStyle );
34:
35:         //    Store parameters...
36:         this.offset = offset;
37:         setImageToUse( imageToUse );
38:     }
39:
40:     /**
41:     * Construct and load an ImagePanel
42:     * @param imageToUse The image to display
43:     * @param offset The x y offset
44:     */
45:     public
46:     ImagePanel( String imageToUse, int offset )
47:     {
48:         this( imageToUse, offset, NONE );
```

continues

Listing 3.3. continued

```
 49:      }
 50:
 51:      /**
 52:       * Construct and load an ImagePanel
 53:       * @param imageToUse The image to display
 54:       */
 55:      public
 56:      ImagePanel( String imageToUse )
 57:      {
 58:          this( imageToUse, 5, NONE );
 59:      }
 60:
 61:      /**
 62:       * Construct and load an ImagePanel
 63:       */
 64:      public
 65:      ImagePanel()
 66:      {
 67:          this( "question.gif" );
 68:      }
 69:
 70:      /**
 71:       * Get the image to use
 72:       */
 73:      public String
 74:      getImageToUse()
 75:      {
 76:      return( imageToUse );
 77:      }
 78:
 79:      /**
 80:       * Set the image to use
 81:       */
 82:      public void
 83:      setImageToUse(String itu)
 84:      {
 85:          imageToUse = itu;
 86:
 87:          //   Open up the image...
 88:          MediaTracker myTracker;
 89:          myTracker = new MediaTracker( this );
 90:
 91:          try
 92:          {
 93:              URL url = getClass().getResource( imageToUse );
 94:              myImage = createImage( ( ImageProducer )url.getContent() );
 95:          }
 96:          catch ( Exception e )
 97:          {
 98:              System.err.println( "Couldn't load the image " + imageToUse +
                 ➥"." );
 99:              myImage = null;
100:              return;
101:          }
102:
```

```
103:            myTracker.addImage( myImage, 0 );
104:
105:        try
106:            {
107:                myTracker.waitForID( 0 );
108:            }
109:            catch ( InterruptedException e )
110:            {
111:                System.out.println( "Error during load: " + e.toString() );
112:            }
113:    }
114:
115:    /**
116:     * Calculates the space needed to nicely enclose any contained
117:     * components
118:     */
119:    public Insets
120:    getInsets()
121:    {
122:        return( new Insets( offset, offset, offset, offset ) );
123:    }
124:
125:    public Dimension
126:    getMinimumSize()
127:    {
128:        int w = 10, h = 10;
129:
130:        if ( myImage != null )
131:            {
132:                w = myImage.getWidth( this ) + ( offset * 2 );
133:                h = myImage.getHeight( this ) + ( offset * 2 );
134:            }
135:
136:        //    Make sure I'm big enough...
137:        if ( w > getSize().width )
138:            setSize( w, h );
139:
140:        return( new Dimension( w, h ) );
141:    }
142:
143:    public Dimension
144:    getPreferredSize()
145:    {
146:        return( getMinimumSize() );
147:    }
148:
149:    /**
150:     * Paint the image
151:     * @param g The Graphics object to paint on
152:     */
153:    public void
154:    paint( Graphics g )
155:    {
156:        //    Let the border paint...
157:        super.paint( g );
158:
159:        if ( myImage != null )
```

continues

Listing 3.3. continued

```
160:            {
161:                g.drawImage( myImage,
162:                    offset,
163:                    offset,
164:                    this );
165:            }
166:        }
167:
168: }    public Dimension
169:      getPreferredSize()
170:      {
171:          return( getMinimumSize() );
172:      }
173:
174:      public void
175:      paint( Graphics g )
176:      {
177:          //    Let the border paint...
178:          super.paint( g );
179:
180:          g.drawImage( myImage,
181:              offset,
182:              offset,
183:              myObserver );
184:      }
185: }
```

This class really has only one constructor, even though there are four total constructors. Three of them call the fourth. This technique is good to use because it keeps all of your construction code together and lets you set defaults accordingly. In the main constructor (Line 29), you call the base class's constructor, and then set the image to use. The accessor method setImageToUse() stores image name and loads the image into memory.

This class uses a MediaTracker to ensure that the images load (Line 88). Although using a MediaTracker is not necessary, doing so ensures that the image is loaded before the component is layed out so that the sizes are correct when the layout manager calls the getPreferredSize() and getMinimumSize() methods. These methods are necessary because this class shrinks to fit around the image, except for the offset from the sides also specified in the constructor.

You extend the getInsets() method as well (Line 119). In this code, you add the offset to the existing insets of the base class. This method tells the graphics engine to leave that much room around the edges. In addition, the paint() method is augmented to draw the image in the proper place after the base paint() method has been called.

Testing ImagePanel

The test program in Listing 3.4 demonstrates the use and features of the ImagePanel class. This program is an applet called ImageTest.

Listing 3.4. The `ImageTest` applet.

```java
import java.awt.*;
import java.applet.*;

public class
ImageTest
extends Applet
{
    public
    ImageTest()
    {
        setFont( new Font( "Helvetica", Font.BOLD, 14 ) );
        setBackground( Color.lightGray );

        BorderPanel myPanel = new BorderPanel( BorderPanel.RAISED );
        setLayout( new BorderLayout() );

        Panel p;

        myPanel.add( p = new ImagePanel( "information.gif", 5,
        ➡ImagePanel.RAISED ) );
        myPanel.add( p = new ImagePanel( "exclamation.gif",15,
        ➡ImagePanel.LOWERED ) );
        myPanel.add( p = new ImagePanel( "question.gif", 25,
        ➡ImagePanel.RIDGED ) );
        myPanel.add( p = new ImagePanel( "stop.gif", 35, ImagePanel.GROOVED ) );

        //    Add to the center...
        add( "Center", myPanel );
    }

}
```

This applet creates a single `BorderPanel`, which it fills with four `ImagePanels`. Each `ImagePanel` increases its size by 10 pixels. Figure 3.6 shows the output of this applet.

Figure 3.6.

The output of the
`ImageTest` *applet.*

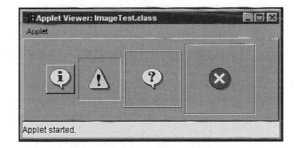

Creating the `TabPanel` Class

One major shortcoming of the stock Java components is the lack of a tabbed panel or folder component. This component presents information one sheet at a time. This new metaphor is common in Microsoft Windows and is becoming popular on other platforms as well.

Sun Microsystems, Inc. noted that this component would catch on, so it provided the `CardLayout` layout manager. This layout presents a stack of components with only one component visible at a time. You must bring one card in the stack to the top to view it. Using the `BorderPanel` component, you can build a new custom component, called `TabPanel`, that uses the `CardLayout` layout manager and provides a tabbed folder component.

The idea behind the `TabPanel` class is easy. Using a `BorderLayout`, you place a strip of tab buttons in the North border and place a `CardLayout` of panels in the Center border. The two line up and appear to be a single control. Figure 3.7 illustrates this point.

Figure 3.7.

The `TabPanel` *concept.*

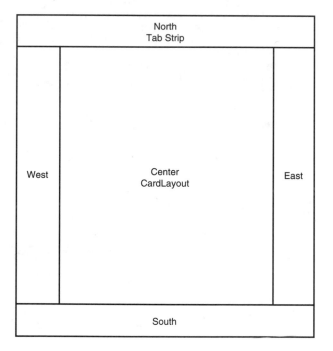

Figure 3.8 shows a tab panel in use.

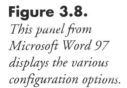

Figure 3.8.

This panel from Microsoft Word 97 displays the various configuration options.

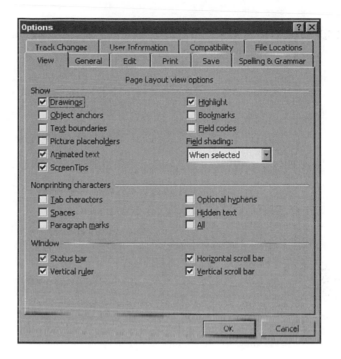

Designing the TabPanel Class

The design of the TabPanel class is a bit complex. The main class, TabPanel, is a manager of two other classes: TabPanePanel and TabStrip. TabPanePanel is the portion that manages the panes in the CardLayout. TabStrip draws and manages the tab buttons along the top of the window. The TabPanel class acts as a message router. It tells the TabPanePanel which tab on the TabStrip was clicked.

A fourth, private class called TabPane belongs to the TabStrip class. This class is used to represent a single pane in the tab panel. Using this class, the TabStrip class can keep track of the names of panes and whether they are enabled.

Managing the Panes

The TabPanePanel class has the job of managing the individual panes. Listing 3.5 shows the source code for this class.

Listing 3.5. The TabPanePanel **class.**

```
import java.awt.*;

public class
TabPanePanel
extends BorderPanel
{

    CardLayout                      myLayout = new CardLayout();

    public
    TabPanePanel()
    {
        super( RAISED );
        setSkipTop( true );
        setLayout( myLayout );
    }

    public void
    addPane( String name, Component comp )
    {
        add( name, comp );
    }

    public void
    selectPane( String paneName )
    {
        myLayout.show( this, paneName );
    }

}
```

This class is simple because you rely on CardLayout to do the management for you. In the constructor, you set the border to a raised style and tell the panel not to draw the top lines. Finally, you set the layout to CardLayout. You also add two methods to this class: addPane() and selectPane(). The addPane() method adds a pane to the card layout, and selectPane() selects a pane from the card layout.

Managing the Tabs

The most complex of the four classes by far is the TabStrip class, which is responsible for drawing and flipping the tabs at the top of the panel. The TabStrip control uses a Vector to keep an array of the panes that it is managing. It provides methods for looking up panes in the array as well.

These methods are necessary because sometimes the number of the pane (0, 1, 2, and so on) is needed. Other times the name of the panel is needed. For example, CardLayout only accepts the names of the components it stores. You need to know which name is associated with the array of panes.

3

This class also provides methods to enable and disable panes. Your programs cannot call these methods directly, however. Only the main class, TabPanel, uses them.

Drawing the Tabs

The most complex portion of the TabStrip class is the drawing routine. This routine is responsible for measuring the tabs, drawing the tabs, and drawing the tab text. All of the drawing is done in the paint() method, which starts with a simple declaration and some variables:

```
public void
paint( Graphics g )
{
    int             tabWidth = 0, tabHeight = 0;
    Dimension       mySize = size();
    FontMetrics     fm = g.getFontMetrics( selFont );
    Color           oldColor = g.getColor();
```

If there are no panes, then there are no tabs. You simply exit the method:

```
//   Don't do anything if there's nothing to do...
if ( panes.size() == 0 )
    return;
```

In the next bit of code, you set the background color and specify a solid background:

```
//   Clear myself off...
g.setColor( Color.lightGray );
g.fillRect( 0, 0, mySize.width, mySize.height );
```

You now need to calculate the width of the tabs. This calculation is necessary so you know how wide to draw the tabs. The TabStrip component supports two types of tabs: proportional and full width. Proportional tabs take up only a little more room than the text inside them. Full-width tabs take up the entire width of the component. Calculating the width of full-width tabs is easy; just divide the total width by the number of tabs, as shown in the following code. Proportional tabs are calculated in the tab drawing loop.

```
//   Calculate the width of the panes...
if ( fullWidthTabs )
    tabWidth = ( mySize.width - panes.size() ) / panes.size();
```

Next you need to calculate the height of the tabs. This measurement is standard across all tabs and is based on the height of the font. Fix the height at eight pixels higher than the font:

```
//   And the height...
tabHeight = fm.getHeight() + fm.getDescent() + 8;
```

Now you resize the object to match the calculated tab widths and height:

```
realWidth = mySize.width;
realHeight = tabHeight;
resize( realWidth, tabHeight );
```

Here is where the real fun begins. First, you start a loop for each tab you need to draw:

```
//    Loop through tabs and draw...
for ( int i = 0, x = 0; i < panes.size(); i++, x += tabWidth )
{
```

Then you grab a pane from the pane array:

```
TabPane myPane = ( TabPane )panes.elementAt( i );
```

At this point in the code, you get the name and calculate the width for proportional tabs:

```
String str = myPane.myName;

if ( !fullWidthTabs )
    tabWidth = fm.stringWidth( str ) + TAB_PIXELS;
```

You want the currently selected tab to pop up. You get this effect by drawing that tab two pixels higher than the others. Setting the offset to 2 here does the trick. The offset is the number of pixels down from the top of the control where the tabs will be drawn.

```
//    Offset to draw...
int offset = 2;
```

If the tab you're coding is the current tab, then you set the offset to 0. This offset pops up the current tab. You also set the font if the selected font is different from the normal font.

```
//    UP a little for selected guy...
if ( currentTab == i )
{
    g.setFont( selFont );
    offset = 0;
}
else
    g.setFont( normalFont );
```

Next, you draw the sides of the tab:

```
//    Draw the left and top sides...
g.setColor( Color.white );

//    Skip left side of next-door neighbor...
if ( i != currentTab + 1 )
{
    //    Draw a line across the top of the tab...
    g.drawLine( x + offset + 2, offset,
        x + offset + tabWidth - 3, offset );
    g.drawLine( x + offset, 2 + offset,
        x + offset, tabHeight - 1 + offset );
    g.drawLine( x + offset + 1, offset + 1,
        x + offset + 1, offset + 1 );
}
else
    //    Extend white line on top...
    g.drawLine( x, offset, x + tabWidth - 1, offset );

//    Skip this side if next to current tab...
```

3

```
if ( currentTab - 1 != i )
{
    //    Draw right side...
    g.setColor( Color.black );
    g.drawLine( x + tabWidth + offset - 2,
        offset + 1, x + offset + tabWidth - 2, offset + 1 );
    g.drawLine( x + tabWidth + offset - 1,
        offset + 2, x + offset + tabWidth - 1,
        offset + tabHeight - 1 );
}

//    Draw inner sanctum...
g.setColor( Color.gray );
g.drawLine( x + tabWidth + offset - 2,
    offset + 2, x + offset + tabWidth - 2, offset + tabHeight - 1 );
```

Then you draw the text:

```
//    Draw the text...
g.setColor( Color.black );

int textWidth = g.getFontMetrics().stringWidth( str );
int textHeight = g.getFontMetrics().getHeight();

//    Leave four pixels on a side...
if ( textWidth < tabWidth - 4 )
{
    if ( myPane.enabled )
    {
        g.drawString( str,
            //    Center horizontally...
            x + offset + ( ( tabWidth - textWidth ) / 2 ),
            //    Center vertically...
            ( ( tabHeight - textHeight ) / 2 ) + textHeight + offset - 1 );
    }
    else
    {
        g.setColor( Color.white );

        //    Draw at a one space offset...
        g.drawString( str,
            //    Center horizontally...
            x + offset + ( ( tabWidth - textWidth ) / 2 ) + 1,
            //    Center vertically...
            ( ( tabHeight - textHeight ) / 2 ) + textHeight + offset );

        //    Draw a dark gray line in its place...
g.setColor( new Color( 128, 128, 128 ) );
        g.drawString( str,
            //    Center horizontally...
            x + offset + ( ( tabWidth - textWidth ) / 2 ),
            //    Center vertically...
            ( ( tabHeight - textHeight ) / 2 ) + textHeight + offset - 1 );
    }
}
```

Finally, you draw a line that extends across the remaining area of the tab. This line serves as the top. You then restore the canvas color:

```
//    If I'm not selected, draw a white bottom...
g.setColor( Color.white );

if ( currentTab != i )
{
    if ( i != panes.size() - 1 )
    {
        g.drawLine( x, tabHeight - 1,
            x + tabWidth - 1, tabHeight - 1 );
    }
    else
    {
        g.drawLine( x, tabHeight - 1,
            mySize.width - 1, tabHeight - 1 );
    }
}
else
{
    g.drawLine( x + tabWidth - 1, tabHeight - 1,
        mySize.width - 1, tabHeight - 1 );
}
}

//    Restore the old color...
g.setColor( oldColor );
}
```

Putting Them All Together

The last class is the `TabPanel` class. Because its subcomponents do most of the work, it is a fairly simple class, as shown in Listing 3.6.

Listing 3.6. The `TabPanel` class.

```
import                      java.awt.*;
import                      java.util.Vector;

public class
TabPanel
extends BorderPanel
{
    protected TabPanePanel    panePanel = new TabPanePanel();
    protected TabStrip        selector = new TabStrip( panePanel );

    public
    TabPanel()
    {
        super( NONE );

        //    Don't draw the northern edge of the box...
```

3

```
        setSkipTop( true );

        //    We need a border layout...
        setLayout( new BorderLayout() );

        //    Add my stuff...
        add( "North", selector );
        add( "Center", panePanel );
    }

    public void
    addPane( String name, Component comp )
    {
        selector.addPane( name, comp );
    }

    public void
    selectPane( String name )
    {
        selector.selectPane( name );
    }

    public void
    enablePane( String paneName )
    {
        selector.enablePane( paneName );
    }

    public void
    disablePane( String paneName )
    {
        selector.disablePane( paneName );
    }

}
```

This class just passes along your requests to its subcomponents. This leverage of work is key in creating usable, powerful custom components.

Testing TabPanel

To test TabPanel, you need to create an applet that creates a TabPanel and places several components inside it. Listing 3.7 shows the code for the applet, TabTest, that does just that.

Listing 3.7. The TabTest applet.

```
import                    java.awt.*;
import                    java.applet.*;

public class
TabTest
```

continues

Listing 3.7. continued

```
extends Applet
{
    //    Create a tab panel...
TabPanel myPanel;

    public
    TabTest()
    {
        myPanel = new TabPanel();
        setBackground( Color.lightGray );
        myPanel.resize( 500, 500 );

        //    Add some panes to it...
        BorderPanel p;
        myPanel.addPane( "Tab 1", p = new BorderPanel( BorderPanel.RAISED ) );
        p.add( new Label( "Panel 1" ) );
        myPanel.addPane( "Tab 2", p = new BorderPanel( BorderPanel.RAISED ) );
        p.add( new Label( "Panel 2" ) );
        myPanel.addPane( "Tab 3", p = new BorderPanel( BorderPanel.RAISED ) );
        p.add( new Label( "Panel 3" ) );
        myPanel.addPane( "Tab 4", p = new BorderPanel( BorderPanel.RAISED ) );
        p.add( new Label( "Panel 4" ) );
        myPanel.addPane( "Tab 5", p = new BorderPanel( BorderPanel.RAISED ) );
        p.add( new Label( "Panel 5" ) );

        myPanel.disablePane( "Tab 3" );

        //    Add to the center...
        setLayout( new BorderLayout() );
        add( "Center", myPanel );
    }

    public boolean
    action( Event evt, Object arg )
    {
        if ( evt.target instanceof TabStrip )
        {
            if ( ( ( Integer )arg ).intValue() == 4 )
            {
                myPanel.enablePane( "Tab 3" );
                myPanel.disablePane( "Tab 4" );
                return( true );
            }

            if ( ( ( Integer )arg ).intValue() == 2 )
            {
                myPanel.enablePane( "Tab 4" );
                myPanel.disablePane( "Tab 3" );
                return( true );
            }
        }

        return( false );
    }

}
```

This simple applet demonstrates the TabPanel class quite nicely. It creates five tabs and places a panel inside each one. Inside each of the panels is a label naming the panel. The action() method in the applet demonstrates the enabling and disabling of tabs. If you click Tab 5, Tab 4 will be disabled. If you click Tab 3 when Tab 4 is disabled, Tab 4 will be enabled. Figure 3.9 shows the output of the TabTest applet.

Figure 3.9.

The output of the TabTest applet.

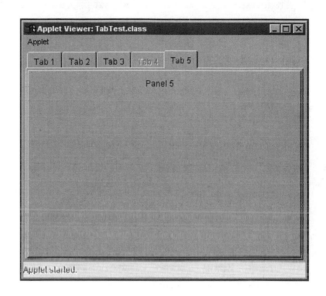

Summary

Today you learned the importance of custom components. You learned how to create your own components and then build upon them to create interesting and unique new tools. You started this process by building a new component that draws a 3-D border around itself. You then enhanced this new class, BorderPanel, to draw images in the ImagePanel class. Finally you took the BorderPanel class and built the TabPanel class, which manages a tabbed folder component. On Day 5, you'll convert this TabPanel into a JavaBean so you can use it with Java GUI builders, such as Visual Café.

Q&A

Q What is a custom component?

A A custom component is a user interface component that does not come with the Java Development Kit. It can be something unique or a combination of two existing components, a button and a list box, for example.

Q What makes custom components visually appealing?

A 3-D borders make custom components visually appealing. Boring, flat 2-D borders just don't cut it in today's world.

Q What is an accessor method?

A An accessor method is a method that provides secure access to a nonpublic member variable. Accessor methods allow you to check for validity in range and value when setting parameters.

Day 4

Foundation Classes and Java Frameworks

by Michael Morrison

When Java was first unveiled a couple of years ago, the initial excitement was over the capability of adding true interactivity to Web pages. Java provided interactivity by enabling developers to create applets that could be embedded directly into otherwise static HTML Web pages. In creating applets, developers relied heavily on the graphics functionality in the Abstract Windowing Toolkit (AWT), which is provided as part of the standard Java API. Once Java started being looked at more seriously as a viable development platform beyond applets, however, weaknesses in the AWT started to show. JavaSoft realized that the graphical user interface (GUI) support in Java would need to be reworked in order to provide a more broad-based development platform for modern applications.

Various efforts immediately began to develop a suite of Java application components, or foundation classes, that could be used to build Java applications with advanced user interface elements and related services. Netscape initially carried the torch and developed the Internet Foundation Classes (IFC). Microsoft soon followed suit and offered its own Application Foundation Classes (AFC). Both of these class libraries offer a wealth of functionality above and beyond the standard Java AWT. You explore each of these class libraries in today's lesson.

Even though the IFC and AFC are powerful and readily available application frameworks, the framework to watch in the coming months is the Java Foundation Classes (JFC), which is JavaSoft's answer to an application framework for Java. Parts of the JFC are present in Java 1.1; other parts are still under development and are expected to be available by the end of 1997. The new parts of the JFC are built upon Netscape's IFC; JavaSoft and Netscape are jointly working on the JFC, which will supercede the IFC upon release. Of the different AWT-based class libraries out there, the JFC stands to be the one most likely to catch on because it will merge with the standard Java API and will be endorsed as the official application framework for Java.

Today's lesson gives you a glimpse of the following frameworks:

- JavaSoft's JFC
- Netscape's IFC
- Microsoft's AFC

You can decide for yourself which one you prefer. Even though the JFC is the newest of the application frameworks, you begin the lesson with it because its core features are similar to many of those found in the IFC and AFC.

JFC : The Future of Java Class Libraries

The JFC is a set of classes and interfaces that facilitate a wide range of GUI features and system functions for Java. Although much of the talk surrounding the JFC has focused on features to come, the JFC is technically already a part of Java 1.1. In fact, the JFC is a superset of the AWT. Granted, JavaSoft didn't exactly have the JFC in mind when it first created the AWT, but in order to make the JFC completely compatible with existing Java code, it only made sense to blend it with the existing AWT. Figure 4.1 shows where the JFC fits into the AWT and Java API.

4

Figure 4.1.

The relationship between the JFC, the AWT, and the Java API.

Although the JFC is present in the Java 1.1 API, many of the more important features promised by the JFC have yet to come. JavaSoft has outlined all of these features in specification form and has even released early implementations of many of them. This lesson takes a look at the current JFC features present in the Java 1.1 API and then shifts gears and explores the forthcoming JFC features that will appear in Java 1.2. Toward the end of the lesson, you test drive a sample application that demonstrates many of the new JFC features.

Before getting into the new functionality promised by the JFC, you should understand the state of the JFC today. The JFC support provided in Java 1.1 can be broken down into the following major categories:

- [ ] Lightweight component framework
- [ ] Delegation event model
- [ ] Printing
- [ ] Clipboard data transfer
- [ ] Desktop colors
- [ ] Mouseless operation

You may be surprised to find out that this support is technically part of the JFC. The Java 1.1 documentation doesn't really mention the JFC, so you wouldn't have any way of knowing the scope of the JFC without digging into the JFC specification. As an example of the unspoken presence of the JFC in Java 1.1, the delegation event model is one of the most significant enhancements in Java 1.1, yet there is no mention of it being a part of the JFC. The reality is that the JFC is more of an organization of functionally related classes and interfaces instead of a distinct technology unto itself.

One of the reasons that the JFC isn't mentioned in Java 1.1 is because the JFC is somewhat of an afterthought. The delegation event model was added to Java 1.1 primarily to facilitate JavaBeans; it just so happens that the JFC is highly Bean-based, and therefore is dependent on the delegation event model. The next few sections uncover the JFC features present in Java 1.1.

4

Lightweight Component Framework

Graphical AWT components in Java 1.0 were based on a *peer* model where an AWT component had an underlying native peer object associated with it. For example, a Java 1.0 button on the Windows platform had a Win32 window associated with it that handled the physical representation of the button. The main reason for using peers in Java was to maintain a native look and feel for Java GUIs. Although this approach worked well for keeping AWT components close to the underlying native GUI, it also meant that the GUI for Java applets and applications could vary widely depending on the native platform. In some situations, this platform inconsistency isn't desirable.

NEW TERM *peer:* A native GUI object used by Java as the underlying support for many AWT components.

To understand how peers can be a problem, suppose you want to create an image button. The logical approach would be to derive a class from `java.awt.Button`, but this approach has a problem because the underlying button peer largely provides the functionality of the `java.awt.Button` class. In other words, the `java.awt.Button` class is more of a wrapper for a native button rather than a complete button implementation in Java. One work-around for this problem is to implement your own Java button by deriving from the `java.awt.Canvas` class. The obvious drawback to this approach is that the button will look the same on all platforms, which can be a bad thing.

To alleviate the problem with peers, Java 1.1 introduced peerless components, which are components with no native peer associated with them. These components are also referred to as *lightweight components*; components with peers are referred to as *heavyweight components*.

NEW TERM *lightweight component:* A component completely implemented in Java, without an underlying native peer.

heavyweight component: A component with an underlying peer that provides some of the component's functionality.

The lightweight component model in Java 1.1 sounds great, but you're still left with the problem of peerless components looking the same on all platforms. This problem is addressed in a new pluggable look-and-feel feature of the JFC that will appear in the next release of Java. You learn about this feature a little later in the lesson.

Delegation Event Model

The Java 1.1 delegation event model marks one of the most important changes in Java 1.1. The delegation event model, which is a core part of the JFC, provides a great deal of flexibility in how events are delivered and processed. Additionally, the delegation event model was pretty much a necessity in making JavaBeans a reality. The event source/listener approach is what makes dynamic interaction between Beans possible. You learned a great deal about the delegation event model on Day 2, "Maximizing the Delegation Event Model," so I won't go into any more detail about it here.

Printing

Prior to Java 1.1, there was no way to print from Java, period. This deficiency is an indication of the original intention of Java—to liven up Web pages. The printing support in Java 1.1 is a sure sign of Java's quick movement toward an all-encompassing development platform. Again, the JFC takes full credit for the presence of printing support in Java 1.1.

Clipboard Data Transfer

Few users of GUIs can discount the power of the cut, copy, and paste operations. This very sentence I'm writing was cut from later in the chapter and pasted in right here (not really). I rely heavily on the cut, copy, and paste clipboard operations in practically every application I use. Support for clipboard operations in Java is yet another piece of the puzzle required for making Java a viable option for full-blown graphical application development.

Desktop Colors

Many of the graphical drawing operations in the Java AWT operate within the context of a color or group of colors. For example, when you draw a line using the Graphics.drawLine() method, the line is drawn in the current color maintained by the Graphics class. You can get and set this color using the Graphics.getColor() and Graphics.setColor() methods. Although the Graphics class certainly allows you to draw in different colors, it doesn't provide a way of applying a consistent system of colors. System colors are used in most graphical environments to give the GUI a consistent look and feel; the result is a set of color schemes a user can choose between.

Java 1.1 remedies the lack of system colors by defining a set of desktop colors. These colors are encapsulated in the java.awt.SystemColor class and include symbolic constants defining colors such as highlight and shadow colors for components. The java.awt.SystemColor class falls within the scope of the JFC.

Mouseless Operation

One notable weakness in Java 1.0 was the lack of support for mouseless operation, which is the use of the keyboard to navigate through a GUI. Keyboard navigation includes moving through components with the Tab key as well as using the Control key to access menu accelerators and command shortcuts. These two types of keyboard navigation have become standard across most GUIs, and most users expect them.

Java 1.1 addresses the lack of keyboard support in Java with provisions for both for component focus and menu accelerators. This support will become more critical as developers build sophisticated GUIs in Java. It's also important in terms of the JFC because of the many new GUI components that will ship in the next version of Java. You learn about these components a little later in the lesson.

Other Miscellaneous Goodies

The JFC makes itself known in some other areas of Java 1.1 that you may not be as familiar with. First off, the enhanced graphics and image handling features in Java 1.1 are a part of the JFC. These features include more versatile clipping regions as well as image scaling and pixel manipulation features. These changes were mainly incorporated into the java.awt.Graphics class.

Another JFC addition to Java 1.1 is support for popup menus, which have become popular more recently in GUIs. As an example, in most windows in Windows 95, you can right-click the mouse to display a popup menu that provides access to context-sensitive menu commands.

Advanced scrolling is the last major JFC-related piece of functionality present in Java 1.1. Java 1.0 supported scrollbars, but much of the details of implementing scroll logic were left up to applications. This kind of support required unnecessary work on the part of developers and resulted in inconsistent scrollbar behavior. The java.awt.ScrollPane class in Java 1.1 directly addresses the scrolling problem by acting as a container for scrollable information. The java.awt.ScrollPane class enables you to add automatic scrolling capabilities to a Java applet or application.

The JFC to Come

So far the lesson has focused on the aspects of the JFC that are already part of the Java 1.1 API. Although these contributions to Java 1.1 are significant, the next wave of JFC features are perhaps the most exciting. Following is a list of the major JFC features expected to become part of Java 1.2:

- ☐ Pluggable look and feel
- ☐ Lightweight component suite
- ☐ Drag-and-drop
- ☐ Advanced 2-D graphics
- ☐ Accessibility for the handicapped

Most of these features will become a part of the java.awt package, which is itself a part of the JFC. As you can see, the scope of these enhancements is broad. Clearly, the next release of Java will be the one to truly position Java as a complete development platform, thanks to the JFC. The following sections explore these new JFC features in a little more detail.

Pluggable Look and Feel

Earlier in the lesson you learned about the conflict between GUIs incorporating characteristics of native platforms and GUIs remaining consistent across different platforms. You found out about lightweight Java components, which are components that don't have an underlying native peer object dictating their appearance. Although lightweight components solve the problem of not being able to extend GUI components, they introduce the problem of GUI components not adhering to a native look and feel.

The JFC will introduce a mechanism known as pluggable look and feel that will provide a means of altering the look and feel of an entire GUI at once. This mechanism will enable developers to scale the look and feel of lightweight components to the native GUI when necessary. The drawback to this approach is that it requires some degree of extra development effort, but it does provide the best of both worlds. Components will be completely independent of the underlying native GUI, yet they can imitate native behavior whenever necessary.

Lightweight Component Suite

Lightweight components have come up numerous times in the discussion of the JFC thus far, but I haven't mentioned anything about specific components. That's because Java 1.1 doesn't ship with any practical lightweight components, it just provides the model for them. The new JFC will include an extensive suite of lightweight components that will bring Java GUIs to a whole new level. These components are based in part on components that were originally included in Netscape's Internet Foundation Classes (IFC), which you explore a little later in the lesson. The new lightweight JFC component suite includes components such as an image button, a toolbar, a tree view, and a progress bar, to name a few. You learn more about these components and how they are used a little later in the lesson.

NOTE

Due to the fact that the JFC will supercede the IFC, Netscape has announced that version 1.1 of the IFC is the final version. They will continue to support this version, but future development efforts will be focused on the JFC.

Drag-and-drop

Drag-and-drop has become a very important feature in most graphical applications, and users therefore expect it as a standard application feature. The new JFC gets Java up to speed with full drag-and-drop support. Providing drag-and-drop support between Java applications isn't much of a problem, but providing support for the drag-and-drop of information between a Java application and a native application is a potentially thorny issue. Even with the potential complexities of supporting native drag-and-drop, drag-and-drop wouldn't be very useful if it were limited only to Java applications. In other words, Java drag-and-drop must work both between Java applications and between a Java application and a native application.

Fortunately, JavaSoft realizes the importance of native drag-and-drop and is incorporating this functionality into the new JFC drag-and-drop mechanism. Additionally, the drag-and-drop API will be completely platform-independent. This means you can write drag-and-drop code to a generic Java API and have it scale appropriately to the underlying native platform. This is precisely the type of abstraction that makes Java such a compelling development platform.

Advanced 2-D Graphics

Although the 2-D graphics support in the Java 1.1 API is by no means bad, it is lacking in a number of ways. By comparison, native 2-D graphics APIs such as the one in the Win32 API are significantly more advanced than the Java 1.1 API's 2-D graphics support. The new JFC will include a completely revamped 2-D graphics API that will bring Java up to the level of native 2-D graphics APIs and possibly beyond.

The new 2-D graphics API will introduce a class named `Graphics2D` that is derived from the `java.awt.Graphics` class. This new class will build upon the `Graphics` class and provide a wide range of advanced 2-D graphics features such as the rotation of images, text, and paths. Additionally, the much needed capability to alter the pen width for drawing operations will be present in this API, along with a host of other 2-D drawing enhancements.

Accessibility for the Physically Handicapped

One of the more practically interesting features in modern GUIs is support for the physically handicapped. Until recently, most application developers took the ability to see a monitor or maneuver a mouse for granted, just as the ability to climb stairs was once taken for granted by architects. However, as GUIs improved to the point of being able to address the physically handicapped, operating system vendors began incorporating special accessibility features such as enlarged mouse pointers and support for alternative input and output devices.

The new JFC includes two primary accessibility features for the physically handicapped: a screen reader and screen magnifier. The screen reader is a textual representation of a GUI that

4

can be communicated to users using a text-to-speech or Braille terminal. Likewise, user responses through an alternative input device can be interpreted just as if they came from a keyboard or mouse. The screen magnifier allows an entire GUI to be magnified up to 16 times the normal size. Additionally, font smoothing and text highlighting serve to complement the screen magnifier in presenting a more visually accessible GUI.

Swinging with the JFC

You now have a good idea about what the JFC is at present along with where it's headed. I mentioned earlier in the lesson that some of the new JFC features are available in early implementation form. JavaSoft has packaged a subset of the new JFC features into a single release that is code-named Swing. Swing consists primarily of the suite of lightweight GUI components you learned about earlier in the lesson. However, in order to make the components work, Swing also includes pluggable look-and-feel support that makes the components adaptable to different GUIs.

NOTE

> Keep in mind that Swing is a code name that refers to a subset of the JFC in beta form. The name Swing will most likely not be used once the JFC nears a final release.

4

In practical terms, Swing is just a bunch of lightweight components that can be used to build sophisticated GUIs. However, from an architectural perspective, there are two other significant parts to Swing: the pluggable look-and feel mechanism and the model-view-controller model used to manage complex GUIs. You learn more about each of these parts of Swing in the next few sections.

Pluggable Look and Feel

The suite of GUI components included with Swing supports a pluggable look-and-feel mechanism that allows the components to operate under a look and feel that can be changed to suit the tastes of different users. The concept of a changeable look and feel may seem strange in today's world of native GUIs, but in the very near future, the concept of a native GUI will blur from the user's perspective. For example, new network computers may be built entirely around the JavaOS operating system, which has no native GUI of its own other than the Java AWT. Users of such a system may demand a familiar Windows or Solaris GUI, in which case they could select a Windows or Solaris look and feel. Pluggable look-and-feel support may seem like window dressing at first, but you have to consider the religious commitment some users have toward their operating system of choice and consequently the GUI employed by the operating system. As an example, I happen to be very accustomed to the Windows 95 GUI and would prefer using it over some generic GUI in a network computer.

It's technically possible to implement a pluggable look and feel without the support provided by the JFC; you just subclass every component you want to change the look and feel of. Clearly, the approach of subclassing every component in a GUI is not a very architecturally sound approach. The JFC's pluggable look-and-feel mechanism not only alleviates the need to subclass a bunch of components, but it allows the look and feel of a GUI to be altered dynamically at runtime. A user can switch GUIs from within an application and see the results immediately.

NOTE

> Swing ships with two pluggable look-and-feel implementations: Windows 95 and Rose. The Windows 95 look and feel, also known as the Basic look and feel, closely imitates the Windows 95 GUI. Likewise, the Rose look and feel is very similar to the Solaris GUI. You see how powerful the pluggable look-and-feel JFC mechanism is later in this lesson when you try out the SwingSet application.

The MVC Architecture

Before getting into the components that make up the Swing component suite, you must understand the Swing's GUI design structure. Swing uses a GUI design known as the model-view-controller (MVC) architecture, which divides a GUI into a model, a view, and a controller. The model represents the state of a component, and the view is responsible for the visual representation of the component. The controller is responsible for handling user input for the component.

NEW TERM

> *model:* The part of the MVC architecture that represents the state of a component.
>
> *view:* The part of the MVC architecture that is responsible for the visual representation of a component.
>
> *controller:* The part of the MVC architecture that is responsible for handling user input for a component.

The best way to understand the MVC architecture is to consider how the different parts interact with each other. A component's state is represented by the model, which is altered by the controller in response to user input. Likewise, the view interacts with the model to provide a visual representation of the component's state. Finally, because the view provides the GUI for the component, it must interact with the controller to pass along user input. Figure 4.2 shows the relationship between the three parts of the MVC architecture.

Figure 4.2.
The relationship between the model, view, and controller in the MVC architecture.

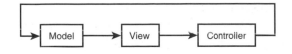

The MVC architecture is an ideal approach to handling complex GUIs, but it isn't always practical. For example, it is sometimes very difficult to completely sever the model, view, and controller into separate entities because of their interdependencies on each other. The JFC solves this problem by combining the view and controller into a single entity known as a *delegate*. Figure 4.3 shows this altered MVC architecture.

NEW TERM

delegate: The view-controller part of the MVC architecture, which is responsible for visually representing a component and handling user input.

Figure 4.3.
The relationship between the model and delegate in the JFC's MVC architecture.

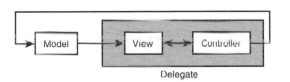

Note that the MVC architecture is only necessary when creating sophisticated GUIs involving Swing components. You are free to use Swing components just as you use AWT components in Java 1.1. However, the MVC architecture provides a more advanced option for complex GUIs that can't be efficiently represented using the existing layouts provided in Java 1.1.

The Swing Component Suite

The real importance of Swing is its component suite, which consists of a surprisingly diverse group of lightweight, JavaBeans-compliant components. As of this writing, the latest release of Swing is version 0.3. Following are some of the more interesting types of components included in this release:

☐ Borders
☐ Buttons

4

- [ ] Combo boxes
- [ ] Icons
- [ ] Labels
- [ ] Lists and list boxes
- [ ] Menu bars
- [ ] Menu items
- [ ] Popup menus
- [ ] Progress bars
- [ ] Tabbed pane
- [ ] Tables
- [ ] Text areas
- [ ] Text fields
- [ ] Trees

Many of these components probably sound familiar from the standard Java AWT. Although many Swing components perform the same function as existing AWT components, the Swing versions are completely different in their implementation. Keep in mind that all of the Swing components are lightweight and support a pluggable look and feel. If you're a little unsure about what this look-and-feel business means, you'll be glad to know that the next section covers the SwingSet sample application, which demonstrates the power of a pluggable look-and-feel GUI.

NOTE

> In addition to completely new components, Swing provides lightweight versions of the standard Java 1.1 AWT components.

The SwingSet: A Swing Tour de Force

If you're anything like me, you're probably thinking that this JFC stuff would make more sense in the context of a real example. Although the focus of this book is to make things hands-on by working through lots of sample code, Swing comes with a sample application that is so thorough it would be difficult to match. So rather than work through sample code, I'm going to take you on a quick tour of the SwingSet application that ships with Swing. You won't be disappointed, trust me!

4

Swing comes with a variety of sample applets and applications that demonstrate various aspects of the Swing component suite. By far the most interesting of all the examples is the SwingSet application, which demonstrates practically every component shipped with Swing. Before you can execute the SwingSet application, you need to set the SWINGHOME environment variable, which is required of all the Swing examples. I installed Swing to the \jdk1.1.3\swing-0.3 directory, so I had to set my SWINGHOME environment variable to this directory.

NOTE

This discussion assumes you have downloaded Swing and installed it on your system. You can download Swing from the Java Developer Connection Web site at http:\\developer.javasoft.com.

With the SWINGHOME environment variable properly set, you're ready to run the SwingSet application. Go to the examples\SwingSet directory beneath the main Swing directory and execute the batch file named runnit.bat. This file executes the SwingSet application in the Java interpreter. Figure 4.4 shows the SwingSet application after first being executed.

Figure 4.4.

The SwingSet sample application.

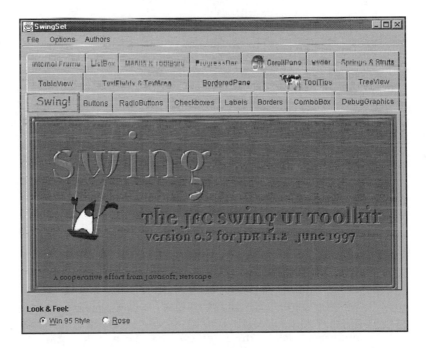

The SwingSet application consists of a bunch of tabbed panes containing examples of the Swing components. Incidentally, the tabbed panes themselves are Swing components. A good pane to start with is the Buttons pane, which contains a bunch of different buttons. Figure 4.5 shows the Buttons pane.

Figure 4.5.

The Buttons pane in the SwingSet sample application.

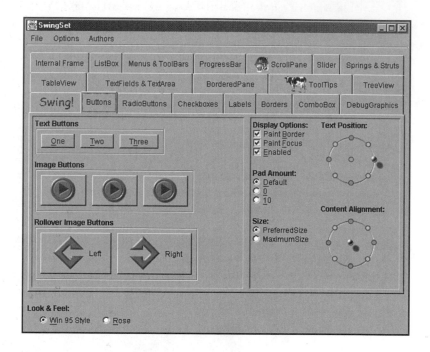

As you can see, the Buttons pane contains three different types of buttons: text buttons, image buttons, and rollover image buttons. Clearly, these buttons are far more versatile than the java.awt.Button class provided in the Java 1.1 AWT. To get an even better glimpse at the versatility of the Swing components, click the Rose radio button near the bottom-left corner of the SwingSet window. This button changes the look and feel of the SwingSet application to take on a Solaris flavor. Figure 4.6 shows the Buttons pane as seen through the Rose look and feel.

The buttons themselves didn't change all that much under the new look and feel, but many of the other components did. For example, the Rose radio button itself completely changed its look. Likewise, the checkboxes and radio buttons on the right side of the pane completely changed their appearances. For an even more dramatic look at how the look and feel affects components, click on the TreeView pane. Then click Jazz in the tree, followed by Miles Davis. Figure 4.7 shows the resulting TreeView pane as seen with the Rose look and feel.

Figure 4.6.

The Buttons pane in the SwingSet sample application with the Rose look and feel.

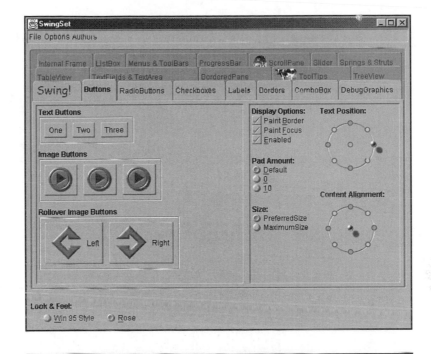

Figure 4.7.

The TreeView pane in the SwingSet sample application with the Rose look and feel.

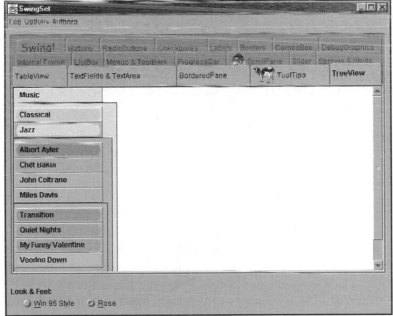

Now change the look and feel back to Windows 95 by clicking the Win 95 Style radio button near the bottom-left corner of the SwingSet application. Figure 4.8 shows the dramatic change in appearance of the TreeView pane under the Windows 95 look and feel.

Figure 4.8.

The TreeView pane in the SwingSet sample application with the Windows 95 look and feel.

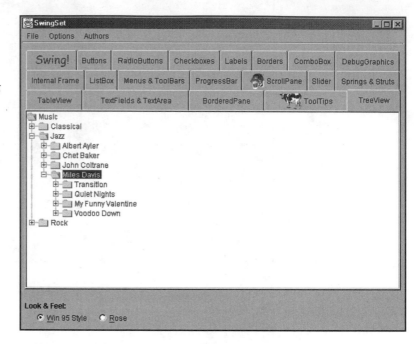

The SwingSet application provides a very comprehensive look at much of the functionality present in the JFC. For this reason, I highly encourage you to spend some time exploring it and seeing how the different components work. It will give you a good indication as to what the next version of Java has in store. Besides, it's one of the most interesting and fun sample applications I've ever seen.

Netscape's IFC

Netscape's Internet Foundation Classes (IFC) are the precursor to the JFC and offer many of the same features as the JFC. The primary difference between the IFC and JFC is that the IFC is designed as more of a third-party class library, whereas the JFC is integrated tightly with the existing Java API. This tighter integration is possible because JavaSoft and Netscape got together and reworked the IFC in order to come up with the JFC. Even though the IFC isn't as tightly integrated with the existing Java API, it provides a wealth of features and is available now. If you are in need of an application framework immediately, the IFC might be your answer.

NOTE

JavaSoft and Netscape claim that IFC applications will be portable to JFC applications without too much effort. This transition definitely will involve code changes, but hopefully nothing extremely drastic. Assuming this claim is accurate, the IFC is a great way to develop applications today that will have longevity as the JFC supercedes the IFC in the near future.

The IFC framework can be broken down into the following functional parts or services:

- **Windowing.** The IFC framework supports a traditional windowing environment within a Java application and supports IFC components in native windows.

- **Application components.** The IFC framework has fundamental GUI application components such as buttons, sliders, and text fields.

- **Composite components.** The IFC framework has advanced GUI application components such as color, font, and file choosers.

- **Drawing/event management.** The IFC framework has event handling for user interface objects and the resulting GUI drawing model.

- **Animation.** The IFC framework supports animation features such as buffered drawing and transparency.

- **Drag-and-drop.** The IFC framework supports dragging and dropping items within an application.

- **Object persistence.** The IFC framework gives objects the capability to save and restore their state to a non-volatile location such as a hard drive.

- **Timing.** The IFC framework supports concurrent behavior without the need to spawn threads.

Some of these services are completely superceded by standard Java 1.1 features. For example, the Java 1.1 API fully supports object persistence, which makes the IFC offering unnecessary. This duplication of features is a result of the fact that the IFC was developed prior to Java 1.1. In fact, the movement of IFC features to the JFC consisted largely of replacing IFC services with standard Java services. That is why the JFC is more tightly integrated with the Java API.

NOTE

Even though the IFC duplicates some of the features of Java 1.1, IFC features are not any less useful than Java 1.1 features. If you want to use the IFC to build applications, then by all means use the IFC features. I just wanted to point the situation surrounding the IFC, JFC, and Java 1.1.

4

The IFC's GUI application features can be broken down into three major groups:

☐ Views and components
☐ Choosers
☐ Windows

The next few sections examine each of these GUI features and what they have to offer in terms of building application user interfaces.

Views and Components

Like the JFC, the core part of the IFC is its suite of GUI application components such as buttons, sliders, scrollbars, and text fields. The IFC components are geared toward building advanced application user interfaces, which alleviates the need to spend a lot of time working on user interface details. IFC components are highly reusable, primarily due to clearly defined override points; these points allow developers to easily modify the functionality of a component to suit their needs. The IFC also lays the groundwork for the pluggable look-and-feel features found in the JFC.

The IFC's GUI components are all based on the concept of a *view*, which is a rectangular entity capable of drawing on the screen and receiving events. The View class provides the implementation of a basic view and serves as the basis for the entire IFC component API. Within a given application, there is a view hierarchy, which is laid out with each view having zero or more subviews, or *descendants*. Before a view can draw or receive events, you must place it within this hierarchy through a call to the addSubview() method. A root view forms the top of the hierarchy in any application; all other views descend from the root view.

> **NEW TERM**
>
> *view:* A rectangular entity capable of drawing on the screen and receiving events.

All IFC components are derived from the View class and are included in the netscape.application package. Because components are subclasses of View, they appear somewhere within the view hierarchy. The view hierarchy allows an object that is a subclass of View to act as a container for other views. This hierarchy lets you treat a container view as a single entity, even though it consists of multiple subviews. A component's position within the view hierarchy is determined by its parent view, or *superview*, which is the view that contains the component. The root view sits atop the view hierarchy of IFC applications and is the superview of all other views. Figure 4.9 shows a typical application view hierarchy.

Figure 4.9.

A typical application view hierarchy.

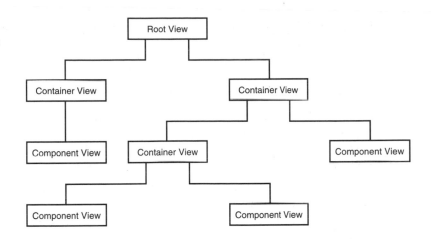

Although views are ultimately rectangular in appearance, they can simulate nonrectangular regions using *transparency*. Transparency allows the underlying background of a view to show through parts of a view that are identified as being transparent. Views can also be buffered, in which case drawing is performed on an off-screen buffer that is then drawn to the screen in a single operation. Buffered drawing alleviates flicker that can occur when a view is drawn repeatedly at a high rate. Animation typically is a major source of flicker, which is why buffered drawing is considered an animation feature.

Applications are built using application GUI components, such as buttons and text fields. Table 4.1 lists the application GUI components provided by the IFC.

Table 4.1. Application GUI components provided by the IFC.

Component	Function
Button	A button that issues commands upon being clicked
CheckBox	A user interface element representing one of two states (on/off)
ColorWell	A color edit component that supports drag-and-drop to modify the colors of other components
ContainerView	A view that can be used as a container for other components
ListView	A list of items that can be selected
Popup	A popup menu from which users can issue commands
RadioButton	A mutually exclusive group of items that allows only one to be selected at a time
Slider	A user interface element that provides a means of incrementally navigating through a range of values

continues

Table 4.1. continued

Component	Function
TextField	A string editing component
TextView	A string viewing component that supports multiple paragraphs and fonts

You may be thinking that some of these components don't sound all that groundbreaking. I mean, doesn't Java already have buttons and checkboxes? Yes, but the IFC components go much farther than the standard Java AWT components in their set of features. For example, IFC buttons support images that are displayed along with the text label of a button.

Choosers

Choosers are an important type of GUI application element in that they provide advanced interfaces for commonly performed application tasks such as selecting files and customizing fonts. The IFC choosers are all implemented as dialog boxes that are displayed as separate windows. The IFC provides the following choosers:

☐ Color Chooser

☐ Font Chooser

☐ File Chooser

The Color Chooser is a dialog box that provides a means of editing the color of any object that accepts dragged colors, such as a color well. Figure 4.10 shows what the IFC Color Chooser looks like. The Color Chooser includes slider components and text edit boxes that you can use to alter the RGB (Red, Green, Blue) values of a color. After mixing a color, you can drag the color from the Color Chooser to a GUI component capable of receiving colors; the component immediately displays the new color.

Figure 4.10.

The Color Chooser.

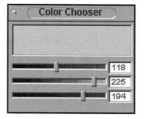

The Font Chooser is a dialog box that provides a means of altering the properties of a font including the font name, point size, and style. Figure 4.11 shows what the IFC Font Chooser looks like. You can use the Font Chooser to modify the font for any text that appears in an editable text view component. To change the font for a text view component, you first select the component and then use the Font Chooser to specify the name, size, and style of the font. Clicking the Set button in the Font Chooser results in the text view component updating its font.

Figure 4.11.

The Font Chooser.

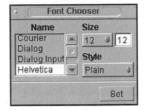

The File Chooser is a little different from the other two choosers in that it relies on a native dialog box to provide a means of finding and selecting files. For example, in Windows 95 the File Chooser is the standard Windows 95 File Open dialog box.

Windows

Windows are user interface objects used to organize data, commands, and user interface components for an application. Windows are different from components in that windows act as frames, meaning that they don't require a parent container. The IFC supports two types of windows: internal windows and external windows. An internal window is a Java-based window that has no dependency on the underlying platform. Internal windows are very much like peerless lightweight components in the Java 1.1 API. External windows have an underlying native window that is platform-specific. An example of an external window is a File Open dialog box, which is provided by the underlying platform.

Drawing with the IFC

The IFC introduces a different drawing model than the one used in applications developed with the Java AWT. The IFC approach doesn't use the update() or paint() methods; instead, it uses a similar pair of methods called draw() and drawView(). The draw() method is called whenever an application is drawn to the screen. The draw() method in turn calls the drawView() method, which is responsible for handling the drawing of an application. To modify the specific way an application is drawn, you override the drawView() method.

Every component derived from the View class implements a drawView() method that handles the drawing of the component. Some components also provide more specific drawView() methods that draw different parts of a component separately. For example, the border of a button is drawn with a special drawing method, drawViewBackground(), that can be overridden to alter the border of the button by itself. You can call the draw() method to update the appearance of a component. However, you typically will never call the drawView() method, because it is automatically called by the draw() method.

> **NOTE**
>
> The IFC graphics model is based on the graphics model provided by the standard Java AWT. An application drawing area is represented by a two-dimensional grid, with its origin in the upper-left corner, the positive x-axis extending to the right, and the positive y-axis extending down.

Calling methods on a Graphics object carries out specific drawing operations. The IFC Graphics object is provided in the netscape.application package and is passed into the drawView() method. When you override the drawView() method, you use this Graphics object to perform graphics operations. The IFC Graphics object maintains a clipping rectangle, which serves as a bounding box for the drawing operations performed on a component.

An IFC Sample Applet

Here you are about two-thirds of the way through the lesson and I've yet to show you a practical example of how to use an application framework. In truth, the application frameworks explored in this lesson could each warrant an entire book's worth of coverage. My only goal is to give you a glimpse at what they each have to offer. Part of that glimpse is provided by a sample applet called IFCDemo, which demonstrates some of the features common to all of the application frameworks discussed today. The IFCDemo applet happens to use the IFC, but you could implement the same applet with roughly the same amount of effort using either the JFC or AFC.

Running the Applet

The IFCDemo applet uses four components to demonstrate some of the features of the IFC. Figure 4.12 shows the applet in action.

Figure 4.12.

The IFCDemo sample IFC applet.

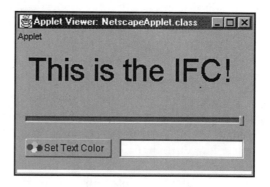

As you can see, the applet consists of a text view component, a slider component, a button component, and a text field component. The latter three components work in concert to provide a means of altering the text displayed in the text view component. Moving the slider results in the font size of the text changing. Pressing the button displays a Color Chooser, which is used to change the color of the text. The text field enables you to enter new text to be displayed. The applet and its source code are available from the companion Web site for the book at http://www.mcp.com/info/1-57521/1-57521-347-8.

Try out the different components to get a feel for how they work. To change the text being displayed, type in the text field and press the Enter or Tab key. Figure 4.13 shows the applet after the text is changed through the text field.

Figure 4.13.

Changing the text using a text field.

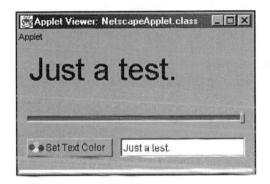

To change the color of the text, select the Set Text Color button. Notice that the button label consists of text along with an image. This combination is something that the standard Java AWT cannot do because of its dependence on an underlying peer window. The peerless approach taken by the IFC allows buttons to do interesting things such as combine text with images. Anyway, getting back to the applet, when you select the button, the Color Chooser is displayed.

The Color Chooser provides an interface to mix a color using sliders and/or text fields. To apply a color mixed in the Color Chooser, click the color in the Color Chooser and drag it to the component you want to color. In the IFCDemo applet, the text view component is designed to accept dropped colors and apply them to the text color. Dragging a color onto the text being displayed will color the text (see Figure 4.14). That's about as intuitive as a user interface can get!

4

Figure 4.14.

Changing the text color using the Color Chooser.

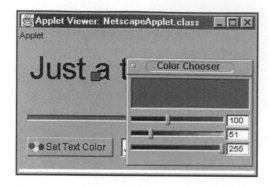

The last feature that the applet supports is using the slider component to change the text size. Try clicking and dragging the slider to modify the text size. Notice that the text is resized dynamically as you drag the slider and that there is no flicker. The lack of flicker is due to the fact that the slider and text view components use double-buffering. Figure 4.15 shows the text being resized with the slider.

Figure 4.15.

Changing the font size of the text using a slider.

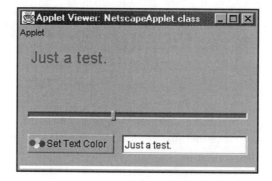

Examining the Applet Code

Now that you know how the applet functions, you're ready to dig into the code and see how it works. Before you do, however, understand that the IFC is a pretty complicated set of classes. I've tried to keep this applet as simple as possible so that it's easier to digest, but even simple IFC applets are still different from normal Java applets in a lot of ways. Enough small talk, let's take a look at the code for the applet! Listing 4.1 contains the complete source code for the IFCDemo applet class.

Listing 4.1. The source code for the IFCDemo applet.

```
 1: import netscape.application.*;
 2: import netscape.util.*;
 3:
 4: public class IFCDemo extends Application implements Target {
 5:    Button        button;
 6:    Slider        slider;
 7:    TextField     textField;
 8:    ColorTextView textView;
 9:
10:    public void init() {
11:       super.init();
12:
13:       // Set the main window background color
14:       mainRootView().setColor(Color.lightGray);
15:
16:       // Create the output color text view
17:       textView = new ColorTextView(10, 10, 280, 60);
18:       textView.setFont(new Font("Helvetica", Font.PLAIN, 40));
19:       textView.setBackgroundColor(Color.lightGray);
20:       textView.setString("This is the IFC!");
21:       textView.setBuffered(true);
22:       textView.setHorizResizeInstruction(View.LEFT_MARGIN_CAN_CHANGE);
23:       textView.setVertResizeInstruction(View.HEIGHT_CAN_CHANGE);
24:       mainRootView().addSubview(textView);
25:
26:       // Create the font size slider
27:       slider = new Slider(10, 80, 280, 30);
28:       slider.setLimits(8, 40);
29:       slider.setValue(40);
30:       slider.setTarget(this);
31:       slider.setCommand("sliderWasMoved");
32:       slider.setBuffered(true);
33:       slider.setHorizResizeInstruction(View.WIDTH_CAN_CHANGE);
34:       slider.setVertResizeInstruction(View.BOTTOM_MARGIN_CAN_CHANGE);
35:       mainRootView().addSubview(slider);
36:
37:       // Create the "Set Text Color" button
38:       button = new Button(10, 120, 110, 24);
39:       button.setTitle("Set Text Color");
40:       button.setImage(Bitmap.bitmapNamed("Color.gif"));
41:       button.setImagePosition(Button.IMAGE_ON_LEFT);
42:       button.setTarget(this);
43:       button.setCommand("buttonWasPressed");
44:       button.setHorizResizeInstruction(View.WIDTH_CAN_CHANGE);
45:       button.setVertResizeInstruction(View.BOTTOM_MARGIN_CAN_CHANGE);
46:       mainRootView().addSubview(button);
47:
48:       // Create the text field
49:       textField = new TextField(130, 120, 160, 24);
50:       textField.setTarget(this);
51:       textField.setCommand("textWasEntered");
```

continues

Listing 4.1. continued

```
52:      textField.setHorizResizeInstruction(View.WIDTH_CAN_CHANGE);
53:      textField.setVertResizeInstruction(View.BOTTOM_MARGIN_CAN_CHANGE);
54:      mainRootView().addSubview(textField);
55:    }
56:
57:    public void performCommand(String command, Object arg) {
58:      if ("buttonWasPressed".equals(command))
59:        mainRootView().showColorChooser();
60:      else if ("sliderWasMoved".equals(command))
61:        textView.setFont(new Font("Helvetica", Font.PLAIN, slider.value()));
62:      else if ("textWasEntered".equals(command))
63:        textView.setString(textField.stringValue());
64:    }
65:
66:    public static void main(String args[]) {
67:      IFCDemo app;
68:      ExternalWindow mainWindow;
69:      Size size;
70:
71:      app = new IFCDemo();
72:      mainWindow = new ExternalWindow();
73:      app.setMainRootView(mainWindow.rootView());
74:      size = mainWindow.windowSizeForContentSize(300, 160);
75:      mainWindow.sizeTo(size.width, size.height);
76:      mainWindow.show();
77:
78:      app.run();
79:      System.exit(0);
80:    }
81: }
```

Perhaps the best place to begin in explaining the source code is the Application class, which is a class provided in the netscape.application package that all IFC applets and applications must derive from. Also notice that the IFCDemo class implements the Target interface, which is the IFC's twist on event handling. You learn more about the Target interface a little later in the lesson.

The IFCDemo class defines four member variables that represent each of the four components used in the applet (Lines 5-8). The last component, textView, is a ColorTextView object, which is not part of the standard IFC class library (Line 8). You learn how the ColorTextView class works a little later in the lesson.

The init() method is used to initialize IFC applets and applications. The first step the init() method takes is to set the background color of the main application window to light gray, which is a little more appealing (to me at least) than the standard white (Line 14). The init() method then takes on the task of creating the different components.

4

The color text view component is created first (Lines 17-24). Notice that it is created using a constructor that takes four arguments. These arguments are the component's X position, Y position, width, and height. This is a fairly standard way to create IFC components. The properties of the component are then set, which includes altering the font, background color, display string, double-buffering support, and sizing attributes. The call to setBuffered() is all that is required to make the component double-buffered, and therefore avoid flicker (Line 21). The sizing attributes allow the component to be automatically sized in proportion to its container window.

The font component is created in a very similar fashion. One noticeable difference is the setting of the slider component's Target and Command properties. These properties dictate the manner in which the component dispatches events. Every IFC component has a default event action that determines when a command event is generated. Table 4.2 lists the default IFC event actions.

Table 4.2. Default IFC event actions.

Component	Event action
Button	Clicking the button
Color well	Dropping a color into the color well
List item	Selecting an item in a list view
List view	Selecting a list view item that does not specify a command
Menu item	Selecting a menu item
Popup menu	Selecting a popup menu item that does not specify a command
Slider	Changing the slider value
Text field	Pressing the Return key, the Tab key, or the Shift+Tab key combination
Timer	The timer's delay elapses

The slider component's target is set to this (Line 30), which means that the applet itself will receive event notifications whenever the slider's value changes. The command sent upon this notification is set to the string sliderWasMoved, which indicates the reason for the event notification (Line 31). This string is caught later and used as a means of isolating slider movement events.

The button is created and customized next and involves roughly the same modifications as the other components. One notable difference is the use of an image along with the textual button label. The image is specified with a call to the setImage() method; the Bitmap class is used to load the image (Line 40). Once the image is set, its alignment with the label is set with a call to `setImagePosition()` (Line 41). The button is also registered as an event source and is assigned the command string `buttonWasPressed` (Line 43).

The last component created is the text field component, which is used to receive text. Similar to the slider and button components, the text field component is registered as an event source (Line 50) and is assigned the command string `textWasEntered` (Line 51).

Events are delivered to the applet through the `performCommand()` method. This method is called whenever an event is sent from a component to an applet. The command string passed into the `performCommand()` method indicates the event being sent, which is compared to different event strings. If a button press event occurs, the `showColorChooser()` method is called (Lines 58-59). If a slider event occurs, the `setFont()` method is called on the text view control (Lines 60-61). If a text entry event occurs, the `setString()` method is called on the text view control (Lines 62-63).

The IFC framework is designed for Java programs to function either as applets or applications. The `main()` method in the `IFCDemo` class is responsible for initializing the program when it runs as an application. The `main()` method first creates an `IFCDemo` object, along with an external window that serves as the application frame (Lines 71-72). The window is then set as the root view for the application, along with being sized and made visible (Lines 73-76). Finally, the `run()` method is called to start the application running (Line 78).

The `IFCDemo` applet uses the `ColorTextView` class as a color text view that accepts colors dropped onto it to change the color of the text being displayed. Listing 4.2 contains the complete source code for the `ColorTextView` component.

Listing 4.2. The source code for the `ColorTextView` component.

```
1: import netscape.application.*;
2: import netscape.util.*;
3:
4: public class ColorTextView extends TextView implements DragDestination {
5:   ColorTextView(int x, int y, int width, int height) {
6:     super(x, y, width, height);
7:   }
8:
9:   public DragDestination acceptsDrag(DragSession dragSession,
   ➥int x, int y) {
10:     if (Color.COLOR_TYPE.equals(dragSession.dataType()))
11:       return this;
12:     else
13:       return null;
14:   }
15:
16:   public boolean dragDropped(DragSession dragSession) {
```

```
17:    Color c = ((Color)dragSession.data());
18:    setTextColor(c);
19:    draw();
20:    return true;
21:  }
22:
23:  public boolean dragEntered(DragSession dragSession) {
24:    return true;
25:  }
26:
27:  public boolean dragMoved(DragSession dragSession) {
28:    return true;
29:  }
30:
31:  public void dragExited(DragSession dragSession) {
32:  }
33: }
```

The whole purpose of the ColorTextView class is to provide drag-and-drop functionality for colors from the Color Chooser. The ColorTextView class extends the TextView class and implements the DragDestination interface to support dropped colors (Line 4). Because the DragDestination interface must be implemented entirely to be able to instantiate the TextView class, you have to provide some methods that you don't necessarily need.

The acceptsDrag() method is overridden to specify the types of data the component provides drag support for. Because color data is the only type supported by the component, the acceptsDrag() method returns the this object only when a color object has been dragged onto the component (Lines 10-11). Otherwise, the method returns null, which indicates that the component doesn't support any other data types (Line 13).

The dragDropped() method is called whenever an object is dropped on a component. The acceptsDrag() method guarantees that the dragDropped() method will only be called with color data. The color data is retrieved in the dragDropped() method and used to set the text color of the component (Lines 17-18). The component is then updated to reflect the color change with a call to the draw() method (Line 19). The other methods in the ColorTextView class are dummy methods that fulfill the need to fully implement the interface.

One more item is required to make the applet work. Listing 4.3 contains the HTML code for the Web page used to test the applet.

Listing 4.3. The HTML code for the IFCDemo applet's test Web page.

```
1: <TITLE>IFC Demo Applet</TITLE>
2: <HR>
3: <APPLET CODE="NetscapeApplet.class" WIDTH=300 HEIGHT=160>
4:   <PARAM NAME="ApplicationClass" VALUE="IFCDemo">
5: </APPLET>
```

Typically an applet's class is provided in the `CODE` argument for the `APPLET` tag. However, the structure of the IFC requires you to use the `NetscapeApplet` class as the startup class for applets (Line 3). This class is what enables applets to use all the same features as applications. When using the `NetscapeApplet` class, the name of the applet class you develop is provided as the value of the `ApplicationClass` parameter (Line 4). That's all it takes to incorporate an IFC applet into a Web page!

Microsoft's AFC

Microsoft's Application Foundation Classes (AFC) represent Microsoft's offering in the Java application framework market. The AFC is a set of application GUI components similar in function to the JFC and IFC. Although the AFC is implemented in Java, it is a little different from the JFC and IFC in that it includes support for some native Win32 features, such as the DirectX multimedia services.

The AFC provides a framework that applications must use if they want to use AFC components and application services. The AFC requires you to use the AFC framework entirely, as opposed to mixing AFC code with standard Java AWT code. However, the AFC provides wrapper classes for AFC components that allow you to use them as JavaBeans components in AWT code.

The AFC consists of the following major services:

☐ **Application components.** This service is an application framework and component suite including advanced GUI components such as trees.

☐ **Graphics effects.** This service provides support for enhanced graphics elements such as glyphs and textures.

☐ **Win32 resources.** This service provides support for Win32 resources.

☐ **CAB files.** This service provides support for cabinet (CAB) files, which are similar in function to Java archives (JAR files).

Application Components

The AFC is a lot like the standard Java AWT in that it is comprised of components, containers, and layout managers. In reality, these elements are common aspects of just about any application framework. Even so, the AFC is designed to be very similar in function to the AWT in order to minimize the learning curve and make things more consistent. The AFC doesn't extend the AWT directly, however.

The AFC is heavily component-based, so the application GUI components form the heart of the AFC. The AFC provides a set of lightweight base classes that serve a similar purpose as the lightweight component model in Java 1.1. Lightweight base classes make derived GUI components much more efficient because they don't rely on underlying native window support. In contrast, standard Java AWT components have the overhead of underlying native window support. Unlike the AWT, the AFC performs all of its own window management.

The end result of the lightweight base classes in the AFC is peerless GUI components. Peerless components, as you learned earlier in the lesson, provide a better cross-platform component solution because they are more streamlined and have a more consistent user interface across different platforms.

The AFC provides the following types of application components:

- ☐ Static controls
- ☐ Button controls
- ☐ Menu controls
- ☐ Choice and list controls
- ☐ Dialog-based controls

Static controls, as their name suggests, don't accept or respond to user input and therefore are typically used to display static text. For example, static text controls are used to represent text in list boxes. Static controls are also used to display images, text, and the combination of an image with text.

The AFC supports a variety of different button components including push buttons, radio buttons, checkboxes, and repeat buttons. The most interesting of these buttons are repeat buttons, which operate like push buttons except that they repeatedly fire events while they are being held down. All of the different buttons support images along with traditional text labels.

AFC menu controls are popup menus that can be used in a variety of different scenarios. The menu components consist of menu items, menu lists, and menu buttons. A menu item can be text, an image, or even another control. Menu lists serve as containers and consist of menu items. Menu buttons act as the user interface for accessing a menu; when you click a menu button, the corresponding menu is displayed.

Choice and list controls are used to provide a list of items for selection purposes. Choice controls function much like Win32 drop-down list boxes in that they display a single item and only provide a selection list when clicked. List controls display a list of items and support the selection of multiple items if necessary.

Dialog-based controls aren't controls in a traditional sense because they are displayed in their own window. However, they are self-contained and can be easily modified and reused like controls, which earns them control status. The AFC supports message box, property sheet, wizard, and text searching dialog boxes.

Graphics Effects

I mentioned earlier that the AFC doesn't directly extend the Java AWT. Although this statement is true with respect to the component and application-level features of the AFC, it doesn't apply to the AFC's advanced graphics features. The AFC provides a set of graphics classes built upon the AWT graphics classes that provide lots of interesting graphics capabilities, such as support for pens when drawing graphics primitives.

Win32 Resource Support

To aid developers in accessing existing Win32 resources from Java applets and applications, the AFC provides support for Win32 resources. This support enables you to use existing .res files common to Windows applications in Java applications. This feature is extremely useful for porting a Win32 application to Java, because it allows you to preserve and directly reuse application resources.

CAB File Services

Microsoft has its own solution to compressed archives that support security through digital signatures: CAB files. CAB stands for CABinet, which is an archive format Microsoft has been using internally for some time. CAB files are functionally equivalent to JAR files in that they provide a file format for distributing applets and applications that supports compression and digital signatures. You learn all about JAR files on Day 17, "Working with Java Archives."

The AFC includes direct support for CAB files, including the packaging of applets and applications in CAB files. This support improves download time for applets because CAB files use compression; additionally, there is only a one HTTP transaction because all the files for an applet are combined into one. CAB files also provide a means of authenticating an applet with a digital signature. You learn about security and digital signatures on Days 18 and 19.

Summary

In this lesson, you learned about application frameworks and why they are important to the future of application development in Java. More specifically, you learned about two existing application frameworks, Netscape's IFC and Microsoft's AFC, along with JavaSoft's forthcoming JFC. Each framework has its own unique approach to providing application components and services. You found out in this lesson exactly what types of features the frameworks provide and how these features relate to the existing Java API.

The first half of the lesson focused on the JFC, which is planned to be a part of the core Java API in its next release. You learned that the JFC is already present in Java 1.1, laying the groundwork for some of the profound GUI features to come. You examined these new GUI features and found out exactly what the JFC encompasses. You got a glimpse of the suite of new components comprising the JFC and saw firsthand how these components, code-named Swing, will change the face of Java in the very near future. If you can't wait for the JFC or you want to try a third-party foundation class solution, the IFC or AFC is for you. The latter half of the lesson covered these two application frameworks.

All three application frameworks provide similar services and will ultimately solve the needs of a Java application developer. Deciding which framework you use has to do with personal taste and gauging which one will serve your needs best in the long haul.

Q&A

Q When will the new JFC features be available?

A The majority of the new JFC features will appear in the next major release of Java, version 1.2, which is expected to ship by the end of 1997. As you are reading this lesson, the JFC should already be released or quickly approaching a release date. Check out JavaSoft's Web site at http:\\www.javasoft.com for up-to-the-minute information on the release of Java 1.2.

Q How is the JFC related to JavaBeans?

A All JFC components qualify as JavaBeans components, meaning that they meet the minimum requirements of JavaBeans components. You learn about these requirements in the next lesson, "Introduction to JavaBeans."

Q Do I have to use the MVC architecture with JFC components?

A No. The MVC architecture is provided as an option for developers implementing complex GUIs. You are totally free to use JFC components however you choose, which includes using them the old-fashioned Java 1.1 AWT way. I guess it's a little early to be calling Java 1.1 old-fashioned, but I think you get the idea.

Q Is it difficult migrating Java 1.1 code to Swing?

A No it isn't, provided that your code uses the Java 1.1 delegation event model for its event-handling needs. The only real changes that have to be made are the names of the component classes, because some Swing components are named differently than their Java 1.1 AWT predecessors.

Q **What's the difference between a Swing component and a JFC component?**

A Nothing. Swing is just a project code name for the early access implementation of the JFC component suite. When the components officially become part of the next version of Java, the Swing name will go away.

Q **How do I get more information about the foundation classes discussed in this lesson?**

A This lesson barely scratched the surface of the JFC, IFC, and AFC foundation class libraries. To get more information on them, please refer to the Web site for the respective foundation class vendors: www.javasoft.com, www.netscape.com, and www.microsoft.com.

4

Day **5**

Introduction to JavaBeans

by Michael Morrison

Today's lesson introduces you to JavaBeans, the much-touted software component model for Java. This lesson essentially picks up where *Teach Yourself Java
in 21 Days* left off by exploring the following topics:

- [ ] The JavaBeans API
- [ ] Usage scenarios
- [ ] The basic structure of a Bean
- [ ] Standard AWT components as Beans
- [ ] Converting your own components to Beans

You also learn in this lesson what functionality makes a class a Bean. (A *Bean* is
a JavaBeans component.) In doing so, you may be surprised at how little
JavaBeans-specific overhead is required for a class to qualify as a Bean. At the end
of the lesson, you will convert two of the AWT components developed on Day
3, "Creating Custom Components," to Beans.

The JavaBeans API Revisited

The JavaBeans API consists of all the classes and interfaces that make JavaBeans such an interesting technology. *Teach Yourself Java in 21 Days* touched on the JavaBeans API; this section quickly recaps its major functions and features. JavaBeans is ultimately a programming interface, which means that all its features are implemented in the java.beans package. The java.beans package is also referred to as the JavaBeans API and is provided as part of the standard Java 1.1 class library.

The JavaBeans API itself is a suite of smaller APIs devoted to specific functions or services. By understanding these services and how they work, you'll have much more insight into the JavaBeans technology. These main component services in the JavaBeans API facilitate the features that make JavaBeans such an exciting technology:

- [ ] Property management
- [ ] Introspection
- [ ] Event handling
- [ ] Persistence
- [ ] Application builder tool support

Property Management

The property management facilities in the JavaBeans API are responsible for handling all interactions relating to Bean properties. Properties reflect the internal state of a Bean and constitute the data part of a Bean's structure. (Beans have two basic parts: a data part and a method part.) More specifically, properties are discrete, named attributes of a Bean that determine its appearance and behavior. Properties are important in any component technology because they isolate component state information into discrete pieces that can be easily modified.

NEW TERM	*property:* A discrete, named attribute of a Bean that determines its appearance and behavior.

To help you get a better idea of the importance of properties, consider some different scenarios that deal with properties. The following are some examples of how Bean properties are accessed:

- [ ] As object fields in scripting environments such as JavaScript or VBScript
- [ ] Programmatically, using public accessor methods
- [ ] Visually, using property sheets in application builder tools
- [ ] Through the persistent storage and retrieval of a Bean

As this list shows, properties come into play in a variety of ways when it comes to Bean access and manipulation. Notice the flexibility properties provide: You can access them through scripting languages such as JavaScript, through full-blown programming languages such as Java, and through visual application builder tools. This freedom to access and manipulate Beans in a variety of ways is one of the critical design goals of the JavaBeans technology; the property management facilities in the JavaBeans API fulfill this goal.

Introspection

The introspection facilities in the JavaBeans API define the mechanism by which components make their internal structure readily available to the outside world. These facilities consist of the functional overhead necessary to enable development tools to query a Bean for its internal structure, including the interfaces, methods, and member variables that comprise the Bean. Although the introspection services are primarily designed for use by application builder tools, they are grouped separately from the application builder services in the API because their role in making a Bean's internal structure available externally is technically independent of builder tools. In other words, you may have other reasons for querying a Bean about its internal structure beyond the obvious reasons used in builder tools.

NOTE

> The introspection facilities in the JavaBeans API are closely linked to the reflection services provided by the Java 1.1 API. You learn about the reflection services on Day 11, "Reflection: Looking Inside."

5

The JavaBeans API introspection services are divided into two parts: low-level services and high-level services. The difference between these two types of services is the level of access they provide to a Bean's internal structure. These two distinct services offer Bean introspection capabilities based on the required level of access.

The low-level API services provide wide access to the internal structure of a Bean. These services are very important for application builder tools that heavily use Bean internals to provide advanced development features. For example, application builder tools often need access to all of the members of a Bean, not just the public members. This type of private Bean access is provided by the low-level introspection services. However, keep in mind that this level of access is inappropriate for application developers.

The high-level API services are more appropriate for application developers. The high-level services use the low-level services behind the scenes to provide access to limited portions of a Bean's internal structure (typically, the Bean's public properties and methods). The high-level services enable access only to the parts of a Bean's internal structure that are specifically designed for external use.

Event Handling

The JavaBeans event-handling facilities use the same delegation event model as the Java 1.1 AWT (which you learned about on Day 2, "Maximizing the Delegation Event Model." The facilities provided by the Java 1.1 AWT delegation event model are critical in that they determine how Beans respond to changes in their state, as well as how these changes are propagated to applications and other Beans.

Persistence

JavaBeans' persistence facilities, which are provided by the Java 1.1 API, specify the mechanism by which Beans are stored and retrieved within the context of a container. The information stored through persistence consists of all the parts of a Bean necessary to restore the Bean to a similar internal state and appearance. These parts generally include all public properties and, potentially, some internal properties, although each particular Bean determines what information is stored. Transient data and references to external Beans, including event registrations, are not stored through persistence. The expectation is that these Bean references will be stored somehow by an application builder tool or through some programmatic means.

By default, Beans are persistently stored and retrieved using the automatic serialization mechanism provided by Java, which is sufficient for most Beans. You learn about this serialization mechanism on Day 12, "Object Serialization." Bean developers are also free to create more elaborate persistence solutions based on the specific needs of their Beans. Like the introspection facilities, the JavaBeans persistence facilities provide both an explicit approach and an automatic approach to carrying out their functions.

Application Builder Tool Support

The final area of the JavaBeans API deals with application builder tool support. The application builder tool support facilities provide the overhead necessary to edit and manipulate Beans using visual application builder tools. Application builder tools rely heavily on these facilities to enable a developer to visually lay out and edit Beans while constructing an application. These facilities fulfill a major design goal of the JavaBeans API: They enable Beans to be used constructively with little or no programming effort.

The application builder tool support for a Bean is required only at design time. Consequently, bundling this support code into a runtime Bean is somewhat wasteful. Because of this situation, the application builder facilities require that builder-specific overhead for a Bean be physically separate from the Bean itself. This separation enables Beans to be distributed by themselves for runtime use or in conjunction with the application builder tool support for design-time use.

Usage Scenarios

In learning about JavaBeans' neat features, you can miss the forest for the trees. What I mean is that knowing how Beans are used in the big picture is essential to understanding JavaBeans. Examining a few Bean-use scenarios should give you a better idea of how Beans fit into the software development process.

Because of Beans' adherence to JavaSoft's goal of *reuse everywhere*, you can use them in several ways. The following sections describe three major development-use scenarios for Beans: using an application builder tool to build an applet, hand-coding an applet, and using a component bridge.

Using Beans with an Application Builder Tool

You can use JavaBeans components with a visual application builder tool to construct applications with minimal programming. You must purchase the builder tool along with whatever Beans you want to use. Of course, you can also develop your own Beans or download freeware Beans developed by others.

Once you have a suitable tool and a suite of Beans, follow these steps to create an application:

1. Lay out the application visually using the builder tool and the Beans.

2. Customize the Beans by editing their properties. To edit the properties, you use visual property editors, which are invoked by the builder tool and supplied by the Beans.

3. Connect the Beans to each other and to the application by wiring events to appropriate handler routines. You perform this process primarily in a visual fashion by virtue of the builder tool. I say "primarily" because it is usually necessary to write *some* code in the event-handling routines.

4. Test everything and iron out the kinks. When you are happy with the outcome, package the application with the Beans and distribute them as one physical unit.

NOTE   I use the term *application* in a general sense throughout this discussion. In Java programming, an application is a stand-alone Java program, as opposed to an applet, which is a Java program that runs within the confines of a Web browser. In this discussion, the term *application* has a more general meaning and refers to both types of programs.

As you can see, the entire development process described requires very little programming. (If you've ever used an object-based visual development tool such as Visual Basic or

PowerBuilder, this process probably seems familiar.) Using Beans with an application builder tool is very convenient and intuitive because it alleviates many of the drudgeries of programming by putting a visual spin on the challenge of application development.

The builder tool provides many of these programming conveniences, but they wouldn't be possible without the internal support provided by the Beans. For example, the builder tool must be able to determine what features a Bean provides; the introspection facilities of the JavaBeans component model provide this information. Also, the Beans provide visual editors so that the Beans can be edited and customized.

Using Beans in Handwritten Code

Using Beans in code you write yourself isn't quite as rosy a scenario as connecting Beans with a builder tool, but you can accomplish just as much. In this handwritten scenario, there is no fancy application builder tool, and nothing is done visually, unless you consider looking at source code a "visual" process. Instead, all the code for the application is written by hand, including the integration of Beans.

This approach typically involves a developer using the standard Java Development Kit provided by JavaSoft, which includes a command-line compiler and debugger. Although these tools aren't fancy, they *are* free. Even though the tools themselves are free, you must still come up with Beans to use in building the application. As in the first scenario, you can buy, borrow, or develop your own Beans.

To use Beans in a handwritten application, follow these steps:

1. Lay out the application by writing code to create and position the Beans appropriately.

2. Customize the Beans by writing code that calls various methods that modify the properties of the Beans. Calling these methods has the same effect as visually editing a Bean with a property editor—you be the judge of which approach sounds easier for the developer.

3. Connect the Beans to the application using event handlers. To accomplish this step, you must write code to register each event listener with the appropriate component so that event notifications can be routed. You then must write code for the event handlers themselves. The visual approach usually requires the event handlers to be written as well, but the event listener registration is typically handled automatically.

4. Test everything and then package the Beans with the application and distribute the results.

This development scenario differs from the first scenario primarily in that you do everything by writing code. Although nothing is wrong with this approach, replacing handwritten code with more visual techniques generally results in a more rapid and intuitive development process. Even so, some developers are more comfortable getting dirty in the details of handwritten code, which is perfectly fine. The beauty of JavaBeans is that it fully enables and even encourages the existence of both scenarios; Java alone only supports the latter.

Using Beans Through a Bridge

The final usage scenario for Beans involves the usage of a component bridge, which allows Beans to be integrated with environments designed for a different type of component, such as ActiveX (a different component technology that originated on the Microsoft Windows platform). Using a bridge, a Bean can be integrated and used in a non-Java development environment such as Visual Basic. This powerful scenario allows developers to worry less about their choice of tools and technologies. Ideally, Beans should run in any environment; bridges are a big step in that direction.

A Bean running in a bridge environment is not much different than a Bean running in an application builder tool that directly supports JavaBeans. The only real difference is that the bridge acts as an intermediary between JavaBeans and the component model being bridged to. For example, the ActiveX bridge allows you to use Beans in any ActiveX environment, such as Visual Basic. When a Bean is using the ActiveX bridge to run in Visual Basic, the bridge is acting as an intermediary between the Bean and an ActiveX wrapper that is visible to Visual Basic. In other words, the bridge enables Beans to appear as ActiveX components in ActiveX environments, which is a pretty significant achievement.

NOTE For more information about using Beans with the ActiveX bridge, check out JavaSoft's JavaBeans Tools for ActiveX Web pages at http://splash.javasoft.com/beans/activextools.html.

5

The Basic Structure of a Bean

You now understand a great deal about the JavaBeans technology and how Beans are used, but you still don't know much about Beans themselves. A Bean, like an object in any object-oriented environment, is comprised of two primary things: data and methods that act on the data. The data part of a Bean completely describes the state of the Bean; the methods provide a way for the Bean's state to be modified and for actions to be taken accordingly. Figure 5.1 shows the two fundamental parts of a Bean.

Just like a normal Java class, a Bean can have methods with different types of access. For example, private methods are accessible only within the internals of a Bean, but protected methods are accessible both internally and in derived Beans. The methods with the most accessibility are public methods, which are accessible internally, from derived Beans, and from outside parties such as applications and other components. In this context, accessible means that an application can call any of a component's public methods. Public methods have a unique importance to Beans because they form the primary communication link between a Bean and the outside world.

Figure 5.1.

The fundamental parts of a JavaBeans component, or Bean.

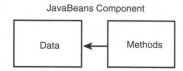

 NOTE

> A Bean also communicates with the outside world through events, which are generated when the internal state of the Bean changes. Event listeners, such as applications, handle and respond to events. Events were covered in great detail on Day 2.

A Bean's public methods are often grouped according to their functionality. Functionally similar groups of public methods are also known as *interfaces*. A Bean exposes its functionality to the outside world through these interfaces. Interfaces are important because they specify the protocol by which a particular Bean is interacted with externally. A programmer only has to know a Bean's interfaces to be able to successfully manipulate and interact with the Bean. Figure 5.2 shows how interfaces expose a Bean's functionality to the outside world.

NEW TERM

> *interface:* A functionally similar group of public methods in a Bean.

Figure 5.2.

The relationship between interfaces and methods in a JavaBeans component.

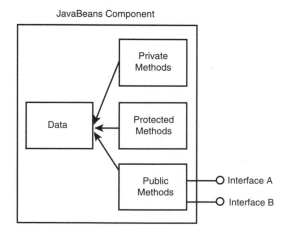

Although Beans are expected to provide support for facilities such as persistence and application builder tool integration, all Beans ultimately boil down to data and methods. These facilities are supported in the form of additional methods, data, and interfaces, which are themselves groups of methods. No matter how complex a Bean looks on the outside, just keep in mind that it is ultimately a combination of data and methods. How simple!

What Constitutes a Bean?

The structure of a Bean sounds simple, but if a Bean is just data and methods, why aren't all Java objects Beans? The answer is that Beans are required to support a minimum level of functionality that isn't always associated with a normal Java class. The question then is, exactly what constitutes a Bean and why? First off, you should understand that a Bean is nothing more than a Java class that supports a minimum set of required features. There is nothing magical about a Bean—any Java class that supports the required functionality qualifies as a Bean.

The following are the minimal requirements for a Java class to qualify as a Bean:

- The class must be instantiable.
- The class must have a default constructor.
- The class must be serializable.
- The class must follow JavaBeans design patterns.
- The class must use the Java 1.1 AWT delegation event model (if it must process or generate events).

The next few sections outline the meanings behind each of these requirements.

Must Be Instantiable

The "must be instantiable" requirement means that a class must be capable of being instantiated as an object in order to qualify as a Bean. This requirement is very straightforward, because an uninstantiable Bean would be of little use. In practical terms, the requirement means that a Bean can't be an abstract class or an interface.

Must Have a Default Constructor

All Beans must have a default constructor, which is a constructor that takes no arguments. The reason for this requirement is that application builder tools must create Beans as default objects because they know nothing about the Bean's other constructors. Additionally, the JavaBeans persistence facility uses the default constructor for a Bean to restore the Bean from its persistent state. Beans must therefore have a default constructor to be usable within application builder tools and to support persistence.

Must Be Serializable

Serialization, a standard feature in Java 1.1, allows objects to be represented as a series of bytes. Serialization serves as the basis for persistence, which gives objects the ability to be stored away to a nonvolatile location for later retrieval. Because persistence is very important for Beans, all Beans are required to be serializable. Meeting this requirement can be as simple as a class implementing the `Serializable` interface and doing nothing more, in which case the class supports serialization automatically. You learn a great deal more about serialization on Day 12.

> **NEW TERM**   *serialization:* The representation of an object as a series of bytes.

Must Follow JavaBeans Design Patterns

Another important requirement for Beans is that they follow standard JavaBeans design patterns. JavaBeans *design patterns* are naming conventions for Bean methods and data that convey information about the functionality of the Bean. Design patterns are important because they help provide an automatic form of introspection, which is the mechanism by which components make their internal structure readily available to the outside world. By conforming to a simple set of design patterns, Beans support introspection without any special overhead.

> **NEW TERM**   *design patterns:* Naming conventions for Bean properties and methods that convey information about the functionality of a Bean.

As an example, consider a Bean with a property named `weight` that is an integer. One type of design pattern applies to methods used to access properties, or *accessor methods*. The design pattern for accessor methods dictates that the method used to set a property should begin with the word `set` followed by the capitalized property name. Likewise, the method used to a get a property should begin with the word `get` followed by the capitalized property name. Therefore, the `weight` property has the following accessor methods:

```
public int getWeight();
public void setWeight(int w);
```

In addition to the design patterns for accessor methods, there are design patterns that specify the method signatures for event registration methods. Design patterns are generally straightforward; they follow the logical naming conventions most Java programmers already use, so most classes meet the design pattern requirement. The JavaBeans specification, available from `http://www.javasoft.com/beans/spec.htm`, has detailed information about the different design patterns supported by JavaBeans.

Must Use the Delegation Event Model

The final requirement for a class to qualify as a Bean is that it uses the Java 1.1 AWT delegation event model, which you learned all about on Day 2. This event model is very different from the Java 1.0 event model and was designed in many ways to specifically support the functionality required of JavaBeans. You should use the new event model for all AWT development anyway, so the requirement for Beans to use it isn't burdensome.

Standard AWT Components as Beans

At this point, you may be thinking that the Bean requirements seem pretty minor in terms of development effort. A lot of Java classes could be classified as Beans according to this minimum set of requirements. The truth is, many classes, including most of the standard Java 1.1 AWT components, are completely legitimate Beans. This fact may seem strange because no one ever mentions them as being Beans, but the idea is for Beans to be very simple to develop and require little extra work to use. It makes sense that the standard Java 1.1 AWT components qualify as Beans because they are promoted as being reusable graphical components.

Speaking of AWT components being Beans, you've already unknowingly developed some Beans of your own! Well, almost. The AWT components you developed back on Day 3 almost qualify as Beans. If you run through the list of requirements, you'll find that the only missing ingredient is that the components aren't serializable. Read on to see how to whip them into shape as Beans!

Converting Your Own Components to Beans

To demonstrate how easy it is to build Beans, you're going to take two of the components you developed on Day 3 and convert them to Beans. There isn't much conversion to be done, because most of the features of JavaBeans are automatic. The two components I'm referring to are `BorderPanel` and `ImagePanel`, which were developed on Day 3 purely as AWT components. With these two components in mind, review the list of requirements for a class to qualify as a Bean:

1. The class must be instantiable.
2. The class must have a default constructor.
3. The class must be serializable.
4. The class must follow JavaBeans design patterns.
5. The class must use the Java 1.1 AWT delegation event model (if it must process or generate events).

Both classes pass the first test with flying colors because they are definitely instantiable. The second requirement is easily met because they both provide a default constructor. The third requirement, however, is a problem; neither of the classes support the `Serializable` interface, which is required for all Beans. You have to address this issue to get the classes working as Beans, but move on now and see whether anything else is missing.

The fourth requirement is potentially thorny, because it dictates how the methods of a class are named. The method names (for the accessor methods) used in the classes conform to the JavaBeans design patterns, however, so you're in luck.

NOTE

The code for the classes was developed for Day 3 by the author of that lesson, Jerry Ablan, without any knowledge that the classes needed to conform to JavaBeans design patterns. This example is a testament to the fact that most Java programmers adhere to a consistent style, which in this case happened to exactly match the JavaBeans design patterns. What can I say, we got lucky!

The final requirement for a class to be a Bean is that it uses the Java 1.1 delegation event model. Of course, this requirement is only necessary if the class uses events. Neither of the classes in question uses events, so this requirement isn't a problem.

Supporting Serialization

Based on the list of Bean requirements, the only missing ingredient for the `BorderPanel` and `ImagePanel` classes is serialization support. Adding serialization support is unbelievably easy. If a class's member data is capable of being serialized, all you have to do to make a class serializable is to have the class implement the `Serializable` interface. The `Serializable` interface contains no methods, so classes have to do nothing more than declare the implementation in their class definition; no methods actually have to be implemented.

To convert the `BorderPanel` class to a Bean, modify its class definition:

```
public class BorderPanel
extends Panel
implements BorderStyle, Serializable
{
   ...
}
```

The only change to the class is the addition of the `Serializable` interface to the `implements` section of the class definition. That's just too easy!

Just so I don't get you thinking that converting all classes to Beans is this easy, let me go over an important issue regarding object serialization. I mentioned earlier that implementing the

Serializable interface is all that is required to convert a class to a Bean, provided that the class' member data is capable of being serialized. What exactly would prevent a class's member data from being of serialized? The answer is object references.

Objects references present a problem for the automatic Java serialization facility because they refer to objects in memory that can move around. References can't be serialized because they wouldn't refer to valid memory when restored. One solution is to serialize the entire object referred to, which would solve the whole reference problem because a new reference would be created when the object is restored. Although this approach works, the automatic class serialization facility in Java doesn't support it. Fortunately, many object references refer to objects that don't need to be serialized anyway. What then?

Java supports *transient member variables*, which are member variables that can't be serialized. When the automatic serialization facility encounters a transient member variable, it skips it. Later, when an object containing a transient member variable is restored serially, the member variable is set to null. Typically, classes are designed so that the constructor initializes all transient member variables appropriately.

NEW TERM | *transient member variables:* A member variable that isn't capable of being serialized.

You declare member variables transient with the transient keyword:

```
public transient Font font;
```

The ImagePanel class has a member variable that must be transient in order for the class to be serializable; this variable is the myImage member variable, which is a reference to an Image object. To make the myImage member variable transient, just use the transient keyword in its declaration:

```
protected transient Image myImage;
```

The ImagePanel class also needs to implement the Serializable interface:

```
public class ImagePanel
extends BorderPanel
implements Serializable
{
    ...
}
```

At this point, the BorderPanel and ImagePanel classes are Beans, but they still must be packaged as Beans in order to be usable in application builder tools.

5

Packaging the Beans

The standard method of distributing Beans involves packaging them into compressed archives called JAR (Java ARchive) files. JAR files are similar to other types of compressed files, such as ZIP or TAR files, except that they are specifically tailored to packaging Java classes and resources. JAR files basically enable you to group the classes and resources for Beans into one compressed unit to organize them and conserve space. Bean resources can include anything from images and sounds to custom resources, such as data files. You learn all about JAR files on Day 17, "Working with Java Archives." For now, I'll just cover the bare essentials necessary to get the BorderPanel and ImagePanel Beans packaged; Day 17 clarifies everything regarding JAR files.

To create a JAR file for a Bean, you have to use the JAR utility, which ships with JDK 1.1. You also need to provide a special file called a *manifest file* that lists the Beans included in the JAR file. This manifest file is necessary to indicate which class in the JAR file is the main Bean class. Additionally, you can package multiple Beans into a single JAR file, in which case the manifest file would specify each Bean class. Following is the manifest file, BorderPanel.mf, for the BorderPanel Bean.

```
Manifest-Version: 1.0

Name: BorderPanel.class
Java-Bean: True
```

The manifest file, which you learn much more about on Day 17, indicates the Bean class. In this case, the Bean class is listed as BorderPanel.class. To create a JAR file containing the BorderPanel Bean using the BorderPanel.mf manifest file, issue the following command in the directory where the BorderPanel classes are located:

```
jar cfm BorderPanel.jar BorderPanel.mf Border*.class
```

This command invokes the JAR utility to create a JAR file containing the Bean. The name of the new JAR file is identified by the first argument; the second argument is the name of the external manifest file. The remaining argument is a wild card specifying the classes to be added to the archive.

That's all it takes to create a JAR file for the BorderPanel Bean. The Bean is now ready to be used in the BeanBox or any other JavaBeans-supported development environment. Packaging the ImagePanel Bean is a very similar process to packaging the BorderPanel Bean. The following is the manifest file, ImagePanel.mf, for the ImagePanel Bean:

```
Manifest-Version: 1.0

Name: ImagePanel.class
Java-Bean: True
```

The only difference between this manifest file and the one for the BorderPanel Bean is the name of the Bean class. To create a JAR file containing the ImagePanel Bean using the

`ImagePanel.mf` manifest file, issue the following command in the directory where the `ImagePanel` classes are located:

```
jar cfm ImagePanel.jar ImagePanel.mf *.class *.gif
```

Notice that two wild cards are provided in this command; the first one is to add all of the classes in the directory to the JAR file, and the second one adds all the GIF images in the directory. The GIF images are required by the `ImagePanel` Bean, as are all the classes. The two Beans are now packaged and ready to use in an application builder tool. You'll have to wait and see them in action in the next lesson, however.

NOTE
The source code, executables, manifest files, and JAR files for the converted `BorderPanel` and `ImagePanel` Beans are included on the companion Web site for this book.

Summary

Today's lesson focused on JavaBeans, the exciting Java-based software component technology. You began the lesson by quickly revisiting the JavaBeans API to learn about the primary functional parts of JavaBeans. You then took a look at the three different ways in which Beans are used to develop applications: visually through application builder tools, programmatically through straight Java source code, and through component bridges.

You then moved on to learning the basic structure of a Bean, along with what a class must have to be considered a Bean. In doing so, you found out that most of the standard Java 1.1 AWT classes are technically Beans. You finished up the lesson on a practical note by converting two of the AWT components developed on Day 3 into Beans. In the next lesson, you learn more about how Beans are used to build applications. You also get to try out the two converted Beans in the BeanBox test container provided with the JavaBeans Development Kit (BDK).

Q&A

Q If a Bean is made up only of data and methods, how does it differ from normal Java classes?

A Although the structure of a Bean is identical to that of normal Java classes, Beans are required to support certain minimal features such as serialization, JavaBeans design patterns, and the Java 1.1 delegation event model.

5

Q Why are design patterns so important to JavaBeans?

A Although design patterns may seem like just a formality imposed on the naming of Bean properties and methods, they are critical to JavaBeans' introspection facilities. When a Bean provides no explicit information about its internal makeup, JavaBeans uses automatic introspection based on design patterns to figure out the functionality of a Bean. In this way, design patterns fully dictate the public appearance, and usage, of most Beans.

Q Is implementing the `Serializable` interface the only option for supporting Bean serialization?

A No. Beans can also implement the `Externalizable` interface, which is an interface derived from `Serializable` that is designed to give objects more control over how they are serialized. You learn more about the `Externalizable` interface on Day 12.

Q Can Beans be used outside of JAR files?

A Yes, but not in application builder tools. Beans must be packaged in JAR files in order to be used in application builder tools. In applications developed through straight coding, however, Beans can be used outside of a JAR file just like normal Java classes.

Day 6

Using JavaBeans Effectively

by Michael Morrison

Now that you have a solid understanding of Beans and how they are used, you're ready to press on to learning how to develop applications with Beans. This lesson picks up where yesterday's lesson left off by looking at the JavaBeans technology from a practical perspective. After today, you should have all the knowledge necessary to begin using Beans productively on your own.

Today's lesson covers the following topics:

- ☐ Using the JavaBeans Development Kit, or BDK, which contains tools and resources necessary to build and test Beans
- ☐ Using the BeanBox, which allows you to test Beans in a visual environment similar to that of application builder tools
- ☐ Testing Beans in the BeanBox
- ☐ Using Beans the old-fashioned way in straight Java code
- ☐ Using Beans through a component bridge, such as the ActiveX Bridge

The JavaBeans Development Kit (BDK)

In addition to the Java 1.1 Development Kit (JDK), JavaSoft also produces the JavaBeans Development Kit (BDK), which includes all the tools and resources necessary to create and test Beans. Although third-party visual Bean development environments are currently in the works, the BDK will remain the standard Bean development toolkit. The BDK is freely available from JavaSoft, and you can download it from JavaSoft's Web site at `http://www.javasoft.com`. Please note that the BDK requires the Java Development Kit (JDK) version 1.1 or later, which provides all the API functionality used by JavaBeans.

NOTE

> Check JavaSoft's Web site to ensure that you have the very latest versions of the BDK and the JDK. Development kits like these tend to evolve rapidly, so new versions are released periodically. Also, you must install the JDK *before* you install the BDK because the JDK has all the core support required by the BDK.

Inside the BDK you'll find a host of useful information to help you develop JavaBeans components. The most useful part of the BDK is the BeanBox test container, which you can use to test Beans in a setting similar to a visual application builder tool. In addition to the BeanBox, the BDK includes a wide range of sample Beans with complete source code, as well as source code for the JavaBeans API. The BDK also has a JavaBeans tutorial that provides a quick overview of the JavaBeans technology.

The BeanBox Test Container

The BeanBox test container is an application that is used to test Beans. You can drop Beans into the BeanBox and try them out in a completely visual manner, just as if you were using them in an application builder tool. The BeanBox is an indispensable tool for testing Beans and seeing how they will work in application builder tools as design time components or in completed applications as runtime components.

NEW TERM

> *design time:* The execution mode where a component is being used to construct an application in an application builder tool.

runtime: The execution mode where a component is included in a completed application.

Sample Beans and Source Code

The BDK includes a variety of different sample Beans with complete source code. These Beans demonstrate many different aspects of the JavaBeans technology. Some of them even include source code in HTML form with color highlights to make certain aspects of the code easier to understand. You can use the sample Beans as starting points for Beans of your own. The BDK also provides the source code for the BeanBox test container.

API Source Code

The BDK includes the complete source code for the JavaBeans API, which is technically part of the core Java 1.1 API. Although this source code is also available with the JDK 1.1, the BDK isolates the specific classes that comprise the JavaBeans API, which are located in the java.beans package.

JavaBeans Tutorial

The JavaBeans tutorial provided with the BDK outlines many of the basic concepts associated with JavaBeans and the BeanBox test container. This tutorial is shipped in both PostScript and Adobe Acrobat formats.

Using Beans in the BeanBox Test Container

One of the key benefits of JavaBeans is the capability for Beans to be used in visual application builder tools. By using BeanBox, you can see this capability in action and learn how to work with JavaBeans in a visual environment. The BeanBox enables you to lay out, edit, and interconnect Beans visually. Although the BeanBox isn't intended to be a fully functional development tool for creating applications with Beans, it does provide a simple example of how you can manipulate Beans visually. The BeanBox is an indispensable tool for Bean development because it provides a simple test bed for trying out Beans.

 Note To use a Bean with the BeanBox, you must package the Bean in a Java archive or JAR file. All of the sample Beans included with the BDK are packaged in JAR files and stored in the jars directory in the main Bdk directory. The details of how to package Beans in JAR files are covered on Day 17, "Working with Java Archives."

The BeanBox is a stand-alone application executed using the JDK interpreter. Instead of running through the interpreter, the BeanBox comes with a batch file, run.bat, which is in the BDK's Beanbox directory and is responsible for setting the CLASSPATH environment variable before executing. You should use this batch file to run the BeanBox because it sets CLASSPATH to values specific to using the BeanBox. The following are the contents of the run.bat batch file used to execute the BeanBox:

```
if "%OS%" == "Windows_NT" setlocal
set CLASSPATH=classes
java sun.beanbox.BeanBoxFrame
```

As you can see, the batch file first sets CLASSPATH to a few different paths; then it executes the BeanBox within the JDK interpreter. Don't worry too much about the CLASSPATH settings; they are based on the internal workings of the BeanBox.

To run the BeanBox, just execute the run batch file. When you run the batch file, the BeanBox executes and displays three different windows. Each of these windows performs a different function within the scope of the BeanBox. The first window is the ToolBox window, which is shown in Figure 6.1.

Figure 6.1.

The BeanBox's
ToolBox window.

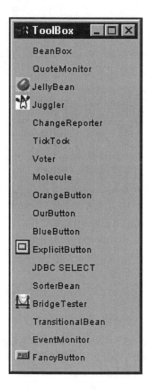

6

The ToolBox window lists a variety of available Beans. These Beans are all sample Beans provided with the BDK to demonstrate the development and use of Beans. Notice that some of the Beans have icons associated with them. These Beans use a Bean information class to specify the icon to be displayed in visual development environments. Other Beans are listed in the ToolBox window by name only.

The second window associated with the BeanBox is the main BeanBox window, shown in Figure 6.2. The BeanBox window is the central window for the BeanBox application because it is where you lay out Beans. The BeanBox window is very similar in function to form windows in other types of visual development environments, such as Visual Basic, in that it serves as a container for Beans. This window has four menu items: File, Edit, View, and Help. You use these menus to load and save BeanBox files and connect Beans together, among other things.

Figure 6.2.

The BeanBox's main BeanBox window.

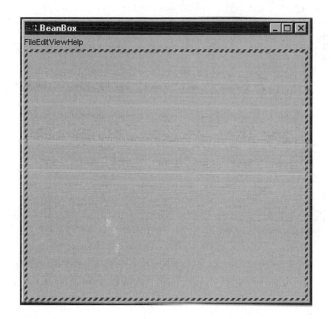

The last window in the BeanBox is the Properties window, which lists the properties associated with the currently selected Bean. The Properties window is responsible for providing the visual editing capabilities of the BeanBox because it displays a property editor for each property defined in a Bean. Figure 6.3 shows the Properties window.

6

Figure 6.3.

*The BeanBox's
Properties window.*

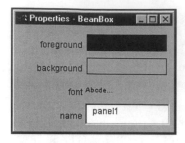

When you first run the BeanBox, the Properties window displays the properties for the
BeanBox container itself. You can try to edit these properties by clicking one of them with
the mouse. For example, click the background property to change the background color for
the container. Figure 6.4 shows the property editor dialog box displayed for changing the
background color.

Figure 6.4.

*The property editor
dialog box for the
background color
property.*

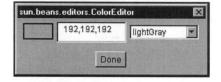

This property editor dialog box enables you to easily change the background color for the
BeanBox container window either by entering RGB (Red, Green, Blue) colors or by selecting
a standard color from a drop-down list. Select a different color and click Done to see how your
choice affects the window.

NOTE

> For Beans that have an associated customizer, the Edit menu in the
> BeanBox includes a Customize command that runs the customizer on
> the Bean. A *customizer* is a visual Bean editor that provides a more
> advanced interface than just a group of property editors. For example,
> many customizers use a wizard-style interface where you customize a
> Bean by answering a series of questions.

6

Working with Beans in the BeanBox

Working with Beans in the BeanBox is easy and demonstrates the real benefit of visual editing with Beans. The first thing you do is select a Bean from the ToolBox window and add it to the main BeanBox window. Click a Bean's name or icon in the ToolBox window; this action turns the mouse pointer into a cross. Then click in the BeanBox window at the location you want to place the Bean. A new Bean appears in that location with a default size and set of properties.

Try laying out one of the sample Beans that comes with the BDK:

1. Click the OurButton Bean in the ToolBox window.
2. Click somewhere in the BeanBox window to place the Bean. The BeanBox window should look similar to Figure 6.5.

Figure 6.5.

The main BeanBox window after adding the OurButton *Bean to the BeanBox.*

Notice that the new Bean is drawn with a hashed border. This border indicates that the Bean is the currently selected Bean, which means that the Properties window reflects the properties for this Bean. Beans are selected by default when you add them to the BeanBox window. To select a different Bean, click anywhere on the Bean you want to select.

You will be using the OurButton Bean you just laid out to control an animation Bean, but first you have to change its label property. You do this using the Properties window. Change the Bean's label property to read Start Animation. Now add one more OurButton Bean using the steps you just went through:

1. Click the OurButton Bean in the ToolBox window.
2. Click somewhere in the BeanBox window to place the Bean.
3. Edit the Bean's label property, and set the value to Stop Animation. The BeanBox window should now look similar to Figure 6.6.

Figure 6.6.

The main BeanBox window after adding two OurButton *Beans to the BeanBox.*

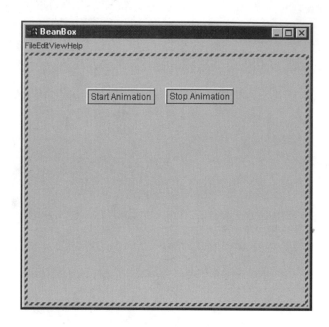

Throw in a little excitement by adding a Bean that displays an animation:

1. Select the Juggler Bean from the ToolBox window.
2. Add the Bean to the BeanBox just below the OurButton Beans. The BeanBox window should look similar to Figure 6.7.

If your Beans aren't lined up quite the way they are shown in the figure, feel free to move them around. To move a Bean, select the Bean you want to move, and then click the hashed border and hold down the mouse button while you drag the mouse. Release the mouse button when the Bean is in the position you want. You can also resize Beans that support resizing by clicking one of the corners on the hashed border and dragging the mouse. You don't need to resize any of the Beans in this example because they automatically size themselves to fit their content.

6

Figure 6.7.

The main BeanBox window after adding a Juggler *Bean to the BeanBox.*

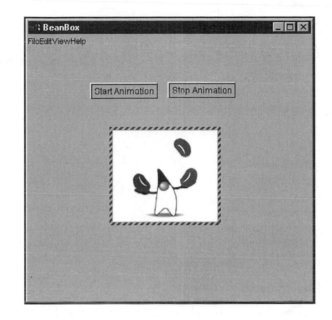

Wiring Beans Together with Events

A particularly useful function of the BeanBox is that you can wire Beans together using events. For example, you can easily connect a Bean's event to a public method defined in another Bean, which effectively ties the two Beans together functionally. The BeanBox enables you to do this task visually, which makes it very simple. As you might guess, the two buttons you've laid out thus far are perfectly situated to control the Juggler animation Bean. Wire them up to see what happens:

1. Select the Start Animation button.

2. Click the Edit menu in the BeanBox.

3. Select the action menu item, and then select the actionPerformed command beneath it. You'll see a line originating from the button that moves as you move the mouse around.

4. Move the mouse over the Juggler Bean and click to connect the button Bean's action event to the Juggler Bean. A dialog box appears that shows the available target methods defined in the Juggler Bean (see Figure 6.8).

5. Select the startJuggling() method from the dialog box to specify it as the receiver of the action event. Now any time you click the Start Animation button, the Juggler Bean's startJuggling() method is called.

Figure 6.8.

*The
EventTargetDialog
dialog box for the
`Juggler` Bean.*

Repeat this procedure to connect the `Stop Animation` button to the `stopJuggling()` method of the `Juggler` Bean. Test the buttons by clicking them to start and stop the animated `Juggler` Bean. It's as simple as that!

Using Runtime Mode

Up to now you've worked with the BeanBox in what is known as design time mode, which means that you have interacted with individual Beans from a design perspective: You've edited their properties and connected them together with events. In a runtime setting such as a Bean residing in a application, none of these design time issues exist. Therefore, it is beneficial to be able to test a Bean in a runtime setting to make sure it behaves properly. The BeanBox supports just such a mode and calls it, appropriately enough, runtime mode.

To test your Beans in runtime mode, select `Disable Design Mode` from the `View` menu in the BeanBox. Notice how the ToolBox and Properties windows disappear when the BeanBox is in runtime mode. To switch back to design time mode, select `Enable Design Mode` from the `View` menu.

Saving Your Work

You can easily save the contents of the BeanBox using the `Save` command from the `File` menu. When you save the contents of the BeanBox, the persistence features of JavaBeans store the state of each Bean. You then can reload the Beans later using the `Load` command from the `File` menu; the persistence features reconstruct the Beans just as you left them.

Testing Your Own Beans in the BeanBox

Now that you have a feel for the BeanBox, you're ready to try out the Beans you converted from AWT components yesterday. The first step to using any Bean with the BeanBox (other than the sample Beans) is to load the Bean into the BeanBox so you can access it from the ToolBox window. You can accomplish this task in one of two ways:

- ☐ Copy the Bean's JAR file to the jars directory, which is located in the main Bdk installation directory. This approach results in the Bean automatically being added to the ToolBox window each time you run the BeanBox.

- ☐ Load the Bean into the current BeanBox session by selecting the LoadJar command from the File menu in the BeanBox.

The first approach is better if you plan on continuing to use the Bean with the BeanBox, but the second approach is better for quickly testing a Bean. You're going to use the second approach to try out the BorderPanel and ImagePanel Beans.

Testing the BorderPanel Bean

Run the BeanBox by executing the run.bat batch file, and then select LoadJar from the File menu to load the Bean. In the dialog box that appears, locate and select the BorderPanel.jar file. After you select the file, the Bean is added to the ToolBox window.

To add the Bean to the BeanBox, select the BorderPanel Bean in the ToolBox window and then click in the BeanBox container window. A small gray box appears; this box is an instance of the Bean (Figure 6-9). You can resize the Bean by clicking a corner of the hashed border surrounding the Bean and dragging the mouse.

Now turn your attention to the Properties window and notice that the Bean's properties are all available for editing. The most interesting property editor is the text box for the borderStyle property. This editor might seem strange because the borderStyle property is usually set to predefined constants in straight Java code. These constants are ultimately just numbers, however, which is all JavaBeans knows about the value of the property. To apply the style, you have to use the numeric value of a border style constant. The following are the numeric values for each border style.

Border style	Numeric value
None	0
Flat	1
Lowered	2
Raised	3
Grooved	4
Ridged	5

6

Figure 6.9.

*The main BeanBox
window after adding
a* BorderPanel *Bean
to the BeanBox.*

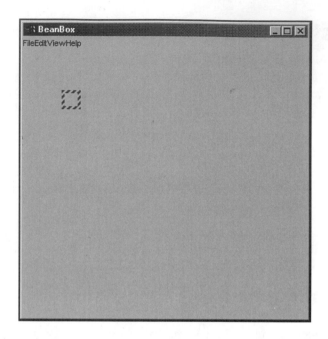

Using the text box property editor, set the borderStyle property to 5, which will make the
border have a 3-D ridge around it. Figure 6.10 shows what the Bean looks like after you resize
it and change its borderStyle property.

Figure 6.10.

*The main BeanBox
window after resizing
and customizing the*
BorderPanel *Bean.*

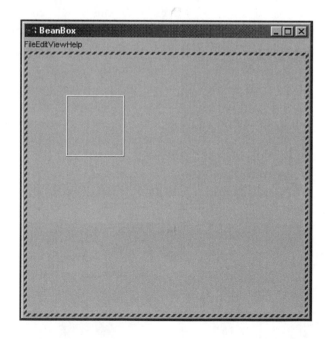

You should now have a good idea about how the BorderPanel Bean works in the BeanBox. Feel free to put the Bean through a more thorough test on your own.

Testing the ImagePanel Bean

Turn your attention to the ImagePanel Bean. Add it to the BeanBox the same way you added the BorderPanel Bean, by using the LoadJar command from the File menu. Notice that the Bean is added to the ToolBox window. Select the Bean in the ToolBox window and add an instance of it to the container window next to the BorderPanel Bean (see Figure 6.11).

Figure 6.11.

The main BeanBox window after adding an ImagePanel *Bean.*

Try customizing the Bean by changing its background color to black, its imageToUse property to Exclamation.gif, and its borderStyle property to 4. Figure 6.12 shows the results of these changes.

Figure 6.12.

The main BeanBox window after customizing the ImagePanel *Bean.*

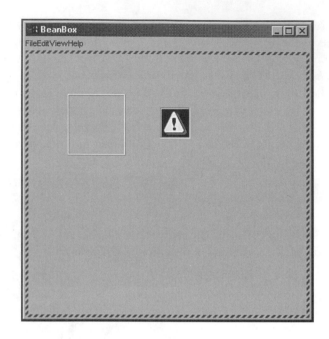

Saving a Bean for Later

Seeing your Beans in action is pretty neat, but you've yet to touch on one of the most interesting aspects of the BeanBox: its capability to save Beans for later. Later in this lesson, you learn how to use the BorderPanel and ImagePanel Beans in a hand-coded Java applet. To make things more interesting, you're going to use a couple of serialized BorderPanel Beans that have been stored in files. You can easily serialize a Bean to a file by selecting the Bean in the BeanBox and then selecting SerializeComponent from the File menu.

Change the background color of the BorderPanel Bean you customized earlier to pink, and then serialize the Bean to a file named PinkBorderPanel.ser. Repeat this process to create another serialized Bean file, but this time change the background color to yellow and name the file YellowBorderPanel.ser. Incidentally, .ser is the standard file extension for serialized Beans. The two files you just created contain the BorderPanel Bean in customized form and are ready to be used later in the lesson when you build a Bean tester applet by hand.

Using Beans the Old-Fashioned Way

You just experienced one of the biggest benefits of the JavaBeans technology through its built-in support for visual layout and editing using application builder tools. Through working with the BeanBox, you should now appreciate the significance of the visual design aspect of JavaBeans. I now want to shift gears and look at a completely different scenario involving JavaBeans: the use of Beans in hand-coded Java programs.

This part of the lesson is devoted to showing you how laying out and editing Beans visually isn't the only approach available to developers. Granted, it's the favored approach to building applications with JavaBeans because it is so incredibly easy to learn, but it may not be for everyone. Plenty of developers feel more at home hacking away at the code level. I have to admit I even like working solely at the code level at times because it ultimately gives you more insight into what's going on in your program. Everyone has their own ideas about what type of development environment works best for them, and JavaBeans promotes their freedom of choice.

Building applications using JavaBeans through straight coding is not mentioned a lot, but you can use Beans directly in source code just like traditional Java classes. Working with Beans at the source level doesn't necessarily provide any higher degree of flexibility, but it might feel more natural for some developers who are accustomed to writing straight Java code. As I mentioned earlier, you can always see exactly what is going on when you work at the source code level. For this reason, you should understand how to use Beans directly in Java source code.

Even though using Beans directly in code is a more involved process than simply pointing and clicking in a visual tool, the task of building Java applications out of Beans at the code level is conceptually similar to using visual tools for the same purpose. The primary difference is that you have to do everything in code that the builder tools enable you to do visually. More specifically, you must perform the following steps to build applets or applications out of Beans in a nonvisual environment:

1. Create the Beans.
2. Customize the Beans.
3. Connect the Beans.

You can think of these steps as the three C's of JavaBeans development: Create, Customize, and Connect. These three steps apply equally well to visual JavaBeans development, but they are more apparent when working at the code level.

 NOTE This discussion focuses on using Beans directly in Java code to build stand-alone applications. Developing applets with Beans is a very similar process, so the discussion applies equally to it. In fact, you build an applet that uses Beans in the next section of the lesson.

Creating Beans Programmatically

In a visual application builder tool, creating an instance of a Bean is as simple as selecting the Bean from a toolbox or palette and clicking in the editing (form) window for the application you are developing. Creating Beans directly in source code isn't much more difficult, but it isn't as elegant or intuitive as pointing and clicking with the mouse. To create a Bean directly in code, you create an instance of the Bean class using a special method provided by the Beans class called instantiate(). You must use this approach instead of the new operator to ensure that the Bean uses the appropriate class loader. Different class loaders come into play when a Bean is created from a serialized file, for example.

Here is the definition for the Beans.instantiate() method:

```
Object instantiate(ClassLoader cls, String beanName) throws IOException,
    ClassNotFoundException
```

The first argument to the instantiate() method is the class loader for the Bean, which can be passed as null to use the default system class loader. It's unlikely that you would want to use a different class loader, unless you are using a custom security manager. The second argument is the name of the Bean class to instantiate, which is the fully qualified class name for the Bean, including package information. The following is an example of creating a Bean using the instantiate() method:

```
OurButton button = (OurButton) Beans.instantiate(null, "OurButton");
```

The instantiate() method always creates Beans using their default constructor, which is why Beans must always provide a default constructor. Because the instantiate() method is capable of throwing exceptions, you must always place calls to it within a try-catch clause.

After you create a Bean in code, you still have to add it to an application's window in order for it to be associated with the application. This requirement is due to the fact that an application class is a container class, which is capable of holding graphical AWT elements such as Beans. To add a Bean to an application, call the application's add() method, which is inherited from the Container class. The following is an example of adding the OurButton Bean to an application by using the add() method:

```
add(button);
```

As you can see, adding a Bean to an application in straight Java code is a very straightforward process. Keep in mind that this code is placed in the application class's constructor along with the Bean creation code. You typically will create all your Beans and then add them to an application in the application class's constructor.

Customizing Beans Programmatically

After you've created and added all of your Beans to an application, you then must customize them to fit the needs of the application. Beans are rarely used with their default settings, so customization is a standard part of using Beans at the code level. Bean customization is just as important as Bean creation because it determines how Beans function and appear in an application.

Customizing a Bean is simply a matter of calling one or more of its public methods with the desired settings. Usually, you use a Bean's accessor methods to customize the Bean by setting its properties to different values. If you recall from earlier in the book, accessor methods are public methods used to get and set the properties of a Bean. The application class's constructor is a good place to handle Bean customization. The following piece of code shows how to customize the OurButton Bean after creating it and adding it to an application:

```
OurButton button = (OurButton) Beans.instantiate(null, "OurButton");
add(button);
button.setLargeFont(true);
button.setLabel("Click me, please!");
```

This code creates and adds an OurButton Bean and then customizes it by setting two of its properties. The setLargeFont() method sets the font property of the Bean. This code also sets the label property, which determines the label text drawn below the button itself.

Connecting Beans Programmatically

JavaBeans uses the same delegation event model as the Java 1.1 AWT does; this model is based on event sources and listeners. You learned all about this event model on Day 2, "Maximizing the Delegation Event Model." Rather than rehash all its details again, let me point out that Beans are connected through the exact same event handling mechanism you learned about on Day 2. From a programming perspective, this similarity means that you have to register an application as an event listener for a particular Bean event and then write code to handle and respond to the event.

Bean customization is a straightforward process of calling the appropriate public methods to get the desired results. Granted, this process is not as fancy as clicking and setting properties in a visual application builder tool, but it accomplishes the same task.

Testing Your Beans the Old-Fashioned Way

Earlier in this lesson you tested out the BorderPanel and ImagePanel Beans in the BeanBox. Now you're going to see how to use these Beans programmatically in straight Java code. If you recall, on Day 3 you developed test applets for the AWT component versions of these Beans. The applet you develop now tests both of these Beans using the programmatic approach to using Beans you've learned about in this lesson. The applet used to test the Beans is called PanelTest because it tests both panel Beans. Listing 6.1 contains the complete source code for the PanelTest applet.

6

Listing 6.1. The source code for the PanelTest applet.

```
1: import java.awt.*;
2: import java.applet.*;
3: import java.beans.*;
4:
5: public class
6: PanelTest
7: extends Applet
8: {
9:   public
10:   PanelTest()
11:   {
12:     setFont( new Font( "Helvetica", Font.BOLD, 14 ) );
13:     setBackground( Color.lightGray );
14:
15:     try
16:     {
17:       BorderPanel myPanel = (BorderPanel) Beans.instantiate( null,
18:         "BorderPanel" );
19:       myPanel.setBorderStyle( BorderPanel.RAISED );
20:       myPanel.setLayout( new GridLayout( 3, 3, 15, 15 ) );
21:
22:       Panel p;
23:       ImagePanel ip;
24:
25:       myPanel.add( p = (Panel) Beans.instantiate( null,
26:         "YellowBorderPanel" ) );
27:       p.add( new Label( "Panel1" ) );
28:       p.add( new Label( "Panel1" ) );
29:       p.add( new Label( "Panel1" ) );
30:       myPanel.add( p = (Panel) Beans.instantiate( null,
31:         "PinkBorderPanel" ) );
32:       p.add( new Label( "Panel2" ) );
33:       p.add( new Label( "Panel2" ) );
34:       p.add( new Label( "Panel2" ) );
35:       myPanel.add( ip = (ImagePanel) Beans.instantiate( null,
36:         "ImagePanel" ) );
37:       ip.setImageToUse( "Exclamation.gif" );
38:       myPanel.add( ip = (ImagePanel) Beans.instantiate( null,
39:         "ImagePanel" ) );
40:       ip.setImageToUse( "Stop.gif" );
41:
42:       //Add to the center...
43:       add( "Center", myPanel );
44:     }
45:     catch (Exception e)
46:     {
47:       System.err.println(e);
48:     }
49:   }
50: }
```

6

NOTE

The source code and executable for the `PanelTest` applet is included on the companion Web page at `http://www.mcp.com/info/1-57521/1-57521-347-8`.

Everything in the `PanelTest` class takes place in the constructor; all the Beans are created and customized accordingly. The overall structure of the `PanelTest` class is similar to that of the `BorderTest` and `ImageTest` classes you developed on Day 3. In this case, you are creating and customizing Beans instead of AWT components, however. The primary difference is that you must use the `Beans.instantiate()` method in `PanelTest` to create the Beans. If you recall from earlier in this lesson, all Beans must be created using `instantiate()` instead of the `new` operator.

The `PanelTest` constructor first creates a `BorderPanel` object using the `Beans.instantiate()` method (Line 17). This panel serves as the container panel to which other panels are added. Notice that the properties of the panel are set with calls to the `setBorderStyle()` and `setLayout()` property methods. After creating the container panel, the constructor moves on to creating more Beans.

The first Bean created after the container is the yellow `BorderPanel` Bean saved in the BeanBox earlier in this lesson. If you recall, this Bean was customized in the BeanBox and then serialized to a file named `YellowBorderPanel.ser`. To create a Bean from the serialized file, the name `YellowBorderPanel` is passed into the `instantiate()` method (Lines 25-26). After the serialized Bean is created, some labels are added to it just for fun (Lines 27-29).

The next Bean is also a serialized `BorderPanel` Bean. This time the Bean saved in the `PinkBorderPanel.ser` file is created with a call to `instantiate()` (Lines 30-31). Some labels are also added to this Bean just to make things a little more interesting (Lines 32-34).

After the serialized `BorderPanel` Beans are created, an `ImagePanel` Bean is created (Lines 35-36). The image for the Bean is then set to `Exclamation.gif` using the `setImageToUse()` property method. The last Bean created is another `ImagePanel` Bean. The image for this Bean is also set using the `setImageToUse()` property method, but this time the image is set to `Stop.gif`.

That wraps up the code for the `PanelTest` applet class. To see the applet in action, open the `PanelTest.html` file in the JDK 1.1 appletviewer. Figure 6.13 shows what the applet looks like while running in the appletviewer.

6

Figure 6.13.
The PanelTest
applet running in the
appletviewer.

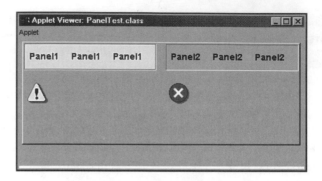

Using Beans Through a Bridge

Although you typically think of Beans as being useful in building applets or applications in Java, a component bridge makes it possible to use Beans in environments that don't necessarily support Java at all. One such bridge is the ActiveX Bridge, which allows Beans to be used as ActiveX components. The ActiveX Bridge lets you integrate Beans into ActiveX-based environments such as Visual Basic. The rest of this section focuses on the ActiveX Bridge because it is the only available component bridge for JavaBeans as of this writing.

NOTE   The version of the ActiveX Bridge as of this writing is Release 1.0 Beta 4. You can download the latest version of the ActiveX Bridge from the following Web site: http://splash.javasoft.com/beans/bridge/.

The ActiveX Bridge consists of the following parts:

☐ Bridge classes

☐ The ActiveX Packager utility

☐ Sample Beans

☐ Documentation

The Bridge classes consist of special Java and C++ classes that act as a translator between JavaBeans and ActiveX. The ActiveX Packager is a utility that builds extra functionality into a Bean so that it is capable of being used as an ActiveX component. The sample Beans are two Beans from the BDK that have already been run through the Packager. The documentation consists primarily of a tutorial on how to use a Bean in Visual Basic.

Using the ActiveX Bridge, JavaBeans components can fire events that ActiveX containers can catch. They also can act as servers for ActiveX method invocation. The first of these capabilities allows a Bean to fire events that are handled in ActiveX containers such as Visual

Basic forms. For example, a Bean button click could be handled and responded to with Visual Basic code. The second capability allows ActiveX environments such as Visual Basic to call Bean methods.

If this discussion seems biased toward Visual Basic as an ActiveX development tool, it's because Visual Basic is currently the most thoroughly tested environment for the ActiveX Bridge. In addition, Visual Basic is a very popular visual development tool that has no direct support for Java or JavaBeans, which makes it an interesting environment for JavaBeans integration.

The ActiveX Bridge is designed to be as automatic as possible. Ideally, a Bean would require no additional code to masquerade as an ActiveX component. (The key word here is *ideally*.) Back in the real world, you have to deal with the issues involved in integrating two very different technologies. The ActiveX Bridge goes a long way toward making the JavaBeans/ActiveX merger a straightforward one. All things considered, Beans require little additional code to be usable as ActiveX components.

With the ActiveX Bridge, Beans require three elements to operate in an ActiveX environment:

1. A type library
2. A registry file
3. Java stub classes

A type library is a binary file that describes the properties, methods, and events of a Bean in ActiveX terms. You can think of a type library as ActiveX's rough equivalent of a Bean information class. The registry file contains information about the Bean, such as the path to the type library. The Java stub classes comprise the actual bridge between a Bean and ActiveX. The ActiveX Packager automatically generates these elements and adds them to the Bean's JAR file.

Bridging Properties

All Bean properties are accessible under ActiveX. The ActiveX Bridge automatically invokes the proper accessor methods for JavaBeans properties. Bound and constrained properties are also supported through similar facilities in ActiveX. Native Java property types are automatically mapped to comparable ActiveX property types. Additionally, some JavaBeans properties are naturally mapped to standard ActiveX properties. Because standard ActiveX property names begin with a capital letter, the Bridge also capitalizes all JavaBeans property names.

Bridging Methods

All public JavaBeans methods can be called from ActiveX, with the exception that overloaded methods aren't fully supported in the Beta 4 release of the Bridge. The overloaded method with the most arguments is the only one accessible in ActiveX. Method arguments and return values are automatically processed and translated appropriately by the Bridge. Exceptions thrown by a method are caught by the Bridge and returned to the ActiveX container in a special package.

Bridging Events

JavaBeans events are fully supported by the Bridge, but they are merged together under one interface. In other words, the Bridge doesn't support multiple event interfaces. This limitation could be a problem if different interfaces contain methods with the same name.

Another big issue regarding events and the ActiveX Bridge is the differing approaches to event processing used by JavaBeans and ActiveX. JavaBeans events are based on the Java 1.1 AWT delegation event model, which relies heavily on event information being represented by an immutable event object, which is an object that can't be modified. ActiveX events, on the other hand, are represented by native data types that are sometimes able to be written to. The ActiveX Bridge supports both types of events; it refers to the ActiveX event type as "cracked," which refers to the fact that the information is broken up into separate entities. You can specify whether you want cracked or uncracked events when packaging a Bean with the ActiveX Packager.

That sums up the major aspects of how a Bean is bridged to another component model. The ActiveX Bridge is a powerful and important JavaBeans-related technology; I encourage you to experiment with it!

Summary

Today you learned a great deal about the applied side of JavaBeans. You began the lesson by learning about the JavaBeans Development Kit (BDK) and what it has to offer for Bean development and testing. You then used the most important part of the BDK, the BeanBox test container, to create, customize, and connect a couple of Beans in a purely visual manner. With some BeanBox experience under your belt, you used the BeanBox to try out the Beans you converted in yesterday's lesson.

To demonstrate that Beans have a life beyond visual application builder tools, the lesson shifted gears and showed how Beans are used programmatically in straight Java code. You used this knowledge to build an applet in straight Java code that tests the Beans converted in yesterday's lesson. The lesson concluded with a look at how Beans are used in component bridges. More specifically, you learned how the ActiveX Bridge allows Beans to masquerade as ActiveX components.

Q&A

Q If the BDK has everything necessary to build and test Beans, why do I need the JDK?

A Although the BDK includes the BeanBox test container and other useful resources for Bean development, you still must have a Java compiler, such as the JDK compiler, to build your own Beans. Additionally, the JavaBeans API is part of the core Java 1.1 API, which is part of the JDK.

Q If a lot of the standard Java 1.1 AWT components are Beans, then why aren't they included in the BeanBox?

A Just because a component meets the minimum requirement of being a Bean, doesn't mean it has all the advanced features of JavaBeans. The sample Beans shipped with the BDK and included in the BeanBox each demonstrate some type of explicit JavaBeans functionality built into a Bean, which is why they are singled out as examples. Of course, Java 1.1 AWT components that qualify as Beans can certainly be included and used in the BeanBox; they just need to be properly packaged into Java archives.

Q How is using Beans programmatically in straight Java code different from using other Java classes?

A Using Beans programmatically is no different than using other Java classes, except for the fact that Beans must be instantiated using the Beans instantiate() method instead of new. This method allows Beans that have been serialized to be loaded from special files. The main reason for pointing out the programmatic usage of Beans in today's lesson was to provide a contrast between the visual usage of Beans in the BeanBox.

Q Why is the ActiveX Bridge necessary? Isn't JavaBeans powerful enough by itself?

A As a component technology, JavaBeans is certainly powerful enough by itself. Power alone is not always the chief consideration to be made in a real-world development effort, however. You have to consider the existing code base for an application as well as how the application is going to be maintained in the long term. You may want to eventually rewrite a Visual Basic application in Java, but you don't have the resources to undertake the task all at once. One solution would be to develop new enhancements to the application as JavaBeans components and use the ActiveX Bridge to integrate the Beans with the original application. Eventually, you could convert the application to Java, and the Beans would still integrate perfectly.

Day 7

Networking with Java

by Jerry Ablan

My favorite thing about Java is the ease of creating network-capable programs. Even if you have never written networking software before, you can pick it up in a few short hours. Many of the networking examples used in books to illustrate the concepts behind this type of programming are simplistic. They don't model real-world applications. I mean, how many telnet clients are you going to be writing in Java?

This chapter takes a more practical approach by teaching you the following:

- ☐ The finer points of Java network programming
- ☐ How to implement a POP3 e-mail reading class
- ☐ How to implement an SMTP e-mail sending class

E-mail and the Internet

I decided to use an e-mail program to teach you about networking in Java because e-mail is one of the largest uses for the Internet today. This seemingly innocuous use of bandwidth has contributed most, after the World Wide Web, to the Internet's growth.

In addition, both of the Internet e-mail protocols (POP3 and SMTP) are *application-level* protocols. This term means that after the connection is made, the communication that goes on between the two parties is largely in a human language rather than a computer language. An e-mail message is just lines of text. This protocol is the appropriate level for the purposes of this chapter.

 TIP

> One neat thing about application-level protocols (such as POP3, SMTP, and HTTP) is that you can use any telnet program and connect to the respective server and hand-enter the commands yourself. You can try this feature by using a telnet program and connecting with port 80 of any Web server. After you get an established connection, type **GET** / and press the Enter or Return key. You'll be amazed at what comes back. (It is the HTML code for the base Web page of that site.)

MIME Encoding

You are probably wondering how people can send pictures and documents through e-mail if it is all just lines of text. The answer is that the pictures and documents are converted into lines of text before they are sent. This conversion is called *MIME encoding*.

MIME stands for Multipurpose Internet Mail Extension. This specification is designed to allow the transport of binary data in ASCII- or text-based messages. This broad, flexible specification encompasses all sorts of data types. You can even add your own types. MIME is an extension of the Internet Text Message format.

Internet Text Messages

MIME was developed for the purpose of allowing client software to recognize the contents of an Internet Text Message. An Internet Message is composed of a *header* and a *body*. The header contains information such as the message's delivery path, the sender, and the recipient. These header *fields* are identified by a type name, followed by a colon and the related data. The entire header section ends with a single blank line; the rest of the message is considered the body.

7

The following is a simple text message header taken from a fictitious Internet e-mail message:

```
Message-ID: <13058A7A.264D@mindbuilder.com>
Date: Mon, 11 Feb 1980 07:17:14 -0800
From: Jerry Ablan <munster@mindbuilder.com>
To: Tony Karwatowicz <tonyk@mindbuilder.com>
Subject: Hi there!
```

As you can see, the header fields in the previous listing are Message-ID, Date, From, To, and Subject; there are many other possible header fields. Each header field identifies a bit of information. Any client software should be able to recognize the header and act upon known header fields. It can safely ignore the ones it doesn't know about, but many of the header field names are standard.

As another example, the following is a header from a Usenet message:

```
Path: ddsw1!news.mcs.net!not for-mail
From: user@host.com (A. User)
Newsgroups: alt.news
Subject: News is cool!
Date: 26 Nov 1995 23:01:56 -0600
Organization: /usr/lib/news/organi[ze]ation
Lines: 12
Message-ID: <40bgn4$hog@news.host.com>
NNTP-Posting-Host: news.host.com
```

Again, you see the simple pattern: header field, colon, and data. The information may be different in the two messages, but the format of the header is standard.

NOTE

For a complete description of the Internet Text Message format, check out http://ds.internic.net/rfc/rfc822.txt.

Reading Mail from a Server

Because all e-mail is lines of text, retrieving it from a server is similar to reading data from a file: you get it a line at a time. On UNIX machines, network connections via TCP/IP are implemented much the same way files are. Sockets and files share the same input and output functions. Sun has tried to capture this wonderful network interface within Java's API. I think Sun did an excellent job!

The Post Office Protocol (POP) is an application-level protocol used to retrieve e-mail from an e-mail server. The server must, of course, be running a POP server for retrieval to work. This protocol is extremely common these days, so you should have access to at least one POP server. If your ISP doesn't have one, then perhaps your office has one.

7

POP is currently in its third version, hence the name POP3. POP1 was introduced in 1984. It contained basic commands to retrieve mail from a mail server; one could only retrieve the entire contents of the mailbox in question, however. There was no way to retrieve only a single message. You could also delete the mail in the mailbox. Again, it was all or nothing. In 1985, POP2 came along. It added acknowledgments (responses to queries) and the capability to retrieve a single message at a time. This protocol was the e-mail king for nearly 10 years.

Then, in 1994, POP3 was proposed. POP3 simplifies e-mail retrieval down to a set of 12 simple commands, and you only need to use half of those to get your mail. Table 7.1 lists the POP3 commands.

Table 7.1. The POP3 commands.

Command	Purpose
USER	Sends the user name
PASS	Sends the password
APOP	Sends the user name and password in an encrypted format
QUIT	Ends the session
STAT	Retrieves the mailbox status
LIST	Lists a mailbox summary
RETR	Retrieves a message
DELE	Deletes a message
NOOP	Does nothing (No operation)
RSET	Resets the session
TOP	Retrieves only the first n lines of a message
UIDL	Retrieves a unique identification for a message

If you want to read the specifications for POP1, POP2, or POP3, you can find them at (respectively):

```
http://ds.internic.net/rfc/rfc918.txt
http://ds.internic.net/rfc/rfc937.txt
http://ds.internic.net/rfc/rfc1725.txt
```

Reading Mail with Java

To read mail from a POP server, you only need to know three things:

1. The host name of the mail server
2. The username
3. The password for the user

Connecting and retrieving e-mail is a trivial matter. The following are the steps necessary to retrieve mail from a POP server:

1. Connect to the server on the POP3 port (110).

2. Send the username and password.

3. Retrieve the number of mail messages available.

4. Retrieve each mail message.

5. Close the connection.

Only five steps to retrieving e-mail! It couldn't be easier, and in this section you create a Java class to do it.

Creating the POP3Reader class

Call the e-mail retrieval class POP3Reader. To begin with, you need to import a lot of classes from the java.io and java.net packages, so just import them all. You also need the StringTokenizer and Vector classes. You use the StringTokenizer class to split up status messages retrieved from the server, and you use the Vector class to hold your retrieved mail.

Here is the code so far:

```
/*
 * Class: POP3Reader.java
 */

import     java.io.*;
import     java.not.*;
import     java.util.StringTokenizer;
import     java.util.Vector;

public class
POP3Reader
extends Thread
```

Notice that you are extending the Thread class. This class allows you to go to sleep while you are waiting for input from the POP server. Sometimes network lag can slow down retrieval, and you need to wait a bit. Being in your own thread is useful so you don't stop the parent application from running.

Next, you need some member variables to hold information about the connection:

```
protected    Socket            popSocket;        //    The socket used
protected    BufferedReader    popIn;            //    The input stream
protected    PrintWriter       popOut;           //    The output stream
protected    String            lastInputLine = "";
                                                 //    A holder for input

protected    boolean           popDelete;        //    Delete mail from server?
protected    boolean           popDebug;         //    Print debug statements?
```

```
protected   String   popHost;          //    Mail server name
protected   String   popUser;          //    Mail user name
protected   String   popPassword;      //    Mail user password
protected   int      popPort;          //    Port to connect on
protected   int      popMessageCount;
                                        //    The number of messages
                                        //    available

protected   Vector   messages;         //    A holder for the
                                                 messages
```

Each of the preceding instance variables hold either information needed to connect to a host or used to hold information retrieved from the host. For instance, you store retrieved messages in a Vector variable called messages. All of these variables are defined as protected. This definition allows descendants of this class to modify them.

The constructor initializes the values for the member variables:

```
public
POP3Reader()
{
    popDebug = false;
    popHost = null;
    popUser = null;
    popPassword = null;
    popPort = 110;
    popMessageCount = 0;
    messages = new Vector();
}
```

Note that you set the popPort to 110. This port is the standard POP3 port. If your POP server is on a different port, use the popPort accessor method to change it.

Speaking of accessor methods, you need to create some for all of your instance variables:

```
//    Get and set the port...
public void setPort( int port ) { popPort = port; }
public int getPort() { return( popPort ); }

//    Get and set the host...
public void setHost( String host ) { popHost = host; }
public String getHost() { return( popHost ); }

//    Get and set the user...
public void setUser( String user ) { popUser = user; }
public String getUser() { return( popUser ); }

//    Get and set the password...
public void setPassword( String password ) { popPassword = password; }
public String getPassword() { return( popPassword ); }

//    Get and set the debug flag...
public void setDebug( boolean debug ) { popDebug = debug; }
public boolean getDebug() { return( popDebug ); }
```

```
//    Get and set the delete flag...
public void setDelete( boolean delete ) { popDelete = delete; }
public boolean getDelete() { return( popDelete ); }

//    Get the message count (read-only)...
protected void setMessageCount( int count ) { popMessageCount = count; }
public int getMessageCount() { return( popMessageCount ); }
```

You may have noticed that the setMessageCount() method is declared as protected. This declaration essentially makes this instance variable read-only to outside classes. You want to do this so that no one can mess with the value. It should only contain a value that represents the number of actual messages on the server.

> **TIP**
>
> You can control the printing of debug information by using an instance variable. The popDebug variable, when set to true, notifies the class to print extra information. This information is useful for debugging or if you want to know what's going on behind the scenes.

Connecting to the Server

Connecting to the server is easy. With the currently set popHost and popPort, you create a new Socket using those values:

```
popSocket = new Socket( popHost, popPort );
```

If something goes wrong, an IOException is thrown. Otherwise, popSocket will contain a reference to your newly created socket.

To communicate on the new socket, the Socket class provides an input and output stream in the form of an InputStream class and an OutputStream class respectively. But using the stock InputStream and OutputStream classes is not easy. They only accept a single data type to send (byte arrays), and their input capabilities are limited. Instead, you'll use two new Java 1.1 API features, the Reader and Writer classes.

The Reader and Writer Classes

Writer is a new class that makes it easy to write data to a stream. It has a complimentary class for reading data from a stream, the Reader class. These classes are abstract and are the basis for several interesting classes. The one you are going to use for writing data is the PrintWriter. This class enables you to treat your output stream as though it were a data file. It even implements the println() method.

To create a PrintWriter class from the output stream, call the constructor passing the InputStream:

```
popOut = new PrintWriter( popSocket.getOutputStream(), true );
```

7

Creating the Reader class is just as easy as creating the Writer class, but you want to take the process one step further. Because your communications are line-based, you should use a line-based Reader. If your Reader automatically could read a line from the stream, that would be killer! A BufferedReader Reader class can do just that. Create the Reader class like so:

```
popIn = new BufferedReader(
    new InputStreamReader( popSocket.getInputStream() ) );
```

You now have two member variables, popIn and popOut, that represent the two halves of the connection to the mail server. These variables are used exclusively to communicate with the server.

Sending Authentication Information

Before you can get mail from the server, you need to send the username and password. To do this step, you use the USER and PASS commands. You use the popOut Writer variable to send this data:

```
popOut.println( "USER " + popUser );
popOut.println( "PASS " + popPassword );
```

The println() method sends the string it is passed and adds a line separator to the end. Depending on which operating system you are running from, this separator can be a carriage return, a line feed, or both.

The server responds with a +OK response if all is well; otherwise, it sends back an error message. You wait for these messages with a method called waitForMessage().

Waiting for a Response

Because you need acknowledgement before going any further, you must wait to make sure the username and password were accepted. You need a method that reads the input stream and looks for an acceptance message. This method is waitForMessage(). The source code for this method and its supporting methods is shown in Listing 7.1.

Listing 7.1. The waitForMessage() method.

```
1:    protected boolean
2:    waitForMessage( String message )
3:    {
4:        String              nextLine;
5:
6:        if ( popSocket == null )
7:            return( false );            → exit to invocation
8:
9:        while ( ( nextLine = getNextLine() ) != null )
10:       {
11:           //    Is this what we want?
12:           if ( message.equals( "*" ) || nextLine.startsWith( message ) )
13:               return( true );
14:
15:           idle();
```

```
16:            }
17:
18:            return( false );
19:        }
20:
21:    protected void
22:    idle()
23:    {
24:        try
25:        {
26:            sleep( 1000 );
27:        }
28:        catch ( InterruptedException e )
29:        {
30:        }
31:    }
32:
33:    protected String
34:    getNextLine()
35:    {
36:        try
37:        {
38:            lastInputLine = popIn.readLine();
39:
40:            if ( popDebug )
41:                System.out.println( lastInputLine );
42:
43:            return( lastInputLine );
44:        }
45:        catch ( IOException e )
46:        {
47:        }
48:
49:        return( null );
50:    }
```

The waitForMessage() (Line 1) method calls the getNextLine() method (Line 9) to retrieve the next line from the input stream. It then compares the retrieved line with the message it is waiting for (Line 12). If the lines match, the method returns true. If the lines don't match, you call the idle() method, which sleeps for a second waiting for more data. If no data is available, or if all of the data available has been read, the method returns false.

The getNextLine() method (Line 33) exists solely to trap the last line retrieved from the input stream. You could just access the popIn variable from the waitForMessage() method. Having the actual data available, however, is useful, as you'll see. The data is placed into the lastInputLine member variable.

Querying the Server

The next step to reading e-mail is to query the server to see whether there is any mail to retrieve. You do this step by using the STAT command. This command returns the number of messages, and the total number of bytes of all the messages. It looks something like this:

```
+OK 1 1063
```

The +OK is the response to the STAT request. The first number is the number of messages; the second is the number of bytes.

Issuing the STAT command is easy with the popOut Writer variable:

```
//    Send stat...
popOut.println( "STAT" );
```

Again, you wait for a response

```
//    Wait for connection reply...
if ( !waitForMessage( "+OK" ) )
    return( popMessageCount );
```

and then parse the response:

```
//    Get the message count and size...
StringTokenizer s = new StringTokenizer( lastInputLine );
s.nextToken();
popMessageCount = Integer.valueOf( s.nextToken() ).intValue();

if ( popDebug )
    System.out.println( "There are " + popMessageCount + " messages available."
);
```

You use StringTokenizer to split up the response. The response has three parts: the response, the message count, and the total bytes of the message. You ignore the first and last parts, concentrating on the second. You grab the integer value of that second part and place it into the member variable popMessageCount.

Here is a place where the last input line received is handy to have. Because the response and the query results come in on the same line, you need that last line for the results. Because you stored it in an instance variable, it is now available. Also, if the popDebug flag is set, you print a line with the message count.

Retrieving Your Mail

Now that you know how many messages are available, you can grab them off the server. You do this step with a simple loop:

```
for ( int i = 0; i < popMessageCount; i++ )
{
    String m = getMessageFromServer( i + 1 );

    if ( m != null )
        messages.addElement( m );
}
```

For each message, you call the getMessageFromServer() method. This method retrieves the message and places it in a string. The string is then added to the Vector for retrieved messages.

This class is quite simple; it was designed for illustrative purposes and not for maximum usefulness. You can, however, enhance it to add any features you want. For instance, you could add functionality that decoded attached files.

The getMessageFromServer() method uses the getNextLine() method to read data from the input stream. Listing 7.2 shows the code for this process.

Listing 7.2. The getMessageFromServer() method.

```
 1:     protected String
 2:     getMessageFromServer( int which )
 3:     {
 4:         String          myMessage = "";
 5:
 6:         if ( popSocket == null )
 7:             return( null );
 8:
 9:         popOut.println( "RETR " + which );
10:
11:         //    Wait for reply..
12:         if ( !waitForMessage( "+OK" ) )
13:         {
14:             System.out.println( "Error retrieving message #" + which +
             ➡" from server" );
15:             return( null );
16:         }
17:
18:         //    Retrieve the message...
19:         String l;
20:         while ( ( l = getNextLine() ) != null )
21:         {
22:             //     End of message?
23:             if ( l.equals( "." ) )
24:                 break;
25:
26:             myMessage += l + "\r\n";
27:         }
28:
29:         if ( popDebug )
30:             System.out.println( "Retrieved message #" + which +
             ➡" from server" );
31:
32:         //     Delete message from server if requested...
33:         if ( popDelete )
34:         {
35:             popOut.println( "DELE " + which );
36:
37:             //     Wait for reply...
38:             if ( !waitForMessage( "+OK" ) )
```

continues

7

Listing 7.2. continued

```
39:                     return( myMessage );
40:
41:             if ( popDebug )
42:                 System.out.println( "Deleted message #" + which +
                    ➥" from server" );
43:         }
44:
45:         return( myMessage );
46:     }
```

This method first checks to see whether you have a connection (Line 6), if not, it returns immediately. You then issue the RETR (retrieve) command to the server (Line 9). This command causes the server to send a response, followed by the text of the message. Finally, the server sends a single period (.) signaling the end of the message. This method retrieves lines until it receives that single period (Line 23). Each line is appended to a master string, which is the string that will be returned (Line 26).

The next part of Listing 7.2 is the popDelete variable handler. This variable is useful if you don't want to keep a copy of your mail on the server after you've read it. When you set this variable to true, you issue the DELE command to the server. This command removes the message permanently. In the final part of Listing 7.2, the message is returned.

Testing the POP3Reader Class

You can test the POP3Reader class with a simple program called POPTest (see Listing 7.3). Because of applet security restrictions, this program is an application. Unless the applet is loaded locally, or your mail server happens to be the same as your Web server, your applet will not be able to connect with the remote host.

Listing 7.3. The POPTest program.

```
1:
2: public class
3: POPTest
4: {
5:     public static void
6:     main( String args[] )
7:     {
8:         new POPTest();
9:     }
10:
11:     public
12:     POPTest()
13:     {
14:         POP3Reader r = new POP3Reader();
15:
```

```
16:            r.setHost( "pophost" );
17:            r.setUser( "user" );
18:            r.setPassword( "password" );
19:
20:            r.retrieveMail();
21:
22:            System.out.println( "There are " + r.getMessageCount() +
              ⮕"message(s) available" );
23:
24:            for ( int i = 0; i < r.getMessageCount(); i++ )
25:            {
26:                System.out.println( r.getMessageAt( i ) );
27:            }
28:        }
29: }
```

In this constructor, you first instantiate a new POP3Reader class. You then set the necessary variables needed to retrieve mail. The retrieveMail() method is then called. This method retrieves all the mail and stores it in the messages Vector. After the retrieval, you iterate through the message list, printing each one.

Sending Mail to a Server

Retrieving mail is harder than sending mail. You can take the POP3Reader class and convert into a mail sender very quickly. You just need to remove a few things and modify a couple of methods to create a different function.

Simple Mail Transfer Protocol

Instead of using POP3 to send mail, the mail-sending class uses SMTP, the Simple Mail Transfer Protocol. SMTP is an application-level protocol used for sending textual e-mail over the Internet. First introduced in 1982, it is arguably one of the oldest surviving Internet protocols. Its use is widespread today. Table 7.2 shows the commands that (minimally) make up SMTP.

Table 7.2. The SMTP commands.

Command	Purpose
HELO	Identifies the sender of the message
MAIL	Initiates a mail transaction
RCPT	Identifies the recipient of the mail message
DATA	Indentifies the beginning of the data transfer
QUIT	Ends the session
RSET	Resets the transaction

7

As you can see, this set of commands is smaller than POP3 and easier to digest. Notice that there are no user and password identification commands. Because SMTP is not based on users, anyone can connect to an SMTP server and send mail.

If you want to read the specifications for SMTP, you can find them at:

```
http://ds.internic.net/rfc/rfc821.txt
```

Sending Mail with Java

To send mail to an SMTP server, you only need to know the host name of the server. There is no username or password to contend with. Connecting and sending is simple. The following are the steps necessary to send mail to an SMTP server:

1. Connect to the server on the SMTP port (25).
2. Send the HELO command.
3. Send the MAIL command.
4. Send the RCPT command.
5. Send the DATA command.
6. Send the data.
7. Send a single period (.).
8. Send the QUIT command.
9. Close the connection.

Only nine steps to sending e-mail! In the following sections, you create and test a Java class called SMTPSender to handle this task.

Creating the SMTPSender Class

Like the POP3Reader class, you need to import a lot of classes from the java.io and java.net packages for SMTPSender, so just import them all:

```
/*
* Class: SMTPSender.java
*/

import     java.io.*;
import     java.net.*;

public class
SMTPSender
extends Thread
```

Next, you need some member variables to hold information about the connection. Each of these instance variables hold either information needed to connect to a host or information used to hold information retrieved from the host.

```
protected    Socket              smtpSocket;    //    The socket used
protected    BufferedReader      smtpIn;        //    The input stream
protected    PrintWriter         smtpOut;       //    The output stream
protected    String              lastInputLine = "";
                                                //    A holder for input

protected    boolean             smtpDebug;     //    Print debug statements?
protected    String              smtpHost;      //    Mail server name
protected    int                 smtpPort;      //    Port to connect on
```

The constructor initializes the values for the member variables:

```
public
SMTPSender()
{
    smtpDebug = false;
    smtpHost = null;
    smtpPort = 25;
}
```

Note that you set the `smtpPort` to 25. This port is the standard SMTP port. If your SMTP server is on a different port, use the `smtpPort` accessor method to change it.

Speaking of accessor methods, you need to create some for all of the instance variables:

```
//    Get and set the port...
public void setPort( int port ) { popPort = port; }
public int getPort() { return( popPort ); }

//    Get and set the host...
public void setHost( String host ) { popHost = host; }
public String getHost() { return( popHost ); }

//    Get and set the debug flag...
public void setDebug( boolean debug ) { popDebug = debug; }
public boolean getDebug() { return( popDebug ); }
```

Connecting to the Server

Connecting to the server is easy. With the currently set `smtpHost` and `smtpPort`, you create a new `Socket` using those values:

```
smtpSocket = new Socket( smtpHost, smtpPort );
```

If something goes wrong, an `IOException` is thrown. Otherwise, `smtpSocket` will contain a reference to your newly created socket.

You use a reader and writer just like the `POP3Reader` class to communicate on the socket:

```
smtpIn = new BufferedReader(
    new InputStreamReader( smtpSocket.getInputStream() ) );

smtpOut = new PrintWriter( smtpSocket.getOutputStream(), true );
```

You now have two member variables, `smtpIn` and `smtpOut`, that represent the two halves of the connection to the mail server. These variables are used exclusively to communicate with the server.

7

Sending the Mail

The SMTPSender class was designed to illustrate the method of sending data to an SMTP server; therefore, it is quite simplistic. You implement the entire connection through data sending in a single method called sendMail(). Listing 7.4 shows this method.

Listing 7.4. The sendMail() method.

```
1:      public boolean
2:      sendMail( String msgTo, String msgFrom, String msgSubj,
        ➥String msgBody,
3:          String ehData )
4:      {
5:          //    Attempt to connect with the host...
6:          if ( smtpHost == null )
7:              return( false );
8:
9:          //    Open the port...
10:         try
11:         {
12:             smtpSocket = new Socket( smtpHost, smtpPort );
13:
14:             smtpIn = new BufferedReader(
15:                 new InputStreamReader( smtpSocket.getInputStream() ) );
16:
17:             smtpOut = new PrintWriter( smtpSocket.getOutputStream(), true );
18:
19:             //    Wait for connection reply...
20:             if ( !waitForMessage( "220" ) )
21:                 return( false );
22:
23:             //    Send a HELO
24:             smtpOut.println( "HELO " +
25:                 InetAddress.getLocalHost().getHostName() );
26:
27:             //    Wait for connection reply...
28:             if ( !waitForMessage( "250" ) )
29:                 return( false );
30:
31:             //    Send MAIL FROM...
32:             smtpOut.println( "MAIL FROM: " + msgFrom );
33:
34:             //    Wait for connection reply...
35:             if ( !waitForMessage( "250" ) )
36:                 return( false );
37:
38:             //    Send TO...
39:             smtpOut.println( "RCPT TO: " + msgTo );
40:
41:             //    Wait for connection reply...
42:             if ( !waitForMessage( "250" ) )
43:                 return( false );
44:
45:             //    Send data...
46:             smtpOut.println( "DATA" );
```

```
47:
48:             //    Wait for connection reply...
49:             if ( !waitForMessage( "354" ) )
50:                 return( false );
51:
52:             //    Send the subject data...
53:             if ( msgSubj != null )
54:                 smtpOut.println( "Subject: " + msgSubj );
55:
56:             //    Send some more info...
57:             smtpOut.println( "To: " + msgTo );
58:             smtpOut.println( "X-Mailer: " + version );
59:             smtpOut.println( "Mime-Version: 1.0\n" );
60:             smtpOut.println( "Content-Type: TEXT/PLAIN; charset=US-ASCII\n"
);
61:
62:             //    Send any additional data the client wants in the header...
63:             if ( ehData != null )
64:                 smtpOut.println( ehData );
65:
66:             //    Now print a blank line to separate the header from the
             message
67:             smtpOut.println();
68:
69:             //    Send the data...
70:             smtpOut.println( msgBody );
71:
72:             //    Send the end of message indicator...
73:             smtpOut.println( "." );
74:
75:             //    Wait for OK reply...
76:             if ( !waitForMessage( "250" ) )
77:                 return( false );
78:
79:             //    Send the end of message indicator...
80:             smtpOut.println( "QUIT" );
81:
82:             //    Wait for connection reply...
83:             if ( !waitForMessage( "221" ) )
84:                 return( false );
85:
86:             disconnect();
87:         }
88:         catch ( IOException e )
89:         {
90:             smtpSocket = null;
91:             return( false );
92:         }
93:
94:         //    Return
95:         return( true );
96:     }
```

The first thing you do in this code is make sure there is a host to connect with. If not, you bail. Next, you create the Socket connecting to the server host given.

This entire method is enclosed in single try/catch clause because if any part of the sending fails, the method fails. If you only send the first half of an e-mail, should that be considered correct? No, of course not. Therefore, if the method doesn't go all the way, then it didn't work.

After you're connected, you create the input reader. The class uses this reader in the getNextLine() method, which was introduced in the POP3Reader class. You copy this reader into the SMTPSender class. You also create an output writer to send data to the server, just as in the POP3Reader class.

Now you can follow the steps for sending e-mail. The first step is sending the HELO command. This command identifies the sending host of the message. The format of this command is as follows, where <host> is the host name of the sender:

```
HELO <host>
```

When this command is accepted, the server issues a reply that begins with the code 250. The method waits for that response; if it doesn't get this response, it returns. Lines 24-29 show this process.

Next, you need to identify who is sending the message by using the MAIL command, as shown in Lines 32-36. If this command is accepted, the server issues a 250 message. You then need to identify the recipient of the message by using the RCPT command, as shown in Lines 39-43. If this command is accepted, the server issues a 250 message.

Now comes the fun part: sending the data to the server. The data is the message body. It is passed into this method in the msgBody variable. You begin sending data by issuing the DATA command and waiting for a 354 response, as shown in Lines 46-50.

In Lines 52-64, you send the subject of the message, if given, and some other miscellaneous header information. The sender may also send extra header information. This information is placed in the ehData variable. If this variable is not null, it is also sent.

Everything sent up to this point was header information. You are now ready to send the data portion. Remember that the header and data are separated by a single blank line. You send this line over on Line 67. On Line 70, you send the body of the message, which can contain any text. Then on Line 73, you send the single period (.) on a line by itself signifying the end of the message. You wait for the 250 acknowledgement message and then send the QUIT command.

Testing the SMTPSender Class

You can test the new class with a simple application. The same applet restrictions apply for this class as for the POP3Reader class. The test program, shown in Listing 7.5, is a bit simpler than POPTest. After you instantiate the SMTPSender class, you only need to set the host, and then call the sendMail() method. This method does all the work.

Listing 7.5. The SMTPTest application.

```
public class
SMTPTest
{
    public static void
    main( String args[] )
    {
        new SMTPTest();
    }

    public
    SMTPTest()
    {
        SMTPSender r = new SMTPSender();

        r.setHost( "smtp.mcs.net" );
        r.sendMail( "munster@mcs.net", "munster@mcs.net", "Hi", "Hi from Java!"
);
    }
}
```

Summary

Today you learned about some real-world Java networking issues. You learned about Internet e-mail and what constitutes an Internet Text Message. This topic led into a discussion of the Post Office Protocol (POP). This protocol is used to retrieve mail from a mail server. You created a class that speaks this protocol and retrieves mail from a server. The retrieved mail is then stored for later use. Lastly, you learned about sending mail and the SMTP protocol. You created a class that sends e-mail using SMTP. This class copied some of the functionality of the POP reader class and added some more.

Q&A

Q What is an application-level protocol?

A An application-level protocol is a method of communications that resembles human language (English) more than computer language (binary).

Q What separates the header and the body of an Internet Text Message?

A A single blank line.

Q What Internet protocol is used to retrieve e-mail from a server?

A The Post Office Protocol version 3, or POP3, is used to retrieve e-mail from a server.

Q What Internet protocol is used to send e-mail?

A The Simple Mail Transfer Protocol, or SMTP, is used to send e-mail.

7

WEEK 2

At a Glance

- ☐ Introduction to Database Programming with JDBC
  A sampling of several Java/database connectivity solutions
  The Java Database Connectivity Package, or JDBC
  Introduction to programming with JDBC
- ☐ Advanced Database Programming with JDBC
  Create some new Java classes that make using JDBC easier
  Write a program to retrieve and display data from a newly created database
  Enhance the basic program to be a complete address book application

☐ Internationalization: Parlez Vous Java?

Global programming

Locales

Resource Bundles

Handling and formatting international data

☐ Reflection: Looking Inside

The basics of reflection

Reflection and security

The Reflection API

☐ Object Serialization

Create a serialized class

Discover how to keep your data from being serialized

Learn about versioning of serialized objects

☐ Remote Method Invocation

Learn about distributed object programming with RMI

Build a small distributed application that demonstrates the principles behind distributed computing

Learn how to use RMI to build distributed Java applications

☐ Building the Object Web with Java and CORBA

Take a whirlwind tour of CORBA

Learn how to select a Java ORB

Follow along with a basic Java/CORBA application

Day 8

Introduction to Database Programming with JDBC

by Jerry Ablan

A computer application is nothing more than a bundle of source code that manipulates a set of data. That data is key to the operation and functionality of the application. The data, however, can come from a variety of places: the user, in-memory defaults, or offline stored databases. Databases and their relationship to Java are the subject of this lesson.

This lesson covers the following topics:

☐ A quick introduction to databases

☐ How Java can interact with databases

☐ A sampling of several Java/database connectivity solutions

☐ The Java Database Connectivity Package, or JDBC

☐ Introduction to programming with JDBC

This lesson sets the stage for Day 9, "Advanced Database Programming with JDBC," where you develop a full-fledged database application.

What Is a Database?

Databases come in all different shapes and sizes. They can be flat files of ASCII data (like Q&A) or complex binary tree structures (Oracle or Sybase). In any form, a database is a *data store*, a place that holds data. The type of data in the store is irrelevant.

The job of the *database management system*, or DBMS, is to keep track of changes to this data. Some DBMSs are *relational*. Those are RDBMSs. The relational part refers to the fact that separate collections of data within the reaches of the RDBMS can be looked at together. The RDBMS is responsible for ensuring the integrity of the database by keeping all that data in line.

NOTE

Very few DBMSs are not RDBMSs these days. Therefore, I refer to any database, be it DBMS or RDBMS, as RDBMS.

So many different types of RDBMSs are available today that it would probably take two full books to give a summary of each one. This overview is a quick start guide for those of you who are not familiar with some newer concepts in data storage. If you are familiar with database technology, you might want to skip forward a little in this lesson.

Database Terminology

In the days of yore, programming database applications was pretty simple. Most databases were mainframe databases; very few microcomputer databases were available. Most of the ones that were available cost an arm and a leg. The cheap ones were, well, you got what you paid for. But all databases had files, records, and fields.

The database terms of yesteryear, however, have been replaced. Some of the bigger database companies, such as Oracle and Sybase, have redefined database terminology. This change is most likely in response to the larger customer base that is not programming-literate. A programmer can deal with files, records, and fields, but more and more nontechnical people are creating database applications and queries these days. Their formal training is in applications. As you'll see, some of the new terms are commonly found in spreadsheet and word-processing programs.

The following list of current database terms will be of relevance to you, the Java programmer:

☐ *Client-server.* Client-server is more of an architecture than a tangible entity. The client is a computer system that requests the services provided by an entirely different computer system. On a smaller scale, the client and server may be separate processes running on the same computer system. The distinction is that there is a service provider (the server) and a consumer of that service (the client). For your purposes here, the server is the RDBMS, and the client is the application that is requesting data from the server.

☐ *Database* or *instance.* The database or instance is the entity, or collection of data, that is created and stored for retrieval and modification. Depending on the RDBMS, several of these entities can exist on a single machine. For instance, multiple Oracle instances can exist on a UNIX server. Each has a distinct area for data, and they have no knowledge of each other unless they are configured in a certain way. A database or instance is comprised of *schemas*.

☐ *Schema.* A schema is a collection of database objects that belong to a single user of the database. Databases have many users.

☐ *Table.* A table is a database object that contains a single set of data. Similar things are stored together in a table. For instance, a company may have an employee table. This table would store all kinds of information about an employee. A table contains *rows* of data.

☐ *Row.* A row of data is a single record in a table. A row is divided into *columns*.

☐ *Column.* A column is the smallest unit of data in a table. It is a part of the row. When data is displayed in a spreadsheet-like fashion, a column would be the up/ down slice of data.

Figure 8.1 is a visual representation of some of the preceding terminology.

Figure 8.1.

A visual guide to the database terminology used in this book.

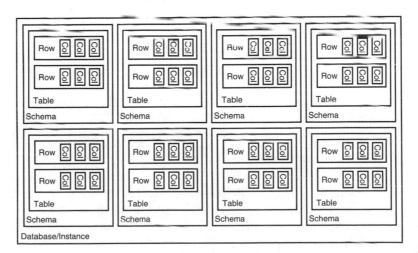

Database Locations

Databases can exist in various places. Larger databases require the horsepower of a multiple CPU server. Smaller databases can get away with only a microcomputer serving data. Wherever the database is stored, the application programmer must know its location. These locations are also referred to as tiers. Multiple tiers sometimes can span multiple locations. As far as programmers are concerned however, there are only two options for database location: local and remote.

Local and Remote

A local database is one that resides on the machine that client applications run. Local databases offer the fastest response time because there is no network traffic between the client (your application) and the server (the RDBMS engine). Some examples of local databases are Paradox from Borland, Access from Microsoft, and Personal Oracle from Oracle.

A remote database, on the other hand, is one that resides on a machine that the client software does not run on. This distinction is important for two reasons:

- ☐ Response time is slower. Even the fastest network connections cannot get you the same response time as a local database. Bear in mind, however, that the difference might be seconds or less.
- ☐ An additional software layer is needed to communicate with the database.

The first item is only relevant for performance-critical applications. Also, although a remote database is generally slower than a local database, a well-tuned RDBMS server can out-perform a poorly tuned local server in some cases.

The second item, however, may cause unexpected grief and headaches. With some database server and client products, a second software layer is necessary to transparently interact with the remote database. This software might be an optional software package that is not included with the server software. I'll get to this layer in the next topic, "Database Access."

TIP

Here are some of the database software vendor Web sites and some excellent sources of database information:

- ☐ Data Access Corporation: `http://www.daccess.com/`
- ☐ Informix Software, Inc: `http://www.informix.com`
- ☐ Free Database List: `http://cuiwww.unige.ch/~scg/FreeDB/FreeDB.list.html`
- ☐ Microsoft Corporation: `http://www.microsoft.com`
- ☐ Oracle Corporation: `http://www.oracle.com`

8

☐ Progress Software Corporation: http://www.progress,com

☐ Sybase, Inc: http://www.sybase.com

Tiering 1-2-3

Today's applications have three basic components: the user interface (application code), the business logic (rules), and the data. The user interface displays the data from the database. The business logic manipulates the data from the database. The data component is the data in the database. Tiering involves moving the logical location of each of these three components.

I have heard about 10 different explanations of the client-server concept of multitiering, and not one of them ever is the same. The following sections explain my take on the single-tiered, two-tiered, and three-tiered architectures.

Single-Tiered

In the single-tiered architecture, the user interface (application code), business logic (rules), and the data reside together logically. An example of a program in this format is a calculator program. Figure 8.2 shows a model of a single tier application.

Figure 8.2.

A single-tier application.

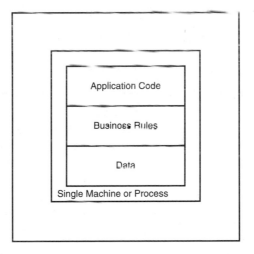

Two-Tiered

In a two-tiered architecture, the user interface (application code) and the business logic (rules) reside in a different logical location than the data. Most database applications fit this format. In fact, most client-server applications fit into this category. Figure 8.3 shows a model of a two-tier application.

Figure 8.3.

A two-tier application.

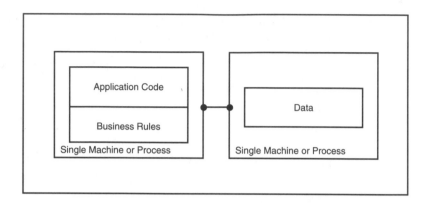

Three-Tiered

In a three-tiered system, all three components, user interface (application code), business logic (rules), and data, reside in different logical locations. To put it another way, the client software makes a call to a remote service. That remote service is responsible for interacting with the data and responding to the client. The client has no knowledge of how and where the data is stored. All it knows about is the remote service. Conversely, the remote service has no knowledge of the clients that will be calling it. It only knows about the data.

This partitioning of logic allows for better data control and reuse of existing code. Three-tier architecture is becoming more widespread because more and more tools are being created that handle the tiering automatically. Figure 8.4 shows a model of a three-tier application.

Figure 8.4.

A three-tier application.

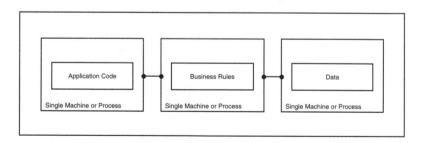

Database Access Methods

In order to "talk" to your database, you need to use some sort of software. Whether the software comes with your server, or you have to write the code yourself, this software is essential for database communications.

Although there are innumerable methods of retrieving and storing data, the following are the most common: native, ODBC, and SQL. SQL is probably the most common data access method, ODBC a close second, and, except for driver creators, native methods are rarely used. Figure 8.5 illustrates the software layers in these three types of methods. The following sections discuss each of the three access methods.

Figure 8.5.

The software layers that can be used to access data.

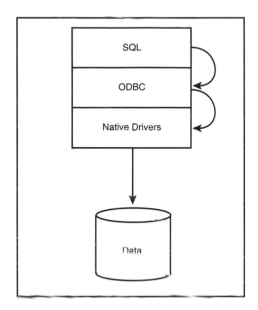

Native Drivers

Native drivers give you the raw power of talking directly to your database. When you make the connection and retrieve data, you are talking right to the file system. An example of a native driver is the Oracle Call Interface (OCI) from Oracle Corporation for Oracle databases. Native drivers are usually statically or dynamically linked into your software at compile time.

The main advantage to native drivers is that data access is lightning fast because the database access code is linked with your program. However, native drivers have two main disadvantages:

☐ Applications created in this manner are usually not portable to other platforms without code modifications.

☐ Because the driver is linked into your application, changes in the driver software require possible recompilation of your application.

ODBC

Open Database Connectivity (ODBC) is a standard developed by Microsoft Corporation. ODBC is an application program interface for accessing data in a standard manner from an abundance of data sources regardless of their type. If the data source is ODBC-compliant, your program can talk to it. ODBC drivers are available for almost every major database vendor.

TIP

> Check out the ODBC home page for some cool ODBC links:
>
> http://ourworld.compuserve.com/homepages/VBrant/

Advantages

ODBC drivers have two main advantages:

☐ Although not as fast as native drivers, ODBC drivers are pretty fast. You have only one additional layer of software to go through to get to your data.

☐ You can use SQL to query the database.

Disadvantages

ODBC drivers also have two main disadvantages:

☐ Applications created in this manner are usually not portable to other platforms without code modifications.

☐ Because the driver stub is linked into your application, changes in the driver software API may require recompilation of your application.

SQL

Although not a layer of access to databases like ODBC or native drivers, the Structured Query Language (SQL) provides a standard method of querying data from different data sources. SQL, usually pronounced like the word *sequel*, was adopted as an industry standard in 1986. SQL was completely overhauled in 1992, and the new language was called SQL92, or SQL2. Work is currently in progress to produce the next generation, SQL3.

SQL uses simple English words to instruct the database to perform certain actions, so you do not need to know how to program to use SQL. SQL can be used with almost every major database product available today. Usually, SQL used to access one RDBMS can be used to access another RDBMS. In addition, you can even use SQL syntax to interact with a data source using ODBC! On the down side, SQL queries can become quite complex and lengthy. Because SQL syntax uses regular English words, typing in these queries can seem quite monotonous.

The following is a short list of SQL commands and their meanings:

☐ SELECT. This command instructs the database to return rows from a table.

☐ UPDATE. This command instructs the database to modify rows in a table.

☐ INSERT. This command instructs the database to insert rows into a table.

☐ DELETE. This command instructs the database to delete rows from a table.

8

☐ COMMIT. Most RDBMSs work with units called *transactions*. A transaction can consist of multiple actions. The COMMIT command instructs the database to record all the actions that you have performed up until this point and to reset the transaction. When you use the COMMIT command, the data is available to everyone who has access. Before the COMMIT occurs, however, only people with access to your schema can see the changes.

☐ ROLLBACK. You use the ROLLBACK command instead of COMMIT. This command instructs the database to remove any changes you've made since the last COMMIT. This command is very useful for long, multiple-table updates. Suppose you need to add 10 rows to a table. After inserting 9 rows, the 10th insert fails. The first 9 rows must be removed for the data to retain its integrity. If you use the ROLLBACK command, the 9 inserted rows will not be recorded.

The following sections go over the syntax of some of the more commonly used SQL commands. This material is by no means an exhaustive SQL syntax review, however. Dozens of books about SQL have been published. The command syntax that follows is general ANSI SQL and might not be correct for your RDBMS. Please check your documentation if there is any doubt.

NOTE
In the syntax examples that follow, any parameter that is enclosed in square brackets ([]) is an optional parameter and may be left out.

TIP
Here are some useful SQL Web sites:
☐ Ask the SQL Pro: http://www.inquiry.com/techtips/thesqlpro/
☐ Introduction to SQL: http://w3.one.net/~jhoffman/sqltut.htm

The WHERE Clause

Most SQL commands act on all the rows of a table at one time. You can restrict these global actions to a limited number of rows by using a WHERE clause. The WHERE clause enables you to specify criteria to limit the number of rows.

The general syntax for a WHERE clause is as follows:

```
COMMAND arguments WHERE [[[schema.]table.]column OPERATOR value]
➡[AND¦OR [[[schema.]table.]column OPERATOR value]]
```

Here's what the different parts of the syntax mean:

☐ The *arguments* are the arguments specific to the *COMMAND*.

☐ The *schema* is the area where the table exists.

☐ The *table* is the table where the column lives.

☐ The *column* is the column name to compare with *value*.

☐ The *value* is a literal or column name to compare with *column*.

Multiple operations may be checked in the WHERE clause. These operations can be linked with either the AND or OR keyword. The *OPERATOR* might be many things depending on the RDBMS in use. Table 8.1 shows the operators that are available in most RDBMSs.

Table 8.1. Commonly available operators.

Operator	Meaning	Example
<	Less than	`emp_id < 10`
>	Greater than	`salary > 50000`
=	Equal to	`can_be_paged = 'Y'`
<=	Less than or equal to	`user_count <= 128`
>=	Greater than or equal to	`user_count >= 0`
<>	Not equal to	`lost_shovels <> 5`
is	For checking NULL values	`name_suffix is NULL`
not	For negating an operator	`name_suffix is not NULL`
like	Allows for the use of wild cards	`first_name like '%MUNSTER%'`

Please note that you cannot use the WHERE clause alone. You must append it to a DELETE, SELECT, or UPDATE command.

INSERT

The INSERT statement enables you to create a new row in a table. The syntax for an INSERT statement is as follows:

```
INSERT INTO [schema.]table [(column[,column…])] VALUES (value[,value])
```

Here's what the different parts of the syntax mean:

☐ *schema* is where the table exists.

☐ *table* is the target table.

☐ *column* is the column name(s) of the data you want to insert.

☐ *value* is the value(s) that you want to insert.

The following code shows the INSERT command in action:

```
INSERT INTO EMPLOYEE ( EMP_ID, LAST_NAME )
   VALUES ( 1, 'Munster' )
```

```
INSERT INTO ADDRESS ( EMP_ID, STREET_ADDRESS )
   VALUES ( 1, '1313 Mockingbird Lane' )
```

DELETE

The DELETE statement enables you to remove a row or rows from a table. The syntax for a DELETE statement is as follows:

```
DELETE FROM [schema.]table [WHERE expression]
```

Here's what the different parts of the syntax mean:

- [ ] schema is the location where the table exists.
- [ ] table is the target table.
- [ ] expression is an expression as outlined in the previous section, "The WHERE Clause."

> **WARNING**
>
> Without a WHERE clause, the DELETE command removes all rows from a table.

Here are two examples of how the DELETE command works:

```
DELETE FROM EMPLOYEE WHERE EMP_ID = 1
```

```
DELETE FROM ADDRESS WHERE CITY LIKE 'CHICAG%'
```

SELECT

The SELECT statement enables you to retrieve a row or rows from a table. The syntax for a SELECT statement is as follows:

```
SELECT [[schema.]table.]column [,[[schema.]table.]column] FROM [schema.]table
➥[WHERE expression]
```

Here's what the different parts of the syntax mean:

- [ ] schema is where the table exists.
- [ ] table is the target table.
- [ ] column is the column or columns to retrieve. You can use an asterisk (*) to indicate that the SELECT statement should return all columns.
- [ ] expression is an expression as outlined in the previous section, "The WHERE Clause."

Here are two examples of how the SELECT command works:

```
SELECT EMP_ID FROM EMPLOYEE
```

```
SELECT LAST_NAME, FIRST_NAME, MID_NAME FROM EMPLOYEE WHERE EMP_ID = 666
```

UPDATE

The UPDATE statement enables you to modify a column or columns in one or more rows in a table. The syntax for an UPDATE statement is as follows:

```
UPDATE [schema.]table SET [[schema.]table.]column = value
➡[,[[schema.]table.]column = value] [WHERE expression]
```

Here's what the different parts of the syntax mean:

- ☐ *schema* is where the table exists.
- ☐ *table* is the target table.
- ☐ *column* is the column or columns to modify.
- ☐ *expression* is an expression as outlined in the previous section, "The WHERE Clause."
- ☐ *value* is the new value that the column should hold.

Here are two examples of how the UPDATE command works:

```
UPDATE EMPLOYEE SET SALARY = SALARY + ( SALARY * .05 )
```

```
UPDATE ADDRESS SET ZIP_CODE = 60805 WHERE ZIP_CODE = 60642
```

JDBC in Depth

JDBC is a rich set of classes that gives you transparent access to a database with a single application programming interface (API). This access is handled with plug-in platform-specific modules, also called drivers. Various database manufacturers provide these drivers. Using these drivers and the JDBC classes, your programs can access consistently any database that supports JDBC, giving you the freedom to concentrate on your applications without worrying about the underlying database.

The JDBC class hierarchy lives in the java.sql package. Many of the classes in the JDBC hierarchy are abstract. It is up to the database vendor to provide implementations of these classes for its customers.

All access to JDBC data sources is handled through SQL. Sun has concentrated on JDBC issuing SQL commands and retrieving their results in a consistent manner. Though this SQL interface makes the JDBC fairly easy to use, you do not have the "raw" database access that you might be used to. Don't start thinking that JDBC is limited, however. With the classes, you can open a connection to a database, execute SQL statements, and do what you want with the results. In addition, SQL statements can include creating database objects such as tables, views, synonyms, triggers, and stored procedures.

The DriverManager **Class**

The cornerstone of the JDBC package is the DriverManager class. The DriverManager class manages the loading and unloading of drivers. For you Bozo fans out there, think of it as Ringmaster Ned. Just as Ringmaster Ned is essential for introducing new circus acts, the DriverManager is instrumental in creating new database connections. You the programmer won't usually see the DriverManager's work, though. This class mostly works behind the scenes to ensure that everything is cool for your connections.

The DriverManager class maintains a Vector that holds information about all the drivers that it knows about. The elements in the Vector contain information about the driver, such as the class name of the Driver object, a copy of the actual Driver object, and the Driver security context. The drivers managed by the DriverManager class are represented by the Driver class.

 NOTE

> The security context is an implementation-dependent object that defines the environment in which the application is running. This information is usually enough for Java to perform security checks. When the DriverManager opens or queries a Driver, the security context of the Driver is checked against the security context of your application. If they don't jibe, the Driver will not be loaded.

Although the DriverManager class is not a static class, it maintains all static instance variables with static access methods for registering and unregistering drivers. Maintaining these variables and methods allows the DriverManager class never to need instantiation. Its data always exists as part of the Java runtime.

The Driver **Class**

If the cornerstone of JDBC is the DriverManager, then the Driver class is most certainly the bricks that build the JDBC. The Driver class is the software wedge that communicates with the platform-dependent database, either directly or using another piece of software. How it communicates depends on the database, the platform, and the implementation. Figure 8.6 illustrates the software layers in a Java JDBC application connection to a database.

You must create each Driver class in your program, or you can have them preloaded for you by specifying the class names of the drivers you want to have preloaded. To do this, you need to specify a value for the system property called jdbc.drivers. This property needs to contain the fully qualified class name of each Driver class separated by a colon (:), which allows the DriverManager to instantiate the class because it knows how to find classes in your CLASSPATH.

Figure 8.6.

The Java-JDBC-database layers.

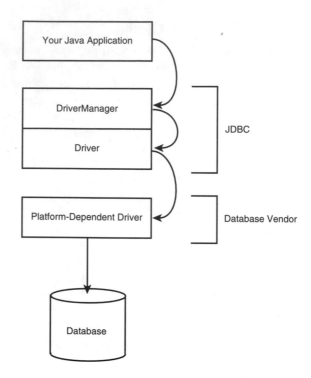

Here is a sample property setting:

```
jdbc.drivers=sun.jdbc.odbc.JdbcOdbcDriver
```

This example loads the JDBC-ODBC bridge drivers. If you were using Sun's HotJava browser, this line would go in your `.hotjava/properties` file. You can also start your programs with the following code as a command-line argument:

```
java -Djdbc.drivers=sun.jdbc.odbc.JdbcOdbcDriver
    MyApplication
```

A second, more direct approach is less flexible. With this approach, you must use the utility class `Class` to force-load a class. Here's how you would use the utility class `Class` to load the JDBC/ODBC bridge class from the previous example:

```
try
    {
        Class.forName( "sun.jdbc.odbc.JdbcOdbcDriver" );
    }
catch ( ClassNotFoundException e )
    {
        System.out.println( "Cannot find JDBC/ODBC driver class" );
    }
```

This method is good in that it ensures that your classes are loaded. If they don't load, you'll catch the `ClassNotFoundException`.

TIP

> You can replace the `Class.forName` method with the following syntax in Java 1.1:
>
> `<classname>.class`
>
> So instead of typing
>
> `Class.forName( "java.applet.Applet" )`
>
> you can simply type this:
>
> `java.applet.Applet.class`
>
> This new syntax is part of the Reflection API. (You'll learn more about the Reflection API on Day 11.) Although this syntax is easier on the eyes, it does not convey its meaning too well. Others unfamiliar with the new syntax may not be sure what you are trying to do.
>
> One more thing: When you use this new syntax, you must assign the return value to a variable like so:
>
> `Class newClass = <classname>.class`
>
> Otherwise, your compiler will generate an error.

After a Driver is constructed, you never need to worry about it again. In fact, if you use the `jdbc.drivers` property as outlined previously, you never even have to create driver objects.

The `Connection` Class

It is the `Driver` class's responsibility to register with the `DriverManager` and connect with the database; the `Connection` class represents those database connections. The `Connection` class encapsulates the database connection into an easy-to-use package. In the foundation building analogy, the `Connection` class is the mortar that binds the JDBC together. The `DriverManager` creates this class when its `getConnection()` method is called. This method accepts a database connection URL and returns a database `Connection` to the caller.

The Database Connection URL

To connect with a JDBC data source, a uniform resource locator, or URL, is used. You are undoubtedly familiar with HTTP URLs. The JDBC URL simply adds a `jdbc` to these URLs. The format follows:

`jdbc:<sub-protocol>:<sub-name>`

In this syntax, `sub-protocol` is the name of the driver set that defines a particular database connectivity method. This method can be represented by several drivers.

The *sub-name* part is the additional information necessary to complete the URL. This information is different depending on the *sub-protocol*.

Suppose you want to connect with an mSQL data source on host `hermy.munster.com` on port `4333`. The instance name is `data`. The connection URL would be as follows:

```
jdbc:msql://hermy.munster.com:4333/data
```

In this example, `msql` is the sub-protocol, and `//hermy.munster.com:4333/data` is the sub-name.

To connect with an Oracle data source with the `jdbcKona` drivers from WebLogic, the following URL is sufficient:

```
jdbc:weblogic:oracle
```

This URL is sufficient because the `jdbcKona` drivers use Oracle's SQL*Net software, which maintains its own set of network addresses for database instances. All it needs to know is the type of database with which it is connecting.

For the JDBC-ODBC bridge, the sub-name is the ODBC data source name representing your data source. The JDBC-ODBC bridge is local only. You cannot create remotely loaded applets that use this bridge. Because it is implemented in a platform-specific manner, it breaks the applet security model.

There is, however, another method of implementing the JDBC-ODBC bridge. Several companies have remote JDBC-ODBC bridge software that allows applets to run against ODBC data sources when loaded remotely. Two of these companies are IDS Software and WebLogic. You can get more information on their products from their Web sites:

IDS Software: `http://www.idssoftware.com`

WebLogic: `http://www.weblogic.com`

Remember that `Vector` that holds driver information in the `DriverManager` class? Well, here's where you'll use it. When you call the `getConnection()` method, the `DriverManager` asks each driver that has registered with it whether the database connection URL is valid. If one driver responds positively, the `DriverManager` assumes a match. If no driver responds positively, an `SQLException` is thrown. The `DriverManager` returns the error `no suitable driver`, which means that of all the drivers that the `DriverManager` knows about, not one of them could figure out the URL you passed to it.

Assuming that the URL was good and a `Driver` stepped up to the plate and said "I can handle this!," then the `DriverManager` will return a `Connection` object to you. What can you do with a `Connection` object? Not much. This class is nothing more than an encapsulation of your

8

database connection. It is a factory and manager object and is responsible for creating and managing Statement objects.

The Statement Class

Picture your Connection as an open pipeline to your database. Database transactions travel back and forth between your program and the database through this pipeline. The Statement class represents these transactions.

The Statement class encapsulates SQL queries to your database. Using several methods, these SQL queries return objects that contain the results of your SQL query. When you execute a SQL query, the data that is returned to you is commonly called a result set. You can choose from several result sets, depending on your needs:

☐ ResultSet executeQuery(String sqlStatement)

This method sends the SQL query contained in sqlStatement and returns a single set of results. This method is best used in sending SELECT statements. These statements typically return a result set.

☐ int executeUpdate(String sqlStatement)

This method sends the SQL query contained in sqlStatement and returns an integer. This method is useful when you send SQL INSERT, DELETE, or UPDATE statements. These commands return a count of rows that were affected by your query. You should not use this statement for queries that return result sets.

☐ boolean execute(String sqlStatement)

This method sends the sqlStatement to the database and returns true if the statement returns a result set or false if the statement returns an integer. This method is best used when multiple result sets can be returned.

Use the following methods to easily navigate the results of a query:

☐ boolean getMoreResults()

This method moves to the next result set in the Statement. This method, like the execute() method, returns true if the next result is a result set or false if it is an integer. If you have already retrieved a ResultSet from the Statement, this method will close it before returning.

☐ ResultSet getResultSet()

This method returns a result set in a ResultSet object. This result set is the current result set.

☐ int getUpdateCount()

This method returns the integer result that an execute() method returned.

By now you are probably wondering what this ResultSet class is all about and how it can possibly hold all that data. Well, it's quite a class, as you are about to see.

The ResultSet Class

As you've probably guessed, the ResultSet class encapsulates the results returned from a SQL query. Normally, those results are in the form of rows of data. Each row contains one or more columns. The ResultSet class acts as a cursor, pointing to one record at a time and enabling you to pick out the data you need.

Gaining Access to a Column's Data

You can gain access to the data within the ResultSet using many different methods. These methods are in the form of get<*type*>(), where <*type*> is the data type of the column. These functions return a new instance of the type that contains the data from the result set. If the column value is NULL, the value returned from these methods is NULL.

NOTE
The NULL value in database lingo is not the same as the NULL value in programming languages. Programming NULLs usually indicate zero or nothing. In database storage, however, the NULL value indicates the lack of a value. This enables you to store zeroes and gives you a clear indication that a column has not been set or modified.

You can access the column's data either by column number or name. These methods give you the flexibility to access the columns either way.

TIP
Accessing the columns by name does present more overhead than accessing them by number. In performance-critical applications, consider accessing your data by column number.

The following list presents the get<*type*>() methods provided by the ResultSet class and their return types:

```
Object getObject()
String getString()
boolean getBoolean()
byte getByte()
short getShort()
int getInt()
long getLong()
float getFloat()
double getDouble()
BigDecimal getBigDecimal()
```

```
byte[] getBytes()
java.sql.Date getDate()
java.sql.Time getTime()
java.sql.Timestamp getTimestamp()
java.io.InputStream getAsciiStream()
java.io.InputStream getUnicodeStream()
java.io.InputStream getBinaryStream()
```

Getting to the Next Row

When you've retrieved all the data you can from a column, it is time to move on to the next row. You move to the next row with the next() method. This method returns a Boolean value indicating the status of the row. Internally, it moves the ResultSet's cursor to the next row, thereby giving access to the data stored in the columns of that row.

When a ResultSet object is created, its position is always before the first row of data it contains. This position makes it necessary to call the next() method before you can access any column data. The first call to next() makes the first row available to your program. Subsequent calls to next() make the next rows available. If no more rows are available, next() returns false.

A JDBC Sample Program

Programming concepts aren't always clear when you read about them; therefore, a small example of JDBC programming is definitely in order. The following program in Listing 8.1 is a sample program that illustrates the concepts presented so far:

☐ Connecting to a JDBC data source

☐ Executing a query

☐ Parsing the results of the query

Listing 8.1. The sample JDBC program.

```
import                          java.sql.*;

public class
JDBCExample
{

    public static void
    main( String args[] )
    throws Exception
    {
        //    Find the class...
        Class.forName( "sun.jdbc.odbc.JdbcOdbcDriver" );
```

continues

Listing 8.1. continued

```
//    Open a connection...
Connection myConnection = DriverManager.getConnection(
    "jdbc:odbc:myDataSource",
    "admin",
    "password" );

//    Create a statement...
Statement myStatement = myConnection.createStatement();

//    Execute a query...
try
{
    //    Execute the query...
    myStatement.execute( "select * from emp" );

    //    Get the result set...
    ResultSet mySet = myStatement.getResultSet();

    //    Advance to the next row...
    while ( mySet.next() )
    {
        //    Get the data...
        int empno = mySet.getInt( "empno" );
        String ename = mySet.getString( "ename" );
        long salary = mySet.getLong( "sal" );

        //    Print it all out...
        System.out.println( Integer.toString( empno ) + " - " +
            ename + " - " + Integer.toString( empno ) );
    }
}
catch ( SQLException e )
{
    System.out.println( "SQL Error: " + e.toString() );
}

//    Close everything up...
myStatement.close();
myConnection.close();
}

}
```

This program uses JDBC-ODBC bridge drivers to communicate with an imaginary database on a local machine. This program retrieves and prints three of the columns from the imaginary emp table.

The Future for JDBC

Even though JDBC seems quite complete, there is room for improvement and extension. JavaSoft plans on building a layer that lives on top of the JDBC API. This layer will transparently map Java objects to database objects (such as rows and columns). It is currently being called Java Object-Relational Mapping and currently has no release date. For more information on JDBC, please visit the JDBC Web site at JavaSoft: `http://www.javasoft.com/jdbc`.

Summary

This chapter was an overview of the databases and database connectivity options that you have at your disposal. I discussed the database terminology that you will be using in the book for the first time. You are now familiar with rows and columns of data. The more you use these terms, the more comfortable you will be using them.

After the terminology discussion, I talked about the differences between local and remote databases. This subject led you right to a discussion about the advantages and disadvantages of various database access methods. Finally, I ended this chapter discussing Java Database Connectivity, or JDBC. JDBC is the preferred database connectivity tool for Java.

Tomorrow, on Day 9, you'll create a fully functional database entry application using your new knowledge.

Q&A

Q What is a three-tiered application?

A A three-tiered application is one where the three basic components of an application (user interface, business logic, and data) are separated into three distinct logical locations. Although they may all exist in one computer, they are not all combined into a single executable unit.

Q What is SQL?

A SQL stands for Structured Query Language. SQL is an English-like language for manipulating data stored in a database. Common words like SELECT, INSERT, UPDATE, and DELETE are used to modify the data.

Q What is the purpose of the Statement class?

A The Statement class exists to carry your SQL commands to the database and return Resultsets.

Day 9

Advanced Database Programming with JDBC

by Jerry Ablan

Now that you have a grasp of what the JDBC is, today you'll tackle a real-world application using Java and JDBC. A *real-world application* is one that connects to a database and actually does something useful. The application you build today stores the names and addresses of your acquaintances—you guessed it, an address book.

In this chapter, you'll do the following:

☐ Create some new Java classes that make using JDBC easier

☐ Write a program to retrieve and display data from a newly created database

☐ Enhance the basic program to be a complete address book application

Making JDBC Easier to Use

JDBC is pretty simple to use. In fact, of all the database programming methods, it is my favorite. But you can make it even simpler to use! In addition, these simplifications can be reused in other database applets and applications. To do this, you'll create a set of interfaces and classes that will greatly simplify your use of JBDC and database programming in general. Figure 9.1 shows the new interface and classes to be constructed today.

Figure 9.1.

An interface and two classes that can make your JDBC connecting simple.

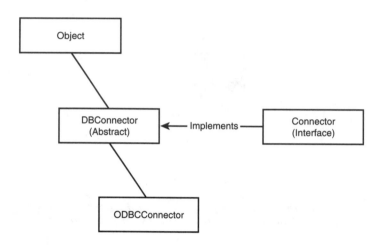

The first item you're going to create is an interface called `Connector`. An *interface*, as you recall, is a framework to which classes must adhere. As you'll see, interfaces can be very useful.

 NOTE

You can find the source code for these classes and programs on the companion Web site for this book.

The `Connector` Interface Methods

The `Connector` interface defines the pattern or template a class must follow to comply with the JDBC database connection standard. However, the standard is defined by this interface for the most part. By extending this interface, you extend the standard. The `Connector` interface is the place to implement the functionality required of your applications.

The `Connector` interface defines four methods:

- [ ] `connect()`—Connects with a data source
- [ ] `disconnect()`—Disconnects from a data source

☐ `connected()`—Indicates the connection status

☐ `getConnectionURL()`—Returns a URL used for connecting to a JDBC data source

The following sections examine each of these interface methods.

The `connect()` Method

The connect method is defined as follows:

```
public boolean
connect( String user, String password, String server );

public boolean
connect();
```

Accepted as input arguments are the user's name, user's password, and the server where the data exists. This third parameter may be optional with some Connector implementations. It has been included here for completeness. A second `connect()` method takes no arguments. This method may be useful for nonsecure database implementations that don't use a password.

The information provided to the `connect()` method is used to connect with a JDBC data source. The `getConnectionURL()` method is responsible for that; the implementor must connect to the database using that method.

The `disconnect()` Method

The `disconnect()` method is defined as follows:

```
public boolean
disconnect();
```

Nothing spectacular here. The implementor must disconnect from the database using this method.

The `connected()` Method

The `connected()` method simply returns true or false, depending on whether the object is currently connected to a database. The method is defined as follows.

```
public boolean
connected();
```

The implementor must keep track of the connection status and report on it using this method.

The `getConnectionURL()` Method

The final method in the Connector interface is the `getConnectionURL()` method. It is defined as follows:

```
public String
getConnectionURL()
```

9

The connection URL is used to connect with a JDBC data source. It is up to the implementor of this interface to return the correct connection URL for the database.

The Connector Interface Code

Listing 9.1 shows the entire Connector interface source code.

Listing 9.1. The source code for the Connector interface.

```
 1: /*
 2: * Class: Connector.java
 3: */
 4:
 5: public interface
 6: Connector
 7: {
 8:
 9:     /**
10:      * Establishes a session/connection with the database
11:      * @param user The user who is connecting
12:      * @param passwd The password of the user
13:      * @param server The host name of where the database resides
14:      */
15:     public boolean
16:     connect( String user, String password, String server );
17:
18:     public boolean
19:     connect();
20:
21:     /**
22:      * Disconnects the currently connected session
23:      */
24:     public boolean
25:     disconnect();
26:
27:     /**
28:      * Returns true if the connection is established
29:      */
30:     public boolean
31:     connected();
32:
33:     /**
34:     * Constructs the JDBC connection URL necessary to connect to a given
35:     * data source
36:     */
37:     public String
38:     getConnectionURL();
39:
40: }
```

Creating New Classes

Now that you've defined the Connector interface, you're probably wondering what the heck you can do with it. You're going to apply the Connector interface to an abstract class called DBConnector. This class implements the methods in the interface and creates a class that manages connections to the JDBC data source. In addition, the DBConnector class will define a single abstract method called getConnectionURL().

The fact that this class is abstract may seem odd to you. However, it is a standard object-oriented programming approach. You put all your base functionality into the lowest, or base, class. That leaves the specific information about connecting to a database for the higher-level classes. The encapsulation of functionality simplifies the construction of higher-level classes.

The new class, DBConnector, implements all the standard things about connecting to a JDBC data source. If you remember back to your JDBC discussion, the only thing that distinguishes one JDBC connection from another is the URL used to connect with the data source. And that URL is what is left out of your new class. The getConnectionURL() method is responsible for creating the proper URL for the data source in question.

The DBConnector Class

The DBConnector class encapsulates a lot of the repetitive tasks required to connect to a JDBC data source. DBConnector is an abstract class, and therefore it is incomplete. You cannot instantiate the DBConnector class directly. Only its derivatives can be instantiated.

The declaration of the DBConnector class is as follows:

```
public abstract class
DBConnector
implements Connector
```

The DBConnector class implements the Connector interface; however, it does not implement the entire interface. Because one method, getConnectionURL(), must be implemented by extenders of this class, the DBConnector class must be declared abstract.

Instance Variables

The DBConnector class has several instance variables that are of much import:

- [ ] protected Connection *myConnection*

  Holds a JDBC Connection object used to talk to the database

- [ ] protected Statement *myStatement*

  Holds a JDBC Statement object for executing SQL queries

- [ ] protected boolean *isConnected*

  Holds an indicator of the connection status

- [ ] protected String *lastError*

  Holds the last error that occurred, if any

All these instance variables are protected. Only *myStatement* is available outside of the
DBConnector hierarchy through the getStatement() method. The users of this class will use
this object to execute queries.

Methods

Inside the DBConnector class, you've implemented three of the four methods defined in your
Connector interface. They are described in the following sections.

The connect() Method

The connect() method connects with the specified JDBC data source passing the name,
password, and optional server. It returns a Boolean indicating whether the connection was
successful. Listing 9.2 contains the source code for the connect() method.

Listing 9.2. The connect() method.

```
 1:    public boolean
 2:    connect( String user, String password, String server )
 3:    {
 4:        //    If we are connected, disconnect first!
 5:        if ( isConnected )
 6:        {
 7:            if ( !disconnect() )
 8:                return( false );
 9:        }
10:
11:        //    Construct a JDBC connection URL
12:        String dbUrl = getConnectionURL();
13:
14:        //    Was there a problem?
15:        if ( dbUrl == null )
16:            return( false );
17:
18:        //    Try to make a connection...
19:        try
20:        {
21:            //    Make a properties object to pass to the JDBC driver...
22:            Properties p = new Properties();
23:            p.put( "user", user );
24:            p.put( "password", password );
25:            p.put( "server", server );
26:
27:            //    Get a connection and statement
28:            myConnection = getConnection( dbUrl, p );
29:            myStatement = myConnection.createStatement();
30:        }
31:        catch ( SQLException e )
32:        {
33:            lastError = e.toString();
34:
35:            System.out.println( "Error during driver initialization: " +
36:                lastError );
37:
```

```
38:              return( false );
39:          }
40:
41:          //   It worked!
42:          isConnected = true;
43:          return( true );
44:      }
```

First off, the connect() method checks to see whether it is already connected with a data source. If so, it disconnects.

Line 12 calls the getConnectionURL() method to get the information it needs to do the actual connection. This getConnectionURL() method is not implemented in this class; it must be implemented in a subclass.

The connect() method then attempts to connect with the data source and creates a Statement for communicating with the data source. If either of these attempts fail, the SQLException is thrown. This exception is stored in the lastError member variable.

Notice that if you fail to connect, you return from this method with a value of false. If you succeed, the logic flows through and sets the isConnected member variable to true. This flag is used in the next method, connected().

You may have noticed the getConnection() helper method. This method hides the DriverManager call from your connect() method. Although this helper method is not necessary, it does reduce the complexity of the connect() method

> **TIP**
>
> When writing methods, a good rule of thumb is to try to keep the length of the method to one or two pages of code. If your methods are longer than this, they are harder to debug. Moreover, you're probably not adhering to object-oriented principles. Of course, this is not always the case; it may be completely necessary to have a several-hundred-line method.
>
> To repeat, here is the general rule: Remember to separate your code into bite-size chunks.

The getConnection() helper method is shown here:

```
public Connection
getConnection( String dbUrl, Properties p )
throws SQLException
{
    return( DriverManager.getConnection( dbUrl, p ) );
}
```

The `connected()` Method

The `connected()` method simply indicates the state of the connection. It is managed by the `connect()` and `disconnect()` methods. The source code is shown in Listing 9.3.

Listing 9.3. The `connected()` method.

```
1:      public boolean
2:      connected()
3:      {
4:          return( isConnected );
5:      }
```

The `disconnect()` Method

The final method in the DBConnector class is the `disconnect()` method. This method disconnects from the data source and resets the `isConnected` flag. The source code is shown in Listing 9.4.

Listing 9.4. The `disconnect()` method.

```
1:      public boolean
2:      disconnect()
3:      {
4:          //   Are we already disconnected?
5:          if ( !isConnected )
6:              return( true );
7:
8:          try
9:          {
10:             myStatement.close();
11:             myConnection.close();
12:         }
13:         catch ( SQLException e )
14:         {
15:             lastError = e.toString();
16:
17:             System.out.println( "Error during DB disconnect [" +
18:                 lastError + "]" );
19:
20:             return( false );
21:         }
22:
23:         isConnected = false;
24:         return( true );
25:     }
```

The method first checks whether you are really connected. (No sense causing unnecessary errors.) If you aren't connected, the method returns.

Next, you close the Statement and Connection objects that were created in the connect()
method. If no error occurs, the isConnected flag is set to false.

The ODBCConnector Class

The next class you create is the ODBCConnector class. This class extends the DBConnector class
and implements the getConnectionURL() method, thus completing the Connector interface.
Because the interface is finally complete, you can instantiate the ODBCConnector class as you
please.

Other than the constructor, the ODBCConnector class has only a single method. The source is
shown in Listing 9.5.

Listing 9.5. The ODBCConnector class.

```
 1: /*
 2: * Class: ODBCConnector.java
 3: */
 4:
 5: public class
 6: ODBCConnector
 7: extends DBConnector
 8: {
 9:     String                      dsInfo;
10:
11:     public
12:      ODBCConnector( String dsInfo )
13:     {
14:         //    Call the initializer...
15:         super();
16:
17:         this.dsInfo = dsInfo;
18:
19:         //    Load the class now...
20:         Class myClass = sun.jdbc.odbc.JdbcOdbcDriver.class;
21:     }
22:
23:     public String
24:     getConnectionURL()
25:     {
26:         //    Return the constructed string...
27:         return( "jdbc:odbc:" + dsInfo );
28:     }
29:
30: }
```

The constructor calls the basc class, stores the data source information, and explicitly loads
the JDBC-ODBC bridge drivers. The getConnectionURL() method is where the URL is
constructed and returned. Because you use the JDBC-ODBC bridge in this class, the dsInfo
variable must hold a valid data source name. A *data source name* is an ODBC configuration
name specified in your operating system configuration.

The code in Listing 9.6 shows a sample class called `OracleConnector`. Although this class also implements the `getConnectionURL()` method, it connects to an Oracle data source using WebLogic's Oracle drivers.

Listing 9.6. The `OracleConnector` class.

```
 1: /*
 2: * Class: OracleConnector.java
 3: */
 4:
 5: public class
 6: OracleConnector
 7: extends DBConnector
 8: {
 9:
10:     public
11:      OracleConnector()
12:     {
13:         //    Call the initializer...
14:         super();
15:     }
16:
17:     public String
18:     getConnectionURL()
19:     {
20:         //    Return the constructed string...
21:         return( "jdbc:weblogic:oracle" );
22:     }
23:
24: }
```

A Simple JDBC Retrieval Program

Now that you have some programming ammunition in your toolbox, it's time to put it to some real-world use. In this section, you'll create a database application that is actually useful—an address book application. You can use this application to keep the names, addresses, phone numbers, and e-mail addresses of your friends, family, and acquaintances. You'll start by creating the user interface and then retrieving a single record and displaying it. If this record does not exist, you'll create the record.

NOTE

This program uses the `tmj.mdb` Microsoft Access database included on the companion Web site for this book. If you are using UNIX or a Macintosh, you probably will not be able to run the sample program.

The Database

This sample program uses a small Microsoft Access database called `tmj.mdb`. It was specifically created for today's programs. Inside the database is a single table called `address`. The `address` table has the following data columns (which are self-explanatory):

```
addressID
firstName
lastName
companyName
address1
address2
city
state
zipPostalCode
country
homePhone
workPhone
emailAddress
```

They are all text fields and are of varying lengths.

The User Interface

I used Symantec Café to create the interface for this application. And it is an *application*, not an *applet*. I used Café because, as you know, it is a pain in the ascot to create attractive user interfaces with Java's default layouts. Using a tool like Café can speed up development; a tool like Visual Café can really get you flying. Figure 9.2 shows the screen for this simple application.

 TIP

> For more information on Café and Visual Café, check out Symantec's Web site at `http://www.symantec.com`.

The interface is simple. You have a series of `TextFields` and `Labels` that hold and label the data. Along the side are a set of buttons. Only the Exit button is enabled in this version of the application. When you enhance this application in the next section, you'll bring life to the other buttons.

Figure 9.2.

The user interface for the sample database program.

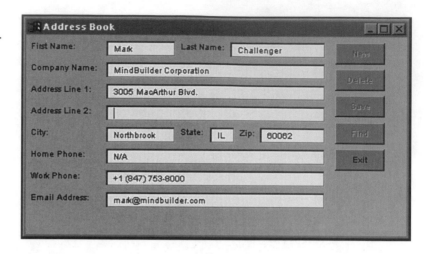

Listing 9.7 shows the non-Café-generated portion of the constructor for the AddressBook class.

Listing 9.7. The hand-coded portion of the AddressBook **class constructor.**

```
 1: public
 2:     AddressBook()
 3:     {
 4:         super( "Address Book" );
 5:         setBackground( Color.lightGray );
 6:
 7:         //   Set the buttons up properly...
 8:         initializeButtons();
 9:
10:         //   Open up the database...
11:         initializeDatabase();
12:         //   Set up a window listener for closing...
13:         addWindowListener( new WindowAdapter()
14:             { public void windowClosing( WindowEvent e )
15:                 { btnExitClicked(); } } );
16:
17:         show();
18:     }
```

Nothing too exciting in here. You simply set the background color to a nice light gray, set up the buttons, and initialize the database. The addWindowListener() method adds an event listener for the windowClosing() event to inform us of when the window was closed.

Events on the Fly

The initializeButtons() method sets the action handlers for all your buttons. Listing 9.8 shows the source code for this method.

Listing 9.8. The `initializeButtons()` method.

```
 1:    void
 2:    initializeButtons()
 3:    {
 4:        //    Add listeners...
 5:        btnNew.addActionListener( new ActionListener()
 6:            { public void actionPerformed( ActionEvent e )
 7:                { btnNewClicked(); } } );
 8:
 9:        btnDelete.addActionListener( new ActionListener()
10:            { public void actionPerformed( ActionEvent e )
11:                { btnDeleteClicked(); } } );
12:
13:        btnSave.addActionListener( new ActionListener()
14:            { public void actionPerformed( ActionEvent e )
15:                { btnSaveClicked(); } } );
16:
17:        btnClear.addActionListener( new ActionListener()
18:            { public void actionPerformed( ActionEvent e )
19:                { btnClearClicked(); } } );
20:
21:        btnFind.addActionListener( new ActionListener()
22:            { public void actionPerformed( ActionEvent e )
23:                { btnFindClicked(); } } );
24:
25:        btnExit.addActionListener( new ActionListener()
26:            { public void actionPerformed( ActionEvent e )
27:                { btnExitClicked(); } } );
28:    }
```

Each button is handled individually. You set up an event handler to listen for a click of the button using an *anonymous local class*. An anonymous local class is one that has no name (anonymous) and is contained within a set of brackets (local). This is an extremely easy technique to use to set up callback routines for buttons and other components. Listing 9.7 used this type of class to create a listener for the windowClosing() event.

Each of these handlers is empty except for the exit handler, which closes the window and exits the program:

```
public void
btnExitClicked()
{
hide();          // hide the Frame
dispose();       // tell windowing system to free resources
System.exit(0); // exit
}
```

You'll fill in these handlers later on in this lesson when you enhance this application.

Initializing the Database

Listing 9.9 shows the code for the database initialization routine `initializeDatabase()`.

Listing 9.9. The `initializeDatabase()` method.

```
1:    void
2:    initializeDatabase()
3:    {
4:        ResultSet          rs;
5:
6:        db = new ODBCConnector( "tmj" );
7:
8:        if ( !db.connect() )
9:        {
10:            System.out.println( "Error: " + db.getLastError() );
11:            return;
12:        }
13:
14:        try
15:        {
16:            rs = db.getStatement().executeQuery( "select * from address " +
17:                "where lastName = 'Challenger'" );
18:
19:            if ( !rs.next() )
20:            {
21:                //    Insert a record into the database...
22:                db.getStatement().execute( "insert into address
                ➥( firstName, " +
23:                    "lastName, companyName, address1, address2, city,
                    ➥state, " +
24:                    "zipPostalCode, country, homePhone, workPhone, " +
25:                    " emailAddress ) values (" +
26:                    "'Mark'," +
27:                    "'Challenger'," +
28:                    "'MindBuilder Corporation'," +
29:                    "'3005 MacArthur Blvd.'," +
30:                    "null," +
31:                    "'Northbrook'," +
32:                    "'IL'," +
33:                    "'60062'," +
34:                    "'US'," +
35:                    "'N/A'," +
36:                    "'+1 (847) 753-8000'," +
37:                    "'mark@mindbuilder.com' )" );
38:
39:                //    Now re-read row...
40:                rs = db.getStatement().executeQuery( "select * from
                ➥address " +
41:                    "where lastName = 'Challenger'" );
42:
43:                if ( !rs.next() )
44:                {
45:                    System.out.println( "Error: " + db.getLastError() );
```

9

```
46:                          return;
47:                     }
48:                 }
49:
50:             displayResults( rs );
51:         }
52:         catch ( SQLException e )
53:         {
54:             System.out.println( "Error: " + db.getLastError() );
55:         }
56:     }
```

Line 6 creates a new ODBCConnector with the data source named tmj. This data source name, or DSN, is set up on my system to point to the tmj.mdb file that contains the address table.

Next, you attempt to connect with the data source. Remember that the connect() method returns true or false to indicate the success or failure of the connection attempt. If you don't connect successfully, you return from this procedure.

Finally, you try to retrieve all the rows and columns from the database where the last name is equal to Challenger. If this query returns no rows, you attempt to insert a single row into the table. This row is then re-read and displayed.

When you "talk" to the database using the SQL language, you use the Statement class. This class has several methods for the conversation, the two important ones are execute() and executeQuery().

The execute() Method

The execute() method of the Statement class accepts a String containing a SQL statement as an argument. This String is then sent on to the database. A ResultSet object is only sometimes generated when you call this method. The return indicates the type of return value. If the execute() method returns true, the result is a ResultSet. Use the getResultSet() method to retrieve the ResultSet object.

If the execute() method returns false, the executed statement returned a value. This value can be retrieved using the getUpdateCount() method, which returns an integer value.

```
Boolean bResult = myStatement.execute( "select * from address" );
    if ( bResult )
    {
        ResultSet rs = myStatement.getResultSet();
        // Handle results
    }
    else
    {
        System.out.println( "Return result was " +
        ➥myStatement.getUpdateCount() );
    }
```

It is possible that the execute() method can return more than one set of results. To handle that, you can use the getMoreResults() method to retrieve the type of results in the next set. The getMoreResults() method returns a Boolean just like the execute() method does.

```
bResult = myStatement.getMoreResults()
if ( bResult )
{
    ResultSet rs = myStatement.getResultSet();
    // Handle results
}
else
{
    System.out.println( "Return result was " + myStatement.getUpdateCount() );
}
```

The executeQuery() Method

The executeQuery() method is a bit different than the execute() method but uses the same idea. It accepts a SQL statement as an argument and sends it to the database. However, the executeQuery() method returns a ResultSet right to the caller. If you are expecting only a single result set from your statements, this is the method to use.

```
ResultSet rs = myStatement.executeQuery( "select * from address" );
if ( rs.next )
{
    // Handle results
}
```

Displaying the Results

Continuing with Listing 9.9, the next thing you do is display the results of the search. This is the last thing done during the database initialization. This is done in the displayResults() method, shown in Listing 9.10.

Listing 9.10. The displayResults() method.

```
 1:    public void
 2:    displayResults( ResultSet rs )
 3:    throws SQLException
 4:    {
 5:        txtFirstName.setText( rs.getString( "firstName" ) );
 6:        txtLastName.setText( rs.getString( "lastName" ) );
 7:        txtCompanyName.setText( rs.getString( "companyName" ) );
 8:        txtAddress1.setText( rs.getString( "address1" ) );
 9:        txtAddress2.setText( rs.getString( "address2" ) );
10:        txtCity.setText( rs.getString( "city" ) );
11:        txtState.setText( rs.getString( "state" ) );
12:        txtZip.setText( rs.getString( "zipPostalCode" ) );
13:        txtHomePhone.setText( rs.getString( "homePhone" ) );
14:        txtWorkPhone.setText( rs.getString( "workPhone" ) );
15:        txtEmailAddress.setText( rs.getString( "emailAddress" ) );
16:    }
```

The ResultSet is passed in to the displayResults() method, and each column is retrieved and moved into its appropriate text field on the screen. You use the getString() method of the ResultSet class to retrieve the data from the ResultSet.

Enhancing the Simple Application

The next thing you're going to do is to enhance the sample application. Your enhancements are as follows:

☐ Add functionality to the buttons

☐ Create the actual code to read and write database records

Because your base application already has event handlers set up, there isn't an enormous amount of work to do.

Providing a Placeholder

The first thing you have to add is a new instance variable to let us know whether you are working with a new record or one retrieved from the database. This variable is useful when creating SQL statements—as you'll see later in this lesson —and holds the addressID column from the database when you retrieve data. Refer back to Figure 9.2 and notice that the addressID column is not displayed.

Here's the code that adds this new variable to the top of the program:

```
//    A holder for our record id.
protected long                         myAddressID;
```

Now you have to set it. When the New button is clicked, it should be set to an invalid value, like 1. When you retrieve a row of data from the table, the button should be set to the actual value of the displayed row. So the two logical places to set the variable are in the New button's click handler, btnNewClicked(), and in displayResults. Here are the changes to the handler routine:

```
public void
        btnNewClicked()
    {
myAddressID = -1;
}
```

In the displayResults portion of the application, you just add a line to the top:

```
myAddressID = rs.getLong( "addressID" );
```

Clearing the Screen

The New button is used to clear any values currently on the screen. You clear the screen by setting to nothing the text of each TextField in the program. Listing 9.11 shows how you do this in the btnNewClicked() method.

Listing 9.11. Clearing the screen in the `btnNewClicked()` **method.**

```
public void
    btnNewClicked()
    {
        int firstField = -1;

        for ( int i = 0; i < getComponentCount(); i++ )
        {
            if ( getComponent( i ) instanceof TextField )
            {
                TextField tf = ( TextField )getComponent( i );
                tf.setText( "" );

                //    Keep track of the first text field...
                if ( firstField == -1 )
                    firstField = i;
            }
        }

        //    Move the focus...
        ( ( Component )getComponent( firstField ) ).requestFocus();
        myAddressID = -1;
        btnDelete.disable();
    }
```

This code uses a neat trick to blank out all the fields. Because the `Frame` that contains your application is a container, you can obtain a list of the components that it contains. By enumerating that list, you can see which ones are `TextFields` and set them to blank.

You also keep track of which component is the first `TextField` on the screen. This useful trick allows you to set the focus at the first field. Finally, you set your new variable to -1 and disable the Delete button. You can't delete a new record because it hasn't yet been stored. If you wish to start over, click the New button again.

Finding Data

To retrieve records to display and edit, you need a method to search for the records. The sample application implements the search capabilities in the `findRecord()` method, which is called from the `btnFindClicked()` method:

```
public void
    btnFindClicked()
    {
        findRecord();
    }
```

The findRecord() method takes the first name and last name fields from the screen and looks them up in the database. If a row exists, it is displayed; otherwise, nothing happens. If more than a single row is returned, only the first row is displayed. Listing 9.12 shows the findRecord() method.

Listing 9.12. The findRecord() method.

```
public boolean
findRecord()
{
    String sql, whereClause = "";

    sql = "select * from address where ";

    if ( !txtFirstName.getText().equals( "" ) )
    {
        if ( !whereClause.equals( "" ) )
            whereClause += " and ";

        whereClause += "firstName = '" + txtFirstName.getText() + "'";
    }

    if ( !txtLastName.getText().equals( "" ) )
    {
        if ( !whereClause.equals( "" ) )
            whereClause += " and ";

        whereClause += "lastName = '" + txtLastName.getText() + "'";
    }

    try
    {
        ResultSet rs = db.getStatement().executeQuery( sql + whereClause );

        if ( rs.next() )
        {
            displayResults( rs );
            return( true );
        }

        System.out.println( "No matching records found." );

    }
    catch ( SQLException e )
    {
        System.out.println( "Error: " + e.toString() );
    }

    return( false );
}
```

You construct a WHERE clause based on the contents of the TextFields. This clause is then appended to the SQL statement and executed. If there is a match, the displayResults() method is called to display the results. Otherwise, an error message is displayed.

Saving Data

To save records that have been edited, you need a save method. The save function is implemented in the saveRecord() method, which is called from the btnSaveClicked() method:

```
public void
    btnSaveClicked()
    {
        saveRecord();
    }
```

The saveRecord() method uses the stored addressID column information and constructs an appropriate SQL statement with the data from the screen. Listing 9.13 shows the saveRecord() method.

Listing 9.13. The saveRecord() method.

```
public boolean
saveRecord()
{
    try
    {
        if ( myAddressID == -1 )
        {
            String sql = "insert into address ( firstName, " +
                "lastName, companyName, address1, address2, city, state, " +
                "zipPostalCode, homePhone, workPhone, " +
                " emailAddress ) values (" +
                "'" + txtFirstName.getText() + "'," +
                "'" + txtLastName.getText() + "'," +
                "'" + txtCompanyName.getText() + "'," +
                "'" + txtAddress1.getText() + "'," +
                "'" + txtAddress2.getText() + "'," +
                "'" + txtCity.getText() + "'," +
                "'" + txtState.getText() + "'," +
                "'" + txtZip.getText() + "'," +
                "'" + txtHomePhone.getText() + "'," +
                "'" + txtWorkPhone.getText() + "'," +
                "'" + txtEmailAddress.getText() + "')";

            db.getStatement().execute( sql );
        }
        else
        {
```

```
        db.getStatement().execute( "update address " +
            "set firstName = '" + txtFirstName.getText() + "'," +
            "lastName = '" + txtLastName.getText() + "'," +
            "companyName = '" + txtCompanyName.getText() + "'," +
            "address1 = '" + txtAddress1.getText() + "'," +
            "address2 = '" + txtAddress2.getText() + "'," +
            "city = '" + txtCity.getText() + "'," +
            "state = '" + txtState.getText() + "'," +
            "zipPostalCode = '" + txtZip.getText() + "'," +
            "homePhone = '" + txtHomePhone.getText() + "'," +
            "workPhone = '" + txtWorkPhone.getText() + "'," +
            "emailAddress ='" + txtEmailAddress.getText() + "' " +
            "where addressID = " + Long.toString( myAddressID ) );
    }

    return( true );
}
catch ( SQLException e )
{
    System.out.println( "Error: " + e.toString() );
}

return( false );
}
```

If the instance variable myAddressID is set to -1, you know that this row was not retrieved from the table. Therefore, an INSERT statement is required to get it into the database. If the myAddressID variable is not equal to -1, you know that the row was retrieved from the table and that an UPDATE statement is required. In either case, the statement is created and executed. Any errors are printed to the console.

Deleting Data

To remove records from the table, you need a delete method. The delete function is implemented in the deleteRecord() method, which is called from the btnDeleteClicked() method:

```
public void
    btnDeleteClicked()
    {
        deleteRecord();
    }
```

The deleteRecord() method, like saveRecord(), uses the stored addressID column and constructs an appropriate SQL statement with the data from the screen. Listing 9.14 shows the deleteRecord() method.

Listing 9.14. The `deleteRecord()` method.

```
public boolean
deleteRecord()
{
    if ( myAddressID != -1 )
    {
        String sql = "delete from address where addressID = " +
            Long.toString( myAddressID );

        try
        {
            db.getStatement().execute( sql );
            btnNewClicked();
            return( true );
        }
        catch ( SQLException e )
        {
            System.out.println( "Error: " + e.toString() );
        }
    }

    return( false );
}
```

You don't do a thing if the `myAddressID` variable is set to -1 (because you don't delete new records). If the variable does not equal -1 (meaning that the record is not new), you construct a DELETE query based on the value of the `myAddressID` variable. This query is executed and any errors are displayed. If the deletion succeeds, the `btnNewClicked()` method is called to clear the screen and reset the `myAddressID` variable to -1—a nice touch for your users.

Summary

Today you covered some advanced JDBC topics. You created some classes to better help us program JDBC applications. These classes hide, or encapsulate, much of the JDBC connection drudgery performed by every application. In addition, these classes are extensible so that you can use them with other databases.

You also created a simple database application. This address book program created and displayed a single record in a table. This application demonstrated some rudimentary JDBC programming issues.

Finally, you enhanced the simple application to implement editing, saving, deleting, and searching for data from the table. Using a building-block approach, you built on your simple address book application and created something truly useful.

Q&A

Q What is an anonymous local class?

A An anonymous local class is one that has no name and is contained within a set of brackets. It cannot be instantiated or used outside of the purpose for which it is created.

Q What is the difference between the `execute()` and `executeQuery()` methods?

A The `execute()` method returns a value indicating the success of the underlying SQL statement. The `executeQuery()` method returns a JDBC `ResultSet` object with the results of the query.

Q Which SQL statement is used to remove data from a table?

A You can remove data from a table by using the `DELETE` SQL command.

9

Day 10

Internationalization: Parlez Vous Java?

by Michael Morrison

There was a time when software developers never had to be concerned with the notion of *international software*. The task of supporting multiple languages and customs in a software application was just too difficult to justify the potential returns of international sales. It shouldn't come as too big of a surprise to find out that times have changed in terms of international software. Rapidly growing international software markets coupled with the Internet have finally given developers a solid reason to be concerned with creating global software.

Java 1.1 provides a wide range of features to facilitate the creation of international software, or global programming. Before Java 1.1, global programming typically involved developing entirely new versions of a program for each target language and set of customs. Java 1.1 ushers in a new approach to global programming that makes it possible to maintain one code base and add support for new languages and customs with minimal effort. This lesson explores Java 1.1 internationalization and how to develop global Java programs. More specifically, you learn about the following topics in today's lesson:

- [ ] Global programming
- [ ] Internationalization and localization
- [ ] Locales
- [ ] Resource Bundles
- [ ] Handling and formatting international data
- [ ] The `WorldExplorer` Sample Applet

Understanding Global Programming

You've no doubt noticed that many of the instructional manuals that come with electronics and appliances include instructions in multiple languages. Although we often take things like this for granted, the languages used in these manuals are carefully selected based on the consumer market. By providing instructions in multiple languages, a company can ensure that a wider range of consumers can understand and use their product. The same situation exists with software—except that software is much more complex than a printed instructional manual. Nevertheless, it's becoming more and more important for software to support multiple languages as the software market turns global.

The development of software for a global market is known as *global programming* and involves the support of multiple languages and customs. When first pondering global programming, most programmers tend to think in terms of languages or countries. However, neither of these approaches alone is sufficient for creating truly global programs; many countries have multiple languages, and many languages differ across the countries in which they are spoken. For example, both English and French are spoken in Canada. Likewise, English is spoken in both the United States and the United Kingdom, but some words are spelled differently and even have a different meaning to people from each country. It simply isn't sufficient to convert English words and phrases to Spanish, for example, and call a program "Spanish ready." Granted, this approach may work in some general situations, but as a complete globalization solution, you simply need more detail.

> **NEW TERM** *global programming:* The development of software for a global market, which involves the support of multiple languages and customs.

To solve the problem of identifying different languages and countries, Java 1.1 introduces the concept of a *locale*, which is a geographical or political region that shares the same language

10

and customs. Locales are used as the basis for creating global programs; you *localize* a program to each locale you want it to support. Even though locales are defined to include both a language and a country, there are still some situations in which the same language varies within the same country. So, locales can be even more specific and define a specific language dialect or area within a country. Suppose that you want to get really serious about locales and divide the U.S. into different English dialects: the North, the South, the Midwest, and a generic locale for the rest of the U.S. In doing so, you could provide different versions of a phrase based on the locale of the user:

☐ Generic: "Yes"

☐ North: "Yeah"

☐ South: "Yep"

☐ Midwest: "You betcha"

NEW TERM | *locale:* A geographical or political region that shares the same language and customs.

Every Java applet or application executes within a given locale; this is the locale used to determine what globally sensitive information is presented to the user and how. In this way, locales are handled automatically by the Java runtime system. The developer's job is simply to provide different localized data sets and then load the data set for the default locale. Most global programs also perform some degree of data processing because there isn't always a one-to-one relationship between words, phrases, and numbers in different languages. Additionally, dates and currencies vary widely from country to country and must therefore be represented correctly in a global program.

Internationalization and Localization

The globalization of a program can be broken into two distinct tasks: internationalization and localization. *Internationalization* is the process of developing a program so that it is prepared to support multiple locales. Internationalization does not involve the direct support of a specific locale; an internationalized program is simply a program that is prepared to handle locale-sensitive information. *Localization* is the process of supporting a specific locale in a program, which primarily involves defining locale-sensitive information. Internationalization and localization work hand in hand to allow programs to support multiple locales.

> **NEW TERM**
>
> *internationalization:* The process of developing a program so that it is prepared to support multiple locales.

> **NEW TERM**
>
> *localization:* The process of supporting a specific locale in a program.

Based on these definitions of internationalization and localization, it may not sound as if developing global programs is all that difficult. However, when you consider how many different things in a program vary based on locale, it's easy to see how internationalization and localization can get very complex. In truth, internationalization is the more difficult of the two because it involves structuring a program so that no locale-sensitive information is hard-coded. Additionally, you have to deal with different meanings and formatting of data such as dates, times, numbers, currency, capitalization rules, and sorting. It's easy to see why many developers have opted in the past to develop completely different versions of a program for different languages and countries.

Because the localization of a program depends greatly on how the program has been internationalized, you should always deal with internationalization first. Internationalized programs are designed so that the current locale can be switched, resulting in the program altering itself accordingly with the new locale-sensitive information. The locale-sensitive information is grouped together separately from the main code of the program (and can even be contained in external data files). This organizational aspect of internationalization and localization allows programs to support multiple locales with a single code base.

It's important to understand from this discussion that internationalization impacts the structure of a program, while localization impacts the organization of the program's locale-sensitive data. This is an important distinction because, from a programming perspective, most of your time is spent internationalizing a program. Once a program is internationalized and ready to support different locales, providing the information for the locales is a pretty straightforward process. This is why the Java API used to develop global programs is referred to as the Internationalization API; because it primarily deals with the programmatic constructs required to internationalize programs.

Internationalization and localization both depend greatly on the data in a program that must be localized. All global programs rely on three main types of data:

- ☐ Program data
- ☐ User data
- ☐ System data

10

Program Data

Program data is data considered part of a program, such as text messages, button labels, icons, images, and sounds. Programs with graphical user interfaces typically have a significant amount of program data because practically every graphical user interface element has a label associated with it—not to mention some that include lists of textual information. Because program data is so tightly linked to the interface of a program, it is often the most difficult to isolate and localize properly.

User Data

User data is data supplied at runtime by the user, such as text messages. A good example of user data is the document a user creates in a word processing program. A word processor must certainly be concerned with the locale of the user if it is to interpret and represent the textual information in the document appropriately. Clearly, localizing user data can be a significant undertaking depending on the specific type of program you are developing.

System Data

System data includes data obtained from the runtime environment, such as date, time, and system information. Because system data is obtained from the Java runtime system, it only makes sense that Java would provide some degree of internationalization support for working with this type of data. In fact, the Java Internationalization API contains a rich set of classes and interfaces for manipulating system data in a locale-sensitive fashion. This makes dealing with system data considerably easier than dealing with program and user data.

Working with Locales

As you learned earlier, a locale is defined as a geographical or political region that shares the same language and customs. In terms of Java, a locale is simply an identifier for a particular combination of a language and a region. In other words, Java locales are numeric identifiers that uniquely identify physical locales. For example, Java provides four different French locales based on countries that use the French language: France, Belgium, Canada, and Switzerland. There is also an English locale for Canada, which is logical because both French and English are spoken in Canada.

The Locale Class

Java locales are represented by the Locale class, located in the java.util package. The Locale class models a locale using a series of string identifiers relating to the language and country for a locale, as well as a variant field that can represent application-specific information about a locale. The best way to understand the manner in which the Locale class models a locale is to look at its constructors:

```
public Locale(String language, String country);
public Locale(String language, String country, String variant);
```

The first argument to both constructors is a lowercase two-character string that corresponds to an ISO language code, as defined by the ISO-639 language standard. An example of such a code is en, which is the ISO language code for the English language. Similarly, the fr code is for the French language, while the es code is for the Spanish language. For a full list of these codes, check out the following Web site:

```
http://www.ics.uci.edu/pub/ietf/http/related/iso639.txt
```

The second argument to both constructors is also a two-character string, but this one is uppercase and represents an ISO country code, as defined by the ISO-3166 country standard. An example of such a code is US, which is the ISO language code for the United States. Similarly, the IT code is for Italy, and the CA code is for Canada. For a full list of these codes, check out the following Web site:

```
http://www.chemie.fu-berlin.de/diverse/doc/ISO_3166.html
```

The third argument to the second Locale() constructor is a string, but it is not limited to two characters and it follows no standard. This argument represents application-specific locale information. For example, if you want to break a locale into more specific dialects, you use this argument. You can also use this argument to subdivide locales according to something not related to languages or customs, such as a computing platform. For example, you may want a program to present different information based on whether a user is on a Macintosh or Windows platform.

You can get the string identifier for a locale using the Locale class; the Locale class returns a string concatenation of the language, country, and variant strings you just learned about, separated by underscores. For example, the string representation of the French Canadian locale is fr_CA. Likewise, the U.S. English locale is en_US, and the same locale on a Windows platform might be en_US_WIN. Keep in mind that the variant piece of a locale string (WIN in this example) is entirely application-specific. Table 10.1 lists the locales supported by the Java 1.1 Internationalization API.

Table 10.1. Locales supported by Java 1.1.

Locale	Language	Country
sq_AL	Albanian	Albania
ar_EG	Arabic	Egypt
be_BY	Belorussian	Belarus
bg_BG	Bulgarian	Bulgaria
ca_ES	Catalan	Spain
zh_CN	Chinese	China

Locale	Language	Country
zh_TW	Chinese	Taiwan
hr_HR	Croatian	Croatia
cs_CZ	Czech	Czech Republic
da_DK	Danish	Denmark
nl_BE	Dutch	Belgium
nl_NL	Dutch	Netherlands
en_CA	English	Canada
en_IE	English	Ireland
en_GB	English	United Kingdom
en_US	English	United States
et_EE	Estonian	Estonia
fi_FI	Finnish	Finland
fr_BE	French	Belgium
fr_CA	French	Canada
fr_FR	French	France
fr_CH	French	Switzerland
de_AT	German	Austria
de_DE	German	Germany
de_CH	German	Switzerland
el_GR	Greek	Greece
iw_IL	Hebrew	Israel
hu_HU	Hungarian	Hungary
is_IS	Icelandic	Iceland
it_IT	Italian	Italy
it_CH	Italian	Switzerland
ja_JP	Japanese	Japan
ko_KR	Korean	Korea
lv_LV	Latvian	Latvia
lt_LT	Lithuanian	Lithuania
mk_MK	Macedonian	Macedonia
no_NO_B	Norwegian (Bokmål)	Norway
no_NO_NY	Norwegian (Nynorsk)	Norway

continues

Table 10.1. continued

Locale	Language	Country
pl_PL	Polish	Poland
pt_PT	Portuguese	Portugal
ro_RO	Romanian	Romania
ru_RU	Russian	Russia
sh_SP	Serbian (Latin)	Serbia
sr_SP	Serbian (Cyrillic)	Serbia
sk_SK	Slovak	Slovakia
sl_SI	Slovene	Slovenia
es_ES	Spanish	Spain
sv_SE	Swedish	Sweden
tr_TR	Turkish	Turkey
uk_UA	Ukrainian	Ukraine

The Locale class includes constants for some of the most commonly used locales. Table 10.2 lists these locale constants.

Table 10.2. Locale constants defined in the Locale class.

Constant Name	Locale Represented
CANADA	en_CA
CANADA_FRENCH	fr_CA
CHINA	zh_CN
CHINESE	zh
ENGLISH	en
FRANCE	fr_FR
FRENCH	fr
GERMAN	de
GERMANY	de_DE
ITALIAN	it
ITALY	it_IT
JAPAN	ja_JP
JAPANESE	ja

Constant Name	Locale Represented
KOREA	ko_KR
KOREAN	ko
PRC	zh_CN
SIMPLIFIED_CHINESE	zh_CN
TAIWAN	zh_TW
TRADITIONAL_CHINESE	zh_TW
UK	en_GB
US	en_US

You may be surprised by the fact that some of the locale constants defined in the Locale class represent only a language and not a language/country combination. Although this may at first appear to go against the very point of using a locale, you have to understand the way locales work to understand why these constants are provided. Along with representing a specific language and region, locales can also be used to represent a language in general. Consider a situation in which you don't want to distinguish between different German dialects; in this case, it makes sense to develop an application based on the German language in general. To do so, you would use the de locale or the Locale.GERMAN locale constant.

Creating Locales

Creating locales is very easy; you simply provide the appropriate language and country code strings to the Locale constructor. For example, the following code creates a locale for Austria:

```
Locale l = new Locale("de", "AT");
```

This locale can then be used to perform locale-specific operations in an application. But what if an application doesn't specifically support the Austria locale? Locales have an interesting and powerful way of dealing with failure; if an attempt is made to use an unsupported locale, Java tries a more general version of the locale by dropping the country. For this example, Java tries the more general German language locale if the Austrian locale fails. If both locales fail, Java resorts to the default locale, which is hopefully supported by the application. If not, a MissingResourceException exception is thrown. You learn more about the meaning of this exception a little later in the lesson when you find out about resource bundles.

 NOTE

> Keep in mind that it isn't necessary to explicitly create a Locale object for locales that have constants defined for them in the Locale class; you can just reference the constant directly. You can also get the default locale by calling the static getDefault() method provided by the Locale class.

Getting Information about a Locale

The Locale class includes methods for retrieving information about a given locale. Following are some of these methods:

```
getCountry()
getLanguage()
getVariant()
toString()
getDisplayName()
getDisplayCountry()
getDisplayLanguage()
getDisplayVariant()
```

The first three methods get the string codes used to specify a locale. For example, the getCountry() method returns the string IT for the Italy locale. The toString() method returns the complete locale name for a locale, which consists of the individual string codes separated by underscores. The last four methods return information in a form that is more readable than the first four methods. For example, the getDisplayCountry() method returns the string Italy for the Italy locale. These methods are used primarily for presenting information about a locale to a user. Listing 10.1 contains the source code for the LocaleInfo application, which uses some of these methods to display information about a locale.

Listing 10.1. The source code for the LocaleInfo application.

```
1: public class LocaleInfo {
2:   public static void main(String[] args) {
3:     Locale locale = null;
4:
5:     // Get the locale
6:     switch (args.length) {
7:     case 0:
8:       locale = Locale.getDefault();
9:       break;
10:
11:     case 2:
12:       locale = new Locale(args[0], args[1]);
13:       break;
14:
15:     case 3:
16:       locale = new Locale(args[0], args[1], args[2]);
17:       break;
18:
19:     default:
20:       System.out.println("Usage: java LocaleInfo
          ➥[LanguageCode CountryCode]" +
21:         " [Variant Code]");
22:       System.exit(0);
23:     }
24:
```

10

```
25:      // Output information about the locale
26:      System.out.println("Code     : " + locale.toString());
27:      System.out.println("Name     : " + locale.getDisplayName());
28:      System.out.println("Language : " + locale.getDisplayLanguage());
29:      System.out.println("Country  : " + locale.getDisplayCountry());
30:    }
31: }
```

NOTE The source code and executable for the LocaleInfo application are available on the companion Web site for this book at http://www.mcp.com/info/1-57521/1-57521-347-8.

The LocaleInfo application accepts the string codes for a locale as arguments and displays information about the locale to standard output. Notice that the toString(), getDisplayName(), getDisplayLanguage(), and getDisplayCountry() methods are used to print information about a locale (Lines 26 through 29). If no arguments are provided to the application, the default locale is used (Line 8).

Following is an example of how to use the LocaleInfo application to get information about the Japanese locale:

```
java LocaleInfo ja JP
```

This command results in the following output:

```
Code     : ja_JP
Name     : Japanese (Japan)
Language : Japanese
Country  : Japan
```

The LocaleInfo application is a good way to find out information about locales. Try it out on a few different locales to see what type of information is displayed about each.

Using Resource Bundles

Although locales certainly play an important role in the globalization of a Java program, they are really only half of the equation. The actual localization of a program is carried out by organizing locale-sensitive data into groups of information that are specific to different locales. These groups of information are called *resource bundles* and consist solely of locale-sensitive data. A resource bundle must be provided for each different locale a program supports. When a program attempts to access information based on a given locale, Java looks for the resource bundle corresponding to the locale. If no resource bundle is found, Java searches for a more general resource bundle—for example, one based only on the language of the locale.

The Java Internationalization API provides a class, ResourceBundle, that facilitates the organization of locale-sensitive data into bundles of information. Locale-sensitive data is bundled by deriving a class from ResourceBundle (or one of its subclasses) and providing the data as class data. This data is then accessed using a special overridden method. The Java Internationalization API provides two classes derived from ResourceBundle—ListResourceBundle and PropertyResourceBundle—that can be used to make the bundling job easier.

The ListResourceBundle class is used to store lists of locale-sensitive resources. Subclasses of ListResourceBundle must override the getContents() method and provide an array of resources; each item in the array is a pair of objects. The first element of each pair is a string key used to access the second object, which is the actual value being stored. The PropertyResourceBundle class is used to store strings in an external property file. A property file contains string keys that must be used with the getString() method to retrieve values.

You must always derive a class from the ListResourceBundle class to provide resource bundles; the name of the class indicates the locale of the data. To bundle resources in a property resource bundle, you must create an external property file whose name indicates the locale of the data. Both approaches are useful, depending on the type of data you are localizing and how it will be accessed.

Resource bundles, whether files or classes, are named using the locale string codes you learned about earlier in this lesson. You form the class or file name for a resource bundle by appending the appropriate locale code to the end of the resource name. For example, if you have a resource bundle named AudioBundle, a French Canadian resource bundle class would be named AudioBundle_fr_CA. The AudioBundle class would serve as the default resource bundle, while the AudioBundle_fr_CA class would apply to the French Canadian locale. You can also specify a more general resource bundle, such as AudioBundle_fr, which would apply to the French language as a whole. You put together some resource bundles of your own later in this lesson when you develop the WorldExplorer applet.

Handling and Formatting International Data

In addition to providing support for locales and resource bundles, the Java Internationalization API also includes support for working with international data such as dates and times. This support is very important to global programming because it provides a way of localizing many types of data with very little effort. For example, the Calendar class has methods that take a Locale object as a parameter; dates and times returned by these methods are automatically localized to the specified locale. Following is a list of the different types of data that have international support in the Java API:

☐ Numbers
☐ Dates and times
☐ Text messages

The Java Internationalization API includes a class called Format located in the java.text package that encapsulates locale-sensitive formatting and parsing. There are three classes derived from Format that address each of the types of data just mentioned: NumberFormat, DateFormat, and MessageFormat. The API also contains subclasses of these classes that provide more specific data formatting support. You learn about some of these classes in the next few sections.

Numbers

The Java Internationalization API provides the NumberFormat class, located in the java.text package, to help facilitate the conversion of binary numbers into locale-specific text strings for meaningful display. The NumberFormat class not only provides support for the formatting of numbers for any locale, but also is capable of parsing numbers displayed in any locale back into binary format. The NumberFormat class is an abstract class that defines the interface through which numbers are formatted. Even though NumberFormat is an abstract class, you can obtain a NumberFormat object using the static getInstance() method; then you can use some of the methods defined in the class to format numbers. Following is an example of how to use a NumberFormat object to format a number for the default locale:

```
double num - 27.0;
String s = NumberFormat.getInstance().format(num);
```

In this example, the format() method is used to format the number for the default locale. The NumberFormat class provides a variety of different format() methods that can be used to control how a number is formatted for a given locale. If you want to format a number for a locale other than the default locale, you use a different version of the getInstance() method that takes the locale as an argument. Following is an example of formatting a number for the Italy locale:

```
Locale italyLocale - new Locale("it", "IT");
double num = 27.0;
String s = NumberFormat.getInstance(italyLocale).format(num);
```

In addition to the NumberFormat class, there is a DecimalFormat class (derived from NumberFormat) that provides formatting support specific to decimal numbers. The DecimalFormat class allows you to use patterns to specify things such as the precision of numbers, whether leading zeros should be printed, and the currency symbols used, among other things. Just as with the NumberFormat class, instances of the DecimalFormat class are typically obtained through a static getInstance() method.

10

Dates and Times

Dates and times represent a significant area of concern for the globalization of programs. The Java Internationalization API includes extensive support for localizing dates and times through a small set of date and time management and formatting classes. More specifically, these classes automatically support these items:

- ☐ Time zones and daylight-savings adjustments
- ☐ Different calendars
- ☐ Different date fields such as the number of the week in the year
- ☐ Patterns for formatting dates and times
- ☐ The parsing of formatted dates and times back into a binary form

The main class for dealing with dates and times is the `Calendar` class, an abstract class that converts a point in time to a set of integer constants representing the year, month, week, and so on. Although the `Calendar` class is abstract, you can obtain a `Calendar` object using its static `getInstance()` method, like this:

```
Calendar now = Calendar.getInstance();
```

This code retrieves a `Calendar` object initialized to the current time. If it seems strange to you that a `Calendar` object stores a time, consider that a traditional calendar is just a general way of keeping track of time. In Java, the `Calendar` class happens to provide a more specific approach—right down to the second!

If you are already familiar with the `Calendar` class, you're probably wondering how it supports globalization. Using the default `getInstance()` method shown in the previous code example, the `Calendar` class automatically localizes the time to the default locale. To localize the time to another locale, you use a different `getInstance()` method. Following is an example that shows how to retrieve the current time localized to the Korea locale:

```
Calendar now = Calendar.getInstance(Locale.KOREA);
```

Notice that the `Locale.KOREA` locale constant is used instead of creating a `Locale` object explicitly. You can use this approach any time a `Locale` object is required for an operation.

The Java Internationalization API addresses the issue of time zones with the `TimeZone` class, which encapsulates time zone offsets as well as daylight-savings time offsets whenever applicable. The `TimeZone` class is abstract, but you can obtain an instance using the static `getTimeZone()` method. The API also provides a `SimpleTimeZone` class, derived from `TimeZone`, that provides simple rules governing daylight-savings time. The `TimeZone` and `SimpleTimeZone` classes are used by the `Calendar` class and its subclasses to convert between localized time and coordinated universal time (UTC), which is the internal format used by Java to store time. Because the `Calendar` class makes use of these classes for you, it is rare that you have to work with the `TimeZone` and `SimpleTimeZone` classes directly.

Dates are formatted for display using the abstract `DateFormat` class. Not surprisingly, you can obtain an instance of the `DateFormat` class using a static method, `getDateInstance()`. This approach should be familiar to you from the earlier discussion of the `NumberFormat` class. Following is an example of using the `DateFormat` class to format the current time for the default locale:

```
Date now = Calendar.getInstance().getTime();
String s = DateFormat.getDateInstance().format(now);
```

You may be curious about the use of the `Date` class, as opposed to the `Calendar` class. Although many of the methods in the `Date` class became deprecated as of Java 1.1, the class itself is still used as a way of representing a specific instant in time, with millisecond precision. The `Date` class represents a raw instant of time with very accurate precision; the `Calendar` class provides a meaningful representation of a time in terms of days, hours, seconds, and so on.

Getting back to date formatting, the `DateFormat` class allows you to format locale-specific dates in a variety of ways. For example, you can specify the formatting style for a date with one of the following constants defined in the `DateFormat` class: SHORT, MEDIUM, LONG, or FULL. These constants determine whether a date is formatted as 10/01/88 or October 1, 1988. Table 10.3 shows how these different constants affect the formatting of a date. If the `DateFormat` class isn't enough, you can use the `SimpleDateFormat` class to specify patterns that determine how a date is formatted.

Table 10.3. Date formatting constants.

Constant	Sample Formatting
SHORT	9/2/97
MEDIUM	02-Sep-97
LONG	September 2, 1997
FULL	Tuesday, September 2, 1997

Text Messages

Although the Java Internationalization API doesn't provide any support for converting text from one locale to another, it does provide a great deal of flexibility in organizing and managing locale-sensitive text. The `MessageFormat` class provides a way of building text messages in a locale-independent manner. Text messages formatted with the `MessageFormat` class can contain strings, numbers, and dates, among other things. The significance of the `MessageFormat` class is that you can specify text messages that don't have locale dependencies. For example, the order of elements in a text message can be rearranged based on different locales, such as a language that reads from right to left instead of from left to right.

Messages formatted with the MessageFormat class are specified using a *pattern* that describes the structure of the message and the order of its elements. The format() method is used to format messages encapsulated by a MessageFormat object. When the format() method is called, the elements of the message are formatted and concatenated appropriately to form the resulting text message.

The Java Internationalization API also provides the ChoiceFormat class, which allows you to associate text with a range of numbers. The ChoiceFormat class is often used with the MessageFormat class to handle plurals.

Text Collation

A particularly thorny area of dealing with localized data is that of *collation*, the comparing and sorting of strings. Sorting strings can be difficult in one language, not to mention how complicated it can get trying to develop a collation mechanism that works for multiple languages. Fortunately, the Java Internationalization API goes a long way in helping you implement localized collation. The Collator class performs locale-sensitive string comparison and is used to build searching and sorting routines for text. The Collator class is an abstract base class from which specific collation classes must derive. The RuleBasedCollator class is a subclass of Collator that provides a simple table collator that maps characters to sort keys.

Text Boundaries

When you think of globalizing a program to a wide set of locales, you must consider how the language structures of the different locales impact your program. For example, consider a text-editing program such as a word processor that must be able to distinguish character, word, sentence, and paragraph boundaries. You're probably thinking that these boundaries are obvious if you're accustomed to dealing with Western languages that share the same Roman alphabet. However, there are plenty of languages whose text boundaries differ greatly from those of Western languages, because of a different alphabet as well as because of accent marks.

The Java Internationalization API includes support for text boundary analysis, which enables programs to provide localized text selection and manipulation. The BreakIterator class supports the detection of various boundaries in text such as character, word, line, and sentence boundaries. There is also a lower-level CharacterIterator interface used by BreakIterator that provides an interface similar to the Enumerator interface for accessing characters in a localized manner.

NOTE

If you feel that I have glossed over some of the internationalization features of Java in this section, it's because I did. The reality is that Java internationalization is a massive topic; hopefully this lesson has provided you with a basic understanding of Java internationalization and how to apply some of it to your own programs. If not, perhaps the WorldExplorer sample applet will help—read on!

The WorldExplorer **Sample Applet**

The rest of the lesson is devoted to the development of the WorldExplorer sample applet, which demonstrates some of the internationalization and localization features of the Java API introduced in this lesson. The WorldExplorer applet displays information about a country and allows you to select different countries to see how the information changes (localizes) to the new country. Figure 10.1 shows the WorldExplorer applet in action with the United States as the selected country.

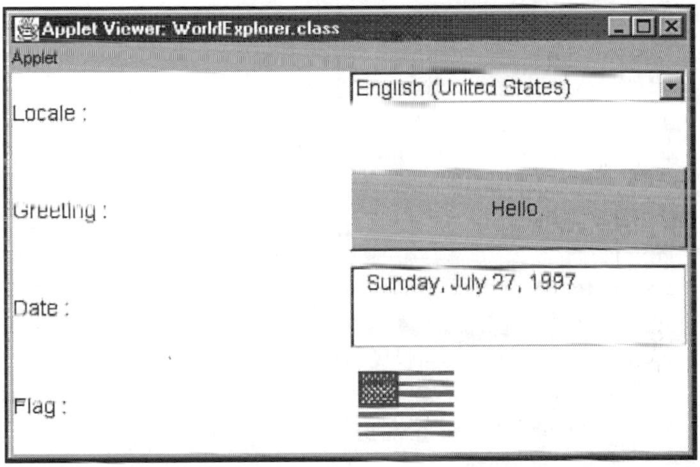

Figure 10.1.

The WorldExplorer *applet with the United States selected.*

As you can see, the applet includes a button with Hello. as its label; this is the greeting of the United States locale. The current date is also displayed using the United States locale format, along with the American flag. If you click the greeting button, an audio clip of the *Hello* greeting is played. Also notice that the labels for each element are in English, which corresponds to the language of the United States locale.

All the elements and their respective labels change whenever you change the locale. Figure 10.2 shows the WorldExplorer applet with France as the selected country. Notice that all the text in the applet changed to reflect the France locale. You can even click the button to hear *Bonjour* spoken in French. As you can see, this applet is a good example of how useful the Java Internationalization API can be in developing global Java applets and applications.

Figure 10.2.

The WorldExplorer *applet with France selected.*

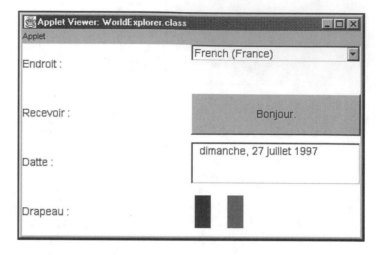

Developing the Main Applet Code

As you learned earlier in this lesson, the best way to develop global programs is to internationalize the main program and then bundle the locale-sensitive data accordingly. Following this approach, let's begin by examining the main applet code for the WorldExplorer applet. Listing 10.2 contains the member variables defined in the WorldExplorer applet class.

Listing 10.2. The member variables for the WorldExplorer applet.

```
 1: private static final Locale[] supportedLocales = {
 2:    Locale.US,
 3:    Locale.FRANCE,
 4:    new Locale("es", "ES"),
 5:    Locale.GERMANY,
 6: };
 7: private ResourceBundle   labels, info;
 8: private Label            localeLabel, greetingLabel, dateLabel, flagLabel;
 9: private Choice           localeChoice;
10: private TextField        dateText;
11: private Button           greetingButton;
12: private ImagePanel       flagImage;
```

The first member, supportedLocales, is a constant array of locales supported by the applet (Lines 1 through 6). This array is used to facilitate the switching of locales in the applet. The labels and info member variables are ResourceBundle objects that represent resource bundles for the current locale (Line 7). You learn more about the data these bundles contain a little later in the lesson. The remaining member variables are all graphical user interface objects used by the applet. The most interesting is the flagImage member, which is an

ImagePanel object (Line 12). The ImagePanel class is the same JavaBeans component you developed in Day 5, "Introduction to JavaBeans." I told you Beans were very reusable!

The initialization of the WorldExplorer applet takes place in the init() method, shown in Listing 10.3.

Listing 10.3. The `init()` method for the `WorldExplorer` applet.

```
 1: public void init() {
 2:    // Initialize the locale and resource bundles
 3:    Locale locale = Locale.getDefault();
 4:    labels = ResourceBundle.getBundle("LabelsBundle", locale);
 5:    info = ResourceBundle.getBundle("InfoBundle", locale);
 6:
 7:    // Create the UI
 8:    setLayout(new GridLayout(4, 2, 0, 10));
 9:    setFont(new Font("Times Roman", Font.PLAIN, 14));
10:    localeLabel = new Label(labels.getString("LocaleLabel"));
11:    localeChoice = new Choice();
12:    for (int i = 0; i < supportedLocales.length; i++) {
13:      localeChoice.add(supportedLocales[i].getDisplayName());
14:    }
15:    greetingLabel = new Label(labels.getString("GreetingLabel"));
16:    greetingButton = new Button(info.getString("GreetingText"));
17:    dateLabel = new Label(labels.getString("DateLabel"));
18:    DateFormat dateFormatter =
19:      DateFormat.getDateInstance(DateFormat.FULL, locale);
20:    String date =
         dateFormatter.format(Calendar.getInstance(locale).getTime());
21:    dateText = new TextField(date);
22:    flagLabel = new Label(labels.getString("FlagLabel"));
23:    try {
24:      flagImage = (ImagePanel) Beans.instantiate(null, "ImagePanel");
25:      flagImage.setImageToUse(info.getString("FlagImage"));
26:    }
27:    catch (ClassNotFoundException e) {
28:      System.err.println(e);
29:    }
30:    catch (java.io.IOException e) {
31:      System.err.println(e);
32:    }
33:    add(localeLabel);
34:    add(localeChoice);
35:    add(greetingLabel);
36:    add(greetingButton);
37:    add(dateLabel);
38:    add(dateText);
39:    add(flagLabel);
40:    add(flagImage);
41:
42:    // Register the applet as an event listener
43:    localeChoice.addItemListener(this);
44:    greetingButton.addActionListener(this);
45: }
```

10

The init() method begins by getting the default locale and loading the resource bundles associated with the locale (Lines 3 through 5). The LabelsBundle resource bundle contains the locale-sensitive names of all the labels for the applet; the InfoBundle bundle contains information such as the greeting text, audio clip, and flag image name. With the locale determined and the localized resource bundles loaded, the init() method moves on to initializing the applet's user interface.

The applet uses a GridLayout object to situate the user interface elements (Line 8). A GridBagLayout object would no doubt have resulted in a more visually appealing layout, but I didn't want to overcomplicate the applet with user interface code. The user interface elements are all initialized with localized strings obtained from the resource bundles. The getString() method is used to retrieve these strings. The only localized data not obtained from a resource bundle is the date, which is obtained using the Calendar class. Notice that the DateFormatter class is used to format the date for the current locale (Lines 18 through 20).

Once all the user interface elements are initialized, the init() method adds them to the applet using the add() method (Lines 33 through 40). The init() method then finishes up by registering the applet as an event listener for item and action events (Lines 43 and 44). Item events are fired by the Choice user interface object whenever the user selects a different country. Action events are fired by the Button user interface object whenever the user clicks it.

Whenever the Choice object fires an item event, the itemStateChanged() event response method is called on the applet. Listing 10.4 shows the source code for the itemStateChanged() event response method.

Listing 10.4. The itemStateChanged() event response method for the WorldExplorer applet.

```
 1: public void itemStateChanged(ItemEvent e) {
 2:   Choice c = (Choice) e.getSource();
 3:
 4:   if (c.equals(localeChoice)) {
 5:     String localeName = new String(e.getItem().toString());
 6:     for (int i = 0; i < supportedLocales.length; i++) {
 7:       if (localeName.equals(supportedLocales[i].getDisplayName())) {
 8:         localizeUI(supportedLocales[i]);
 9:         break;
10:       }
11:     }
12:   }
13: }
```

10

Because the itemStateChanged() method is called whenever the user selects a different country, that method is responsible for changing the current locale and updating the applet appropriately. The itemStateChanged() method first checks to make sure that the localeChoice member is the object that fired the event (Line 4). This step isn't really necessary because localeChoice is the only object in the applet capable of firing item change events, but it is good programming practice (in case you ever add another Choice object to the applet in the future).

The itemStateChanged() method loops through the supportedLocales member array to find the locale selected by the user (Line 6). This search is accomplished simply by comparing the display names of the locales. Once the locale is determined, the localizeUI() method is called and passed the locale as its only argument (Line 8). Listing 10.5 contains the code for the localizeUI() method.

Listing 10.5. The localizeUI() method for the WorldExplorer applet.

```
 1: private void localizeUI(Locale l) {
 2:   // Get the new resource bundles
 3:   labels = ResourceBundle.getBundle("LabelBundle", l);
 4:   info = ResourceBundle.getBundle("InfoBundle", l);
 5:
 6:   // Update the UI
 7:   localeLabel.setText(labels.getString("LocaleLabel"));
 8:   greetingLabel.setText(labels.getString("GreetingLabel"));
 9:   greetingButton.setLabel(info.getString("GreetingText"));
10:   dateLabel.setText(labels.getString("DateLabel"));
11:   DateFormat dateFormatter =
12:     DateFormat.getDateInstance(DateFormat.FULL, l);
13:   String date = dateFormatter.format(Calendar.getInstance(l).getTime());
14:   dateText.setText(date);
15:   flagLabel.setText(labels.getString("FlagLabel"));
16:   flagImage.setImageToUse(info.getString("FlagImage"));
17:   flagImage.repaint();
18: }
```

The localizeUI() method is responsible for updating the applet's user interface to reflect a given locale. Much of the code in the localizeUI() method should look familiar from the init() method because localizeUI() is performing many of the same tasks. The localizeUI() method first loads new resource bundles based on the new locale and then sets the user interface elements using localized data obtained from the resource bundles.

The other event response method used by the WorldExplorer applet is the actionPerformed() method, which is called whenever the greeting button is clicked. Listing 10.6 contains the source code for the actionPerformed() event response method.

Listing 10.6. The `actionPerformed()` event response method for the `WorldExplorer` applet.

```
 1: public void actionPerformed(ActionEvent e) {
 2:   Button b = (Button) e.getSource();
 3:
 4:   if (b.equals(greetingButton)) {
 5:     // Play the localized greeting sound
 6:     AudioClip audio = getAudioClip(getCodeBase(),
 7:       info.getString("GreetingSound"));
 8:     audio.play();
 9:   }
10: }
```

The `actionPerformed()` method plays a locale-sensitive audio clip in response to the user clicking the greeting button. The object firing the event is checked against the `greetingButton` member to make sure that the greeting button is the event source (Line 4). Similar to the `itemStateChanged()` method, this check isn't necessary but is good programming practice. The `actionPerformed()` method gets the audio clip by obtaining the locale-sensitive name of the clip and then calling the `getAudioClip()` method. The clip is then played using the `play()` method.

That wraps up the code for the applet itself. At this point, the applet is internationalized, but it doesn't have any localized data to work with. Read on to see how easy it is to localize the applet!

Bundling the Locale-Sensitive Data

The locale-sensitive data for the `WorldExplorer` applet is contained within two resource bundles: `LabelsBundle` and `InfoBundle`. These bundles are implemented as classes derived from `ListResourceBundle`. If you recall from earlier in the lesson, the `ListResourceBundle` class is used to bundle lists of strings. The list of strings stored in the `LabelsBundle` class consists of user interface labels. The `InfoBundle` class, on the other hand, contains a list of strings with information about each country such as the name of the flag image.

The easiest way to understand how resource bundles work is to look at one. Listing 10.7 contains the source code for the `LabelsBundle` class.

Listing 10.7. The source code for the default U.S. `LabelsBundle` class.

```
 1: public class LabelsBundle extends ListResourceBundle {
 2:   static final Object[][] contents = {
 3:     // Localized U.S. labels
 4:     { "LocaleLabel",    "Locale :" },
 5:     { "GreetingLabel",  "Greeting :" },
```

```
 6:     { "DateLabel",      "Date :" },
 7:     { "FlagLabel",      "Flag :" },
 8:   };
 9:
10:   public Object[][] getContents() {
11:     return contents;
12:   }
13: }
```

As you can see, the label strings are stored in a static array that is accessible through the
getContents() method. This is the standard protocol for bundling string lists in a
ListResourceBundle object. The bundle contains pairs of strings; the first string in each pair
is the key, and the second string is the locale-sensitive information. The string keys are what
the WorldExplorer applet uses to obtain locale-sensitive information from the resource
bundle. Consequently, the key part of the string list is the same across all locales.

Speaking of other locales, the LabelsBundle class appears to only identify data for one locale.
In fact, the LabelsBundle class identifies locale-sensitive data for the default locale, which just
so happens to be the United States. To bundle data for another locale, you create a new class
whose name consists of the resource bundle name with the locale code appended to the end.
For example, the LabelsBundle class for the French language is named LabelsBundle_fr. Its
source code is shown in Listing 10.8.

Listing 10.8. The source code for the French LabelsBundle_fr class.

```
 1: public class LabelsBundle_fr extends ListResourceBundle {
 2:   static final Object[][] contents = {
 3:     // Localized French labels
 4:     { "LocaleLabel",    "Endroit :" },
 5:     { "GreetingLabel",  "Recevoir :" },
 6:     { "DateLabel",      "Datte :" },
 7:     { "FlagLabel",      "Drapeau :" },
 8:   };
 9:
10:   public Object[][] getContents() {
11:     return contents;
12:   }
13: }
```

The LabelsBundle_fr class is practically identical to the LabelsBundle class except for the
locale-sensitive information provided in the string list. Notice that the keys are exactly the
same as the ones used in the LabelsBundle class; it's very important that the keys match
exactly.

The neat thing about resource bundles is that they are associated with a locale solely by name. In other words, you don't have to do anything special when bundling the data except name the class correctly. The task of finding a bundle based on a given locale is handled automatically by Java.

The InfoBundle class contains data such as the image name of the flag for the default locale. Listing 10.9 contains the code for the InfoBundle class.

Listing 10.9. The source code for the default U.S. English InfoBundle class.

```
 1: public class InfoBundle extends ListResourceBundle {
 2:    static final Object[][] contents = {
 3:      // Localized U.S. info
 4:      { "FlagImage",     "Flag.gif" },
 5:      { "GreetingText",  "Hello." },
 6:      { "GreetingSound", "Hello.au" },
 7:    };
 8:
 9:    public Object[][] getContents() {
10:      return contents;
11:    }
12: }
```

The structure of this class is very similar to that of the LabelsBundle class except that the string keys and values are different. Here, the string keys refer to the flag image name, greeting text, and greeting audio clip name, respectively. Keep in mind that this information is for the default U.S. English locale. Listing 10.10 contains the source code for InfoBundle_fr class, which is for the French language locale.

Listing 10.10. The source code for the French InfoBundle_fr class.

```
 1: public class InfoBundle_fr extends ListResourceBundle {
 2:    static final Object[][] contents = {
 3:      // Localized French info
 4:      { "FlagImage",     "Flag_fr.gif" },
 5:      { "GreetingText",  "Bonjour." },
 6:      { "GreetingSound", "Hello_fr.au" },
 7:    };
 8:
 9:    public Object[][] getContents() {
10:      return contents;
11:    }
12: }
```

The only differences between the InfoBundle_fr class and the InfoBundle class are the string values, which reference data specific to the French locale. For example, the greeting text in this class is Bonjour.

Included on the companion Web site for this book along with the source code for the WorldExplorer applet are LabelsBundle and InfoBundle classes for the Spanish and German languages. All the resource bundle classes are compiled just like any other Java classes.

Summary

This lesson introduced you to the Java Internationalization API, which provides interfaces and classes you can use to build global programs. You learned that the globalization of a program consists of two tasks: internationalization and localization. The Java Internationalization API includes all the necessary support for building internationalized programs that rely on localized data to support multiple locales. This support includes special formatting classes for localizing numbers, dates, times, and text messages, as well as classes for bundling locale-sensitive information for easy access. After learning about these classes, you put some of them to work by building an applet that supports four different languages.

Q&A

Q What exactly are the differences among globalization, internationalization, and localization?

A Globalization is the process of supporting multiple languages and sets of customs in a program; it consists of two parts: internationalization and localization. Internationalization is the process of isolating the locale-sensitive code in a program from the rest of the program code. Localization is typically performed after a program has been internationalized, and is the process of adapting the program for use in a specific locale.

Q How does Java support non-Roman alphabets in languages such as Japanese and Arabic?

A Unicode! Unicode is a 16-bit international character-encoding standard that can represent over 65,000 characters—sufficient space for the vast majority of languages around today.

Q Is it possible to localize system-level information such as exception messages?

A Yes, the Internationalization API supports the retrieval of exception messages from a resource bundle, therefore making the exceptions localized.

Q **This lesson made mention of a default locale. What exactly is the default locale and how does it impact the globalization of a program?**

A The default locale is the locale used by the Java runtime environment and is determined by the browser (for applets) or the stand-alone Java runtime (for applications) you are using. For example, if you are using the German version of Netscape Navigator, the default locale is German. The default locale impacts a global program to the extent that the program relies on it. This means that a program can be designed to always use the default locale, or it can be designed so that a user can change the locale manually. In other words, nothing forces a program to use a certain locale unless the developer wants the program to behave that way.

Day 11

Reflection: Looking Inside

by Michael Morrison

This lesson explores an interesting feature of Java 1.1 known as reflection. Although reflection was touched on in *Teach Yourself Java in 21 Days*, this lesson digs deeper to show you exactly what reflection has to offer and why by exploring the following topics:

☐ The basics of reflection and the types of applications that require it

☐ How reflection affects some fundamental parts of the Java technology

☐ Reflection and security

☐ The Reflection API, which is part of the standard Java 1.1 API

☐ A practical sample application that uses reflection to report information about classes

Reflection Basics

Reflection is the process of examining classes and objects at runtime. Using reflection, a Java program can determine the makeup and functionality of a Java object or class at runtime. Additionally, reflection allows a program to examine and modify the contents of an object's member variables (fields), invoke methods on an object, and even create new instances of classes and arrays. The significance of reflection is that all of this capability takes place at runtime, which gives programs an amazing amount of power to examine and manipulate Java classes and objects.

NEW TERM	*reflection:* The process of examining classes and objects at runtime.

Although reflection is a fairly low-level service, it plays a critical role in Java. Reflection provides a means of dissecting a class or object to learn how it works, as well as providing support for dynamically manipulating objects. Dissecting and manipulating classes and objects sounds great, but what types of applications need this type of support? Two fundamental types of applications rely on reflection as a core part of their functionality:

☐ Applications requiring public member access

☐ Applications requiring complete member access

NOTE	The term *application* is used here in a general sense. Applications of reflection could come in the form of API services, Java applets, or Java applications.

Applications Requiring Public Member Access

Although reflection provides a means of determining information about all of a class or object, many applications only need to determine public information. In other words, many applications specifically don't want to know about the protected and private portions of a class or object. A good example of this type of application is JavaBeans, which must be able to ascertain the public member variables, methods, and events that an object supports. JavaBeans relies heavily on Java's reflection services, but its need for information never goes beyond the public members of an object.

The significance of this type of application is the level of access it requires, which in turn affects the type of security restrictions it must adhere to. An application requiring public access to objects is free to execute in a much wider range of environments than one that needs lower-level access to an object. You learn more about security and its role in reflection a little later in the lesson.

Applications Requiring Complete Member Access

The other type of application reliant on Java reflection uses reflection to examine and manipulate all members of an object, including private and protected methods and member variables. A good example of this type of application is a debugger, which must have intimate knowledge of classes and objects at runtime. Another application relying heavily on low-level reflection is Java serialization, which analyzes objects to determine how to serialize them as a stream of bytes. You learn about serialization in the next lesson, "Object Serialization."

As you may have already guessed, this low-level type of reflection carries with it a significant responsibility in terms of security. For this reason, only stand-alone Java applications and built-in Java services such as serialization have the capability of using this type of reflection, according to the JDK 1.1 security policy. Stay tuned for more on this topic later in the lesson.

The Significance of Reflection

You now understand the two major types of applications requiring reflection, or at least you understand the manner in which they rely on reflection. You still may not understand the practical significance of reflection and why it is so important to Java, however. The basic significance of reflection is that it gives applications the capability to learn about classes and objects in a given environment. This capability opens the door for applications to dynamically assess and alter the environment in which they are executing. To get a better idea as to the practical importance of reflection, take a look at two fundamental services provided by the Java 1.1 API: JavaBeans and serialization.

The Role of Reflection in JavaBeans

You learned a great deal about JavaBeans on Days 5 and 6, and you hopefully now have an idea as to how reflection made some of what you learned possible. You know that a critical part of JavaBeans is its support for object introspection, which is the capability to determine information about the public properties, methods, and events supported by an object. Based on this description of introspection, you might think that JavaBeans relies entirely on reflection to fulfill its introspection needs. However, as you may recall from Days 5 and 6, JavaBeans provides introspection in two different forms: automatic and explicit.

Automatic introspection occurs when a Bean doesn't explicitly provide any information about its public members. In this case, a Bean must conform to a series of design patterns that dictate the naming of property accessor methods and event listener registration methods. When the JavaBeans introspector analyzes a Bean using automatic introspection, it relies on high-level reflection to determine the public object members. Thanks to reflection, obtaining the public members of an object is a breeze. The introspector uses this reflected information to determine property accessor methods and event listener registration methods based on design patterns. As long as Bean developers conform to JavaBeans design patterns, this approach works like a charm.

The other introspection approach supported by JavaBeans involves a Bean explicitly including information about its public members. In this case, the JavaBeans introspector asks a Bean for information, and the Bean provides it. Because a Bean is willingly providing information about itself, there is no need to use reflection.

The interesting thing about JavaBeans introspection is that it supports a mixture of these two approaches (see Figure 11.1). Bean developers are free to explicitly provide as much or as little information about a Bean as necessary and then rely on automatic introspection for whatever they don't provide. JavaBeans introspection is a great example of reflection and how it is used in a practical application.

Figure 11.1.

The role of reflection in JavaBeans intro-spection.

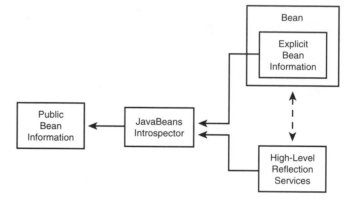

The Role of Reflection in Java Serialization

Serialization is another major part of Java that relies heavily on reflection. Serialization requires a low-level form of reflection because it must have access to all of an object's members, including those that are private and protected. To understand how serialization needs reflection, you have to understand some basics about serialization. You don't learn all the details of serialization until tomorrow's lesson, but for the purposes of this discussion, I'll cover the basic premise behind serialization.

Serialization is the facility that allows Java classes to be represented as a stream of bytes that can be stored to a nonvolatile location such as a hard disk and then later restored. The key to serialization is the capability to accurately represent an object's state as a series of bytes that can later be used to create an identical object. Because an object's state is determined by its member data, it stands to reason that serialization involves the storage and retrieval of a class's member data. This statement is basically true, except for the fact that static and transient member variables can't be serialized and therefore aren't included.

Nevertheless, the general idea behind serialization is the saving and restoring of an object's member data as a series of bytes. At this point, you no doubt can see the implications of reflection on serialization; reflection must be used to access an object's member data. However, the public member data of an object isn't guaranteed to be enough to represent its state, so serialization can't rely on the same high-level reflection used by JavaBeans. Rather, serialization must take advantage of low-level reflection to access all of an object's member data, not just its public data.

In addition, serialization uses reflection beyond the access of member data. Reflection fulfills the following requirements of serialization:

- [ ] Must traverse the inheritance tree for an object
- [ ] Must see whether an object implements a given interface
- [ ] Must access all member variables, or fields, for an object
- [ ] Must get modifiers for all fields to avoid static and transient fields

The Java serialization facility must traverse the inheritance tree of an object in order to access inherited member data. To support serialization, an object must implement the Serializable interface. The Serializable interface contains no methods; it basically serves as a signal indicating that a class wants to support serialization. Therefore, the serialization facility must be able to see whether an object implements this interface in order to provide serialization services. The Java reflection services support both inheritance tree traversal and interface determination for an object or class.

Serialization also requires access to all of the member variables, or fields, of an object so that fields can be read from an object when the object is being stored serially or written to an object when the object is being reconstructed serially. Because not all fields can be stored serially, the serialization facility must know the modifiers for all fields; all static and transient fields are skipped whenever serialization takes place.

The Reflection API

The Java 1.1 Reflection API is responsible for making reflection a reality. This API is a subset of the Java 1.1 API and provides all the support necessary to provide the reflection services you've learned about thus far. The Reflection API consists of the following classes and interfaces:

- [ ] The Class class
- [ ] The Member interface

- ☐ The `Field` class
- ☐ The `Method` class
- ☐ The `Constructor` class
- ☐ The `Array` class
- ☐ The `Modifier` class

Actually, the `Class` class is not technically part of the Reflection API in an organizational sense. The `Class` class is part of the `java.lang` package, and the rest of the reflection classes and the one interface are part of the `java.lang.reflect` package. This difference is a result of backward compatibility because the `Class` class was in the `java.lang` package in Java 1.0. Nevertheless, the `Class` class plays such an important role in Java reflection that you have to consider it part of the Reflection API at least in terms of function. The next few sections examine the Reflection API classes and its one interface.

The `Class` Class

The `Class` class represents a runtime class or interface and serves as the central interface through which reflection information is obtained for a class or object. The `Class` class has no public constructors, which means that you can't create instances of it. `Class` objects are created by the Java virtual machine automatically whenever a new class type is loaded. As a result, every object executing in the Java virtual machine is associated with a `Class` object that can be used to obtain information about the object.

The `Class` class provides a lot of information about a given class. The following are some of the more important pieces of information that `Class` provides:

- ☐ The name of a class type
- ☐ The superclass of a class type
- ☐ The modifiers for a class type
- ☐ The fields, methods, and constructors for a class type
- ☐ Whether an object represents a primitive or an array

To get an instance of a `Class` object for a given class, you use the static `forName()` method:

```
Class c = Class.forName("java.awt.Color");
```

You can then use this `Class` object to get information about the class provided to the `forName()` method:

```
String className = c.getName();
String superclassName = c.getSuperclass().getName();
```

This code gets the name of a class along with the name of its superclass; the `getSuperclass()` method returns a `Class` object representing the superclass. You see the `Class` class in action toward the end of the lesson when you build the `ClassDissector` application.

The Member Interface

The Member interface defines functionality required for three of the primary reflection classes: Field, Method, and Constructor. For example, the Member interface defines a method called getName(), which returns the name of a class member. The interface also defines two other methods, getModifiers() and getDeclaringClass(). The getModifiers() method is used to get the modifiers for a class member, and the getDeclaringClass() method is used to get a Class object representing the class declaring the member. The Member interface also defines two static constants, PUBLIC and DECLARED, which are used by the security manager to determine member access for a class.

The Field Class

The Field class represents a single field (member variable) of a class. A field represented by a Field object can be either a static class field or an instance field. Like Class objects, Field objects can be created only by the Java virtual machine. Unlike Class objects, Field objects are created only when they are specifically asked for. You obtain a Field object by calling the getField(), getFields(), getDeclaredField(), or getDeclaredFields() method on a Class object.

Once you've obtained a Field object, you can use it to get and set the values of the field it represents. When getting or setting an instance field, you must provide the object to which it belongs as an argument to the get() or set() method. For static fields, this object is set to null. This example increments the width field of a Rectangle object using the Field class:

```
Rectangle rect = new Rectangle(10, 20);
Class rectClass = rect.getClass();
Field[] rectFields = rectClass.getFields();
for (int i = 0; i < rectFields.length; i++) {
  if (rectFields[i].getName().compareTo("width") == 0) {
    int width = rectFields[i].getInt(rect);
    rectFields[i].setInt(rect, ++width);
  }
}
```

The fields for the Rectangle object are retrieved using the getFields() method on a Class object. The fields are then looped through in order to find the one named width. The value of the width field is retrieved by calling the getInt() method on its Field object. Notice that the rect object must be passed into this method so that the method knows which object instance to get the field value from; there likely are other Rectangle objects in the system. Finally, the field is set using the setInt() method, which takes the rect object and the new field value.

Admittedly, this example might seem a little silly because you could just change the width property directly, but you have to consider that you can use this approach on any runtime object that exists in the virtual machine, including those that you find out about solely through reflection.

11

The Method Class

The Method class represents a single method of a class. Similar to fields, a method represented by a Method object can be either a static class method or an instance method. Method objects always represent individual methods, which means that multiple Method objects are required to represent overloaded methods. Similar to the Field and Class objects, Method objects can be created only by the Java virtual machine. You obtain a Method object by calling the getMethod(), getMethods(), getDeclaredMethod(), or getDeclaredMethods() method on a Class object.

Once you've obtained a Method object, you can use it to determine the return type, arguments, and exceptions thrown by the method it represents. You can also call a method using the Method object's invoke() method. When calling an instance method, you must provide the object to which it belongs as an argument to the invoke() method, as well as the arguments for the method itself. For static methods, this owner object is set to null. This example prints all the methods supported by the java.awt.Color class using the Method class:

```
Class c = Class.forName("java.awt.Color");
Method[] methods = c.getDeclaredMethods();
for (int i = 0; i < methods.length; i++) {
  System.out.println(methods[i].getName());
}
```

This code results in the following output:

```
testColorValueRange
testColorValueRange
getRed
getGreen
getBlue
getRGB
brighter
darker
hashCode
equals
toString
decode
getColor
getColor
getColor
HSBtoRGB
RGBtoHSB
getHSBColor
```

Notice that only the methods declared in the Color class are printed; no inherited methods are printed. The reson for this is that the getDeclaredMethods() method was used instead of getMethods(). You're probably thinking this code isn't all that amazing considering the fact that you can easily look up the methods for the Color class in the Java documentation. But consider this code's usefulness with a class that you know nothing about.

11

The Constructor **Class**

The Constructor class represents a single constructor of a class. Similar to methods, Constructor objects always represent individual constructors, which means that multiple Constructor objects are required to represent overloaded constructors. Similar to the other member objects, Constructor objects can be created only by the Java virtual machine. You obtain a Constructor object by calling the getConstructor(), getConstructors(), getDeclaredConstructor(), or getDeclaredConstructors() method on a Class object.

Once you've obtained a Constructor object, you can use it to determine the arguments and exceptions thrown by the constructor it represents. You can also create new instances of a class using the Constructor object's newInstance() method.

The Array **Class**

The Array class provides a means of dynamically creating and manipulating arrays. Unlike the Field, Method, and Constructor classes, the Array class doesn't represent an array member. Rather, the Array class is provided as a helper class to facilitate the dynamic creation of arrays and array element access. The Class class doesn't provide any getArray() or setArray() methods, so arrays manipulated by the Array class are always created with the Array class's newInstance() method.

The Modifier **Class**

The Modifier class is a helper class that is used to get the modifiers for a class member. All of the methods defined in the Modifier class are static, which means the class is just an organizational class; you never use an instance of the Modifier class. The Modifier class provides a series of integer constants that represent the different modifiers a class member can have, along with methods for determining each type of modifier. This example uses the Modifier class to print the modifiers of the pixel_bits field in the ColorModel class:

```
c = Class.forName("java.awt.image.ColorModel");
Field field = c.getDeclaredField("pixel_bits");
System.out.println(field.toString());
```

This code results in the following output:

```
protected int java.awt.image.ColorModel.pixel_bits
```

This example printed out all the modifiers of a field, which is interesting but often not as useful as looking for specific modifiers. The Modifier class provides the following methods for querying a member for specific modifiers:

```
isAbstract()
isFinal()
isInterface()
isNative()
```

11

```
isPrivate()
isProtected()
isPublic()
isStatic()
isSynchronized()
isTransient()
isVolatile()
```

All of these methods are static and take an integer as their only argument. This integer is typically obtained from a call to `Class.getModifiers()` and can contain multiple modifiers. The methods in the `Modifier` class decode a particular modifier from the integer to see whether it applies to the member.

Reflection and Security

Quite obviously, the very idea of reflection raises some serious concerns regarding security. When should an application be given access to reflective information about an object? How much information about an object should an application have access to? These questions are addressed head-on by the `Class` class, which communicates directly with the system security manager about when reflection access is granted. Any time an attempt is made to obtain an instance of a `Field`, `Method`, or `Constructor` object, the `Class` class calls the `checkMemberAccess()` method on the system security manager to see whether access is granted. If access is denied, the security manager will throw a `SecurityException` exception.

That's the simple answer to the question about reflection security. The specifics of who has access to what and when are summarized in the following list:

- [ ] Untrusted code has access to all public members of public classes loaded by the same class loader as the untrusted code
- [ ] Untrusted code has access to all public members of public system classes
- [ ] Untrusted code has access to all declared members of all classes loaded by the same class loader as the untrusted code
- [ ] Trusted code has all of the same access as untrusted code plus access to all members of system classes
- [ ] System code has all of the same access as trusted code plus access to all classes loaded by all class loaders

This security access list may not make too much sense to you if you don't understand the difference between trusted and untrusted code. You learn all the details of trusted versus untrusted code on Day 18, "Introduction to Digital Security and the Java Security API." For the purposes of understanding reflection security, let me give you a quick primer. Untrusted

11

code is any code that can't be verified as being safe, such as unsigned applet code. Java 1.1 supports digital signatures, which are a means of signing applet code so that its origin can be verified, and therefore trusted, at least ideally. Another example of trusted code is a stand-alone application, which is trusted by virtue of the fact that it is loaded locally rather than through a network connection.

Trusted code includes signed applets and applications, and untrusted code includes unsigned applets. Once you know this, it's easy to understand why untrusted code is kept on a tight leash in terms of reflection privileges. At the other end of the spectrum, trusted code is given great liberties as to how it can use reflection. Keep in mind in this whole discussion that the standard access control provided by the Java language still applies; the public, private, and protected modifiers are still enforced.

ClassDissector : A Complete Reflection Example

Now that you've explored Java reflection from a few different angles, it's time to break away from the theory and get into the practical. The rest of this lesson is devoted to a sample application that uses the Reflection API to dissect classes and output detailed information about them. You'll probably find the example surprisingly simple because the Reflection API is so easy to use. The application is called ClassDissector and is executed in the Java interpreter like this:

```
java ClassDissector ClassName
```

The following is an example of the output provided by the ClassDissector application when it dissects the java.awt.Dimension class:

```
NAME            : java.awt.Dimension
CLASS/INTERFACE: Class
SUPERCLASS      : java.lang.Object
MODIFIERS       : public synchronized
INTERFACES      : java.io.Serializable
FIELDS :
public int java.awt.Dimension.width
public int java.awt.Dimension.height
private static final long java.awt.Dimension.serialVersionUID
CONSTRUCTORS :
public java.awt.Dimension()
public java.awt.Dimension(java.awt.Dimension)
public java.awt.Dimension(int,int)
METHODS :
public java.awt.Dimension java.awt.Dimension.getSize()
public void java.awt.Dimension.setSize(java.awt.Dimension)
public void java.awt.Dimension.setSize(int,int)
public boolean java.awt.Dimension.equals(java.lang.Object)
public java.lang.String java.awt.Dimension.toString()
```

11

As you can see, the application provides just about everything you could want to know about a class. Listing 11.1 shows the code for the ClassDissector application:

Listing 11.1. The source code for the ClassDissector application.

```
 1: public class ClassDissector {
 2:    public static void main(String[] args) {
 3:       Class c = null;
 4:
 5:       if (args.length > 0) {
 6:          try {
 7:             c = Class.forName(args[0]);
 8:          }
 9:          catch (ClassNotFoundException e) {
10:             System.err.println("Couldn't find class " + args[0] + ".");
11:             System.exit(0);
12:          }
13:
14:          if (c != null) {
15:             // Print general class information
16:             System.out.println("NAME            : " + c.getName());
17:             System.out.println("CLASS/INTERFACE : " + (c.isInterface() ?
18:                "Interface" : "Class"));
19:             System.out.println("SUPERCLASS      : " +
               ➥c.getSuperclass().getName());
20:             System.out.println("MODIFIERS       : " +
21:                Modifier.toString(c.getModifiers()));
22:
23:             // Print interfaces
24:             System.out.print("INTERFACES      : ");
25:             Class interfaces[] = c.getInterfaces();
26:             if (interfaces.length > 0) {
27:                for (int i = 0; i < interfaces.length; i++)
28:                   System.out.print(interfaces[i].getName() + " ");
29:             }
30:             else
31:                System.out.print("None");
32:             System.out.println();
33:
34:             // Print fields
35:             System.out.println("FIELDS :");
36:             Field fields[] = c.getDeclaredFields();
37:             if (fields.length > 0) {
38:                for (int i = 0; i < fields.length; i++)
39:                   System.out.println(fields[i].toString());
40:             }
41:             else
42:                System.out.println("None");
43:
44:             // Print constructors
45:             System.out.println("CONSTRUCTORS :");
46:             Constructor constructors[] = c.getDeclaredConstructors();
47:             if (constructors.length > 0) {
48:                for (int i = 0; i < constructors.length; i++)
```

11

```
49:                 System.out.println(constructors[i].toString());
50:           }
51:           else
52:             System.out.println("None");
53:
54:           // Print methods
55:           System.out.println("METHODS :");
56:           Method methods[] = c.getDeclaredMethods();
57:           if (methods.length > 0) {
58:             for (int i = 0; i < methods.length; i++)
59:                 System.out.println(methods[i].toString());
60:           }
61:           else
62:             System.out.println("None");
63:         }
64:     }
65:     else {
66:       System.out.println("Usage: java ClassDissector ClassName");
67:     }
68:   }
69: }
```

The ClassDissector application uses much of what you've learned throughout the lesson to provide a complete class dissection utility. The application begins by obtaining a Class object representing the class whose name was passed in as a command-line argument (Line 7). This Class object is used throughout the application to retrieve reflection information about the class. The first information obtained about the class is general class information, which includes the class name (Line 16), whether it's a class or interface (Lines 17-18), the class' superclass (Line 19), and class modifiers (Lines 20-21).

The interfaces implemented by the class are then determined by using the getInterfaces() method on the Class object (Line 25). This method returns an array of interfaces that are looped through in order to print out each one (Lines 27-28). If the class doesn't implement any interfaces, ClassDissector lists the interfaces as None (Line 31).

Next stop on the class dissection is the fields for the class, which are obtained by calling the getDeclaredFields() method on the Class object (Line 36). This method returns an array of Field objects that are each printed inside a loop that iterates through the array (Lines 38-39).

The methods and constructors for the class are retrieved in a manner very similar to that used to retrieve the fields. To output all of this class information, the toString() method is used on the different reflection objects. This method is nice because it lists all the information about a class member including the modifiers, type, name, and so on. The application could just as well have retrieved this member information separately and used it to provide more elaborate output, but I thought the simpler approach would be easier to comprehend. The point is that the Reflection API allows you to get as detailed as you want in determining information about a class or object.

Summary

In this lesson you learned about one of the most important features in Java 1.1, reflection. You began the lesson with an introduction to reflection and the theory behind what it does and why. You then moved on to finding out the significance of reflection in terms of Java. From there, you tackled the Java Reflection API, which consists of an interface and a set of classes used to provide reflection services for Java classes and objects. You learned that the Reflection API is your interface to finding out just about anything you need to know about a Java class or object at runtime. With the Reflection API fresh on your mind, you delved into the important topic of security and how it affects Java reflection.

Toward the end of the chapter, you broke away from the theory and learned how to develop an application that takes advantage of some of the services offered by the Reflection API. This application, `ClassDissector`, showed how easy it is to use the Reflection API to find out detailed information about a class. More importantly, it showed you the practical side of reflection and how it can be used.

Q&A

Q Does the JavaBeans BeanBox test container use reflection?

A Absolutely. The nature of the BeanBox requires it to interact with JavaBeans components at a very intimate level, which therefore makes the BeanBox heavily reliant on reflection.

Q Do classes ever have to explicitly provide information to facilitate reflection?

A No. Reflection is a mechanism that operates entirely on the standard Java class structure and requires no additional information on behalf of Java classes. The idea is that all classes should support reflection equally, which is only possible if reflection requires no special effort on behalf of developers.

Q Is it possible to reverse engineer an executable application or applet using the Java reflection services?

A Not really. Although you can certainly find out detailed information about a class's members, this information is hardly sufficient to reverse engineer the implementation of a class. A number of developers have had success analyzing Java bytecodes to reverse engineer Java executables, however. This success has spawned the development of Java "decompilers," which are applications that generate Java source code from executable bytecode.

11

Day 12

Object Serialization

by Jerry Ablan

The Java 1.1 specification has delivered substantial tools to the developer. These tools are in the form of extensions to the basic language and include GUI enhancements, database connectivity, and internationalization, to name a few. But one of the more overlooked, yet important, tools in the Java 1.1 API is object serialization.

In this lesson, you learn about object serialization and how you can create programs and classes that use this new technology. Specifically, you will:

- ☐ Be introduced to serialization
- ☐ Learn how serialization can be used in your programs
- ☐ Create a serialized class
- ☐ Discover how to keep your data from being serialized
- ☐ Learn about versioning of serialized objects

Introduction to Serialization

Serialization is, put simply, the process of creating a copy or clone of something suitable for transmitting. The recipient of the transmission can be a simple file or a computer in Belgium. The key point is that the data created by the serialization is a representation of your data, not the data itself. Once this representation is created, your original object can be reconstructed based on the information stored in the representation. If this sounds a lot like *Star Trek*, you're not too far off.

NEW TERM *serialization:* The process creating a copy of an object suitable for passing to another object.

Object serialization is similar to beaming people aboard a starship. The transporter beam envelops the target of the transmission. The computer then deconstructs the target and transmits it to its destination. On receipt, the recipient reconstructs the target. A perfect duplicate.

You *Star Trek, The Next Generation* fans may recall the episode in which the crew of the *Enterprise* found a copy of Commander Riker. This copy was a result of a transporting mistake in which a copy was left behind. This copy was William Riker—stranded on that planet for years.

Copies of Objects and Clones, Oh My!

When you serialize an object, you actually leave a copy behind because the serialized object is frozen at that moment and transmitted to its destination. The original is left to change and grow different. The copy, once received and reconstituted, is also free to change and grow different. Figure 12.1 shows this process.

NOTE Your objects aren't really copied, only their state is. That means that the data that makes your objects unique is the only thing used by the serialization routines. The actual bytecodes of your object are not part of the serialized object.

Figure 12.1.
*Serializing an object
and its results over
time.*

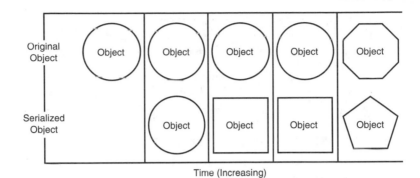

The figure shows several steps in time. The first is before serialization: There is no serialized object. The next step is the serialization step: There are two objects, both circles. In the next step, the serialized object changes to a square, and the original object remains a circle. This is one of the points regarding serialization: There is no guarantee that the objects will remain the same.

Finally, the original object changes into an octagon, and the serialized object becomes a pentagon. You must be careful if you want your serialized objects to match your original objects. Your best bet is to serialize right before destruction. This approach guarantees that the serialized version of your object is a clone of your original.

Persistence

Now that you have this ability to transmit the state of an object, you are probably thinking it's of no use to you. Well, it can be. What serialization gives you is the ability to store and retrieve Java objects. The storage of these objects is called *object persistence*. It means that your objects persist, or remain, after your program has completed. In fact, persistence is the main point of serialization!

object persistence: The ability of an object's data to live on, or persist, after the object has been destroyed.

Think of the possibilities with object persistence! You can create classes that "remember" everything they knew before they were destroyed. For example, you can create a persistent class that remembers where it is placed on the screen.

In addition, when you serialize an object, you are also serializing any objects it refers to. This process is called the *object graph*. It's like a map of all the classes that interconnect with the one you are serializing. When you deserialize the object, the referenced ones come with it.

You've learned about serialization and persistence, both of which describe the process taking place. What you haven't covered is the *medium*, the space in which the objects travel. Where is that space? How do serialized objects get from place to place?

Input and Output Streams

Serialized objects are transmitted and received in streams. These streams are similar to the streams used in Day 7, "Networking with Java." If you read the first book in this series, *Teach Yourself Java in 21 Days*, you know that Day 19, "Java Streams and I/O," was devoted entirely to streams.

I'll quickly summarize streams in case you're a little rusty. There are two basic types of streams: input and output. Input streams are for retrieving, and output streams are for sending. Think of streams as programmatic pipelines that send and receive data.

These little pipelines are smart in that they sometimes know what type of data they are working with. If they do, they can sometimes help in the transmission or reception of that data. If you have ever used the `System.out.println` method before, you've used a stream! The `out` object of the `System` class is an output stream connected to the Java console. Anything you output to that stream is sent to, and received by, the console.

 NOTE

> On UNIX machines, the `out` object is connected to `stdout`, which is part of the operating system.

Although input and output streams are both streams, they have different characteristics. Let's review each type of stream.

InputStream **Features**

The `InputStream` is an abstract class defined in the Java API. This class describes the manner in which data is retrieved from a stream. Who sent it or where it is coming from doesn't matter. Regardless of where the stream came from, once you have it, you use it the same way. An `InputStream` from a file looks just like an `InputStream` from a network connection. `InputStreams` deal strictly with streams of bytes. `InputStream` is the granddaddy of all input stream classes.

What if you want to read characters or strings? You use an abstract class called `Reader` to do just that. This class is identical to the `InputStream` class but it expects to retrieve characters instead of bytes.

Although InputStream has many methods, the read() method is the most important. It is responsible for actually retrieving data from the stream.

The read() Method

The read() method is responsible for getting data out of the InputStream. This method can read either a single byte or an array of bytes. It then returns the number of bytes read. Here's a quick example:

```
InputStream inStream = someObject.getInputStream();
int bytesRead = inStream.read();
```

This method is enhanced in almost every subclass of InputStream. In the Reader class, the read() method retrieves characters instead of bytes.

OutputStream Features

The OutputStream class is the exact opposite of the InputStream class. It is an abstract class that describes the manner in which information is to be written to a stream. OutputStreams deal only in bytes. The OutputStream class is the superclass of all output stream classes.

The Reader class has a corresponding output stream class: the Writer class. The Writer class is used to write characters of data to the stream instead of bytes. The OutputStream and Writer classes are identical except for the data unit they use. They both have several methods, but the most important is the write() method.

The write() Method

The write() method is responsible for moving data to the stream from your program. The following code is implemented to write a single byte of data:

```
byte b = 'A'
OutputStream outStream = someObject.getOutputStream();
int bytesWritten = outStream.write( b );
```

If you want to write an array of bytes, you can use code like this:

```
byte[] b = new byte[ 1024 ];
OutputStream outStream = someObject.getOutputStream();
int bytesWritten = outStream.write( b );
```

The write() method is augmented in the subclasses to perform useful data output capabilities.

Object Streams

Input and output streams are very nice classes. However, they are limited in that they work only with bytes and characters. What you need to serialize objects are input and output streams that deal with objects. Well, the folks at JavaSoft thought of this when they were designing object serialization. They provided two new classes that implement output and input streams for objects: the ObjectOutputStream and ObjectInputStream classes.

12

The `ObjectOutputStream` Class

The `ObjectOutputStream` class is used to write out, or *serialize*, to a stream. This class extends the `OutputStream` class and adds these important methods:

```
public void writeBoolean()
public void writeByte()
public void writeChar()
public void writeDouble()
public void writeFloat()
public void writeInt()
public void writeLine()
public void writeLong()
public void writeObject()
public void writeShort()
```

As you will see, these methods are the counterparts to the methods defined in the `ObjectInputStream` class. They allow you to write the primitive Java types to a stream.

The following code snippet writes some objects to a file:

```
FileOutputStream fos = new FileOutputStream( "myFile" );
ObjectOutputStream oos = new ObjectOutputStream( fos );
oos.writeObject( "I'm a string!" );
oos.writeObject( new Frame() );
oos.writeObject( new Date() );
```

As you can see, you opened a file and wrote a `String`, a `Frame`, and a `Date` out to the file.

The `ObjectInputStream` Class

The `ObjectInputStream` class is used to reconstruct, or *deserialize*, an object received from an input stream. This class extends the `InputStream` class and adds the following methods (among others):

 NEW TERM

> *deserialize:* To convert an object from its serialized form back into its object form.

```
public boolean readBoolean()
public byte readByte()
public char readChar()
public double readDouble()
public float readFloat()
public int readInt()
public String readLine()
```

12

```
public long readLong()
public Object readObject()
public short readShort()
```

These methods are the most important because they allow you to retrieve the basic primitive Java types from a stream.

The following code snippet retrieves the objects you wrote out in the previous example:

```
FileInputStream fos = new FileInputStream( "myFile" );
ObjectInputStream ois = new ObjectInputStream( fos );
String myString = ( String )ois.readObject();
Frame myFrame = ( Frame )ois.readObject();
Date myDate = ( Date )ois.readObject();
```

As you can see, you opened a file and read in a String, a Frame, and a Date. You may notice that I had to cast the readObject() method to the desired class because readObject() returns a generic Object.

WARNING

This example brings up a good point. When serializing objects, be sure to keep the order straight. If you retrieve the wrong object into the wrong type, it results in an error. In the preceding examples, if you had read in the Date as the first object, an exception would have been thrown because the types are not the same.

Serializing Your Own Classes

To create classes that can write themselves to a stream, or read themselves from a stream, you must adhere to one of two interfaces: the Serializable or Externalizable interface.

The Serializable Interface

The Serializable interface is a template that describes what your class must do to be serialized. This interface is special because it doesn't define anything but its name. The declaration of the Serializable interface is like this:

```
public interface
Serializable
{
}
```

The purpose of this interface is to mark your class for serialization. The Serializable interface is similar to the Clonable interface: It defines no methods, just marks your class.

You may, optionally, define the following two methods:

```
private  void writeObject(java.io.ObjectOutputStream out)
   throws IOException
private  void readObject(java.io.ObjectInputStream in)
   throws IOException, ClassNotFoundException;
```

Once implemented, these methods are called when your class is to be serialized and deserialized. If you do not implement these methods, but implement the interface, one of two special methods is called: `defaultReadObject()` or `defaultWriteObject()`.

The `defaultReadObject()` and `defaultWriteObject()` Methods

The `defaultReadObject()` and `defaultWriteObject()` methods, defined in the `ObjectOutputStream` and `ObjectInputStream` classes, provide a simple mechanism to write and read the data of a class to the output or input stream. They simply use reflection (see Day 11, "Reflection: Looking Inside") to get a list of the member variables eligible for serialization.

As you'll see, when you create classes that require serialization, you should call these methods in your `readObject()` and `writeObject()` methods. Here's a quick example:

```
public class
MySerialClass
Implements Serializable
{
    String      myString = "I'm a String";
    Date        myDate = new Date();

    public
    MySerialClass()
    {
    }

    private void
    writeObject( java.io.ObjectOutputStream out )
    throws IOException
    {
        out.defaultWriteObject();
        out.writeString( myString );
        out.writeObject( myDate );
    }

    private void
    readObject( java.io.ObjectInputStream in )
    throws IOException, ClassNotFoundException
    {
        in.defaultReadObject();
        myString = in.readString();
        myDate = ( Date )in.readObject();
    }
}
```

You simply call the default read or write method to handle your data and then you serialize your class's data.

TIP

Even if you want to use only the stock serialization routines, you may find the default methods useful. You can use them as notification that your object has been serialized or deserialized. This notification may be desirable if your serialization and deserialization occur on different platforms. For example, if you have to recompute a value based on a serialized value, you should place your recomputational code in the default method.

The Externalizable Interface

The Externalizable interface is an extension of the Serializable interface. It exists so that you can have complete control over the way your class is serialized. If, perhaps, you are creating an object database and want to store your object in a special way, you would implement the Externalizable interface.

Unlike the Serializable interface, the Externalizable interface defines two methods. Here is the interface:

```
public interface
Externalizable
extends java.io.Serializable
{
    void writeExternal(ObjectOutput out) throws IOException;
    void readExternal(ObjectInput in) throws IOException, ClassNotFoundException;
}
```

As you can see, the Externalizable interface extends the Serializable interface and adds the two methods writeExternal() and readExternal().

NOTE

If you implement this interface, you must use the methods from the DataInput and DataOutput classes to serialize your data.

The writeExternal() and readExternal() methods are what the serialization system actually calls when it wants to write data out or read data in. If you don't define these methods, the default serialization method is used. If you define these methods, your serialization methods are used. By defining them, you simply override the functionality of the serialization system of Java.

12

Protecting Data from Serialization

If you were paying attention in the last section, you noticed that Java's serialization system uses reflection. That means the system looks inside your class to see the names and types of your member variables. It then uses this information to serialize your class. But what if you have sensitive data you don't want serialized? There are some options.

Making transient Data

Your first option to avoiding serialization is the simplest. You can make your sensitive information transient. The transient keyword does not imply that your data is homeless; rather, it marks your data as being nonpersistent. This is an important distinction because *nonpersistent data* is ignored by the serialization routines. Remember that the purpose of serialization is persistence. The transient keyword is not new to Java 1.1. It was in the Java 1.0 API—however, it was unused.

Making static Data

By making your data static, you remove it from the eyes of the serializer. This is your second option. Static data exists once for all copies of the object. Because it is persistent by definition, it is not necessary to store. However, using this option is not always possible.

Implementing the Externalizable Interface

Your third option to avoiding serialization is to implement the Externalizable interface. By implementing this interface, you can create your own object input and output format. For example, you can encrypt and decrypt your information as it is written and read from the object stream.

Not Implementing the Serializable Interface

Your last option to avoiding serialization is to not implement the Serializable interface at all. Unfortunately, this may defeat your purpose entirely. But it is, by far, the safest way of not having your information serialized.

WARNING

> Be warned that the Component class implements the Serializable interface. Therefore, if you create a custom component that contains sensitive information, make it transient or static so that it won't be serialized!

Versioning Serialized Objects

When you serialize an object, you store its current state, and the object continues to thrive. However, what if you serialized some objects last week, but changed the class this week and removed a portion or added more data to the class?

That's where versioning comes in. *Versioning* allows you to stamp a version number on your class; this version number is used by the serialization routines when serializing and deserializing your data.

NEW TERM

versioning: The process of stamping your object with a unique identifier that indicates the revision of your object.

You can apply a versioning number by adding a single member variable to your class:

```
static final long serialVersionUID = <unique ID>;
```

This variable holds a unique identifier (UID) that represents the version number of your class. It is written to the stream when you serialize your object. When you deserialize, if the version of your current class doesn't match the version in the stream, the data is not deserialized.

Obviously, adding this version number is optional. If you choose not to add a version number, the ObjectOutputStream class creates one for you. It computes the version number based on the make-up of your class. It looks at the member data, methods, extensions, and interfaces implemented by your class and generates a unique number that actually represents your class. If you change your class in any way, this number changes as well.

However, that functionality is not always desirable. Suppose that you are working on a class that is serialized. But you keep making changes. If you let the system generate your IDs for you, your stored data will always be invalid. By creating your own version number, the data does not automatically become invalid. You can pick and choose your serialized information.

Look at this snippet of code from the Component class. This readObject() method pulls out only the information it wants from the stream:

```
private void readObject(ObjectInputStream s)
    throws ClassNotFoundException, IOException
{
    s.defaultReadObject();
```

12

```
Object keyOrNull;
while(null != (keyOrNull = s.readObject()))
{
    String key = ((String)keyOrNull).intern();
    if (componentListenerK == key)
        addComponentListener((ComponentListener)(s.readObject()));
    else if (focusListenerK == key)
        addFocusListener((FocusListener)(s.readObject()));
    else if (keyListenerK == key)
        addKeyListener((KeyListener)(s.readObject()));
    else if (mouseListenerK == key)
        addMouseListener((MouseListener)(s.readObject()));
    else if (mouseMotionListenerK == key)
        addMouseMotionListener((MouseMotionListener)(s.readObject()));
    else // skip value for unrecognized key
        s.readObject();
}
}
```

You can employ this technique yourself when creating serialized classes. It gives you more control over what is retrieved and from where.

Generating Version Numbers

You generally don't want to use just any value for your version number because it could possibly conflict with another object. You could read in bad data if you tried to deserialize such an object and the version matched.

To remedy this, the Java 1.1 Software Development Kit comes with a program called serialver. This program generates a line of code that you can cut and paste right into your class. The program is written in Java and accepts the name of the class for which you want a version number:

```
$ serialver java.awt.Component
java.awt.Component:     static final long serialVersionUID =
➡-7644114512714619750L;
```

You can optionally display the tool as a GUI by invoking it with the -show option, like this:

```
$ serialver -show
```

Figure 12.2 shows the serialver program in action running with a GUI. Type the name of your class and click the Show button. The results are displayed in the Serial Version text box (see Figure 12.3).

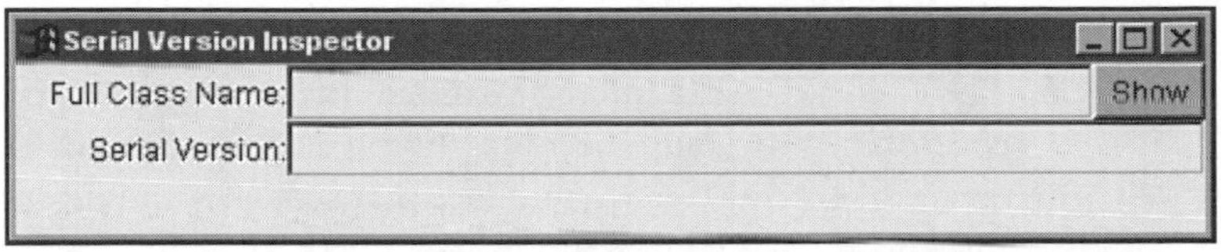

Figure 12.2.

The serialver *window.*

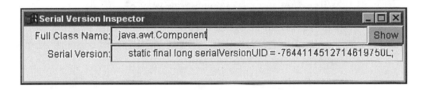

Figure 12.3.

The serialver *window, with a generated version number.*

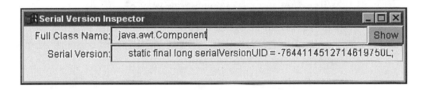

NOTE

> The serialver program is smart. If you select a class that is not serializable, the program does not generate a number for you.

Summary

Today you learned all about object serialization and how it is used. First you learned just what serialization means. This definition led to a discussion of input and output streams. Because serialization uses object input and output streams, you examined these classes and some examples of their use.

Then you learned how to add serialization to your own classes. You created a simple class that implemented serialization and deserialization. I followed this up with a discussion of how to hide your data from being serialized. Finally, I talked about versioning and how to keep track of what version of data is serialized and deserialized.

In tomorrow's lesson, you'll learn about Remote Method Invocation (RMI). RMI relies on the serialization of objects if it is to operate properly.

Q&A

Q What is deserialization?

A Deserialization is the process of reconstructing an object that has been previously serialized.

Q What is the purpose of the Externalizable interface?

A The Externalizable interface exists so that you as a programmer can completely control the way your object is serialized and deserialized. You could, for example, create an Externalizable interface that serializes and deserializes from an archive format such as ARJ or ZIP.

Q What does the serialver program do?

A The serialver program enables you to create version numbers for your objects. These numbers are necessary for serialization to work properly, and they uniquely identify your objects to the world.

Day 13

Remote Method Invocation

by George Reese

Java is centered on the idea that "the network is the computer." The simple concept behind this slogan is the idea that a team of computers working together can accomplish much more than a single computer can by itself. For example, there is no way your little personal computer with 4 gigabytes of storage could store a full database of all the movie information there is to know. The Internet, however, provides you with immediate access to everything you might ever want to know with the help of other machines like those at the Internet Movie Database.

You may have some experience with network programming using sockets. This kind of programming is the first step along the road to Java nirvana. *Socket programming* is a way of building systems in which you divide tasks into processes that run on different machines. These processes talk to each other using *sockets*—a special abstraction that represents a stream of data flowing from one process to another. Socket technology is what allows you to access movie information across the Internet.

The basic conceptual unit in socket-based programming is the application process. In a Web application, you have a Web browser process that talks to a Web server process. In many cases, that Web server process in turn speaks to a database process.

In Java programming, however, the basic conceptual unit is the object. A Java application is nothing more than collection of objects working together to perform a specific task. Although socket programming fits the slogan of the network as the computer, sockets require a conceptual shift akin to fitting round pegs into square wholes. What you really want is a tool that allows your Java objects to talk to each other no matter where they exist on the network. Java provides that tool in the form of Remote Method Invocation (RMI).

In this lesson, you do the following:

- ☐ Learn about distributed object programming with RMI
- ☐ Build a small distributed application that demonstrates the principles behind distributed computing
- ☐ Learn how to use RMI to build distributed Java applications

Distributed Computing with Java

No matter how you look at it, network communication boils down to sockets. The Java RMI exists to hide the tedious details of socket programming and provide you with a pure object framework for building your application. With RMI, you use the same syntax to call methods in objects on remote machines as you use to call methods in any other object.

NOTE

In this lesson, when I refer to a "remote machine," I actually mean a different virtual machine. In the most common case, you can have a client GUI on a PC talking to a database back end on a server machine. Both applications clearly require different Java virtual machines in which to run. It is possible, however, to have a distributed application running on the same machine. To run the examples in this lesson, it probably makes sense to run the "server" application and "client" application together on your PC. They still form a distributed system because they are running in two separate virtual machines.

RMI and CORBA

In addition to providing a pure object framework in which you can work, RMI enables objects to be moved almost seamlessly from machine to machine; little or no code changes are required to move an object from one machine to another. RMI accomplishes this task by using a simplified version of the industry standard CORBA specification. CORBA (Common Object Request Broker Architecture) is a complex specification that enables systems to be built in many different languages, yet still communicate as a single system. CORBA is not necessarily a "remote method" call specification because it supports nonobject programming languages such as C. CORBA's power lies in giving a Java application the capability to call C functions in a remote C application using Java syntax. This power, however, comes at a cost: CORBA is a complex architecture with a steep learning curve for distributed application developers. Lesson 14, "Java and CORBA" is a good place to get started if your distributed computing needs require CORBA.

You can think of RMI as a "pure Java" CORBA. RMI simplifies distributed application development for homogeneous Java systems. Because it is built into the Java language, RMI offers additional benefits such as distributed garbage collection.

Should I Use RMI or CORBA?

This is probably the most frequently asked question by people tasked with creating a distributed system or who are interested in learning about distributed computing in Java. The question is best rephrased as: Am I building a pure Java solution that will never have components in other languages? If the answer is *yes*, RMI is your best bet because of its simplicity and automatic distributed garbage collection. If the answer is *no*, you probably want CORBA.

A Network of Objects

You are probably familiar with the traditional way of looking at applications—as a flow of processes. For an airline reservation system built the traditional way, we can view the system in terms of booking seats and accepting payments. The Java way—the object-oriented way— is different. We briefly touched on that difference in the introduction to this lesson. In an object-oriented application, you view an application as a system of objects that work together. Instead of writing the "flight booking module," you write the "flight object."

A distributed application simply locates the various objects that make up the system on different machines. You can, for example, keep the flight and seat objects on one machine and the customer and employee objects on another machine. The objects on these machines then work together to form a single flight reservation system that is distributed across your network.

13

Placing the Objects on the Network

Because you are a Java programmer, you probably have been building applications in this object-oriented manner. In other words, you are familiar with the object paradigm and understand the semantics of hiding object data and calling object methods. In the distributed world, you have to make one more decision: How do you determine which objects go where?

The simplest division of work is based on functionality. Display-oriented objects, such as GUI widgets, belong on the client machine that interacts with the user. Business objects—objects that encapsulate the logic that makes up the application—belong on a common server machine that all clients use. By sharing the business objects among clients, we are certain that when one customer books a seat, all other customers immediately see the booking of that seat.

Among the advantages of distributed computing is your ability to scale an application with ever-increasing resource needs without changing any code. In plain English, when you run out of CPU power on the server, you can move some of the business objects to another machine—an option that is generally cheaper than buying a more expensive machine.

Look again at the airline reservation system; if our airline grows fast, it may outgrow the capability of a small UNIX server to handle the volume of traffic and data. At that point, our options include these:

- [ ] Buy a more powerful machine at twice the cost of the original and trash the original
- [ ] Buy a similar machine and distribute our server objects

Either option may suit our needs, but the second option is both cheaper and more flexible. The trick is to distribute the objects so that you actually enjoy the benefits of distributed computing.

The most important rule of distributing objects is minimizing communication across virtual machine boundaries. A remote method call is always slower than a local method call. In a flight reservation system, it therefore makes little sense to locate flight objects and seat objects on different machines; we expect these two objects to communicate with one another quite a bit because a flight is made up of seats. It could be, however, that customer objects rarely call methods in flight or seat objects. We can use this minimal interaction as a basis for moving the customer objects to a different machine.

Locating Distributed Objects with RMI

The first step in using RMI is to understand how you find objects located on other machines. In the flight reservation system, the client knows that there is a flight object on the server. To the client system, this flight object is a remote object. To the server system, however, it is a local object. RMI enables the client system to access that flight object in one of three ways:

☐   By a lookup using an RMI URL

☐   As a return value from a call to a method in another object on the server

☐   As a parameter to a method in a client object called by the server

With either of the last two approaches, an initial lookup on some other object must have already been performed. For example, to get a remote object as a return value from a method call in another remote object, you must have a reference to the object whose method returns the desired remote object. Only the first approach enables you to start from scratch and get an object reference.

An RMI URL looks much like any other URL. It comes in the following form:

```
rmi://host:port/object
```

As you see later in this lesson, the default RMI port is 1099. If the object server is using the default port, you can omit the *port* argument from the RMI URL when performing an object lookup.

You may immediately wonder how the `object` part of the RMI URL identifies an object—a fair question because I skipped over *object binding*, the process by which an object is bound to a URL. When a server wants to make an object available for URL lookups, it must bind that object instance to a string representing the object name. You can literally choose any string you want to represent the object name—it is wholly unimportant.

The following code fragment provides an object server that binds a remote object to a URL:

```
public void bindFlight(Flight flight, int number) {
    try {
        java.rmi.Naming.rebind("Flight" + number, flight);
    }
    catch( java.net.MalformedURLException e ) {
        e.printStackTrace();
    }
    catch( java.rmi.RemoteException e ) {
        e.printStackTrace();
    }
}
```

The first argument to `rebind()` is an RMI URL. In addition to the default port of 1099 for an RMI URL, it also defaults to the local host as the server. Because you will be binding objects to the machine on which the process runs, you generally will never have to specify a machine name.

13

What's Going on at Port 1099?

Part of what makes RMI work is a separate application called rmiregistry. This application runs on your machine, listening to port 1099 (or whatever port you specify). Its job is to serve as a registry for distributed object lookups. You can actually have multiple applications bind objects on a single machine. Therefore, before you can run any application that supports object binding, you must start up the rmiregistry application that comes with your Java virtual machine. To start it, issue the command rmiregistry & (on Windows, use the start rmiregistry command).

The object is now ready for lookups. When a client tries to look up flight 186, it uses the following code:

```
public RemoteFlight getFlight(int number) throws RemoteException) {
    return (RemoteFlight)Naming.lookup("rmi://athens.imaginary.com//Flight" +
      number);
}
```

The lookup() static method in the Naming class goes to the object server noted by the RMI URL passed to it and returns a reference to the remote object bound there. You probably are wondering what the RemoteFlight class is. It is a special kind of interface implemented by the Flight class. You learn about these remote interfaces in detail in the next section.

Deep Inside RMI

So far, we have dealt with RMI at a high level, covering the design issues involved in distributing objects across a network and then using RMI to find them. Conceptually, a remote object appears the same to the client machine as it does to the server machine; this is what is meant by *maintaining object semantics*. The fact is, however, that the flight object is located out on the server and the object we now have on the client is something else.

Remote Objects

A remote object is any Java object that can be accessed by a remote process. In your application, you must specify which objects are remote. Making an object remote is simple: you just make it implement an interface that extends java.rmi.Remote. The java.rmi.Remote interface is a standard Java class that looks like this:

```
public interface Remote {
}
```

There is nothing more; Remote is an interface that describes no methods. Its job is to flag an object as a remote object. When you build your remote objects, you create your own interface that extends Remote. The RemoteFlight class mentioned earlier might look like this:

```
public interface RemoteFlight extends java.rmi.Remote {
    public abstract int getFlightNumber() throws java.rmi.RemoteException;
}
```

Your remote object then is any object that implements this interface and provides a body for the getFlightNumber() method. That object may define any number of other methods, but only getFlightNumber() can be called remotely.

The remote object also must export itself (that is, make itself available to the world) using the UnicastRemoteObject.export() method. This static method in the java.rmi.server.UnicastRemoteObject class takes the object passed to it and exports it to remote processes. You can accomplish this export in one of two ways:

- By calling UnicastRemoteObject.exportObject() explicitly
- By extending UnicastRemoteObject, which calls exportObject() in its constructor

The method you choose really depends on your object model. If your object already has another base class, you cannot extend UnicastRemoteObject. To continue the flight reservation example, the Flight class might look like this:

```
public class Flight extends java.rmi.server.UnicastRemoteObject
implements RemoteFlight {
    int flight_number;
    public Flight(int number) throws java.rmi.RemoteException {
        super();
        flight_number = number;
    }
    public int getFlightNumber() {
        return flight_number;
    }
}
```

The only thing about this constructor that differs from nonremote objects is the use of the RemoteException exception.

Whenever you make a call to a method in a nondistributed environment, you know exactly what can go wrong, and you know whether it is even reasonable for it to go wrong in that situation. For example, when converting a String to an int, the parseInt() method throws NumberFormatException, letting you know that if certain conditions are not met, you get an error condition. Furthermore, you probably know where you got the String to begin with (user input, generated earlier from an int, and so on), so you know whether you are even likely to encounter the exception.

13

In a distributed environment, however, there are no such guarantees. Anything can go wrong; in many cases, things you never imagined do go wrong—the network fails, the server crashes, and so on. `RemoteException` is a sort of all-purpose exception that handles errors related specifically to making remote method calls. Every method in a remote interface, therefore, must declare itself as throwing `RemoteException`.

Stubs and Skeletons

When you make a normal method call in Java, the method arguments are placed on the stack, and program control moves to the method you call. When you call a method in an object located somewhere else on the network, however, things get a little more complex. As mentioned earlier, you are not actually calling a method in the remote object directly; you are calling that method through some other object handed to you when you do the lookup. This object is a special object called a *stub*. Like your remote object, the stub implements your remote interface. Instead of performing business logic, however, the implementation of the interface methods perform networking routines that send your method call across the wire to the real implementation in the remote object.

But you also need an object on the remote system that listens for method calls, takes them from the network, and sends them to the true remote object method. Figure 13.1 shows the full flow of a remote method call.

Figure 13.1.

The flow of a remote method call.

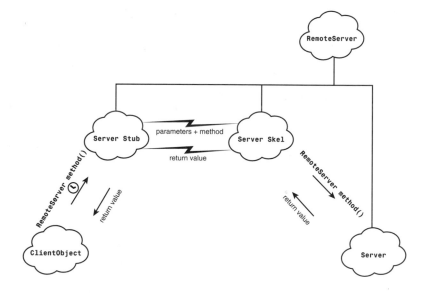

All remote objects are implementations of at least one remote interface. When a client does a lookup() or gets a reference to a remote object in any of the other ways mentioned earlier, it actually gets an instance of a special object called a stub that implements the same remote interface as the object being looked up. In the flight reservation system, the Flight class implements RemoteFlight, which extends Remote. When we do the lookup, we get an instance of a class called Flight_Stub that also implements RemoteFlight. The stub simply implements the RemoteFlight methods in a very different way.

Suppose that RemoteFlight specifies the method public int getNumber(). A Flight object then has an attribute that stores the flight number with getNumber() returning that attribute's value. Flight_Stub, on the other hand, has a bunch of networking code built into it. When getNumber() is called from the client in the Flight_Stub class, that method sends data to the server telling it to call the getNumber() method in the appropriate Flight instance. When it gets the return value—the flight number—from the server, the Flight_Stub returns that value as the return value for getNumber().

The primary job of a stub is therefore to serve as a dummy reference for client systems. It takes method calls destined for remote objects, translates the parameters into network format and sends the call to the proper remote system. After receiving a return value or an exception from the server, the stub translates that return value or exception back into Java objects and either returns a return value or throws an exception.

A *skeleton* object handles the server end of the system. It receives network data destined for a particular object and translates that data into Java objects before calling the target method. After getting a return value or an exception, the skeleton translates the return value or exception into network format for the waiting client stub.

Generating Stubs and Skeletons

I hope you aren't panicking at the thought of writing stub and skeleton classes. The reason you shouldn't panic is that you don't have to— Java has a special tool to write those classes for you. The JDK comes with a special program called rmic that generates skeletons and stubs for remote objects. In the example of the Flight class, after you have compiled the Flight class successfully, all you have to do is issue the following command line:

```
rmic Flight
```

The rmic command generates the Flight_Stub.class and Flight_Skel.class classes. Your objects are all ready!

13

NOTE

The `rmic` tool works like a hybrid of the `java` and `javac` commands. Specifically, it takes the same options as the `javac` command, but its arguments are fully qualified Java class names, not source filenames. If you want to generate stubs and skeletons for classes found in a package, you must issue a command like this one:

```
rmic -d /java/lib COM.imaginary.example.SomeObject
```

This command puts the stub and skeleton classes in `/java/lib/COM/imaginary/example` based on the `SomeObject` class file found in your `CLASSPATH`.

It is also important to note that any special development environment such as VisualCafé or JBuilder may provide their own tools for generating support for stubs and skeletons.

Passing and Returning Data

With local method calls, objects are passed by reference, and primitive data types are passed by value. This is not true for remote method calls. In remote method calls, remote objects are passed by reference; serializable objects and primitive data types are passed by value. Other objects simply cannot be used as parameters or return values.

You already know that a remote object is one that implements a remote interface. Similarly, a serializable object is one that implements the `java.io.Serializable` interface that is part of the Object Serialization API. Being *serializable* means that Java knows how to take the object and turn it into a data stream. You then can use that stream to save an object to a file or, in the case of RMI, send it across a network. This means that when a serializable object is passed to a remote method, it is copied in whole to the other side. Any changes made to the copy on the server are not reflected in the copy on the client.

RMI Programmer's Checklist

Here is a small checklist of things you need to do when writing a distributed Java application using RMI:

- ☐ Write the remote interface
- ☐ Write the remote object
- ☐ Compile the remote object
- ☐ Generate the stub and skeleton
- ☐ Run `rmiregistry`
- ☐ Run the application

13

Serialization Basics

Most of the core Java classes are already serializable. Built into Java 1.1 is the capability for any object to turn itself into an ObjectStream—a type of stream that streams an entire object. Any object you write can automatically be serialized; you simply have to indicate that you want it to be so by making the object implement the java.io.Serializable interface. The following code sample shows how you can normally send an object across a network without RMI:

```
public void send(Socket s) {
    try {
        ObjectOutputStream output =
          new ObjectOutputStream(s.getOutputStream());
        output.writeObject(this);
    }
    catch( Exception e ) {
        e.printStackTrace();
    }
}
```

This send() method tells the object to send itself to the receiving end of the socket it is passed. When you do this, all data is serialized unless it either is specifically marked with the keyword transient or is not serializable.

In an RMI environment, you do not have to know the intimate details of object serialization. Instead, you simply should be aware that serialization is the way in which nonremote objects are passed and returned using RMI. For a more detailed discussion of object serialization, take a look at Day 12, "Object Serialization."

Designing an RMI Application

You may have noted that binding each flight object every time your application server starts up can be impractical, especially if you are talking about a very dynamic system with lots of flights. There are certainly more practical ways in which to design an RMI application; and there are also many special design considerations for RMI applications.

Minimizing Object Lookups

You want to minimize object lookups for two reasons. First, as stated earlier, lookups are impractical on a large scale because they require the server to know *a priori* what objects potential clients will want, and lookups require all the objects to be loaded into memory. In addition, you perform lookups on objects located in a specific place on the network. Any object you have to look up must have a known location, making it harder to move that object to other servers.

13

One of the ways you can most easily minimize object lookups is by providing centralized object servers that are aware of and can control the location of different objects across a distributed server. With the flight object, for example, each client searches for that object on a specific server, athens. Wouldn't it be nice to have the application server spread across multiple servers and have the location of individual flight objects be a runtime configuration issue for the server?

You can accomplish this freedom by providing clients with a single interface to the distributed server. Let's call this single interface the object server, ObjServer. Listing 13.1 shows an example of what an object server might look like.

Listing 13.1. The source code for ObjServer.java.

```java
import java.net.MalformedURLException;
import java.rmi.Naming;
import java.rmi.RemoteException;
import java.rmi.server.UnicastRemoteObject;
import java.util.Hashtable;

public class ObjServer extends UnicastRemoteObject implements RemoteObjServer {
    static public void main(String[] args) {
        try {
            ObjServer server = new ObjServer();
            Naming.rebind("ObjServer", server);
        }
        catch( MalformedURLException e ) {
            e.printStackTrace();
        }
        catch( RemoteException e ) {
            e.printStackTrace();
        }
    }

    private Hashtable flights = new Hashtable();

    public ObjServer() throws RemoteException {
        super();
    }

    public RemoteFlight getFlight(int number) throws RemoteException {
        Integer i = new Integer(number);
        synchronized(flights) {
            if( flights.containsKey(i) ) {
                return (RemoteFlight)flights.get(i);
            }
            else {
                Flight f = new Flight(number);

                flights.put(i, f);
                return (RemoteFlight)f;
            }
        }
    }
}
```

13

I want to draw your attention very quickly to the fact that getFlight() is synchronized on the flights attribute. You should remember that whether or not you have written your application in a multithreaded fashion, remote calls occur asynchronously. You therefore must protect access to any data structures through remote calls in the same way you would synchronize any multithreaded application.

As you can see, a single object worries about the location of all flight objects. In this example, it so happens that all the flight objects are located on a single server. You nevertheless could distribute flights 0 through 999 on one server and flights 1000 and over on another server. Clients still access this object server and call getFlight() to get those flights. The only thing you need to add is some logic in ObjServer for finding those flights. In the original code in which you accessed the flight objects through direct lookups, changing the location of a flight object meant you had to change client code.

Callbacks

So far, we have been discussing clients calling methods in object servers. The paradigm discussed so far does not work well with server-to-client calls. RMI requires a minimal level of administration at the server level for running rmiregistry and managing object distribution. Because Java is supposed to provide a zero administration client environment, it therefore provides a transparent callback mechanism with RMI.

The callback mechanism enables object servers to access remote objects located on clients connected to the servers. For example, you may have a Customer object located on the client machine representing the customer looking at those flights. If the customer decides to purchase a seat, the client calls flight.purchase(customer). According to the rules of RMI, Customer has to be either a remote or serializable object. In this case, you want it to be a remote object because you want changes by the server to be reflected on the client. RMI enables applications to do this transparently without running any special tools such as rmiregistry.

Callbacks have two main limitations:

☐ Only those object servers to which the client already has connected can call methods in a remote client object.

☐ Object servers can get remote object references only as method parameters or return values. They cannot do lookups.

Security

Java developers, especially applet developers, immediately start thinking of security issues whenever sockets are discussed. The first security issue a developer often encounters is the existence of firewalls, especially on the client end. Simply put, everything I have described thus far falls apart when there is a firewall on the client end because few firewalls allow clients to connect to random ports.

13

RMI tries two connection methods when a client attempts to perform a remote method call. The first method is a direct TCP/IP socket connection to the `rmiregistry` port. If that fails, as it would when a firewall is present, RMI then attempts to use a CGI `POST` on the object server's HTTP port. You then can have a CGI on the Web server translate the remote method call into a Java remote method call.

Although this bit of smoke-and-mirrors enables you to get around firewalls on client-to-server calls, it cannot enable server-to-client calls. In fact, there is currently no mechanism for this type of communication when firewalls are present. For that reason, you should not deploy applets on the Internet that require callbacks.

A Simple RMI Application

Now you have all the basics of RMI; it's time to put them together into an RMI application. It seems people everywhere are aching to put chat servers up on their Web sites. For this reason, I have chosen to use as an example an extremely simplistic chat server that uses RMI as its transport mechanism.

The client consists of two classes: `Client` and `RemoteClient`. You probably already recognize `RemoteClient` as the remote interface for the `Client` class. To use the client, a user issues the command `java Client` *username*. At that point, the `main()` method creates a `Client` object and exports it. It then does a lookup on the `ChatServer` object on the server using the URL `rmi://localhost/Server`.

Compiling an RMI Application

When compiling the following `Client` class (as well as any RMI object), keep in mind that order is important. For the `Client` class, issue the following commands:

```
javac RemoteClient.java
javac Client.java
rmic Client
```

Of course, as with any Java application, you must have already compiled any dependencies (such as RemoteChatServer), or you can compile them all together:

```
javac RemoteClient.java Client.java RemoteChatServer.java
```

Once connected with the server, the client goes into a loop in which it accepts user input and sends it to the server. The only input not sent to the server is the quit command. Listing 13.2 shows the `Client` class.

Listing 13.2. Client.java, the client's remote object.

```java
import java.io.BufferedReader;
import java.io.IOException;
import java.io.InputStreamReader;
import java.rmi.Naming;
import java.rmi.RemoteException;
import java.rmi.server.UnicastRemoteObject;

public class Client extends UnicastRemoteObject implements RemoteClient {
    static public void main(String[] args) {
        String url = "rmi://localhost/Server";
        Client client;
        RemoteChatServer server;
        BufferedReader input;
        if( args.length != 1 ) {
            System.out.println("Syntax: java Client NAME");
            return;
        }
        try {
            client = new Client(args[0]);
            System.out.println("Looking up: " + url);
            server = (RemoteChatServer)Naming.lookup(url);
            server.connect(client);
            System.out.println("Done.");
            input = new BufferedReader(now InputStreamReader(System.in));
        }
        catch( Exception e ) {
            e.printStackTrace();
            System.exit(-1);
            return;
        }
        System.out.print("> ");
        while( true ) {
            String str;

            try {
                str = input.readLine();
            }
            catch( java.io.IOException e ) {
                e.printStackTrace();
                System.exit(-1);
                return;
            }
            if( str.equals("quit") ) {
                System.exit(-1);
                return;
            }
            try {
                server.sendMessage(client, str);
            }
            catch( RemoteException e ) {
                e.printStackTrace();
                System.exit(-1);
                return;
```

continues

Listing 13.2. continued

```
            }
            System.out.print("> ");
        }
    }

    private String client_name;

    public Client(String nom) throws RemoteException {
        super();
        client_name = nom;
    }

    public String getClientName() {
        return client_name;
    }

    public void receiveMessage(String msg) {
        System.out.println(msg);
    }
}
```

The remote interface calls for the getClientName() and receiveMessage() methods that the ChatServer class uses to find the name the user specified on the command line and then sends it messages from other clients. Any time a user enters a new line, the Client sends it to the server through the sendMessage() method in the ChatServer. You may think that method would immediately relay the message to all the other clients. Because a remote method call blocks processing until it finishes, however, you do not want to the method to relay the message to all clients. If sendMessage() did that, any time you sent a message, you could not enter a new message until every client received the first message. Because you are working with a network, it could take a long time because some clients might have become unreachable since the last message.

Another issue created by the blocking nature of remote method calls is that you cannot turn around and call a client method from a server method being invoked from that client. In the case of the ChatServer class, you actually send each message to *all* clients, even the one that sent the message. If you tried sending the message inside sendMessage(), the server would hang when it attempted to call back to the sending client because that client is waiting for the return from sendMessage() to complete.

You can get around this knot by queuing up messages and then sending them in a separate thread. In a more robust chat server, you might even have a separate thread for each client connected. With this arrangement, one client's slow connection does not affect the rest of the connected clients. Listing 13.3 shows how this is handled.

Listing 13.3. `ChatServer.java,` **the server class.**

```
import java.rmi.Naming;
import java.rmi.RemoteException;
import java.rmi.server.UnicastRemoteObject;
import java.util.Enumeration;
import java.util.Vector;

public class ChatServer extends Thread implements RemoteChatServer {
    static public void main(String[] args) {
        try {
            ChatServer server = new ChatServer();
            Naming.rebind("Server", server);
            server.start();
        }
        catch( Exception e ) {
            e.printStackTrace();
        }
    }

    private Vector clients  = new Vector();
    private Vector messages = new Vector();

    public ChatServer() throws RemoteException {
        super();
        UnicastRemoteObject.exportObject(this);
    }

    public void connect(RemoteClient client ) {
        synchronized( clients ) {
            if( clients.contains(client) ) {
                return;
            }
            clients.addElement(client);
        }
        sendMessage(client, "connected");
    }

    public void sendMessage(RemoteClient client, String msg) {
        synchronized( messages ) {
            messages.addElement(new Message(client, msg));
        }
    }

    public void run() {
        while( true ) {
            Message[] msgs;

            try { Thread.sleep(500); }
            catch( InterruptedException err ) { }
            synchronized( messages ) {
                if( messages.size() > 0 ) {
                    msgs = new Message[messages.size()];
                    messages.copyInto(msgs);
                    messages.removeAllElements();
```

continues

Listing 13.3. continued

```
                                }
                                else {
                                    continue;
                                }
                            }
                        for(int i=0; i<msgs.length; i++) {
                            RemoteClient c = msgs[i].getClient();
                            String msg = msgs[i].getMessage();
                            Enumeration targs;
                            String nom;
                            try {
                                nom = c.getClientName();
                            }
                            catch( RemoteException err ) {
                                err.printStackTrace();
                                continue;
                            }
                            targs = clients.elements();
                            while( targs.hasMoreElements() ) {
                                RemoteClient target = (RemoteClient)targs.nextElement();
                                try {
                                    target.receiveMessage(nom + ": " + msg);
                                }
                                catch( RemoteException err ) {
                                    synchronized( clients ) {
                                        clients.removeElement(target);
                                    }
                                }
                            }
                        }
                    }
                }
            }
        }

class Message {
    private RemoteClient client;
    private String       message;

    public Message(RemoteClient c, String msg) {
        super();
        client = c;
        message = msg;
    }

    public RemoteClient getClient() {
        return client;
    }

    public String getMessage() {
        return message;
    }
}
```

The Message class at the end of the listing is simply a special holder class that lets you stick together the Client and message sent in the message queue.

Summary

The remote method call paradigm is very powerful for enabling developers to build network systems using an already familiar communication concept, the method call. In particular, RMI makes networking relatively easy in a pure Java environment. As long as you keep in mind the special limitations associated with a remote method call, there is really nothing new in terms of coding that you have to understand. The new stuff is simply process-oriented changes involved in running rmic and rmiregistry as well as creating interfaces for remote objects.

In this lesson, you learned how a single server object can be shared by multiple clients. When it comes to developing more complex systems, the concept of shared objects can be much more important. Imagine a manufacturing system in which all client purchasers were looking at the same inventory items. When one client makes a purchase, the others can immediately see that a purchase was made so that they do not try to buy a nonexistent product.

Q&A

Q How do I get RMI to work through a firewall?

A Make sure that the java-rmi.cgi CGI script that comes with JDK 1.1 is in your Web server's CGI directory. With the script safely there, RMI will attempt to work through port 80 using this script if a firewall prevents connecting to other ports.

Q How do I make callbacks if the client is behind a firewall?

A You don't. Callbacks can only be made if the server can open up a connection on an arbitrary socket to the client.

Q I made a small change to one of my classes. It compiles and rmic works, but the application errors when I run it. What is wrong?

A You must remember to shut down and restart rmiregistry. Otherwise, it will be running against an old copy of the class in question.

Q Can my RMI application inter-operate with CORBA?

A Not today, but in the future. RMI currently uses a proprietary wire protocol to talk between the client and server. In the future, JavaSoft intends to support IIOP (Internet Inter-Orb Protocol) in addition to its proprietary protocol. IIOP is an open protocol that allows different CORBA ORBs to inter-operate. By supporting IIOP, RMI will gain the capability to work in a CORBA environment.

13

Q Can I distribute my application server across multiple server machines?

A Yes. The only restriction you need to bear in mind is the restriction on applet access to multiple hosts. If, for example, you wanted to have a StateProvince and Country object server on one machine and your application objects on another, you can pass these objects between the servers or to clients without any problem. If one of those clients is an applet, however, that applet can only talk to objects that reside on the Web server. If the application objects exist on the Web server, then your applet will not be able to access the StateProvince or Country objects, even if they are passed to the client indirectly through the application object server.

13

Day 14

Java and CORBA

by Bryan Morgan

Unlike nearly all the other topics covered by the lessons in this book, this lesson deals with a technology that subsumes Java, is not owned by Sun Microsystems, is language independent, and is operating-system independent.

In this lesson, however, you will see that Java and the CORBA technology merge almost perfectly, which is why CORBA is finally seeing tremendous interest and growth after being an open standard since 1990. This lesson introduces you to the Common Object Request Broker Architecture (CORBA) and, in particular, the use of the Java programming language in building CORBA-compliant applications. Because CORBA can be an extremely complex topic, the purpose of this lesson is to give you a high-level overview into the current state of CORBA and how you can effectively use Java to build mobile, platform-independent, distributed, object-oriented applications that are scalable beyond the boundaries of Java itself. Before doing that, I'll introduce the current Web programming model and its inherent limitations.

In this lesson, you'll do the following:

- ☐ Learn about the worldwide object web
- ☐ Take a whirlwind tour of CORBA
- ☐ Understand why you should use Java with CORBA
- ☐ Learn how to select a Java ORB
- ☐ Follow along with a basic Java/CORBA application
- ☐ Compare DCOM to CORBA
- ☐ Compare Java RMI to CORBA

The World Wide Object Web

As you undoubtedly know, the World Wide Web consists of a galaxy of interconnected HTTP, FTP, Mail, and Gopher servers that dynamically serve, create, or route information based on user requests. Because of their popularity, Web servers have evolved to become application-development platforms through the use of CGI scripts or proprietary Web application servers. Any developer who has tried to build applications using CGI, for example, realizes the inherent limitations involved with this technology. After years of dramatic progress that had many developers using Rapid Application Development (RAD) tools to develop powerful object-oriented applications, the World Wide Web thrust us back to the Stone Age of software development. This happened because CGI, NSAPI, and ISAPI scripts or Web application servers all communicate using parameters passed through URLs. In other words, if I wanted to call the script `CapitalQuery.cgi` to retrieve the capital of Florida, I might issue the following URL request:

```
http://www.myserver.com/CapitalQuery.cgi?State=\"FL
```

The server could return an HTML page that contains this text:

```
State Name = Florida
Capital Name = Tallahassee
```

The problem you run into is that HTTP (the protocol of the World Wide Web) was designed from the ground up to be a "stateless" protocol. What does this mean? Imagine that after you found the capital of Florida, you wanted information on the city of Tallahassee. The only practical way to do this is to have the `CapitalQuery.cgi` CGI script encode a link behind the word `Tallahassee` in the preceding text; that link then runs the CGI script `CityQuery.cgi` as follows:

```
http://www.myserver.com/CityQuery.cgi?State=\"FL\"&City=\"Tallahassee\"
```

You are forced to resend the state parameter and issue an entirely new request because the state retrieved from the previous request was lost. In other words, no process sits on the server to remember that you just passed it State=FL. This is an example of what is meant when we say that the Web is stateless. Programmers used to simple constructs such as local variables are forced to rethink the way they build applications. On top of these limitations, performance of server scripts is notoriously poor because of the overhead involved in starting and executing a new process for each user request.

These limitations have prompted many to ponder the future existence of a Web of objects, where developers could instantiate remote objects on Web servers and use those objects as if they were located on the local machine. In Java, you can simply retrieve information about a capital city using pseudo-code that looks something like this:

```
StateObject State = new StateObject("FL");
CityObject City = State.getCapital();
CityInformationObject CityInfo = City.getCityInformation();
```

This code uses three imaginary objects: StateObject, CityObject, and CityInformationObject. These objects are manipulated in code just as if they were located locally (and they may be). However, using distributed object technologies such as Java Remote Method Invocation (RMI) and CORBA, these objects can be located anywhere on the Internet. If you use CORBA, you can use these objects even if they're not written in Java!

The premise behind this lesson and, in a larger sense, CORBA itself, is that the Web cannot truly flourish as an application development medium until it becomes an "object web" capable of supporting enterprise-level concepts such as directory naming, services, security, transactions, and architecture-independent and language-independent objects (so that legacy code can be reused). As you see in this lesson, CORBA is the only technology currently available that fulfills these needs.

CORBA: A Whirlwind Tour

Before beginning to build even the simplest CORBA application, you should have a fundamental understanding of what CORBA is and is not, and how the different "pieces" of the CORBA specification work together. To start with, CORBA is a specification for distributed objects created in part by nearly every major computer software manufacturer. Pieces of CORBA were contributed by Sun Microsystems, Hewlett-Packard, IBM, Netscape, Oracle, Digital, and Apple among many others. All these companies jointly belong to an organization known as the Object Management Group (OMG). The most glaring omission among the many CORBA supporters is Microsoft, who touts the Component Object Architecture (COM) in competition with CORBA.

14

The Object Management Group (OMG)

The Object Management Group (OMG) can be thought of as the caretaker of CORBA. All members of the OMG—nearly 700 companies to date—receive voting privileges and are free to contribute new specifications as they are requested. This process happens when the OMG issues a Request For Proposal (RFP) for a specific CORBA technology, such as transaction services. Companies can issue proposals on how they think this technology should be designed; the OMG decides which proposal or proposals should be incorporated into future versions of CORBA. Member companies can also push for new extensions to CORBA instead of waiting for the OMG to independently extend it. For example, Netscape, Sun, IBM, and Oracle recently jointly recommended to the OMG that the JavaBeans component architecture be named the standard component model for CORBA development. If enough support is generated, a vote on this request should take place sometime in late 1997 or 1998.

CORBA Defined in One Long Paragraph

Thanks to the OMG, CORBA remains an open specification that defines how distributed objects can communicate across a network. These objects can be written in any programming language supported by a CORBA software manufacturer (including C, C++, Java, Ada, and Smalltalk). These objects can also exist on any platform supported by a CORBA software manufacturer (including Solaris, Windows 95/NT, OpenVMS, Digital UNIX, HP-UX, and AIX, among others). This means that you can have a Java application running under Windows 95 that dynamically loads and uses C++ objects stored across the Internet on a UNIX Web server. Language independence is made possible through the construction of interfaces to objects using the Interface Description Language (IDL). IDL allows all CORBA objects to be described in the same manner; all you need then is to make available a "bridge" between the native language (C/C++, COBOL, Java, and so on) and IDL. These objects communicate with each other using an Object Request Broker (ORB) as an intermediary and can communicate over many popular networking protocols (such as TCP/IP or IPX/SPX). ORBs from different vendors communicate over TCP/IP using the Internet Inter-Orb Protocol (IIOP), which is part of the CORBA 2.0 standard (the latest version). The OMG originally defined the Object Management Architecture (OMA) in 1990, which gave birth to what we know today as CORBA. The Object Management Architecture (OMA) defines the four major parts that make up a CORBA installation:

☐ The Object Request Broker, which acts as a software bus for objects to communicate on.

☐ CORBAServices, which define system-level services added on to the ORB, such as security, naming, and transactions.

14

☐ CORBAFacilities, which define application-level services such as compound documents and other vertical facilities.

☐ Business objects, which describe "real-world" objects and applications such as an `Airplane` or `BankAccount`.

The following sections discuss some of the details of the CORBA 2.0 specification including the ORB, CORBAServices, and the IDL used to describe interfaces to underlying CORBA objects.

The Object Request Broker

The most important piece of the Object Management Architecture is the Object Request Broker (ORB). The ORB is the only portion of CORBA that is required to be present if you are to build a CORBA-compliant application. Many ORBs ship without any of the CORBAServices or CORBAFacilities, and business objects are usually created by yourself or by third-party developers. However, without the ORB, a CORBA application cannot function.

The most visible function of a CORBA ORB is to respond to requests from your application or from another ORB. During the life cycle of your running CORBA application, your ORB may be asked to do many different things, including these:

☐ Look up and instantiate objects on remote machines

☐ Marshall parameters from one programming language (such as C++) to another language (such as Java)

☐ Handle security across your machine's local boundary

☐ Retrieve and publish metadata on objects on the local system for another ORB

☐ Invoke methods on a remote object using static method invocation described by a downloaded stub

☐ Invoke methods on a remote object using dynamic method invocation

☐ Auto-start objects that aren't currently up and running

☐ Route callback methods to the appropriate local object that it is managing

The great thing about the ORB is that nearly all the implementation details for all these duties are hidden from the software developer. Simply by providing the appropriate "hooks" in your code to initialize the ORB and register your application with the ORB, you open your application to an entire galaxy of distributed objects.

14

Using CORBA Server Callbacks

Notice that one of the bullets in the list describing ORB duties mentions the routing of a callback message. A CORBA object can simultaneously act as a client and a server. Although you are probably familiar with the operations performed by a client in a client/server application, you may have never built a piece of software that acts as both a client and a server! A CORBA application can register callback methods with an ORB so that these methods are called when a remote object sees fit. In this situation, your client application suddenly begins to act like a server being manipulated from a remote location. The ability to perform callbacks on remote objects allows extremely powerful applications to be built using the CORBA infrastructure.

To help you visualize a simple use of server callbacks, imagine that you built a CORBA digital clock to float on your desktop (similar in appearance to the infamous XWindows clock or the Clock application included with Microsoft Windows). This clock is much more capable, however, because it is interfaced to an official atomic clock run by the U.S. government guaranteed to be absolutely correct. Fortunately for us, this "official" clock has exposed its functionality using CORBA interfaces. You've spent a little time laying out your Java GUI and now want to get your clock going by forcing the second hand to tick each time a second goes by. Without server callbacks, you would have to run a separate thread within your application that continually polls the "ClockServer" and waits for a new second to occur. When that happens, you can tick the second hand forward by one second. This solution requires you to write a lot of extra code and probably suffers from poor performance, but there is no other way for the ClockServer to notify you of an event.

Using a CORBA callback, however, you can register an interface supported by your Clock object. This interface may contain a method named Tick() that updates the GUI each time it is called. If this interface is registered with the ClockServer ORB, each time a new second rolls over, the ClockServer can iterate through its list of registered servers and call each one's Tick() method. This is a much more elegant way to turn your client into a server and is fully supported by most CORBA 2.0 ORBs including Joe, OrbixWeb, and VisiBroker for Java.

How an ORB Works

At its most basic, an ORB is essentially responsible for managing a group of software objects. As you have learned, the code behind these objects can be written in C++, Ada, Java, Smalltalk, or even COBOL. The magical unifying property that all these objects have in common is that they are described using a separate language known as IDL. (IDL is discussed

14

in greater detail later in this lesson in "Object Description Using IDL.") You run the IDL description through an IDL compiler, which then produces a set of stub and skeleton files used to describe that object in the language of your choice. For example, if you want to build your objects in Java, you use an IDL-to-Java compiler on your IDL file. (These IDL compilers are included with the ORB when you purchase it.) The *stub files* are used on the client as placeholders for the remote object to be instantiated. The *skeleton files* are produced for you to fill in the appropriate code to make the object complete (again, more on this later in this lesson).

Many ORBs include an *Interface Repository* that acts as a library for all IDL interfaces managed by the ORB. The Interface Repository can be queried using the ORB's Dynamic Invocation Interface (DII) so that objects can be built dynamically at runtime. ORBs allow both static object invocations (through the use of stubs) or dynamic invocations (through the use of the DII). The Basic Object Adapter (BOA) is included with all ORBs and is responsible for instantiating, tracking, and assigning IDs to objects. Because the BOA is part of the CORBA specification, at a minimum, the BOA must be supported by an ORB. Some manufacturers include their own object adapters which extend the BOA and provide the developer with other useful features such as load balancing.

The State of the ORB Market

The CORBA 2.0 specification, finalized in 1994, allows ORBs from different vendors to interoperate using IIOP. IIOP was an absolutely necessary extension to the base CORBA technology. Without IIOP, CORBA development was possible only on a project-by-project basis; an entire object web would have been impossible to build. Although clusters of different vendor's ORBs may have been available on the Web, you have been forced to have the necessary ORB installed on your client machine so that it could communicate with a particular vendor's server ORB. The current state of the CORBA 2.0 ORB market allows a Visigenic ORB on a client to connect to a Digital ORB on a server. By the same token, a Digital ORB client can connect to a Sun Joe ORB server. All this interoperability gained by IIOP allows you, the software developer, to choose the best ORB for the job. As you see in the next section, the Visigenic VisiBroker ORB is built into the Netscape Navigator 4.0 browser, which may help simplify your decision-making process.

Currently, ORBs complying to the CORBA 2.0 specification are available from many vendors. All these ORBs limit your choice of operating system platform, programming language, or both, and each ORB does some things a little differently than others. For example, some ORBs may include an Interface Repository; others may not. Newer ORBs may support IIOP; older CORBA 1.0 ORBs may not. Because of the differences in the ORBs on the market, the CORBA developer must make sure that thorough research is done before choosing an ORB for use in application development.

14

Object Description Using IDL

For CORBA to maintain its vendor-neutral and programming-language neutral position, there must be some intermediary between C++ CORBA server code, for example, and a Java CORBA client. This intermediary is IDL. Related methods and properties supported by an underlying object are grouped together into a single interface using IDL. Once the IDL interface is complete, you can compile it into the language of your choice in the form of both stub and skeleton code. IDL compilers are included with all ORBs. For example, a Java/IDL compiler is included with the Visigenic VisiBroker for Java ORB, and a C++/IDL compiler is included with the Visigenic VisiBroker for C++ ORB.

Although this lesson is not intended to be an intensive tutorial on IDL, suffice it to say that IDL is much easier to work with than a standard object-oriented programming language such as C++ or Java. This is because IDL cannot be used to specify actual implementation of classes or the methods within them. Instead, IDL is used only to describe the *interface* to the underlying objects. This section provides you with enough of an IDL overview so that you will be familiar with the language and can understand the examples presented later in the lesson. For a more thorough presentation on IDL, visit the OMG Web site at http://www.omg.org.

Just as properties and methods are grouped together into related classes in Java, IDL groups these items in *modules*. You can define one or more *interfaces* in each IDL module. Listing 14.1 shows a simple IDL module named TheModule that contains a basic interface named TheInterface. This interface contains a single variable (TheVariable, of course) defined to be an integer value.

Listing 14.1. The simplest IDL module possible.

```
Module TheModule
{
    interface TheInterface
    {
        long TheVariable;
    };
};
```

Compiling this IDL module using an IDL-to-Java compiler (such as Visigenic's idl2java) results in the Java interface presented in Listing 14.2.

14

Listing 14.2. The Java equivalent of the IDL module, TheModule.

```
package TheModule;
public interface TheInterface
{
    public int TheVariable;
}
```

Each Java data type maps to a specific IDL data type as shown in Table 14.1.

Table 14.1. IDL-to-Java data type mappings.

IDL Type	Java Type
boolean	boolean
char	char
wchar	char
octet	byte
string	java.lang.String
wstring	java.lang.String
short	short
unsigned short	short
long	int
unsigned long	int
long long	long
unsigned long long	long
float	float
double	double

Variables are declared in IDL using the IDL data type you want to correspond to the resulting Java data type. IDL also supports user-defined data types and constructed data types (such as enums, structs, unions, sequences, and arrays), which are converted to Java.

Methods can be declared in IDL as well. The method by which parameters are passed to these methods is controlled by the use of the in, out, and inout keywords. The in keyword specifies that the parameter is to be passed from the caller to the object; out specifies that the parameter is to be passed from the object to the caller; and inout specifies that the parameter is to be passed in both directions. Listing 14.3 shows a basic IDL method named TheFunction that passes a parameter subtly named TheParameter.

14

Listing 14.3. A simple IDL interface with a method.

```
Module TheModule
{
    interface TheInterface
    {
        void TheFunction(in long TheParameter);
    };
};
```

IDL supports many more advanced features such as interface inheritance, exception handling, and typedefs. For the examples you will be building in this chapter, however, a basic knowledge of IDL is sufficient.

Taking Advantage of CORBAServices

CORBAServices are specific categories of system-level services currently being described and finalized by the OMG. Table 14.2 shows the 16 services currently standardized by the OMG with a brief description of each. Note that no ORB supports all these services. In fact, many ORBs support none of them! At the time this book went to press, most ORB vendors were simply trying to comply with the base CORBA 2.0 specification and also trying to add Java capabilities to their products. As time progresses and (of course) the amount of money involved becomes larger, shrink-wrapped CORBA versions of each of these services will begin to appear on the market.

Table 14.2. A description of CORBAServices.

Service	Description
Security	Framework for distributed object security
Transaction	Two-phase commit transaction service
Trader	Queryable object capabilities publication service
Time	Distributed time-synchronization service
Startup	Service to allow auto-start of requests
Properties	Global distributed properties service
Query	Query service based on SQL3 and the Object Query Language
Licensing	Distributed software license management
Concurrency Control	Service that manages locks across objects
Relationship	Service to dynamically build object associations
Externalization	Service that supports streaming of data between components

Service	Description
Event	An event alerter for registered objects
Naming	Service that allows object location through naming
Life Cycle	Service that manages the life cycle of objects
Persistence	Service that stores components persistently on OODBS, RDBMS, and file systems
Collection	Service that allows objects to interface to collections

All these services are currently under development and will at some point be provided in conjunction with an ORB or sold as a stand-alone product. For example, Visigenic currently offers the naming and event services as separate products from its VisiBroker ORB.

Why Use Java with CORBA?

If you didn't know it before purchasing this book, you know by now that Java allows the software developer to quickly build applications that were previously thought impossible or that required a huge programming effort. Two features—the Java virtual machine and the ability to download code on the fly—allow you to build platform-independent, object-oriented, dynamic applications using a wonderful language. If you have been given the task to build applets for use within a Web page, Java is obviously the language of choice.

However, CORBA was around long before Java; many CORBA products are designed for use with other languages, notably C++. Therefore, your manager may ask you at some point: "Why should we use Java on this CORBA project?" It turns out that Java is an almost ideal language for use in CORBA development, which is why interest in CORBA has grown significantly since the introduction of Java. Java allows pieces of CORBA applications to be downloaded as the user sees fit, eliminating the need to update application installations. And as you now know, IDL maps very well to the Java language—particularly the notion of using interfaces to describe an object's capabilities (something built into the base Java language). Because the Java language is fully object-oriented, CORBA objects can be instantiated and used very simply, as you see later in this lesson. Finally, Java's built-in garbage collection and its capability to perform tasks in multiple threads make CORBA development much, much simpler than corresponding CORBA programs written in C++. On top of all of these advantages, you get platform independence, which means that you can write an industrial-strength, multitiered, object-oriented application and then tell your boss it can run on any platform in your organization! CORBA's designers are no doubt thrilled at both the design and ensuing success of the Java programming language because, in the long run, CORBA itself will benefit greatly from it.

14

Selecting a Java ORB

Most ORBs were originally designed to be used with the C++ programming language because it was (until the birth of Java) the object-oriented programming language of choice for most developers. ORBs are also available for Ada, Smalltalk, and COBOL. Currently, only three vendors sell Java ORBs: Sun Microsystems' Joe, Iona Technologies' OrbixWeb, and Visigenic's VisiBroker for Java.

NOTE

> Both OrbixWeb and VisiBroker are explained in greater detail later in this lesson; some examples using the VisiBroker ORB are also provided.

Although Joe is a very capable Java ORB, it still requires all server code to be written in C++, and its server runs only on the Solaris operating system at the time of this writing. Joe also lacks some of the more advanced (but necessary) features that both OrbixWeb and VisiBroker offer (such as dynamic method invocations and an Interface Repository). At the time this book goes to press, it appears that Visigenic is beginning to gain momentum with its ORB after announcing licensing deals with Oracle, Netscape, and Novell, to name a few. The fact that the Visigenic VisiBroker for Java ORB is bundled with the Netscape Navigator 4.0 browser makes it an easy choice for use as a client-side ORB in Web applications.

Web Browser Support for CORBA

As just mentioned, the Netscape Navigator 4.0 browser includes an embedded version of the Visigenic VisiBroker for Java ORB. This arrangement allows CORBA applet developers to simply place their applets and CORBA stub class files on the Web server. All remaining Java ORB files are already located on the client, greatly reducing download time and therefore increasing performance.

You can use the OrbixWeb ORB, for example, and allow its required Java class files to be downloaded dynamically with your applet. The total size of the OrbixWeb Java distribution is around 100 K. Also remember that with Java 1.1, all necessary class files can be packaged together into a JAR file and stored locally on the client's file system. (Microsoft Internet Explorer also supports the use of CAB file download, similar in concept to the Java 1.1 JAR file.)

An Evaluation of Java Object Request Brokers

This section compares the two most popular Java ORBs on the market: Visigenic VisiBroker for Java and Iona Technologies' OrbixWeb. Both of these ORBs allow client-side and server-side CORBA objects to be built in Java, and both ORBs are CORBA 2.0-compliant. Following this brief study, you will build a simple CORBA-based Java application using both ORBs.

Visigenic VisiBroker for Java

The first Java ORB to examine is the Visigenic VisiBroker for Java. Other related CORBA products from Visigenic are also discussed here. At press time, the latest version of Visigenic VisiBroker is 3.0, which adds support for Visigenic's Caffeine technology (explained later in this section), more scalability features such as multithreaded management and server connection management, IIOP over SSL (the Secure Sockets Layer), and the Object Database Activator for integration with popular object databases. The Visigenic VisiBroker product comes in both C++ and Java versions and is supported on a variety of computing platforms including Windows NT, Solaris, IRIX, and other UNIX variants.

Perhaps the most exciting feature of the VisiBroker ORB is its availability. Many leading software companies (including Netscape, Oracle, and Novell) have already licensed VisiBroker so that they can embed it in their products. For example, Netscape is currently shipping VisiBroker with its Navigator 4.0 browser and Enterprise Server 3.0. Novell will be including VisiBroker in upcoming releases of its IntranetWare product line. This wide show of support may make VisiBroker the default choice for many developers working with these products.

VisiBroker supports object instantiation through both a Static Invocation Interface (through the use of stubs) and a Dynamic Invocation Interface (using DII). An Interface Repository (IR) complete with an object interface to itself is included for storage and retrieval of interfaces from structured storage. Visigenic's SmartAgent technology adds important scalability capabilities to VisiBroker, and the Visigenic Gatekeeper can be used as an IIOP proxy (an important feature for Java applet developers). Finally, the Web Naming feature allows objects to be referenced using standard Uniform Resource Locators (URLs), a feature not found in any other ORB.

Notable Product Features

One of the reasons the VisiBroker product has been so successful is its scalable and fault-tolerant SmartAgent technology. SmartAgent, also known as osagent after the name of the agent's executable, is a service that runs "within" the ORB. A SmartAgent is responsible for locating, instantiating, and managing objects as well as cooperating with other SmartAgents running on remote machines to locate objects. If more than one SmartAgent is running on a network, and one SmartAgent becomes unavailable, all the objects it is managing are

14

"handed off" to another SmartAgent on another machine. This feature provides important fault tolerance required by mission-critical distributed applications. Additional fault-tolerant features can be taken advantage of by starting copies of an object on multiple hosts. If a connection is lost between a client and an object implementation, the connection is routed to another instance of that object on another server. All this connectivity is transparent to the user.

The IIOP Gatekeeper included with VisiBroker acts as an IIOP proxy for Java applets running within Web browsers. As an added convenience during development, the Gatekeeper can also act as an HTTP Web server, eliminating the need to run a standard Web server on your local development machine. (The server is implemented in Java and is not recommended for production use in high-traffic environments.) As you know, for security reasons, Java applets are limited to communicating only with the server from which they are retrieved. CORBA applications, however, must often communicate with a variety of object servers for performance concerns or other reasons. The purpose of the Gatekeeper is to give the client Web browser the appearance of connecting to its originating server while transparently rerouting communications to the appropriate CORBA server. The Gatekeeper approach has its disadvantages, however, particularly in the area of security. For this reason, although Netscape licensed the VisiBroker ORB for use within Netscape Navigator 4.0, it disabled the Gatekeeper functionality for applets within the Navigator browser. Future versions of the browser plan to add support for encryption and verification in order to make Gatekeeper more palatable from a security standpoint.

The Web-naming service allows a Uniform Resource Locator (URL) to be associated with a CORBA object. This service is extremely important; it (or one like it) may eventually become a CORBA standard. This service is provided because many ORBs do not supply the CORBA naming service. Consequently, objects are accessed through these ORBs using proprietary naming techniques that make it difficult for one vendor's ORB to access an object managed by another vendor's ORB. By using a common URL, these objects can be referenced in a standard manner.

Visigenic's Caffeine technology includes the Web-naming service, the java2iiop tool, and the java2idl compiler. By using the java2iiop tool, you can generate IIOP-compliant stubs and skeletons directly from Java code without having to write IDL code in between. The java2idl compiler builds IDL directly from existing Java code. Caffeine has been licensed by Netscape and is included with VisiBroker for Java as well as the Netscape Enterprise Server 3.0.

CORBAServices Support

As discussed earlier in this lesson in "Taking Advantage of CORBAServices," CORBAServices are important services defined by the OMG but are not required to be part of a CORBA-compliant ORB. However, some of these services (such as the transaction and naming services) are very important to developers building enterprise-class applications. Visigenic markets implementations of several of the CORBAServices to complete its CORBA product line. (Note that these services are sold separately from the VisiBroker ORB.) Some of these services are currently available for sale; others are under development and will be available in the near future. Table 14.3 shows the services Visigenic plans to support in the near future and their expected release dates.

Table 14.3. CORBAServices supported by Visigenic.

Service	Availability
Event	Available
Naming	Available
Trader	Fourth Quarter 1997

In addition to these three CORBAServices, Visigenic also will offer (in the first quarter of 1998) their integration service for integration into transaction processing environments, a messaging service for asynchronous communications between objects, and a data access service for providing ODBC and JDBC database access capabilities.

VisiBroker also allows developers to choose between a thread-per-session threading model and a thread-pool model for improving the performance and stability of server applications. In all, VisiBroker is an extremely capable Java ORB that fully conforms to the CORBA 2.0 specification. A number of useful services may also be purchased separately from Visigenic to fulfill specifications for many of the defined CORBAServices. The fact that VisiBroker is included for free with the Netscape browsers and servers may make it the ORB of choice for enterprise CORBA development.

The next section describes the OrbixWeb ORB; you will see that Iona supports several other useful features not currently supported by Visigenic.

Iona Technologies' OrbixWeb

OrbixWeb is the name of the Java ORB from Iona Technologies. Iona has developed a full range of CORBA 2.0-compliant ORBs that allow development in C++, Java, Ada95, Smalltalk, and Microsoft OLE-compliant languages such as Visual Basic, PowerBuilder, and Delphi. The Iona Orbix ORB is supported on over 15 operating systems including Windows 95/NT, Solaris, HP/UX, AIX, IRIX, Digital UNIX, UnixWare, SCO, MVS, and (interestingly enough) several real-time operating systems such as pSOS, VxWorks, and QNX. In July 1993, Iona gained recognition for being the first vendor to fully support the OMG's CORBA specification on Windows NT, Solaris, and IRIX. Other notable achievements by Iona include the development of the first ORB to run under Windows 3.1, the signing of licensing agreements with Sun and SGI, and the formation of strategic partnerships with Apple and IBM to further CORBA technology.

14

Notable Product Features

The OrbixWeb ORB is the Java version of the Iona Technologies Orbix ORB. This ORB is CORBA 2.0-compliant, which means that it can be addressed by any other CORBA 2.0-compliant ORB using IIOP. Orbix ORBs can also communicate using the proprietary Orbix protocol that was used before the OMG standardized on IIOP. The Orbix architecture is designed in an open manner so that third-party developers can add protocol support by extending the base Orbix API.

Orbix allows developers to access CORBA objects through the standard static interface using stubs. As does VisiBroker, Orbix supports the Dynamic Invocation Interface (DII) for constructing a request manually and then invoking it from a client. In addition to the DII, Orbix goes a step further by supporting what is called the Dynamic Skeleton Interface (DSI). The DSI is the server-side equivalent of the DII. In other words, a server object can be dynamically constructed on the fly using the DSI. According to Iona, the purpose behind the creation of the DSI was to aid programmers in the creation of gateways for interfacing the server to another CORBA system or even to a non-CORBA system.

OrbixWeb supports an Implementation Repository for linking a server's name with the specific Java class that implements the server. OrbixWeb also supports an auto-start feature, with which objects are dynamically loaded when they are referenced if they haven't already been loaded.

CORBAServices Support

With the release of the OrbixNames service, Iona fully supports the OMG's naming specification. As a fully compliant CORBAService, OrbixNames enables the association of meaningful names with object references within contexts. In addition, the OMG's CORBA events service is fully supported with the OrbixTalk product. Iona also sells a transaction service named Orbix Object Transaction Service (OTS), which complies with the OMG's transaction specification. This service allows the creation of applications with transaction management features to ensure the integrity of data being used by your CORBA applications. As a leader in the CORBA field, Iona is expected to continue to roll out additional CORBAServices as the market demands them. For now, Iona's support of the naming, transaction, and events services, combined with the company's wide language and operating platform support, allows the Iona Orbix product line to fulfill the needs of professional CORBA developers.

If you are still curious about CORBA after reading this lesson, go to either the Iona site (www.iona.com) or the Visigenic site (www.visigenic.com) and download the latest versions of their Java ORBs. (Free trial versions are available for download from both of these sites.)

A Basic Java/CORBA Application

In this section, you will build a basic CORBA application in Java that demonstrates the following concepts:

- ☐ Interface declaration in IDL
- ☐ ORB interoperability using IIOP
- ☐ Commercially popular Java ORBs
- ☐ CORBA Interface Repositories
- ☐ CORBA stubs and skeletons

The application to be constructed is a little more complicated than the basic "Hello, world!" application commonly demonstrated, but is still simple enough to keep from overwhelming you. This application, CapitalQuery, allows the user to enter a U.S. state's abbreviation and then determines that state's capital. A server object is instantiated and used to look up the appropriate capital. For example, if the user enters CA, the capital of California, Sacramento, is returned.

For the simple CapitalQuery application, you must follow several basic steps to build your CORBA objects. These same steps are required in every Java CORBA application that uses any ORB, no matter how simple or complex the application is. Here are the necessary steps:

1. Set up the development/runtime environment by modifying the PATH and by setting several environment variables.
2. Write a specification for each object using IDL.
3. Compile the IDL code to produce client stub code and server skeleton code.
4. Write the client application code.
5. Write the server object code.
6. Compile the client and server code.
7. Start the server.
8. Run the client application.

The following sections follow these steps using both the Visigenic VisiBroker for Java ORB and the Iona Technologies OrbixWeb ORB. After these two examples, you will take advantage of IIOP and interchange these two ORBs to show CORBA 2.0's interoperability features.

Building CapitalQuery Using VisiBroker

The first step to be completed before using VisiBroker is to set up your development environment properly. Under Windows 95/NT, this process involves adding the VisiBroker bin directory to your path and setting two additional environment variables: VBROKER_ADM and

14

CLASSPATH. Set the `VBROKER_ADM` environment variable equal to the location of the `adm` directory in the main VisiBroker installation directory. Then locate the `classes` directory in the main VisiBroker installation directory and add this directory name to the `CLASSPATH` environment variable. You can make these modifications by editing the `AUTOEXEC.BAT` file under Windows 95/NT. Under Windows NT, you can make these modifications more easily by using the System Control Panel application to modify your environment without rebooting.

Now that the environment is set up for VisiBroker, it is time to define your server object using IDL. For this simple application, you define one method that accepts a string containing the state abbreviation and that returns a string containing the state capital city's name. Listing 14.4 shows this simple IDL file, named `Query.IDL`.

Listing 14.4. The `Capital` interface in `Query.IDL`.

```
module Query
{
    interface Capital
    {
        string GetCapital(in string State);
    };
};
```

This exact interface can be reused regardless of which ORB or programming language you use because it is defined in IDL. For example, you can reuse the `Query.IDL` file if you rewrite this application using the OrbixWeb ORB. For now, the next step to be taken is to compile the IDL source code to produce both Java client stub code and server skeleton code. You can compile this source code using the Visigenic `idl2java` compiler. Simply execute the following command at a command prompt:

```
idl2java Query.IDL
```

When this command is executed, eight Java files are created within a `Query` subdirectory. These eight files are `Capital.java`, `CapitalHolder.java`, `CapitalHelper.java`, `_st_Capital.java`, `_sk_Capital.java`, `CapitalOperations.java`, `_tie_Capital.java`, and `_example_Capital.java`.

NOTE

The `Query` subdirectory is created because you defined the `Capital` interface within a module named `Query`. Recall from earlier discussions that an IDL module is the equivalent of a Java package. Therefore, all Java files are located within a directory named `Query`, which is how Java differentiates between packages.

14

As you may have guessed, the Capital.java file contains the Java version of the Capital interface declaration, but what do the other Java classes do? The CapitalHolder.java file contains a holder class used when passing parameters; the CapitalHelper class defines various utility functions. The _st_Capital class defines the client stub; the _sk_Capital class defines the server skeleton class. The CapitalOperations and _tie_Capital classes are used to implement a tie mechanism (a VisiBroker feature designed to allow the implementation class to inherit from a class other than the skeleton class). You do not use these classes directly within this example. Finally, the _example_Capital file contains a sample server object that can be extended to build the server application. Listing 14.5 shows the contents of the Capital.java file, complete with HTML source code comments generated by the idl2java tool.

Listing 14.5. The contents of the Capital.java file.

```
package Query;
/**
<p>
<ul>
<li> <b>Java Class</b> Query.Capital
<li> <b>Source File</b> Query/Capital.java
<li> <b>IDL Source File</b> Query.IDL
<li> <b>IDL Absolute Name</b> ::Query::Capital
<li> <b>Repository Identifier</b> IDL;Query/Capital:1.0
</ul>
<b>IDL definition:</h>
<pre>
    interface Capital {
      string GetCapital(
        in string State
      );
    };
</pre>
</p>
*/
public interface Capital extends org.omg.CORBA.Object {
  /**
  <p>
  Operation: <b>::Query::Capital::GetCapital</b>.
  <pre>
    string GetCapital(
      in string State
    );
  </pre>
  </p>
  */
  public java.lang.String GetCapital(
    java.lang.String State
  );
}
```

14

As you can see, this file contains a lot of comments and one Java interface, `Capital`, that defines one Java method, `GetCapital()`. The eight Java classes created by the IDL compiler give us the framework (in the form of helper classes, a stub, a skeleton, and an interface) to construct our own client/server CORBA application in Java. The next step is to create a client application that takes a command-line argument, instantiates a `Capital` object from the server, and calls its `GetCapital()` method to determine the state capital.

Creating the Client Application

If your client application is to request the VisiBroker ORB to retrieve an object from a server, you must first initialize the ORB in code and then request an object from the server by name. Once you have that object, you write standard Java code to call the `GetCapital()` method and print out the state capital's name. Listing 14.6 shows the code used to do all these operations.

Listing 14.6. The `Client` class.

```
public class Client {

   public static void main(String args[]) {
    try {
      // Initialize the ORB.
      org.omg.CORBA.ORB orb = org.omg.CORBA.ORB.init();
      // Locate a Capital object.
      Query.Capital capQuery= Query.CapitalHelper.bind(orb, "CapitalQuery");

      if (args.length < 1)
      {
          System.out.println("Usage:  Client <State Abbreviation>");
      }
      else
      {
          String state = args[0];
          // Query to determine the state capital.
          String City = capQuery.GetCapital(state);
          System.out.println("The capital is " + City + ".");
      }
    }
    catch(org.omg.CORBA.SystemException e) {
      System.err.println(e);
    }
  }
}
```

There are three key lines of code in the `Client` class. The first key line of code is Line 6, where the `org.omg.CORBA.ORB.init()` method is called to initialize the ORB. This statement causes the application to register itself with the locally running ORB. If this ORB cannot be located, an error message results, and the application exits. If the ORB is initialized, a `Query.Capital` interface is retrieved by calling the second key statement: `CapitalHelper` class' `bind()`

method. When this method is called, a `CapitalQuery` object is retrieved from the server ORB. Once again, if this object cannot be retrieved from the server, a `SystemException` is thrown with an error message, and the application exits. Once the `Capital` interface is retrieved, it is an elementary step to call the third key statement (the `GetCapital()` method) in order to retrieve a state capital and print the name out.

Creating the Server Application

Now that the client application is created, you have to create a corresponding server application that registers a `CapitalQuery` object with the server ORB. This new object extends the created skeleton class and also implements the `Capital` interface. Therefore, you need two new classes for the server: one to define the server object and implement the `Capital` interface and another to register this object with the server ORB. Listing 14.7 shows the `Server` class, which registers the `CapitalQuery` object with the ORB. Listing 14.8 shows the `CapitalQuery` class, which implements the interface and, therefore, the `GetCapital()` method.

Listing 14.7. The `Server` class.

```
public class Server {
  public static void main(String[] args) {
    try {
      // Initialize the ORB.
      org.omg.CORBA.ORB orb = org.omg.CORBA.ORB.init();

      // Initialize the BOA.
      org.omg.CORBA.BOA boa = orb.BOA_init();

      // Create the CapitalQuery.
      CapitalQuery serverQuery = new CapitalQuery("CapitalQuery");

      // Export the newly created object.
      boa.obj_is_ready(serverQuery);
      System.out.println(serverQuery + " is ready.");

      // Wait for incoming requests
      boa.impl_is_ready();
    }
    catch(org.omg.CORBA.SystemException e) {
      System.err.println(e);
    }
  }
}.
```

14

Listing 14.8. The `CapitalQuery` **class.**

```
import java.util.*;

class CapitalQuery extends Query._sk_Capital {

  String[][] StateCapitals =
      {{"AL","LA","MS","GA","FL","TN","SC","NC","VA","KY","TX"},
       {"Montgomery","Baton Rouge","Jackson","Atlanta","Tallahassee",
       "Nashville","Columbia","Raleigh","Richmond","Frankfurt","Austin"}};

  CapitalQuery(String name) {
    super(name);
  }

  public java.lang.String GetCapital(java.lang.String State)
  {
    String tempString, Name;

    Name = "not in the database!";
    for(int i=0; i < 10; i++)
    {
        tempString = StateCapitals[0][i];
        if (tempString.equals(State))
        {
            Name = StateCapitals[1][i];
            break;
        }
    }
    return Name;
  }
}
```

Now that all the necessary code has been created, all that is left to do is get the Visigenic ORB up and running so that the client and server objects can communicate with each other!

Running the `CapitalQuery` Application

After successfully compiling the `Server.java` and `Client.java` source files, you have three Java class files of your creation (`Server.class`, `Client.class`, and `CapitalQuery.class`) to go along with four class files resulting from the code created for you by the IDL compiler (`Capital.class`, `CapitalHelper.class`, `_st_Capital.class`, and `_sk_Capital.class`). Now you run the VisiBroker ORB runtime, known as SmartAgent or osagent (the name of the executable). Assuming that your path has been set properly, simply type **osagent** at the command prompt to start the VisiBroker ORB running on your machine. Once you do that, start the `Server` application using the VisiBroker Java interpreter, `vbj`. Do this by typing the following command at a command prompt:

```
vbj Server
```

After you enter this command, you see a message stating that the server is ready. To run the `Client` application, open another command window and pass a state abbreviation to the `Client` application using the vbj interpreter, like so:

```
vbj Client FL
```

The following message prints out at the prompt:

```
The capital is Tallahassee!
```

Wow! Although you ran both the client and server on the local machine for simplicity reasons, the server can actually be running under Solaris on a Sun UltraSparc in Tibet. For that matter, the server could have been written in C++, and the client would not have known the difference! To quickly review, here is what just happened:

1. You defined the `Capital` interface in IDL and compiled it using the idl2java compiler to create a set of client and server Java classes.

2. You built a simple `Client` application that made use of the `CapitalHelper` class to retrieve a `Capital` object from the server. You then called this object's `GetCapital()` method to retrieve a state capital city's name.

3. You built a simple `Server` application that initialized the ORB and the Basic Object Adaptor (BOA). Then you instantiated a new `CapitalQuery` object and registered it with the server.

4. You started up the ORB and ran both the client and the server. The client passed the state's abbreviation you gave it and returned a city name that printed out for the user to see.

The Missing Link

If you think about this example a little deeper, questions may start popping up in your head. If you have ever written a client/server application that uses a database connectivity layer (Oracle SQL Net, for example), you will remember that on each client machine you had to set up configuration files that specifically told client applications which server to connect to. This direction was in the form of an IP address, a NetWare file server name, or a NetBUI computer name. After your application looks up this address, messages are sent directly to that server.

Nowhere in the previous example did you tell your client application exactly where to look to pass messages to the ORB on a server. How did the client know where the ORB was? The answer varies from vendor to vendor, but the VisiBroker ORB dynamically locates other ORBs on the local network using a broadcast message. The first ORB to respond to the message that also serves the requested object is used for all further messaging with that object. Once this connection has been established, VisiBroker uses the point-to-point communications of the UDP protocol. Multiple ORBs (or SmartAgents, to use the Visigenic term) can

14

be started on a local network, and each ORB can serve the same objects or different objects. One great feature of VisiBroker is that, should one of these ORBs become unavailable, all object implementations registered with that agent are reregistered with another agent. This takes place without the knowledge of any client applications.

For one SmartAgent running on one local network to connect to another SmartAgent on a separate network, some configuration is required. VisiBroker uses a local file named `agentaddr` that contains several configuration settings, one of which is the environment variable `VBROKER_ADM`. This variable can be set to the IP address of the remote server to which you want to force your local ORB to connect. Note that the `agentaddr` file can contain multiple server addresses.

In the case of Java applets downloaded from a Web server and running within a Web browser client, the rules are somewhat different because of the security restrictions involved with running an applet within a browser. (Recall that a Java applet can connect only to the server from which it was retrieved.) For Java applets, VisiBroker supplies the Gatekeeper application, which can act as both a Web server and a IIOP proxy. The Gatekeeper also supports HTTP tunneling, which allows IIOP to be run "on top of" HTTP for environments in which a firewall prevents everything but HTTP messaging. When using the Gatekeepeer, all standard CORBA capabilities are supported from Web client (the browser) to Web server (HTTP server) except for callbacks when the Gatekeeper uses HTTP tunneling. In that case, callbacks from server to client are not allowed. You use Gatekeeper later in this chapter when you build a Java application using VisiBroker.

The following section builds the same `CapitalQuery` application but adds a graphical user interface and encapsulates the client portion of the application within a Java applet.

Building `CapitalQuery` as a Java Applet

It is entirely possible to access the `Server` portion of the `CapitalQuery` application through a graphical user interface in a Java applet. Currently, the most popular use of Java is to construct applets running within Web pages to query databases, draw charts, or perform multimedia operations without installing a browser plug-in. In this section, you add a simple GUI to the `CapitalQuery` application that allows the user to point and click on a list of state names to retrieve each state's capital.

This application requires a Java-capable Web browser (such as Microsoft Internet Explorer Version 3.0 or later, or Netscape Navigator 3.0 or later). Note that this application does not require a Java 1.1-compliant browser such as Netscape Navigator 4.0. The VisiBroker classes are Java 1.0 classes and can be downloaded dynamically to your browser if you are connecting from a remote machine. On the server (which can be the same machine as your development machine), you must have installed the Gatekeeper software with the VisiBroker ORB. A separate HTTP server is not a requirement. However, if you plan to use the Gatekeeper as a Web server, you must connect to it through port 15000 on your machine. Standard Web servers always operate on port 80, the default port used when no other port is given to your browser. To access the Gatekeeper Web server through port 15000, use the following syntax to load the page sample.html from www.myserver.com:

```
http://www.myserver.com:15000/sample.html
```

Listing 14.9 shows the code for the client application: ClientApplet.java. All stubs, skeletons, and server code from the previous Java application example remain the same.

Listing 14.9. The ClientApplet Java class.

```
/*
    A basic extension of the java.applet.Applet class
 */

import java.awt.*;
import java.applet.*;

public class ClientApplet extends Applet
{
    Query_Capital capQuery;

    public void init() {
        super.init();

        setLayout(null);
        addNotify();
        resize(412,110);
        StateList = new java.awt.Choice();
        StateList.addItem("AL");
        StateList.addItem("LA");
        StateList.addItem("MS");
        StateList.addItem("GA");
        StateList.addItem("FL");
        StateList.addItem("TN");
        StateList.addItem("SC");
        StateList.addItem("NC");
        StateList.addItem("VA");
        StateList.addItem("KY");
        StateList.addItem("TX");
        add(StateList);
        StateList.reshape(12,12,88,21);
        QueryButton = new java.awt.Button("Query");
        QueryButton.reshape(12,48,85,30);
        add(QueryButton);
        StaticLabel = new java.awt.Label("State Capital Is:");
        StaticLabel.reshape(120,12,286,24);
        StaticLabel.setFont(new Font("Dialog", Font.PLAIN, 18));
        add(StaticLabel);
        CapitalLabel = new java.awt.Label("?");
        CapitalLabel.reshape(120,48,287,34);
        CapitalLabel.setFont(new Font("Dialog", Font.PLAIN, 20));
```

14

continues

Listing 14.9. continued

```
            add(CapitalLabel);

        try
        {
            // Initialize the ORB (using the Applet).
            org.omg.CORBA.ORB orb = org.omg.CORBA.ORB.init(this);

            // Create the CapitalQuery.
            capQuery= Query.CapitalHelper.bind(orb, "CapitalQuery");
        }
        catch(org.omg.CORBA.SystemException e)
        {
            System.out.println(e);
        }
    }

    void QueryButton_Action(Event event)
    {
        try
        {
            String State = StateList.getSelectedItem();
            String City = capQuery.GetCapital(State);
            CapitalLabel.setText(City);
        }
        catch(org.omg.CORBA.SystemException e)
        {
            System.out.println(e);
        }
    }

    public boolean handleEvent(Event event)
    {
        if (event.target == QueryButton && event.id == Event.ACTION_EVENT)
        {
            QueryButton_Action(event);
            return true;
        }
        return super.handleEvent(event);
    }

    java.awt.Choice StateList;
    java.awt.Button QueryButton;
    java.awt.Label StaticLabel;
    java.awt.Label CapitalLabel;
}
```

The new ClientApplet applet has the advantage of using a graphical user interface to allow
the user to select state abbreviations from a list box. When the user has selected the desired

state, he or she can click the Query button to call the getCapital() method on the server-based Capital object. In the previous Java application, recall that the user could enter a state abbreviation only at the command line to query the server. What is most interesting for the CORBA developer, however, is that the ORB is initialized and the server object is instantiated in only two lines of code. As before, you can retrieve an org.omg.CORBA.ORB object using the init() method. However, this time you pass the this variable to pass the init() method a Java applet class. This action opens a connection to the Gatekeeper running on the server from which this applet was retrieved. Once this connection has been made and the ORB has been initialized, the next line of code binds the CapitalQuery server object to the local capQuery variable. Run the Server application using the vbj interpreter included with VisiBroker using the following command:

```
vbj Server
```

Running the Applet

Compile the ClientApplet.java file to produce a standard Java 1.0-compliant class file that can be loaded in any Java Web browser. For the applet to connect to the server, the Gatekeeper as well as the SmartAgent must also be running on the server. Start the SmartAgent as you did earlier when you ran the Java application, and then start Gatekeeper by executing the gatekeeper command at the command prompt. Now that the SmartAgent, Server application, and Gatekeeper are all running on your server, load the ClientApplet.html file in the appletviewer tool to verify that it works. Figure 14.1 shows the ClientApplet applet running in the appletviewer.

Figure 14.1.

The ClientApplet *Java applet.*

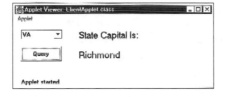

Being able to dynamically download CORBA clients using Java applets is perhaps the single biggest reason for the tremendous amount of new interest in CORBA development. No longer do application developers have to worry about installing and licensing ORBs to place on individual client machines. Instead, client applications can be built in an operating system-independent manner using a great language (Java) and can connect to platform-independent and language-independent servers using CORBA.

The following sections address two "competitors" to CORBA (DCOM and Java RMI) and compares their strengths and weaknesses to CORBA 2.0.

14

Comparing DCOM to CORBA

Currently, Microsoft includes their own ORB with their Microsoft Internet Explorer browser. However the Microsoft ORB is a Distributed Component Object Model (DCOM) ORB and not a CORBA ORB. DCOM is Microsoft's competing distributed objects strategy, currently available in Microsoft Windows NT 4.0 and later and Windows 98. A detailed technical comparison of DCOM and CORBA could literally fill an entire book and is not appropriate here, but you should know a little about your alternatives to CORBA. Although DCOM and CORBA have some things in common, some basic differences between the technologies make CORBA a much better choice at the current time.

To begin with, CORBA and DCOM are both designed to do essentially the same thing: provide an infrastructure for the interoperability of distributed objects across a network. The Java developer can use Java to build both CORBA and DCOM applications. Using Microsoft's Visual J++ Java compiler, the developer can use Java to both build DCOM objects and also access DCOM objects created in other programming languages. (Shameless plug: For more information on Visual J++, see *Visual J++ Unleashed*, published by Sams Publishing.) However, it requires a great deal more configuration and tinkering with the system to get a Java DCOM application working as opposed to a Java CORBA application. In addition, Java CORBA applications are 100 percent pure Java and can run on any Java virtual machine on any platform. Java DCOM applications, on the other hand, work only with Microsoft Internet Explorer 3.0 (or later) on the 32-bit Microsoft Windows platforms.

At a finer level of detail, the CORBA and DCOM object models differ significantly. Although CORBA objects can be persistent in between connections, DCOM objects are pointers to defined DCOM interfaces and disappear once the connection is broken. Because the DCOM communications model is not standardized or open, there is currently zero interoperability with DCOM and CORBA. In fact, the entire DCOM standard is closed at the current time, although Microsoft is submitting DCOM to several standards committees for inclusion in a standards-making process. Unlike Java/CORBA, DCOM does not support the downloading of dynamic stubs. DCOM also does not scale nearly as well as CORBA. Many CORBA ORBs support connection pooling, configurable threading models, and load balancing as well as automatic startup of referenced objects. These features—in addition to the ability to run CORBA on extremely capable hardware platforms (Sun UltraSparc and Tandem computers for example)—allow CORBA applications to scale well beyond department-level client/server applications.

CORBA is also several steps ahead of DCOM in the area of supported services. As you learned earlier in this lesson in the section titled "Taking Advantage of CORBAServices," CORBA defines a number of system-level services you can use and access in an object-oriented manner. DCOM services basically consist of the Windows NT operating system services (such as security) and are not extensible by outside software vendors because DCOM is not an open standard. The fact that very little code currently exists that makes use of DCOM tilts the playing field in favor of CORBA. Microsoft is making a huge effort to extend DCOM so that it can better compete with other object technologies, particularly CORBA, because the future of Web application development hangs in the balance. Microsoft has promoted the concept of a DCOM-to-CORBA bridge with all client ORBs using DCOM and the (fewer) back-end server ORBs using CORBA. Meanwhile, the OMG stresses the need to build a vendor-neutral, language-neutral architecture that can scale for the future. Microsoft has the advantage of building DCOM into all future versions of its operating systems, but CORBA has the advantage of being a better technology that meshes extremely well with Java. This competition will be played out over the next three to five years before one technology takes a clear lead. In terms of industry support, however, CORBA clearly has a huge lead!

Comparing Java RMI to CORBA

There has been some confusion in the software industry about the benefits of Java RMI versus those of CORBA. Some developers have stated that they see no need for CORBA when they have RMI, but many others have stated just the opposite. If you build very small distributed-object applications in Java, CORBA is undoubtedly overkill. For developers in that class, RMI is sufficient. However, for developers who require reliable, scalable systems that can potentially take advantage of the CORBAServices mentioned earlier in this lesson, CORBA remains the only high-performance, secure, scalable, distributed object solution on the market today.

As does CORBA, Java RMI provides an infrastructure for building distributed-object applications in Java. Unlike CORBA, Java RMI is a "Java-only" solution that uses its own wire protocol to instantiate and use objects located on remote machines. In comparison, the CORBA IIOP protocol was designed so that any CORBA 2.0-compliant ORB can converse with any other CORBA 2.0-compliant ORB, regardless of the vendor or underlying programming language used.

JavaSoft has recently announced that future versions of RMI will support IIOP as a communications protocol, a move that will allow RMI and CORBA to interoperate. When this version of RMI is released, it will essentially become a "poor-man's CORBA." Although it may be free, RMI remains an unscalable, fault-intolerant infrastructure not really suitable for medium-to-large scale application development. Its introduction has caused such confusion in the world of distributed objects that many CORBA-watchers have expressed hopes that it will disappear completely. In their words, while open-systems vendors are spending time pondering the pros and cons of RMI and the existing CORBA standard, Microsoft continues to add message and transaction services to DCOM, improving its capabilities so that it can better compete with CORBA.

14

After reading this lesson, each developer should decide whether he or she requires the "high-end" features supported by CORBA. Will the application use any legacy code (C, C++, COBOL, and so on)? Is transaction support required? Once you think through these requirements, the proper decision will probably be self-evident.

Summary

CORBA is the only truly complete distributed-object technology available to the Java developer today. You have seen that you can build client/server CORBA applications in Java using several different commercially available ORBs such as the Visigenic VisiBroker for Java and the Iona Technologies OrbixWeb ORBs. The foundation for CORBA is the Object Request Broker (ORB), which acts as a software bus that allows the interaction of distributed objects on disparate platforms. In addition to the ORB, CORBA also defines a set of services known as CORBAServices that can be optionally supported by the ORB for extended functionality. The Interface Definition Language (IDL) is used to describe interfaces to CORBA objects and can be compiled for any CORBA programming language using an IDL compiler. Because IDL is only an object description language, it is quite simple in syntax.

You saw that CORBA objects can be created in Java using a number of different ORBs; this lesson focused on the Visigenic VisiBroker and Iona OrbixWeb ORBs. You also learned that these two ORBs can interoperate and exchange objects without skipping a beat by using IIOP. For more information on the CORBA standard as it progresses, visit the OMG Web site at http://www.omg.org.

Q&A

Q Does Microsoft plan to support CORBA in upcoming releases of their products?

A Microsoft is, at the time of this writing, totally committed to DCOM and is working with third-party vendors to port DCOM to other operating systems. In cases where CORBA is necessary, Microsoft has recommended the use of DCOM on the client and a DCOM-to-CORBA bridge on the server, thus ensuring the continuing use of their operating systems on the client and server.

Q Which Java development tools support CORBA development?

A At the time of this writing (Fall, 1997), Borland is shipping the Jbuilder Client/
Server Suite, which includes the Visigenic VisiBroker For Java ORB. Netscape also
includes the VisiBroker For Java ORB with its client (Communicator 4.0) and
server (Enterprise Server 3.0) software. Of course, because all of the ORBs mentioned in this chapter are "Pure Java," they can be used with all popular commercial Java development tools.

Q Are there any Java/CORBA applets available for demonstration on the Web?

A Yes. Visit the OMG Web site for an up-to-date listing of Web demos. Also, the
CORBANet demo site provides an excellent demo of CORBA/IIOP by allowing
the user to select which client and server ORBs will be used to run a room-booking
system. Visit this site at `http:// corbanet.dstc.edu.au/`.

14

WEEK

3

15

16

17

18

19

20

21

At a Glance

☐ Introduction to the Java Web Server and Servlets
  Discover the Java Web Server
  Learn about servlets and the Servlet API
  Look at a sample servlet called `HelloWorldServlet`
☐ Programming with the Java Servlet Development Kit
  Examine the servlet life cycle
  Discover the two basic types of servlets
  Create a servlet
☐ Working with Java Archives
  Use the JAR utility to create and manipulate JAR files
  Package Beans for distribution using the JAR utility

☐ Introduction to Digital Security and the Java Security API

Cryptography and two of the main types of encryption: conventional encryption and public-key encryption

The Java Security API and what it has to offer Java programs

☐ Creating Signed Java Objects

Use the `javakey` security tool

Sign JAR files with `javakey`

☐ Things You Can't Do in Java: Using the Java Native Interface

Generate native headers with `javah`

Map Java data types

Access Java information from native code

☐ Things to Come in Java 1.2

Java core enhancements

Standard Java extensions

Other Java technologies, such as PersonalJava, EmbeddedJava, and JavaBeans migration tools

Day 15

Introduction to the Java Web Server and Servlets

by Jerry Ablan

Until now, you probably thought Java was good only for writing applets and applications that run locally. JDBC allows remote computing to some degree— that is, it allows access to databases that may reside on a remote server—but everything is running at the client. There is really no Java running at the server to provide a service for you. With the introduction of the Java Web Server and servlets, creating remotely executed Java objects is now possible. The best part is that creating servlets is as easy as creating applets!

Today you'll do these things:

- ☐ Discover the Java Web Server
- ☐ Learn about servlets and the Servlet API
- ☐ Look at a sample servlet called `HelloWorldServlet`

The Java Web Server

You're probably thinking that there are enough Web servers on the market, and that JavaSoft didn't have to go and write one. Well, you're correct…but how else could the company show off Java doing cool server things?

The Java Web Server is a powerful server written entirely in Java. More importantly, it can be extended and enhanced with server applets called *servlets*. We'll talk more about servlets later in this chapter.

servlet: A distinct Java program that runs at the server level. It has no user interface to speak of and executes behind the scenes.

The beauty—and power—of the Java Web Server is that it scales so well. In other words, if you need more horsepower, get a bigger machine. It matters not what type of machine it is because if you stick to writing servlets, everything will be written in Java, and Java is platform-independent.

Well, that's what JavaSoft says. In reality, you can't buy just any machine. But you've got a wide range of systems to choose from. If you start out on a Windows 95 machine, you can move to a Windows NT server on a DEC Alpha. From there, you can move to a small UNIX box. In all these cases, your Web site moves without any changes.

Note

You can download the Java Web Server from the JavaSoft Web site at `http://jserv.javasoft.com`. It runs on Windows 95, Windows NT, and a variety of UNIX platforms. The current version as of this writing is 1.0.1.

Installing the Java Web Server

You can install the server alongside most other Web servers. There should be no conflict because the Java Web Server defaults to port 8080; most other Web servers run on port 80. The port selection was very thoughtful on JavaSoft's part. The Java Web Server also sets up the administration tool on port 9090. You can select the directory in which you want to install the product. The default directory is `C:\JavaServer1.0.1`. The following subdirectories are installed:

- [ ] `admin`

  This directory contains all the classes required for the Java Web Server administration utility (a Java applet that allows you to configure the Web server).

- [ ] `bin`

  This directory contains all the programs required to run the Java Web Server.

- [ ] `cgi-bin`

  This is the standard `cgi-bin` directory for your Web server. All CGI scripts and programs should be placed here.

- [ ] `lib`

  This directory contains supportive libraries and classes for the Java Web Server.

- [ ] `logs`

  This directory holds all your log files.

- [ ] `properties`

  This directory contains all the property files used by the Web server. Although these configuration files are usually managed by the administrative utility, you may sometimes have to change them manually.

- [ ] `public_html`

  This is the server's root directory. All Web pages that are served start in this directory.

- [ ] `realms`

  This directory holds the security mappings for the Web server.

- [ ] `servlets`

  This directory holds servlets that can be served by your server.

15

☐ srcdemos

This directory contains the source code to some interesting sample servlets and applets.

☐ system

This directory is also used by the administrative utility for file storage.

These are the default directories. You can always change them after you've installed the product.

WARNING

One note about the servlets directory: Any servlet you place in this directory is considered *trusted*, or secure. Before you place a servlet class into this directory, make sure that you know what it does and where it came from.

Administering the Java Web Server

The Java Web Server is easy to administer because it comes with a Java applet to do the job. The administration applet starts when you contact the server on port 9090 (the default port, which can be changed). Figure 15.1 shows the login screen for the administration utility.

Figure 15.1.

The login screen for the Java Web Server administration utility.

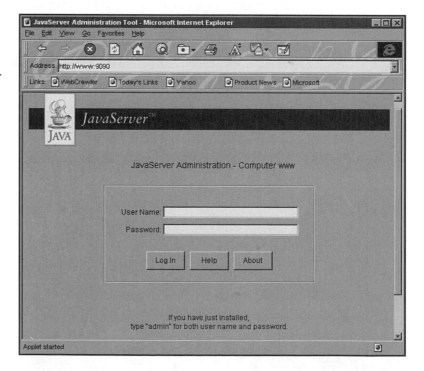

15

Once you log in, you are given a selection of services to administer (see Figure 15.2).

Figure 15.2.

The services you can administer are displayed.

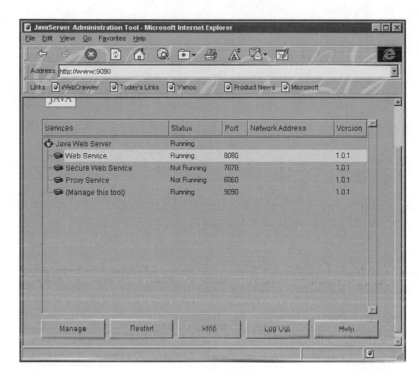

The Java Web Server provides three basic services:

☐ HTTP service

☐ Secure HTTP service

☐ HTTP and FTP proxy service

You can administer each of these services by selecting the appropriate line. We'll take a look at the HTTP service administration just to give you an idea of what it looks like. Once you select a service, you see a new window with the options for that service. Figure 15.3 shows the window for the HTTP service.

Figure 15.3.

The basic service configuration window.

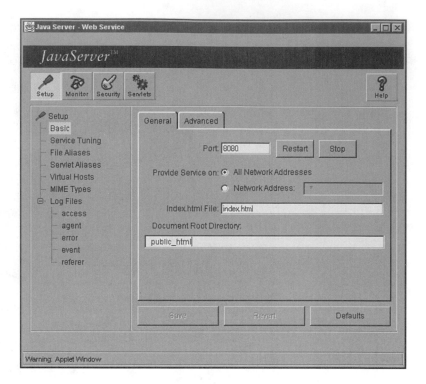

Across the top of the service configuration window are four buttons, representing the four areas of administrative authority: Setup, Monitor, Security, and Servlets. Each area has different options and settings. All these values are stored in property files in the properties directory.

The main point of this discussion is to point out the servlet configuration area. When you click the Servlets button, the screen in Figure 15.4 appears. You use the Servlet configuration area to add servlets to your server. You can also identify servlets in your system with this tool. From this configuration window, you can add servlets, assign names to them, and identify remote servlets.

Figure 15.4.

The Servlet configura-
tion window.

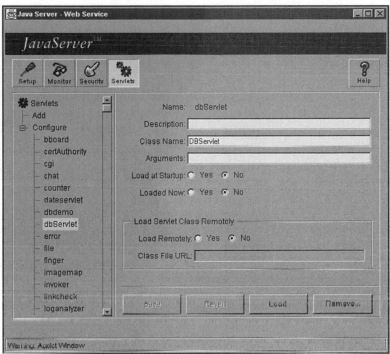

Isn't a Servlet a Napkin?

No, you're probably thinking of a *serviette*. Although they are similar in name, they are two completely different things. A serviette is good for removing food from one's face. A server applet, or *servlet*, is a JavaSoft creation that is essentially a server-side applet. A servlet is a distinct Java program that runs at the server level. It has no user interface to speak of and executes behind the scenes.

The whole notion of servlets came from a need to extend the basic services provided by generic servers. This is not a unique idea: Netscape has an extension development kit for their Web server called Netscape Server API, or NSAPI, and Microsoft has the Internet Server API, or ISAPI. Extending a core service through plug-ins or modules is a very object-oriented and modular approach. It's also easier to debug. As you add code to any program, you run the risk of breaking it. As you add code, your program becomes more complex, and your risk of introducing bugs increases. By adding code in modules, however, you limit the scope of the potential bugs and make them easier to eradicate. Servlets are the ultimate in modular programming: They are self-contained programs that interact with other self-contained programs.

Extensions are an effective and productive way of extending a core service program such as a Web server. Servlets fit the bill as extensions because they are easy to create, they are supported on a variety of platforms, and they benefit from being written in Java.

Here are some of the benefits of programming extensions to service programs as Java servlets:

- ☐ **Platform independence.** Servlets can run on any platform (such as UNIX, Windows, and so on) that support servlets.
- ☐ **Crash prevention.** Servlets can't crash your Web server because they run in the protected realm of the Java virtual machine.
- ☐ **Memory leaks.** Servlets can't leak memory because they are running in the Java virtual machine.

Servlets exist within services. A *service* is a set of processes that performs a function for a client. For example, Web servers perform the service of retrieving HTML pages. Servlets are extensions of services that were created with the Java Service API. The Java Web Server itself is a service created with the Java Service API. Therefore, you can use servlets to extend the functionality of the Java Web Server. This lesson deals with the Service API after it covers servlets in more depth.

NEW TERM	*service:* A set of processes that performs a function for a client.

You can also think of servlets as server plug-ins. Once written and plugged in to a server, servlets provide a service much like a CGI script or program. Servlets can be called with normal HTML and can accept input from a Web browser.

NOTE	At the behest of a browser, the Web server invokes CGI scripts and programs. These programs process the data given to them and return information in the form of HTML. This HTML-coded information is then returned to the browser for display.

Servlets were created to extend Web servers and provide services in an object-oriented and modular manner. The first Web server to work with servlets was the Java Web Server from JavaSoft (described later in this chapter). Servlets can also be used with the following Web servers:

- ☐ Apache 1.1.3 servers (UNIX)
- ☐ Microsoft Internet Information Server versions 2 and above (Windows NT)

15

☐ Netscape Enterprise 2.*x* and 3.0 servers (UNIX/Windows NT)

☐ Netscape FastTrack 2.*x* servers (UNIX/Windows NT)

Another interesting notion about servlets is that they do not have to reside on the disk where the server runs; they can live on a remote network. Just like applets, servlets can be retrieved, loaded, and invoked from a remote location. In addition, you can carry the effects of one servlet into another servlet, a technique called *chaining*. When you chain, you essentially take the output of one servlet and feed it to another servlet as input. You can repeat the chaining process as often as you like to create a kind of filter.

> *chaining:* A technique where you carry the effects of one servlet into another servlet.

Servlet Security

Servlets, like applets, are restricted in the system resources they can use. Depending on their disposition, servlets can have complete control or limited control of system resources. As with an applet, a servlet's disposition can be trusted or untrusted.

Trusted servlets are loaded locally and reside in a specific controlled server area. Trusted servlets are granted all access privileges. *Untrusted servlets* are loaded over a network. They can reside anywhere, on any network. Once loaded, however, they run in a security "sandbox." This sandbox is like a play area for servlets. Fortunately, the servlets can't escape the sandbox. Inside the sandbox, servlets can perform only a certain set of operations and have no access to local files or remote network services.

> *trusted servlet:* A servlet that's loaded locally and resides in a specific controlled server area. Trusted servlets are granted all access privileges.
>
> *untrusted servlet:* A servlet that's loaded over a network. Untrusted servlets can perform only a certain set of operations and have no access to local files or remote network services.

There is one catch to being untrusted: An untrusted servlet can become trusted. To become trusted, a servlet must be digitally signed inside a special file called a Java ARchive Format (JAR) file. You learn more about JAR files in Day 17, "Working with Java Archives." Digital signing is covered in Day 19, "Creating Signed Java Objects."

Once a servlet (or applet, for that matter) is digitally signed, it is considered trusted when it is loaded over a network. The signature is a guarantee that some authority ensures that the object in question is what it claims to be. The signature is not actually secure, but you can rest assured that the object is from where and what it claims.

The Java Servlet API

Creating servlets is almost as simple as creating applets. You simply extend one of the servlet classes and add your specific code. What are those servlet classes? I'm glad you asked.

The classes that enable you to create Java servlets are called the Java Servlet API and are contained in the Java Servlet Development Kit, or JSDK. The JSDK can be downloaded for free from JavaSoft at http://jserv.javasoft.com. As of this writing, JavaSoft has not decided whether they are going to include the Servlet API as part of the core Java language or whether it will be an extension.

NOTE

As this book goes to press, the current version of the JSDK is 1.0.1. A later version may be available soon. Check the JavaServer Web site at http://jserv.javasoft.com for more information.

After you install it, the JSDK provides you with the API classes, the source code to the classes, several demonstration servlets, and a program that allows you to run servlets. This program is like the appletviewer program that comes with the Java Development Kit. However, the JSDK runs only servlets. As of this writing, JavaSoft has not decided whether they are going to include the Servlet API as part of the core Java language or whether it will be an extension.

The JSDK also includes information for installing servlet support for Web servers other than the Java Web Server. Servlets can run on the Apache, Microsoft's Internet Information, and Netscape Enterprise and FastTrack servers. But you don't need a server to write servlets—the servlet runner program is all you need. The server runner program acts like a Web server and services servlet requests.

NOTE

Because the JSDK is apparently based on the Java 1.0 API specification, some things may not work as you expect if you are used to the Java 1.1 API. But servlets do require a runtime environment compatible with Java 1.0 if they are to operate properly.

The Servlet API Classes

The JSDK consists of two packages: `javax.servlet` and `javax.servlet.http`. All together, both packages contain only 14 classes. As you'll see, using them is easy.

Here is the list of classes in the `javax.servlet` package:

GenericServlet (abstract class)
Servlet (interface)
ServletConfig (interface)
ServletContext (interface)
ServletException (class)
ServletInputStream (class)
ServletOutputStream (class)
ServletRequest (interface)
ServletResponse (interface)
UnavailableException (class)

Notice that most of these classes are interfaces or abstract. That is so you have complete control over the creation of your servlet code.

You can create and use the ServletInputStream and ServletOutputStream classes. These classes extend InputStream and OutputStream. However, they add only simple reading and writing methods (such as readLine, print, and println).

NOTE The ServletInputStream and ServletOutputStream classes will probably be converted to Reader and Writer derivatives when the JSDK is brought into line with the Java 1.1 API.

Here is a list of classes from the javax.servlet.http package:

HttpServlet (abstract class)
HttpServletRequest (interface)
HttpServletResponse (interface)
HttpUtils (class)

In this package, the classes are interfaces and abstract. None of them are of any use by themselves. You must derive your own class and augment one of the methods.

NOTE

> Installed with the standard JSDK classes are the sun.servlet package classes. These classes are undocumented and are not recommended for use.

The Servlet Interface

Servlets work in a request/response atmosphere. You make a request of a servlet, and the servlet provides a response. This approach makes servlets the logical choice for request/response protocols like HTTP and FTP.

For your class to become a servlet, at the least it must implement the Servlet interface. This interface defines the following methods:

```
void init(ServletConfig config)
ServletConfig getServletConfig()
String getServletInfo()
void destroy()
void service(ServletRequest req, ServletResponse res)
```

The init() method is the entry point for your servlet. Once the servlet is loaded, this method is called before any other method. The init() method is guaranteed to be called before the service() method is invoked. The init() method is not called again unless the servlet is unloaded, destroyed, and then reloaded. At the least, the init() method should keep a copy of the configuration parameters passed to it. These parameters should then be used by the getServletConfig() method as a return value. This approach provides your servlet with access to the configuration parameters even after they have been initialized.

The getServletConfig() method should return a ServletConfig object that was stored from the one passed in to the init() method. The getServletInfo() method is the counterpart to the getAppletInfo() method of the java.applet.Applet class. getServletInfo() is a freeform method that allows the dissemination of version, copyright, or other information about the servlet.

You use the destroy() method to uninitialize your servlet. Any resources you are using should be released. This method is called when your servlet is unloaded. It is not called again until the servlet is reloaded and then unloaded.

The service() method is the main method of the Servlet interface. This method is where it all happens. Each time a request for your servlet is received by the host service, the service() method is called. The ServletRequest argument passed in provides information about the request. The ServletResponse argument is used to return information to the requester.

15

Implementing the `Servlet` Interface

The `Servlet` interface is partially implemented by the `GenericServlet` class. The `GenericServlet` class defines everything but the `service()` method.

The `HttpServlet` class extends the `GenericServlet` class. The `HttpServlet` class is the class you'll most likely use the most when creating servlets. It provides a wrapper around servlets and the HTTP protocol. Remember that servlets adhere to a request/response protocol. The HTTP protocol is a request/response type of protocol.

The `HttpServlet` Class

If you are writing Web server servlets or CGI replacement servlets, the `HttpServlet` class will be the basis for all your servlets. This class provides a protocol-handling framework for the HTTP protocol. HTTP, as you probably know, is the language of the World Wide Web and Web servers.

When an HTTP client (browser) requests a page from an HTTP server (Web server), the client issues a GET command. It looks like this:

```
GET /index.html
```

This command is followed by a line feed, carriage return, or both. The results of the request are returned. In fact, you can try out the GET command yourself by using a telnet program. Use telnet to get to your local Web server on port 80 and issue the command. Here's what the exchange will look like (what you type is in **bold**):

```
Jupiter:~$ telnet www.mindbuilder.com 80
Connected to www.mindbuilder.com.
Escape character is '^]'.
GET /
<!DOCTYPE HTML PUBLIC "-//IETF//DTD HTML//EN">
<html>
<head>
</head>
<body background="images/bgstrip.gif" bgcolor="#FFFFFF"
text="#000000" link="#0000D0" vlink="#0000A0" alink="#FF0000">
<p> </p>
</body>
</html>
```

The GET command is more commonly referred to as a method. One other method is supported by all Web servers: the POST method. This method is used to submit information to the Web server. If you've ever been to a Web site that asks for information and then makes you click a "submit" button, that "submit" button invokes a POST method. And when you create Web pages that contain HTML forms, the forms are usually submitted to the server using a POST method.

15

In any case, the HttpServlet class implements the service() method for you and decides what to do based on the method used to invoke the servlet. If the GET method was used, the doGet() method of the servlet is called. If the POST method was used, the doPost() method is called.

To successfully extend the HttpServlet class, you must implement one of the methods (doGet() or doPost()) in your class. Let's look at the simplest servlet possible: the "Hello World!" servlet.

The HelloWorldServlet Servlet

The HelloWorldServlet servlet is shipped with the JSDK and is provided as an example of a simple servlet. Once invoked, it returns an HTML page that simply says Hello World. The source code for the HelloWorldServlet servlet is shown in Listing 15.1.

TIP

> Remember that servlets that respond to HTTP requests most likely have to return information in HTML format.

Listing 15.1. The HelloWorldServlet.

```
 1: /*
 2:  * @(#)HelloWorldServlet.java    1.9 97/05/22
 3:  *
 4:  * Copyright (c) 1995-1997 Sun Microsystems, Inc. All Rights Reserved.
 5:  *
 6:  * This software is the confidential and proprietary information of Sun
 7:  * Microsystems, Inc. ("Confidential Information").  You shall not
 8:  * disclose such Confidential Information and shall use it only in
 9:  * accordance with the terms of the license agreement you entered into
10:  * with Sun.
11:  *
12:  * SUN MAKES NO REPRESENTATIONS OR WARRANTIES ABOUT THE SUITABILITY OF THE
13:  * SOFTWARE, EITHER EXPRESS OR IMPLIED, INCLUDING BUT NOT LIMITED TO THE
14:  * IMPLIED WARRANTIES OF MERCHANTABILITY, FITNESS FOR A PARTICULAR
15:  * PURPOSE, OR NON-INFRINGEMENT. SUN SHALL NOT BE LIABLE FOR ANY DAMAGES
16:  * SUFFERED BY LICENSEE AS A RESULT OF USING, MODIFYING OR DISTRIBUTING
17:  * THIS SOFTWARE OR ITS DERIVATIVES.
18:  *
19:  * CopyrightVersion 1.0
20:  */
21:
22: import java.io.*;
23:
```

```
24: import javax.servlet.*;
25: import javax.servlet.http.*;
26:
27: /**
28:  * Hello World. This servlet simply says hi.
29:  *
30:  * This is useful for testing our servlet admin tool, since
31:  * this servlet isn't started up by default when Jeeves starts up.
32:  * Load it by going to http://<server>/admin/servlet.html
33:  * and giving it the name "hello" and the class "HelloWorldServlet".
34:  * Then, invoke by using the URL http://<server>/servlet/hello
35:  */
36:
37: public
38: class HelloWorldServlet extends HttpServlet {
39:
40:     public void doGet (HttpServletRequest req, HttpServletResponse res)
41:     throws ServletException, IOException
42:     {
43:     res.setContentType("text/html");
44:
45:     ServletOutputStream out = res.getOutputStream();
46:     out.println("<html>");
47:     out.println("<head><title>Hello World</title></head>");
48:     out.println("<body>");
49:     out.println("<h1>Hello World</h1>");
50:     out.println("</body></html>");
51:     }
52:
53:     public String getServletInfo() {
54:     return "Create a page that says <i>Hello World</i> and send it back";
55:     }
56: }
```

The servlet extends the HttpServlet class as discussed earlier and implements the doGet() method. The doGet() method is the simplest method to implement because it usually returns only information. Servlets that only provide information are excellent candidates for this type of implementation.

The first thing the servlet does is specify the type of content it is about to return. You can specify any valid MIME type as your content type. Next, a reference to the ServletOutputStream object is retrieved. This is used to output the HTML to the client that requested the service in the first place. This servlet sends back a standard HTML page that prints Hello World. The results, seen with a browser, are shown in Figure 15.5.

Figure 15.5.

The results of calling the `HelloWorldServlet` *servlet are not very exciting.*

Servlets can be much more complex than `HelloWorldServlet`, and they have more interesting aspects. Those issues are dealt with in tomorrow's lesson, which covers programming with the Java Servlet Development Kit.

Summary

Until today, you've been focusing on the client side of Java programming. Today, you ventured into the server side of things. You first had a quick overview of the Java Web Server. You learned that it is a regular Web server, written entirely in Java, that can be extended with server applets called *servlets*. You then took a look at the administrative tool used to administer the Java Web Server. The administrative tool is an applet that can be run with any Java-enabled Web browser.

Next, you learned about servlets. Servlets are the programs that extend the functionality of HTTP servers. They can also add value to any existing Web service. You learned about the Java Servlet Development Kit and the Servlet API.

Finally, you looked at one of the demonstration servlets that comes with the Java Servlet Development Kit. This "Hello World" program was described and its results displayed. Tomorrow, you're going to create some interesting things with the Servlet Development Kit.

Q&A

Q What is the purpose of servlets?

A A servlet is used to extend services written in Java. The Java Web Server is a service written in Java. You can create servlets that extend the Java Web Server.

Q What is the Java Servlet Development Kit?

A The Java Servlet Development Kit, or JSDK, is a set of classes and utilities that allow you to create servlets in Java.

Q What is an `HttpServlet`?

A An `HttpServlet` is a generic-type servlet that is invoked via HTTP calls.

15

Day 16

Programming with the Java Servlet Development Kit

by Jerry Ablan

Yesterday, you learned about the Java Web Server and about server extensions called servlets. These server applets are used to enhance, augment, and beautify dreary old Web server services. Best of all, servlets are written in Java! So once you write one, you can move it to any platform.

But yesterday's look at servlets was cursory at best. Today, you're going to delve deeper into servlets and how to create them. Specifically, you'll do these things:

☐ Examine the servlet life cycle

☐ Discover the two basic types of servlets

☐ Create a servlet

The Servlet Life Cycle

Servlets live on a Web server somewhere (usually, your local Web server). Sometimes, however, you may have servlets on an offsite server such as a corporate Web server or your intranet server. In any case, the servlet is confined to the Web server on which it lives.

Not much is said about the life of a servlet. Once invoked, the servlet provides its service and then dies. Still, it is always good to know how something works when you're going to write code to use it.

Loading Servlets

Servlets are loaded when a request comes in for their services. This loading style is called *dynamic*. Dynamically loaded servlets conserve resources because they are loaded only when they are needed. Imagine having 100 servlets on a Web server that all load when the server starts. But if you use only one of the servlets, the other 99 are left with nothing to do except consume resources. Not very efficient.

The following figures explain how a servlet loads. Figure 16.1 shows the client and the server. Figure 16.2 shows the client making a request of the server. Notice that no servlet is loaded yet. Figure 16.3 shows the client receiving a response from the server. Before responding, the server loads the servlet and passes the necessary information to the servlet. The response from the servlet is passed on to the requesting client.

Figure 16.1.

The client and server are about to dance.

Client

Server

Figure 16.2.

The client asks the server to dance.

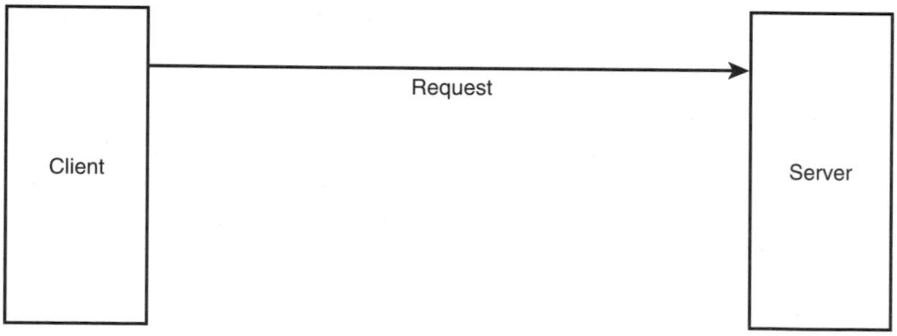

Client

Request

Server

16

Figure 16.3.
The server accepts and asks its little brother to help out.

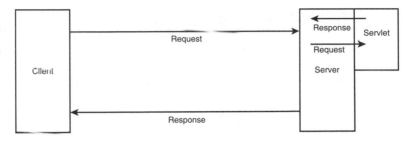

You can also force a servlet into memory by using an administrative method provided by the server. With the Java Web Server, you use the administrative utility. In addition, you can mark a servlet so that it loads with the server at startup.

NOTE

> Forcing a servlet into memory is simply done by clicking the loaded checkbox in the Servlet Administration Utility.

You can load servlets from the local file system or from a remote URL because the Java runtime system uses the same class-loading system for all classes. Because servlets are just another class, they can make use of that feature.

Running Servlets

After the servlet loads, it is ready to service requests. However, one thing must happen before the servlet is set to go: the initialization of the servlet. The servlet is initialized in the init() method.

The init() Method

The entry point to a servlet is the init() method. This method is called only when the servlet is first loaded into memory. Not until it is unloaded, destroyed, and reloaded is this method called again. In your own init() method, you should place any resource intensive or startup code. This code includes things such as establishing network links, opening database connections, allocating memory, reading in data, and so on. Because this method is called only once for the entire life of the servlet, it is a good place to put these types of activities.

Handling Initialization Errors

If you can't start your servlet for some reason, simply throw the UnavailableException. This exception indicates that your servlet is now unavailable. Your servlet can report this condition at any time. However, it is most useful during initialization.

Your servlet may declare one of two states of unavailability. The first is a temporary unavailability, caused, for example, because a resource you require is unavailable or because the CPU load is too high. Temporary unavailability usually corrects itself. Here's a temporary unavailability exception:

```
public void
init( ServletConfig sc )
{
    if ( !someInitialization() )
        throw new UnavailableException( 10, this, "Reason" );
}
```

This code says that the servlet is unavailable for 10 seconds because of "Reason".

The second type of unavailability is a permanent unavailability. Permanent unavailability means that your servlet is dead and requires system administrator intervention to correct it. Examples of permanent unavailability are corrupt data, misconfiguration, and hardware failure. Here is an example of a permanent unavailability exception:

```
public void
init( ServletConfig sc )
{
    if ( !someInitialization() )
        throw new UnavailableException( this, "Reason" );
}
```

This code says that the servlet is unavailable because of "Reason".

The `ServletConfig` Class

The `init()` method receives a `ServletConfig` object as an argument. This object describes, to some degree, the configuration of the servlet. The `ServletConfig` class is a gateway to the information used to load the servlet.

The `ServletConfig` class contains the following methods:

☐ `public ServletContext getServletContext()`

This method returns the context for the servlet, which is useful in gauging security needs.

☐ `public String getInitParameter(String name)`

This method retrieves initialization parameters that may have been loaded with the servlet. You can specify parameters to your servlets.

☐ `public Enumeration getInitParameterNames()`

This method retrieves a list of all the initialization parameters.

The get InitParameter() method is similar to the getParameter() method of the Applet class. It retrieves parameters that were sent in as arguments to the servlet. Listing 16.1 shows a small servlet that demonstrates the methods of the ServletConfig class. The servlet prints the initialization parameters if any were received.

Listing 16.1. A small servlet to showcase the methods of the ServletConfig class.

```
1: import java.io.*;
2: import java.util.Enumeration;
3:
4: import javax.servlet.*;
5: import javax.servlet.http.*;
6:
7: public class
8: ShowInitParamsServlet
9: extends HttpServlet
10: {
11:     protected String              servletName = "ShowInitParamsServlet";
12:
13:     public void
14:     doGet( HttpServletRequest req, HttpServletResponse res )
15:         throws ServletException, IOException
16:     {
17:         ServletOutputStream out = res.getOutputStream();
18:
19:         //    Set content type
20:         res.setContentType( "text/html" );
21:
22:         // Write the data of the response
23:         out.println("<HEAD><TITLE>" + servletName + "</TITLE>
            ➥</HEAD><BODY>");
24:
25:         out.println("<h1>" + servletName + " Output </h1>");
26:
27:         ServletConfig sc = getServletConfig();
28:
29:         if ( sc != null )
30:         {
31:             Enumeration e = sc.getInitParameterNames();
32:
33:             if ( e.hasMoreElements() )
34:             {
35:              out.println( "<P>The following parameters were
                ➥specified:<p>");
36:
37:                 while( e.hasMoreElements() )
38:                 {
```

continues

16

Listing 16.1. continued

```
39:                        String iparam = ( String )e.nextElement();
40:
41:                        out.println( "<h3>" + iparam + " = " +
42:                        sc.getInitParameter( iparam ) + "</h2><p>" );
43:                    }
44:                }
45:            else
46:                out.println( "<P>No initialization parameters were
                   ➥specified." );
47:
48:            while( e.hasMoreElements() )
49:                out.println( "<h2>" + e.nextElement() + "</h2><p>" );
50:            }
51:
52:        out.println("</BODY>");
53:        out.close();
54:    }
55:
56: }
```

This small servlet extends the HttpServlet class. It is a simple servlet to create because you need only provide one method: doGet(). As you can see, that's exactly what I did. The doGet() method is called when someone tries to retrieve the servlet. The servlet does nothing more than print the values given to it in the initialization parameters.

> **TIP**
>
> Almost any servlet you write that responds to a Web browser client is descended from the easy-to-use HttpServlet class. In fact, all the sample servlets that come with the JSDK extend the HttpServlet class.

The values for the initialization parameters are usually specified with the Java Web Server administration utility. In the Servlet area of this utility, each servlet has an arguments field that holds a comma-delimited list of properties or parameters to send to the servlet.

Listing 16.1 used the getInitParameterNames() method to retrieve an enumeration of the valid parameter names. The code then called getInitParameter() to get the value associated with each parameter. Figure 16.4 shows the output of this servlet.

Figure 16.4.

The output of the ShowInitParamsServlet *servlet.*

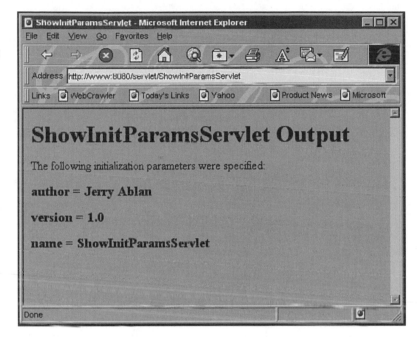

Servicing Requests

After the init() method returns successfully, the servlet is considered to be loaded and initialized. When requests come into your servlet, they are dispatched to the service() method. This method is where it all happens. Here is a sample service() method:

```
public abstract void service( ServletRequest req, ServletResponse res )
        throws ServletException, IOException
    {
        //      handle service request…
    }
```

The service() method receives two arguments. The first is the ServletRequest object, which defines the nature of the request as well as any miscellaneous information passed in along with the request. From the ServletRequest object, you can retrieve a ServletInputStream object.

The second argument received by the service() method is the ServletResponse object. This object is used to respond to the invoker of your service. From this object, you can retrieve a ServletOutputStream object.

Unless you stray from writing HTTP servlets, you probably won't use the service() method much. It is defined for you in the HttpServlet class and is presented in Listing 16.2.

Listing 16.2. The code for the `service()` method.

```
1:      protected void service (HttpServletRequest req,
        ➥HttpServletResponseresp)
2:      throws ServletException, IOException
3:      {
4:          String              method = req.getMethod ();
5:
6:          if (method.equals ("GET")) {
7:              long        ifModifiedSince;
8:              long        lastModified;
9:              long        now;
10:
11:             //
12:             // HTTP 1.0 conditional GET just uses If-Modified-Since fields
13:             // in the header.  HTTP 1.1 has more conditional GET options.
14:             //
15:             // We call getLastModified() only once; it won't be cheap.
16:             //
17:             ifModifiedSince = req.getDateHeader ("If-Modified-Since");
18:             lastModified = getLastModified (req);
19:             maybeSetLastModified (resp, lastModified);
20:
21:             if (ifModifiedSince == -1)
22:                 doGet (req, resp);
23:             else {
24:                 now = System.currentTimeMillis ();
25:
26:                 //
27:                 // Times in the future are invalid ... but we can't treat
28:                 // them as "hard errors", so for now we accept extra load.
29:                 //
30:                 if (now < ifModifiedSince ¦¦ ifModifiedSince < lastModified)
31:                         doGet (req, resp);
32:                 else
33:                         resp.sendError
                            ➥(HttpServletResponse.SC_NOT_MODIFIED);
34:             }
35:
36:         } else if (method.equals ("HEAD")) {
37:             long        lastModified;
38:
39:             lastModified = getLastModified (req);
40:             maybeSetLastModified (resp, lastModified);
41:             doHead (req, resp);
42:
43:         } else if (method.equals ("POST")) {
44:             if (req.getContentLength () == -1)
45:                 resp.sendError (HttpServletResponse.SC_BAD_REQUEST,
46:                     "POST bodies must specify content length");
47:             else
48:                 doPost (req, resp);
49:
50:         } else {
51:             //
```

16

```
52:                  // Note that this means NO servlet supports whatever
53:                  // method was requested, anywhere on this server.
54:                  //
55:                  resp.sendError (HttpServletResponse.SC_NOT_IMPLEMENTED,
56:                      "Method '" + method + "' is not defined in RFC 1945");
57:              }
58:      }
```

Listing 16.2 examines the HTTP method used when invoking this service. If the HTTP method was GET, the servlet redirects the program to the doGet() method. If the HTTP method was POST, the servlet is redirected to the doPost() method. In addition, this routine responds to the HEAD HTTP method. The HEAD method returns only the header information about an HTTP request; the content is not transmitted.

Shutting Down

Your servlet continues to live and provide services until its destroy() method is called. At that point, all resources are freed, and the class can then be garbage collected. To do special processing before your servlet is unloaded, simply implement the destroy() method:

```
public void destroy() {
    //    Cleanup…
    }
```

Servlet Types

A servlet is a servlet, but you have a choice of the type of servlet from which you can base your own servlets. The distinction between types is quite clear; you won't be agonizing for days wondering whether you made the wrong choice. The two choices are GenericServlet and HttpServlet.

The GenericServlet Class

The first type of servlet is a GenericServlet. This class implements almost everything you need for a servlet—it does not provide the service() method. That is your job as a servlet author. You can use GenericServlet servlets for any purpose. They can answer requests, retrieve data from databases, provide three-tier network services, and so on. They are truly generic.

The HttpServlet Class

The second type of servlet is an HttpServlet. This servlet class descends from the GenericServlet class and adds the service() method. However, it creates two new methods, doGet() and doPut(), one of which you must implement in your child class.

To reiterate what was covered in Listing 16.2 and the discussion of the service() method earlier in this chapter, the service() method dispatches to one of three methods based on the type of HTTP request that was received. Table 16.1 shows the HTTP requests and their designated methods.

Table 16.1. HTTP request methods and their related service() methods.

HTTP Request Method	Dispatch Class Method
GET	protected void doGet(HttpServletRequest *req*, HttpServletResponse *resp*) throws ServletException, IOException
POST	protected void doPost(HttpServletRequest *req*, HttpServletResponse *resp*) throws ServletException, IOException
HEAD	private void doHead(HttpServletRequest *req*, HttpServletResponse *resp*) throws ServletException, IOException

If you are writing a servlet that works in conjunction with an HTTP server, HttpServlet is the class on which you should base your servlet. The HttpServlet class adds much value to the GenericServlet class, as described in the following section. Because most servlets use the HTTP protocol, you'll focus your attention on creating a sample servlet using HttpServlet as the base class.

NOTE

As far as I can tell, there is no way to invoke a servlet other than with the servlet runner or a compatible Web server. Therefore, servlets are always invoked by an HTTP request. It only makes sense to use the HttpServlet class as your base. The HttpServlet class doesn't degrade your servlet, and you lose no information. However, you gain a lot by using it: What you get for free is information about the client and its request.

When your doGet() or doPost() method is invoked, it is passed an HttpServletRequest object and an HttpServletResponse object. The following sections detail each of these objects.

The HttpServletRequest **Interface**

The HttpServletRequest interface defines information pertaining to the request made by the client. The information contained in this class corresponds to many of the environment variables used for CGI programming. Table 16.2 lists the methods that have CGI counterparts.

Table 16.2. The HttpServletRequest **methods that have CGI programming equivalents.**

Method	CGI variable
getMethod()	REQUEST_METHOD
getServletPath()	SCRIPT_NAME
getPathInfo()	PATH_INFO
getPathTranslated()	PATH_TRANSLATED
getQueryString()	QUERY_STRING
getRemoteUser()	REMOTE_USER
getAuthType()	AUTH_TYPE

Other information can be passed in to the servlet (or CGI script) from the URL using the query string. The *query string* is the information passed to the servlet after its name. Examine the following URL:

```
http://www/servlet/DoSomething?name=Herman&page=3&type=Computer+Programmer
```

This URL invokes the DoSomething servlet. It passes in three pieces of information along with its request: name, page, and type. These three values are separated by ampersands (&); spaces are replaced with plus (+) signs. This special encoding allows the Web server to pass along the data intact. But how do you retrieve it from within your servlet? Simple: You use the HttpServletRequest class's getParameter() method.

The getParameter() **Method**

You will use the HttpServletRequest class's getParameter() method a lot. It allows you to retrieve a parameter value from the query string passed in to the servlet. Although it is analogous to the Applet class's getParameter() method, the way information is passed in is different.

The HttpServletRequest class's getParameter() method accepts a String with the name of the parameter to retrieve and returns a String. If you want a number, you must convert it yourself. This sample code shows how to retrieve the information from the URL presented in the preceding section:

```
String myName = req.getParameter( "name" );
String myPage = req.getParameter( "page" );
String myType = req.getParameter( "type" );
```

The HttpServletResponse Interface

The HttpServletResponse interface defines methods used to return information to the client. This information is usually returned in the form of an HTML page. Here are the methods defined by the HttpServletResponse interface:

- ☐ public boolean containsHeader(String *name*)

  This method indicates that the response message header contains a field with the specified *name*.

- ☐ public void setStatus(int *statusCode*)

  This method sets a status code for this response.

- ☐ public void setStatus(int *statusCode*, String *statusMessage*)

  This method sets a status code and a status message for this response.

- ☐ public void setHeader(String *name*, String *value*)

  This method adds a header field to this response. *Header fields* are like extra information embedded in the page. You can place anything you want in a header field, and you can add as many header fields as you want.

- ☐ public void setIntHeader(String *name*, int *value*)

  This method is similar to the setHeader() method except that it accepts an integer value for the header value.

- ☐ public void setDateHeader(String *name*, long *date*)

  This method is similar to the setHeader() method except that it accepts a date value for the header value.

- ☐ public void sendError(int *statusCode*) throws IOException

  This method sends an error code back to the client.

- ☐ public void sendError(int *statusCode*, String *statusMessage*) throws IOException

  This method sends an error code and a message back to the client.

- ☐ public void sendRedirect(String *location*) throws IOException

  This method sends a redirection to the client, which makes the client load the page specified in *location*.

Several of the methods just listed use a status code. Table 16.3 lists the status codes, their values, and their meanings.

16

Table 16.3. The status codes used by the methods in the HttpServletResponse interface.

Status Code	Value	Meaning
SC_OK	200	Request was successful
SC_CREATED	201	Request was successful and a new resource was created
SC_ACCEPTED	202	Request was accepted but is not yet complete
SC_NO_CONTENT	204	Request was successful but there is nothing to return
SC_MOVED_PERMANENTLY	301	Requested resource no longer resides here
SC_MOVED_TEMPORARILY	302	Requested resource is not here at the moment
SC_NOT_MODIFIED	304	Requested resource has not changed
SC_BAD_REQUEST	400	Request was not in proper format
SC_UNAUTHORIZED	401	Request not allowed
SC_FORBIDDEN	403	Request refused
SC_NOT_FOUND	404	Requested resource was not found
SC_INTERNAL_SERVER_ERROR	500	A server error occurred, causing the request to fail
SC_NOT_IMPLEMENTED	501	Request not supported
SC_BAD_GATEWAY	502	Response from proxy/gateway was invalid
SC_SERVICE_UNAVAILABLE	503	Request failed because server is too busy

You'll probably recognize some of these status codes (particularly the 404 and 500 codes) because they are standard HTTP server status codes.

Writing a Servlet

Now that you have an understanding of the HttpServlet class and the request and response objects, it's time to put that knowledge to work. To highlight some of the finer points of servlet writing, you'll create a demonstration servlet, which is based on the HttpServlet class.

Servlets should be created to add value to or extend a Web server. Your first servlet fits the bill by checking e-mail for a user. This servlet uses the POP3 protocol to check a mail server for mail. The first servlet uses the POP3Reader class created in Day 7, "Networking with Java." This class allows us to check mail on any POP3 server.

WARNING

This servlet passes the user's password in an insecure manner. Although this approach is usually fine for internal Web sites, external use of this servlet is not recommended.

Servlet Design

Before you start coding the servlet, think about how it will work. You want the users to load an HTML page and input certain information including username, password, and server name. You'll accept this information in a form from a Web page. Figure 16.5 shows what the Web form looks like.

Figure 16.5.

The POPChecker Web page accepts user input.

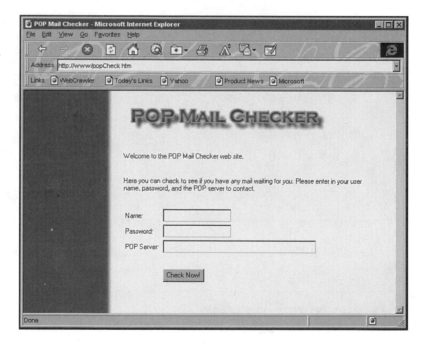

After receiving this information, you'll call your mail-checking routines and display the results. Initially, you use the POST HTTP method to feed your servlet. However, as you'll see later in this discussion, you can eliminate the need for the HTML page if you use the GET method. Figure 16.6 shows what happens after the user fills out the information and submits the form.

Figure 16.6.
I guess I don't have any mail.

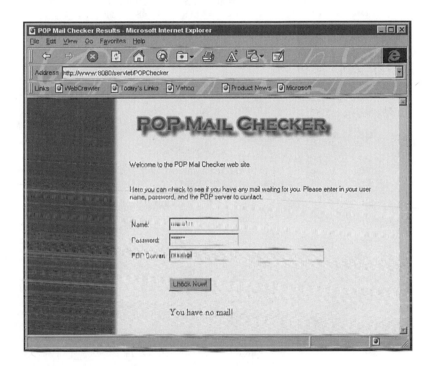

Servlet Implementation

Implementing the servlet to check for mail is simple. You must create a new servlet and extend the HttpServlet class. You then override the doPost() method and do your stuff. Listing 16.3 shows the code for the POPChecker servlet.

Listing 16.3. The POPChecker servlet.

```
1: import java.io.*;
2:
3: import javax.servlet.*;
4: import javax.servlet.http.*;
5:
6: public class
```

continues

Listing 16.3. continued

```
 7: POPChecker
 8: extends HttpServlet
 9: {
10:     protected String          servletName = "POPChecker";
11:     protected POP3Reader       myReader;
12:     protected String           results;
13:
14:     public void
15:     init( ServletConfig config )
16:         throws ServletException
17:     {
18:         super.init( config );
19:
20:         //    Create a new reader
21:         myReader = new POP3Reader();
22:     }
23:
24:     public void
25:     doPost( HttpServletRequest req, HttpServletResponse res )
26:         throws ServletException, IOException
27:     {
28:         String user = req.getParameter( "userName" );
29:         String pass = req.getParameter( "password" );
30:         String server = req.getParameter( "popServer" );
31:
32:         if ( user != null && pass != null && server != null )
33:         {
34:             //    Set values for the check...
35:             myReader.setUser( user );
36:             myReader.setPassword( pass );
37:             myReader.setHost( server );
38:
39:             //     Only get counts...
40:             myReader.setPeek( true );
41:             myReader.retrieveMail();
42:
43:             int cnt = myReader.getMessageCount();
44:
45:             if ( cnt > 0 )
46:             {
47:                 results = "You have " + myReader.getMessageCount() +
                    ➥" message";
48:
49:                 if ( myReader.getMessageCount() != 1 )
50:                     results += "s";
51:
52:                 results += " available on the server!";
53:             }
54:             else
55:             {
56:                 results = "You have no mail!";
57:             }
58:         }
```

```
59:          else
60:              results = "";
61:
62:
63:          ServletOutputStream out = res.getOutputStream();
64:
65:          //    Set content type
66:          res.setContentType( "text/html" );
67:
68:
69:          out.println( "<html>" );
70:          out.println( "<head>" );
71:          out.println( "<title>POP Mail Checker Results</title>" );
72:          out.println( "</head>" );
73:          out.println( "" );
74:          out.println( "<body background='/images/pmcback.gif'
             ➥bgcolor='#FFFFFF'>" );
75:          out.println( "<div align='left'>" );
76:          out.println( "" );
77:          out.println( "<table border='0' width='600'>" );
78:          out.println( "    <tr>" );
79:          out.println( "          <td width='160'><font size='1'
             ➥face='MS Sans Serif'></font> </td>" );
80:          out.println( "          <td width='440'><font size='1'
             ➥face='MS Sans Serif'><img" );
81:          out.println( "          src='/images/pmc.gif' width='361'
             ➥height='58'></font></td>" );
82:          out.println( "    </tr>" );
83:          out.println( "    <tr>" );
84:          out.println( "          <td width='160'><font size='1'
             ➥face='MS Sans Serif'></font> </td>" );
85:          out.println( "          <td width='440'><font size='1'
             ➥face='MS Sans Serif'></font> </td>" );
86:          out.println( "    </tr>" );
87:          out.println( "    <tr>" );
88:          out.println( "          <td><font size='1' face='MS Sans Serif'>
             ➥</font> </td>" );
89:          out.println( "          <td><font size='1'
             ➥face='MS Sans Serif'>Welcome to the" );
90:          out.println( "          POP Mail Checker web site.</font></td>" );
91:          out.println( "    </tr>" );
92:          out.println( "    <tr>" );
93:          out.println( "          <td><font size='1' face='MS Sans Serif'>
             ➥</font> </td>" );
94:          out.println( "          <td><font size='1' face='MS Sans Serif'>
             ➥</font> </td>" );
95:          out.println( "    </tr>" );
96:          out.println( "    <tr>" );
97:          out.println( "          <td><font size='1' face='MS Sans Serif'>
             ➥</font> </td>" );
98:          out.println( "          <td><font size='1' face='MS Sans Serif'>Here
             ➥you can" );
99:          out.println( "          check to see if you have any mail waiting for
             ➥you. Please" );
```

continues

16

Listing 16.3. continued

```
100:          out.println( "              enter your user name, password, and the POP
              ➡server to" );
101:          out.println( "              contact.</font></td>" );
102:          out.println( "       </tr>" );
103:          out.println( "       <tr>" );
104:          out.println( "              <td><font size='1' face='MS Sans Serif'>
              ➡</font> </td>" );
105:          out.println( "              <td><font size='1' face='MS Sans Serif'>
              ➡</font> </td>" );
106:          out.println( "       </tr>" );
107:          out.println( "       <tr>" );
108:          out.println( "              <td><font size='1' face='MS Sans Serif'>
              ➡</font> </td>" );
109:          out.println( "              <td><form action='http://www:8080/servlet/
              ➡POPChecker'" );
110:          out.println( "              method='POST' name='popCheck'>" );
111:          out.println( "                 <div align='left'><table border='0'>" );
112:          out.println( "                    <tr>" );
113:          out.println( "                       <td><font size='1'
              ➡face='MS Sans Serif'>Name:</font></td>" );
114:          out.println( "                       <td><font size='1'
              ➡face='MS Sans Serif'><input" );
115:          out.println( "                          type='text' size='20'
              ➡name='userName' value='" + user +"'></font></td>" );
116:          out.println( "                    </tr>" );
117:          out.println( "                    <tr>" );
118:          out.println( "                       <td><font size='1'
              ➡face='MS Sans Serif'>Password:</font></td>" );
119:          out.println( "                       <td><font size='1'
              ➡face='MS SansSerif'><input" );
120:          out.println( "                          type='password' size='20'
              ➡name='password' value='" + pass + "'></font></td>" );
121:          out.println( "                    </tr>" );
122:          out.println( "                    <tr>" );
123:          out.println( "                       <td><font size='1'
              ➡face='MS Sans Serif'>POP" );
124:          out.println( "                          Server: </font></td>" );
125:          out.println( "                       <td><font size='1'
              ➡face='MS Sans Serif'><input" );
126:          out.println( "                          type='text' size='50'
              ➡name='popServer' value='" + server + "'></font></td>" );
127:          out.println( "                    </tr>" );
128:          out.println( "                    <tr>" );
129:          out.println( "                       <td><font size='1'
              ➡face='MS Sans Serif'></font> </td>" );
130:          out.println( "                       <td><font size='1'
              ➡face='MS Sans Serif'></font> </td>" );
131:          out.println( "                    </tr>" );
```

```
132:            out.println( "                       <tr>" );
133:            out.println( "                         <td><font size='1'
          ➥face='MS Sans Serif'></font> </td>" );
134:            out.println( "                         <td><font size='1'
          ➥face='MS Sans Serif'><input" );
135:            out.println( "                           type='submit' name='Submit'" );
136:            out.println( "                           value-'Check Now!'></font></td>" );
137:            out.println( "                       </tr>" );
138:            out.println( "                       <tr>" );
139:            out.println( "                         <td><font size='1'
          ➥face='MS Sans Serif'></font> </td>" );
140:            out.println( "                         <td><font size='1'
          ➥face='MS Sans Serif'></font> </td>" );
141:            out.println( "                       </tr>" );
142:            out.println( "                       <tr>" );
143:            out.println( "                         <td><font size='1'
          ➥face='MS Sans Serif'></font> </td>" );
144:            out.println( "                         <td><font size='3'
          ➥face='MS Sans Serif'></font>" + results + "</td>" );
145:            out.println( "                       </tr>" );
146:            out.println( "                   </table>" );
147:            out.println( "                 </div>" );
148:            out.println( "         </form>" );
149:            out.println( "         </td>" );
150:            out.println( "   </tr>" );
151:            out.println( "</table>" );
152:            out.println( "</div>" );
153:            out.println( "</body>" );
154:            out.println( "</html>" );
155:
156:
157:            // Write the data of the response
158:            out.close();
159:        }
160:
161: }
```

First you declare some variables. The important one is myReader, which will hold an instance of the POP3Reader class. myReader is the real workhorse for this servlet because it doesn't really do anything but relay information.

You then override the init() method. In this method, you instantiate a POP3Reader class. You'll be using this object over and over again, so there is no sense in creating a new one each time. That can be slow and inefficient.

Next, you override the doPost() method, which is called when the servlet is invoked. This method pulls out the parameters that were passed in, configures the POP3Reader, and then retrieves the mail counts. The counts are then formatted into a string. That string, results, is then output with a complete copy of the original calling HTML page.

16

An Alternative Servlet That Uses the GET Method

Earlier, I mentioned you could use the GET method to eliminate the HTML page. You need the HTML page with the POST method because you cannot initiate a POST method with a browser alone—you need a form. Because all HTTP requests are GET methods, you can change the doPost() method in Line 25 of Listing 16.3 to doGet() and change the HTTP method in Line 110 from POST to GET to call the servlet instead of loading the HTML page.

Because the variables passed in were null, no results are displayed. The reason for not displaying any results is so that you don't have to maintain two sets of HTML code. If you decide to change the layout of the POP mail-checker Web page, just change the HTML code in this servlet.

Summary

Today was an exciting one—you learned more about servlets and how to write them. You examined the life cycle of a servlet. You looked at the init() method and its argument, the ServletConfig class. From there, you looked at the service() method and wound up with the destroy() method.

Then this lesson discussed the two types of servlets you can create: generic or HTTP based. The lesson covered the differences between the two and then examined the methods provided by the HttpServlet class. Finally, you took your new knowledge and created a servlet that checks your e-mail for you. This servlet uses the POP3Reader class created in Day 7, "Networking with Java."

Tomorrow, you learn how to package your Java classes in the Java ARchive, or JAR, format.

Q&A

Q How can servlets be loaded?

A Servlets can be loaded dynamically or forced. Dynamically loaded servlets load and execute when they are called by the Java Web Server. Force-loaded servlets are configured to run whenever the Java Web Server is running.

Q What is the purpose of the service() method?

A The service() method is the entry point into your servlet from the Java Web Server. When a request comes in for your servlet, this is the method that is notified of the request.

Q **Why would I use the `GenericServlet` class as a base class for my own servlets?**

A Well, you probably won't. But it can be useful for developing servlets for non-Java Web Server applications. For example, if you write your own service in Java with the Java Service API, you would use the `GenericServlet` as a base for all your servlets.

16

Day 17

Working with Java Archives

by Michael Morrison

Before Java 1.1, there was no way to bundle for distribution the various files that comprise Java applets and applications. Seeing a critical need for such a feature, JavaSoft developed Java archives, which are special files capable of holding multiple compressed files such as Java class files, images, and sounds. Not only did JavaSoft create a tool—the JAR utility—for building and manipulating Java archives, they also included a compression API as part of Java 1.1. This API, which is based on the popular ZIP file format by PKWare and which provides access to archive compression features, is located in the java.util.zip package.

You learn the following in this lesson:

- ☐ Why Java ARchives, or JAR files, are important and how they work
- ☐ How to use the JAR utility to create and manipulate JAR files
- ☐ Why JAR files are important to JavaBeans
- ☐ How to package Beans for distribution using the JAR utility

Understanding Java Archive Basics

Java archives are commonly referred to as *JAR files* and are a powerful means of compressing and storing multiple files in a single unit. JAR files are based on the popular ZIP file format; the only difference is that JAR files support a way to add security authentication to an archive. JAR files are useful to Java developers in a variety of ways. Following is a list of some of the benefits JAR files offer:

- [ ] Fewer HTTP transactions
- [ ] Efficient file storage
- [ ] Security
- [ ] Platform independence
- [ ] Backward compatibility with Java 1.0
- [ ] High extensibility

Fewer HTTP Transactions

One of the most obvious benefits of JAR files is the improved download performance afforded applets that are embedded in Web pages. The traditional way of distributing an applet is to put all its class files and related resources into a directory somewhere on a Web site. Because the files are all stored individually, each imposes the overhead of an HTTP transaction when downloaded to a client browser. JAR files greatly improve this situation by allowing you to bundle all of an applet's class files and resources into a single archive. The result is that you have only one HTTP transaction—regardless of how many files comprise an applet.

Efficient File Storage

If reducing to one the number of HTTP transactions isn't enough, the fact that JAR files are *compressed* improves download efficiency even more. Depending on how well the files within a JAR file compress, you can save 50 percent or more of storage space, and therefore download time, by JAR compression alone. This significant improvement makes it easier to integrate Java with Web pages because developers can be a little less concerned with download times.

Security

Another big feature supported by JAR files is *digital security signatures*. Don't worry if you aren't familiar with them because you learn more about JAR security and digital signatures tomorrow. For now, just understand that signing a Java applet allows the applet to bypass some of the stringent security limitations imposed by the Java security model. For example, signed Java applets can write files, which has traditionally been a major no-no for applets. Before JAR files, this applet security capability wasn't possible.

Platform Independence

JAR files are completely platform-independent because the JAR standard is written entirely in Java. Platform independence has been an important goal of the Java technology from the beginning and is clearly still a major issue in newer Java technologies such as JavaBeans. Platform independence means that JAR files, such as Java applets, can be built and distributed on any platform that supports Java.

Backward Compatibility

JAR files are backward-compatible with earlier releases of Java. This means, for example, that you can package applets written in Java 1.0 into JAR files. This seemingly inconsequential issue highlights an important point about JAR files: JAR is basically a standard for archiving files. Contrast this with other Java technologies, which are typically programming APIs as well as standards. The only real programming API for JAR is the underlying compression API it uses.

High Extensibility

The final point to be made about JAR files is that they define an open standard that is highly extensible. This means that the JAR standard can grow and evolve to support future enhancements to Java. Because the Java technology is in a constant state of evolution, this is an important requirement of JAR files.

That pretty much wraps up the basics surrounding Java archives and how they fit into Java. Let's move on and find out how Java archives maintain information about the files they contain.

Understanding Manifest Files

Unlike normal ZIP and TAR archives, Java archives support the inclusion of a special file that lists information about the files contained within an archive. This file is the *manifest file*, a text file placed in a JAR file that lists information about the files contained within the archive file. Manifest files are primarily used to specify digital signature information about the files packaged in a JAR file. Manifest files are also used to identify JavaBeans components within a JAR file. It's important to understand that not all files in a JAR file must be listed in the manifest file (for example, the manifest file itself is not listed). However, the main class file for JavaBeans components must be listed, along with any digitally signed classes. Figure 17.1 shows how a manifest file identifies the digitally signed classes and Bean classes in a JAR file.

NEW TERM

> *manifest file:* A text file placed in a JAR file that lists information about the files contained in the JAR file.

Figure 17.1.

A manifest file identifies digitally signed classes and Bean classes in a JAR file.

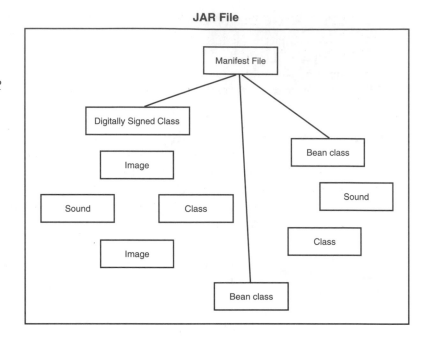

The structure of a manifest file is very simple. Every manifest file begins with a preliminary section that contains, at a minimum, the JAR version number. This version number corresponds to the version of the JAR standard used to create the JAR file; in Java 1.1, the JAR version is 1.0. The preliminary section of a manifest file looks like this:

```
Manifest-Version: 1.0
```

You can optionally specify the JAR version required for using the JAR file. If the actual version is higher than the required version, JAR extensions may be used. Here is an example of how to specify a required version:

```
Required-Version: 1.0
```

Following the preliminary section are the entries for each individual file in the JAR file. Each entry corresponds to a single file in the archive, which is typically either a file with a digital signature or a JavaBeans class file. A JAR file that contains only one Bean and no digital signatures has only one entry in its manifest file. Each Bean entry in the manifest file consists of two required pieces of information: the name of the Bean's class file and a flag indicating that the class is, in fact, a Bean. Following is an example of how these two pieces of information are specified:

```
Name: MyBean.class
Java-Bean: True
```

17

Each Bean entry can also contain digital signature information for security purposes, but that's a topic best left to tomorrow's lesson. A complete manifest file including the MyBean entry looks like this:

```
Manifest-Version: 1.0
Name: MyBean.class
Java-Bean: True
```

As you can see, the complete manifest file for a single Bean is very simple: you basically provide the name of the Bean class and specify that it is a Bean. If you want to include more Beans in an archive file, just add more entries to the manifest file. It's important to note that every JAR file contains a manifest file, regardless of whether you explicitly provide manifest information. At this point, you may be wondering exactly how a manifest file of your own is associated with a JAR file. Hang on, because that answer is coming right up.

NOTE

> Although this discussion of manifest files has been slanted somewhat toward JavaBeans, understand that manifest files are equally important for digitally signing normal Java classes. However, digital signature information is automatically added to a manifest file by the javakey utility; JavaBeans information must be manually provided by the developer. This issue becomes clearer during the next two lessons when you learn about digital signatures and how to sign Java objects.

Using the JAR Utility

You're no doubt eager to start learning exactly how JAR files are created. JAR files are created and modified with the JAR utility (jar), which ships with the JDK 1.1. The JAR utility works very much like the ZIP or TAR utility in that it enables you to combine and compress multiple files into a single archive. However, the JAR utility is specifically geared toward creating archives that support Java and has a special provision for including digital signature information. The syntax for jar is given here:

```
jar Options Files
```

The *Files* argument specifies the files used when working with a JAR file and varies based on the options in the *Options* argument. The *Options* argument specifies options related to how the JAR utility manipulates a JAR file. Following is a list of the jar options:

Option	Description
c	Specifies that a new archive is to be created.
m	Specifies that the manifest file for the archive is to be created using an external manifest file. The external manifest file is provided as the second file in the *Files* list following the options.
M	Specifies that no manifest file is to be created for the archive.
t	Lists the contents of an archive.
x *Files*	Extracts all the files in an archive; extracts just the named files if additional files are specified.
f	Specifies the name of the archive to be accessed, where the name is provided as the first file in the *Files* list. The f option is used in conjunction with all the other options.
v	Causes the JAR utility to generate verbose output, which results in more information being displayed regarding the actions performed on an archive.
0	Stores files in an archive without using compression.

NOTE　Unlike most command-line utilities, the jar utility doesn't require the use of a / or - when specifying options.

Examining an Existing Archive

To get a better idea of how the JAR utility works, examine the JAR file for one of the Beans shipped with the JavaBeans Development Kit (BDK). You learned all about the BDK back on Day 6, "Using JavaBeans Effectively." The Juggler Bean is one of the demo Beans provided with the BDK and has a corresponding JAR file, Juggler.jar, located in the \Bdk\jars directory.

NOTE　This discussion assumes that you have installed the BDK to the default \Bdk directory. If you installed the BDK to some other directory, look for the Juggler.jar file in the jars directory beneath your BDK installation directory.

The following jar command lists all the files stored in the Juggler.jar archive:

```
jar tf Juggler.jar
```

17

The results of executing this command follow:

```
META-INF/MANIFEST.MF
sunw/demo/juggler/Juggler.class
sunw/demo/juggler/JugglerBeanInfo.class
sunw/demo/juggler/Juggler0.gif
sunw/demo/juggler/Juggler1.gif
sunw/demo/juggler/Juggler2.gif
sunw/demo/juggler/Juggler3.gif
sunw/demo/juggler/Juggler4.gif
sunw/demo/juggler/JugglerIcon.gif
```

As you can see, the Juggler Bean requires two classes and a variety of images. Although the listing of the JAR file doesn't tell you exactly which class is the Bean class, you can certainly guess. To find out for sure, you can extract the manifest file from the archive. To make things easier, you can extract all the files in the archive with the following command:

```
jar xf Juggler.jar
```

This command results in all the Bean's files being extracted to the relative paths specified in the JAR file. In other words, the files are placed in subdirectories beneath the \Bdk\jars directory. Figure 17.2 shows what the \Bdk\jars directory looks like after you've executed the extraction command.

Figure 17.2.

The \Bdk\jars directory listing after extracting the contents of the Juggler Bean's JAR file.

As you can see in the figure, there are two new directories: META-INF and sunw. Look back at the JAR file listing and notice that these directories correspond to the relative paths for each file in the archive. To see the manifest file for the Bean, change to the new \Bdk\jars\META-INF directory, where you'll find a file called MANIFEST.MF. This is the manifest file just extracted from the Juggler Bean's JAR file. Listing 17.1 shows this file in its entirety.

Listing 17.1. The Juggler Bean's manifest file.

```
Manifest-Version: 1.0
Name: sunw/demo/juggler/Juggler.class
Java-Bean: True
Digest-Algorithms: SHA MD5
SHA-Digest: HvNgDbu0tEItNQrN2FxtnLHUB/g=
MD5-Digest: lodCaNW4vjtpiyVtqQojAg==
Name: sunw/demo/juggler/JugglerBeanInfo.class
Digest-Algorithms: SHA MD5
SHA-Digest: aVi52xkXvbrqrBBkW4lmI9GJvSo=
MD5-Digest: cy2MF8RT8c8AncXB7ZKtVA==
Name: sunw/demo/juggler/Juggler0.gif
Digest-Algorithms: SHA MD5
SHA-Digest: BoXVBkl+aKR7/2+f80rqxYbltTc=
MD5-Digest: SOLrOrGbrm+3aJNgJgIwdQ==
Name: sunw/demo/juggler/Juggler1.gif
Digest-Algorithms: SHA MD5
SHA-Digest: BoXVBkl+aKR7/2+f80rqxYbltTc=
MD5-Digest: SOLrOrGbrm+3aJNgJgIwdQ==
Name: sunw/demo/juggler/Juggler2.gif
Digest-Algorithms: SHA MD5
SHA-Digest: vf+oWwJoCJXwd0FTwIAOqBwShc8=
MD5-Digest: 0UQOpDSyiy7ziKGuk8o2xQ==
Name: sunw/demo/juggler/Juggler3.gif
Digest-Algorithms: SHA MD5
SHA-Digest: 5ngCVC3l4zj4zefuY5V0zWjGKAM=
MD5-Digest: 0XIiV4Hs97ZLE6Vh5wYH3g==
Name: sunw/demo/juggler/Juggler4.gif
Digest-Algorithms: SHA MD5
SHA-Digest: 7/z73JtPbxHmsn61TQp1q2cvuDs=
MD5-Digest: GY6JSNxiIabXhvoK2ZjjYQ==
Name: sunw/demo/juggler/JugglerIcon.gif
Digest-Algorithms: SHA MD5
SHA-Digest: Irqj25Pd5hgucribaj3QUIU3UAc=
MD5-Digest: BS0b0MJ3J+/tI4G/NFxVEw==
```

Because you probably understand all the information in the manifest file, let's move on. Just kidding! Although the manifest file for this JAR file appears pretty messy, if you look carefully at Listing 17.1, you can find the familiar information about manifest files described earlier: a preliminary section with the JAR version number (1.0), the name of the Bean class (Juggler.class), and the True flag stating that the class is a Bean. The rest of the information in the manifest file specifies digital signatures for all the files in the archive, which you learn more about in tomorrow's lesson. This manifest file was associated with the Juggler Bean's JAR file using the m option to the JAR utility. The m option allows you to specify an external (user-defined) manifest file.

Creating a New Archive

Now you know how to examine an existing JAR file, but you haven't learned how to create a new archive. Creating new JAR files is surprisingly simple: You just use the c option to the

JAR utility and specify the files you want to include. For example, if you have a directory of GIF images you want to package into a new JAR file named Images.jar, execute the following command in the directory containing the images:

```
jar cf Images.jar *.gif
```

The c and f options are used in this example to specify that a JAR file is to be created with the name Images.jar. The wildcard *.gif is used to add all the GIF files in the directory to the archive.

This approach works fine for creating generic JAR files, but it doesn't address the issue of the manifest files required for Beans. To create a JAR file for a Bean, you have to use an additional option: the m option. This example creates a JAR file for a Bean called StringBean, whose manifest file is named StringBean.mf:

```
jar cfm StringBean.jar StringBean.mf *.class *.gif
```

As you can see, it takes three options (cfm) to create a JAR file for a Bean. The name of the new JAR file is identified by the first argument; the name of the external manifest file is provided as the second argument. The remaining two arguments are wildcards used to add all the classes and images in the current directory to the archive.

That's all it takes to create a JAR file for a Bean. Once you've built a JAR file for a Bean, you can distribute the Bean however you want. Users of the Bean can incorporate it into their own applets and applications using application-builder tools.

Extracting Files from an Existing Archive

Extracting files from an archive is very simple. To extract all the files from an archive, use the x option to the JAR utility with no additional parameters, like this:

```
jar fx Images.jar
```

This command results in all the files contained within the Images.jar file being extracted to the current directory. Keep in mind that all JAR files contain a manifest file listing the files contained within the archive. If you use the x option with no parameters to extract all the files in an archive, the manifest file is extracted as well. In addition, extracted files automatically retain any directory structure they have in the JAR file. For example, the manifest file for a JAR file is always stored in the META-INF directory, which means that this directory is created if the manifest file is extracted.

If you want to extract only selected files, you can use the x option and list the files as parameters after the name of the JAR file, like this:

```
jar fx Images.jar Me.gif You.gif
```

This command extracts two images (Me.gif and You.gif) to the current directory. That's all there is to extracting files using the JAR utility.

Using JAR Files

Because the whole point in using JAR files is to improve the distribution of Java applets and JavaBeans components, it's about time you learn how to use JAR files for this purpose. Let's start off with how JavaBeans components are distributed with JAR files because that is something of a no-brainer.

JavaBeans components are typically plugged into an application-builder tool and then used to construct applications visually. Application-builder tools typically provide a command for adding new components. Because the tools fully expect Beans to be packaged in JAR files, there really is nothing to do except follow the specific tool's instructions for adding new components.

For Java applets, however, you have to do a little more work to use a JAR file. Still, I think you'll find it a very simple and straightforward task. Java applets are typically embedded in Web pages using the HTML `<applet>` tag. A new attribute has been added to the `<applet>` tag to facilitate JAR files: `archive`. The `archive` attribute specifies that one or more JAR files should be downloaded with the applet. To specify multiple JAR files, you simply separate them with commas.

WARNING

> Whenever you use the `archive` attribute with the `<applet>` tag, keep in mind that you still have to use the `code` attribute to specify which class file is the main applet class.

When an applet is embedded in a Web page using the `<applet>` tag and `archive` attribute, the applet always looks to the archive first whenever it searches for a class or resource, such as image and sound files. If the applet doesn't find a file in the archive, it contacts the HTTP server and requests the file just as it does if you don't use a JAR file.

Following is an example of using the `archive` attribute to specify that an applet can be found in a pair of JAR files:

```
<applet code="MyApplet.class"
  archive="MyArchive.jar, AnotherArchive.jar"
  width=200
  height=300>
</applet>
```

17

Understanding JAR Files and JavaBeans

This lesson mentioned JavaBeans a few times during the discussion of JAR files. It's important to understand why JAR files are so important to JavaBeans. JAR files enter the picture with JavaBeans when it comes time to package a Bean for distribution. In short, the standard technique for compressing and packaging Beans for distribution is provided by JAR files. Using JAR files, you can group the classes and resources for a Bean into one compressed unit to organize them, conserve space, and (in some cases) provide a measure of security. Bean resources can include anything from images and sounds to custom resources such as Bean-specific data files. Grouping the classes and resources for a Bean cleans up the delivery of the Bean a great deal because it eliminates the task of keeping up with lots of different support files.

If bundling beans in JAR files doesn't sound like all that big a deal, consider that there is a higher motive at work here. The benefits of better organization, faster Web-file transfers, and security are important, but the primary reason to use JAR files with Beans is because application-development tools *require* them. Application-builder tools that support the integration of Beans fully expect to see Beans packaged as JAR files. This expectation exists because JAR files are the standard packaging scheme for Beans. The bottom line is that all Beans should be packaged in JAR files unless there is some good reason why you don't want a Bean to be used in an application-builder tool.

An example of a tool that requires Beans to be packaged in JAR files is the BeanBox test container, which you learned about on Day 6. The BeanBox recognizes only JAR files when it assembles its toolbox of Beans. This brings up a good question about JAR files and Beans: How do application-builder tools know which Beans are included in a JAR file? Because JAR files are ultimately just a bunch of files compressed together and can potentially include multiple class files, it isn't readily apparent which class files are Beans. The answer to the question of which class files are Beans is hopefully apparent to you at this point: manifest files.

NOTE

A single JAR file can store multiple Beans. This arrangement allows you to package an entire library of related Beans together in one JAR file. The manifest file is responsible for formally listing all the Beans contained in a JAR file.

Summary

Today you learned about Java ARchives, or JAR files, which constitute an important new Java 1.1 technology. You learned what Java archives have to offer and why they are so important to both Java applets and JavaBeans components. You got some hands-on experience with the JAR utility, the tool used to create and manipulate Java archives. You also learned how to package Java applets in JAR files and embed them in Web pages for greater efficiency in downloading. Finally, you wrapped up the lesson by learning about the significance of JAR files to JavaBeans.

Q&A

Q If Java archives are based on the popular ZIP file format, does that mean I can use the JAR utility to create and modify ZIP files?

A Yes. Although this capability is rarely mentioned, the JAR utility directly supports ZIP files.

Q If the JAR utility supports ZIP files, does that also mean that ZIP utilities support JAR files?

A Yes. JAR files use the standard ZIP file format, with the additional requirement that they have manifest files describing the files that the archives contain. If you want to hand code your own manifest file (to package a JavaBeans component, for example), you can use any archiving utility that supports the ZIP file format.

Q Can I use JAR files as a way to store files for use by my own applets and applications?

A Yes. The primary purpose of JAR files is to improve the distribution of Java applets and JavaBeans components, but the compression API used by JAR files is part of the Java 1.1 API and can be used in your own applets and applications however you choose. If you have some type of data you want to keep in a compressed form, you can package the data files in a JAR file and then use the classes in the `java.util.zip` package to extract and use the data files in an applet or application.

Day 18

Introduction to Digital Security and the Java Security API

by Michael Morrison

Security has always been a major issue with Java because Java applets are dynamically downloaded and executed and can pose potentially serious security risks. Fortunately, JavaSoft has been extremely attentive in addressing security risks and making sure that Java is as secure as possible. The Java 1.1 API includes a complete API devoted solely to providing advanced security features for the Java platform. The Security API includes support for public-key encryption, which is an extremely powerful way of handling information in a secure fashion.

This lesson dives into the Java Security API and shows you how to use many of the security classes and interfaces. You will learn about the following topics:

- ☐ Cryptography and two of the main types of encryption: conventional encryption and public-key encryption
- ☐ The Java Security API and what it has to offer Java programs

Cryptography 101

The Java Security API is based on *cryptography*, which is defined as the science of secret writing. What does this mean? Well, it means that cryptography provides a way of secretly encoding information so that it can be read only by someone who knows how to decode it. In cryptography, the process of encoding a piece of information is known as *encryption*; the process of decoding the information is known as *decryption*. More specifically, encryption is defined as the process of taking data (*cleartext*) and a short key string and producing data (*ciphertext*) that is meaningless to a third-party who does not know the key. Likewise, decryption is the process of taking ciphertext and a short key string and producing cleartext. Clearly, decryption is the logical complement of encryption.

> **NEW TERM**
>
> *encryption:* The process of taking data (*cleartext*) and a short key string or number and producing data (*ciphertext*) that is meaningless to a third-party who does not know the key.

> **NEW TERM**
>
> *decryption:* The process of taking ciphertext and a short key string or number and producing cleartext; this process is the complement of encryption.

Encryption and decryption can be traced back to the Roman empire when Caesar's messengers delivered messages that were protected through a simple form of encryption. The form of encryption employed by Caesar involved shifting each letter in a message by a given amount. For example, every letter in a message might have been shifted up two letters. Using this approach, the letter *m* becomes *o*, *t* becomes *v*, and so on. This is a very rudimentary form of encryption, but in its day I'm sure it worked quite well. Modern forms of encryption are just as simple in purpose, but their actual encryption implementations can be very complex.

Modern approaches to encryption rely on extremely heavy mathematical formulas that are virtually impossible to solve. The idea is to remove the possibility of breaking an encrypted message using a brute-force approach, because no computers are powerful enough (yet) to

18

try every possible key combination in a reasonable amount of time. Let's hope microprocessors don't improve too rapidly, or our sense of security may quickly vanish!

Two of the main types of encryption around today are conventional encryption and public-key encryption. Java uses the latter, but it's important to understand them both. The next few sections explore these two types of encryption and how they relate to each other.

Conventional Encryption

Conventional encryption, also known as *symmetric encryption*, was the primary type of encryption used before public-key encryption, which you learn about in a moment. Conventional encryption involves the use of a single key to encrypt and decrypt a given message. The *key*, in this case, is a number known to both the sender and receiver of a message and is used to encrypt the message on the sending end and decrypt the message on the receiving end. As long as the sender and receiver both have the key, conventional encryption works like a charm. For example, the encryption used by Caesar was conventional in that it involved a single key—the number of times the letters in a message are shifted. The sender and receiver of the message both have to know the number of shifts (key) for the message to get through. However, a significant problem arises if they don't already share the key; a secure communication channel is required for one of them to give the key to the other.

Consider the situation where the sender and receiver of a message are physically located on opposite sides of the globe (a common scenario on the Internet). To communicate with each other using conventional encryption, they must share the key that they will use to encrypt and decrypt secure messages. One of them is capable of creating the key to start with, but how does he or she get the key to the other one? If the key isn't transferred in a completely secure fashion, the security afforded by conventional encryption is compromised. The point I'm making is that conventional encryption completely depends on there being a secure channel at some point for sharing keys. In this hypothetical example, the sender and receiver would almost have to physically meet to be absolutely certain that the key is shared through a secure channel.

A popular implementation of conventional encryption is the Data Encryption Standard (DES). DES has been used for years by the U.S. government and can be very powerful—provided that keys are carefully shared between communicating parties.

Public-Key Encryption

The weakness of conventional encryption (having to share keys through a secure channel) is addressed by public-key encryption. *Public-key encryption* is an encryption approach that uses two keys: a public key and a private key. Any individual or entity that wants to engage in public-key encryption must have its own public and private keys, which are known as a *key pair*. Unlike keys in conventional encryption, which must be kept completely private, a *public key* in public-key encryption is freely available to anyone who wants to have secure interactions with the owner of the key. Every public key has an associated *private key* that must be kept secret.

| NEW TERM | *public key:* A number associated with an entity (individual or organization) that is available to anyone who wants to have trusted interactions with the entity. |

| NEW TERM | *private key:* A number known only to a particular entity that is always associated with a single public key; private keys must be kept secret. |

The idea behind public-key encryption is that someone encrypts a message using his or her secret private key; the message then can be decrypted by anyone with the corresponding public key. That doesn't exactly sound secure, does it? To make a message secure, the sender must encrypt it using the public key of the recipient. The recipient can then decrypt the message with his or her private key. This arrangement involves two levels of encryption:

1. The sender encrypts a message with his or her private key to signify that the message is coming from him or her. Anyone can decrypt the message at this point, but they must use the sender's public key, which effectively validates that the sender is the true sender of the message.

2. The sender encrypts a message with the recipient's public key to prevent the message from being decrypted by anyone but the recipient. At this stage, the message can be decrypted only by the recipient because the recipient's private key is required.

Digital Signatures

The idea behind the two levels of encryption is to both provide a secure way of transmitting "secret messages" as well as a validation mechanism for making sure that the source of a message is who they say they are. This validation mechanism is known as a *digital signature* and is one of the main applications of public-key encryption. A digital signature is a way of marking a piece of information to signify that the information came from a particular source. In this way, digital signatures are very similar conceptually to handwritten signatures; they provide a way of validating an entity, be it a person or organization.

| NEW TERM | *digital signature:* A way of marking a piece of information to signify that the message came from a particular source. |

There are plenty of parallels between digital signatures and handwritten signatures:

☐ The authenticity of digital signatures can be verified

☐ Digital signatures cannot be forged, assuming that the private key isn't compromised

☐ Digital signatures depend on the information being signed and thus can't be misrepresented as signatures for other information

☐ Because digital signatures depend on the data being signed, the signed data cannot be changed, or the signature is no longer valid

Digital signatures differ from handwritten signatures in that digital signatures are purely digital constructs. In other words, digital signatures are just numbers, so they don't have any visible connection to an individual like a handwritten signature does. You have no intimate connection with your digital signature and no way to distinguish it from other people's signatures beyond your public and private keys. However, when you really think about what sets apart handwritten signatures, digital signatures make more sense. Can you honestly isolate the specific aspects of your handwritten signature that make it unique to you? Okay, maybe you dot your *i*s with smiley faces, but other than that, handwritten signatures are hard to pin down in terms of what makes them individualistic. Likewise, the individual aspects of a digital signature are hidden in the numeric code of the signature.

Certificates

You learned that one of the uses of public key encryption is in providing a way of verifying the source of a message. The approach offered by public-key encryption involves a sender using his or her private key to encrypt a message, in which case, his or her public key can be used by a recipient to decrypt the message. The fact that the public key was used verifies that the message was originally encrypted by them. But what stops someone from generating a falsified key pair and sending a message claiming to be someone else? Nothing. Without a way of registering and certifying public keys, there is no way to know whether a public key is legitimate.

Well, that pretty much blows a hole in public-key encryption, right? Not exactly. All that is required to remedy this problem is a public-key certification system, which requires entities (again, people or organizations) to register themselves and their public keys through a certificate. A *certificate* is a digitally signed statement from a third party verifying that your public key in fact belongs to you. In other words, certificates require a third party to verify the association between an entity and its public key.

> **NEW TERM**
>
> *certificate:* A digitally signed statement from a third party verifying that your public key in fact belongs to you.

18

Of course, you must trust the entity doing the verifying if the certificate is to make sense; otherwise a second con man could validate a bogus certificate for the first one passing a bogus public key around! To facilitate this trust, there are *certification authorities*, organizations devoted solely to the management of key certification. Certification authorities are responsible for issuing new key pairs and certificates, storing a copy of each user's private key, responding to certificate query requests, and keeping an updated list of invalid certificates. Two popular certification authorities are VeriSign, Inc. (www.verisign.com) and Entrust Technologies (www.entrust.com).

NEW TERM	*certification authorities:* Organizations devoted solely to the management of key certification.

Message Digests

Because signatures are used only to verify the source of a message, it isn't necessary to be able to extract the complete message from a signature. In fact, it is extremely inefficient to encrypt a large message solely for the purpose of generating a digital signature (which, in the case of a large file, could itself be quite large). Consider the small size of a handwritten signature within the context of a multipage contractual agreement. Digital signatures should similarly be as compact as possible. Additionally, encryption algorithms are very heavy computationally and can be very slow in processing a large amount of information. Therefore, it is important to try to keep the size of encrypted data small for efficiency.

The solution to generating efficient signatures is to base a signature on a smaller representation of the data being signed. For example, you can calculate a numeric representation of a piece of data that is much shorter than the data itself. Java uses such a facility (known as *hash codes* or *checksums*) when managing strings. The Java Security API provides a stronger implementation of hash codes known as message digests. A *message digest* is a fixed-size representation of arbitrary-sized data that uniquely identifies the data.

NEW TERM	*message digest:* A fixed-size representation of arbitrary-sized data that uniquely identifies the data.

The important aspect of message digests is that it is computationally infeasible to generate the same digest with different input data. In this way, a message digest acts as a "digital fingerprint" for data. Additionally, message digests don't reveal anything about the data used to generate them. The Java Security API uses message digests to create digital signatures of data with much greater efficiency than if the data had been signed in its original form.

18

Applet Authentication

The security features provided by Java 1.1 sound pretty interesting, but you still may be curious about their purpose. Every piece of functionality in Java has a reason for being, and the security features you've learned about this far in this lesson are no different. The Java cryptography features are primarily used for authenticating Java applets. An authenticated applet, or *trusted applet*, is an applet whose source has been validated. The source of an applet is the company or individual who developed the applet or who takes responsibility for the applet.

NEW TERM	*trusted applet:* An applet whose source has been validated.

The idea behind trusted applets is that users typically aren't afraid of using software published by reputable companies. This is evidenced by the fact that the vast majority of software is purchased without any concern for security—most people don't think of off-the-shelf software as being dangerous. The primary reason for this trust (at least for those who have ever questioned the security of off-the-shelf software) is because it is very clear who the publisher of off-the-shelf software is and therefore who is responsible for the software if there is a problem. Incidentally, there have been isolated cases in which viruses were unknowingly shipped in off-the-shelf software; in these cases, the publishers quickly addressed the problem with patches and fixes.

Java applets put an interesting twist on software distribution by allowing themselves to be distributed dynamically over the Internet with little or no interaction from users. This creates a dangerous situation in which hostile applets can wreak havoc on a user's system. Fortunately, JavaSoft was keenly aware of the risks associated with applets and enforced an extremely stringent security model on applets. To make absolutely sure that applets can't monkey around with a user's system, applets are limited to the point that they cannot perform such simple tasks as writing to a file. The security restrictions placed on applets have presented a problem for developers who want to add functionality to applets that simply isn't allowed.

The solution to this dilemma lies in trusted applets. A trusted applet can bypass the stringent security model imposed by Java because the source of the applet is validated. Users have the freedom to pick and choose sources so that they can give trust to sources selectively. Admittedly, this solution pushes a great deal of responsibility onto the user, but taking care of our own security is just a fact of life; software security isn't much different. Therefore, the new security features in Java aren't there so much to automatically protect you from evil, but instead are there to empower you with technologies you can use to protect yourself. These technologies include key pairs, digital signatures, certificates, message digests, and access control lists, all of which are used to facilitate trusted applets.

18

Access Control Lists

Authentication answers an extremely important Java security need by allowing users to verify the source of applets. However, authentication isn't the single answer to all of Java's security problems. The discussion about security in the preceding section alluded to the elimination of all security barriers for trusted applets. In other words, an applet either operates under a very stringent security model or a very lax security model, depending on whether it is trusted. In practice, this approach is too extreme; there may be situations in which you want to limit the access rights of an applet even though it is trusted. With authentication alone, this type of access control simply isn't possible.

Where a need arises, Java provides an answer. In this case, the Security API provides *access control lists*, lists of access permissions assigned to entities to control their access privileges. An access control list is assigned to a given entity and consists of a list of access control entries. These entries in turn contain permissions for different types of access available to the entity, such as the ability to write to a file. Each permission in an access control entry is positive or negative, which corresponds to the permission being granted or revoked.

NEW TERM	*access control list:* A list of access permissions assigned to entities to control their access privileges.

An entity can be an individual or an organization. An "organization" in this sense doesn't necessarily have to correspond to a company; it may make sense to identify organizations of people within a company and to create access control lists for them.

The Java Security API

Now that you have a conceptual handle on the kinds of features provided by the Java Security API, it's time to dive into the API itself and find out more specifics. The Java Security API is spread across three packages in the Java core API:

- ☐ `java.security`
- ☐ `java.security.acl`
- ☐ `java.security.interfaces`

The `java.security` package includes the majority of the functionality in the Security API. The `java.security.acl` package contains classes and interfaces relating to access control lists. The `java.security.interfaces` package contains interfaccs used to facilitate Digital Signature Algorithm (DSA) encryption.

18

The Java Security API introduces the notion of an *engine class,* a class that provides the functionality of a type of encryption algorithm. Examples of engine classes include `KeyPairGenerator`, `Signature`, and `MessageDigest`. The significance of engine classes is the manner in which they support multiple implementations of encryption algorithms. Engine classes defined in the Security API function as interfaces to a given algorithm type, such as the message digest algorithm; specific implementations of the algorithm are carried out in engine subclasses. This two-tiered approach to managing encryption algorithms is what allows different algorithm implementations to be integrated into the Security API with ease.

NEW TERM	*engine class:* A class that provides the functionality of an encryption algorithm.

The Security API can be functionally divided into different parts, which helps in understanding the structure of the API as a whole. Following are the major functional parts of the API:

- ☐ Providers
- ☐ Keys
- ☐ Digital signatures
- ☐ Message digests
- ☐ Access control lists

Providers

A *provider* is a package or set of packages that implement one or more engine classes for different security algorithms. The Java Security API always operates within the context of a provider, because providers provide the way by which encryption is possible. The default provider shipped with the JDK is named SUN; it supplies implementations of the DSA signature algorithm, the MD5 message digest algorithm, and the SHA-1 message digest algorithm. It's not critical that you understand any specifics about these algorithms other than that they offer different approaches to solving the same problems. With Java security, variety is the key to happiness.

NEW TERM	*provider:* A package or set of packages that implement one or more engine classes for different security algorithms.

The Provider class represents a security provider and provides methods for getting information about a provider. Listing 18.1 contains source code for the ProviderInfo application, which uses some of the methods defined in the Provider class to display information about all the providers present on a system.

Listing 18.1. The source code for the ProviderInfo application.

```
 1: public class ProviderInfo {
 2:   public static void main(String[] args) {
 3:     Provider[] p = Security.getProviders();
 4:     for (int i = 0; i < p.length; i++) {
 5:       System.out.println(p[i].getName());
 6:       System.out.println(p[i].getVersion());
 7:       System.out.println(p[i].getInfo());
 8:       System.out.println();
 9:     }
10:   }
11: }
```

The ProviderInfo application uses the getProviders() method defined in the Security class to get an array containing the providers installed in the system (Line 3). The application loops through this array so that information about each provider can be displayed to the user (Line 4). The getName(), getVersion(), and getInfo() methods are used to carry this out (Lines 5 through 7). Executing the ProviderInfo application on my Windows 95 system under JDK 1.1 yielded the following results:

```
SUN
1.0
SUN Security Provider v1.0, DSA signing and key generation, SHA-1 and MD5
message digests.
```

This output shows the default provider, which is the only one present on my system. The name of the default provider is SUN and the version is 1.0; the provider information lists the types of algorithms supplied by the provider.

As the ProviderInfo application demonstrated, security providers are managed by the Security class. The Security class consists entirely of static methods and is therefore never instantiated. The primary use of the Security class is to manage providers, but it also provides support for managing security properties.

Keys

A variety of classes and interfaces are used to represent and manage keys in the Java Security API:

- ☐ Key interface
- ☐ PublicKey and PrivateKey interfaces
- ☐ KeyPair class

☐ KeyPairGenerator class

☐ Identity and IdentityScope classes

The Key interface serves as the basic interface that defines functionality common to all keys. Specific types of keys are represented by the PublicKey and PrivateKey classes. Interestingly enough, the PublicKey and PrivateKey classes don't implement any methods; they are used solely for type safety and identification. The KeyPair class is an organizational class used to hold a key pair, which always consists of a public key and a private key. The KeyPairGenerator class is an engine class used to generate key pairs. Following is an example of how to create a pair of keys using the KeyPairGenerator class:

```
KeyPairGenerator keyGen = keyPairGenerator.getInstance("DSA");
keyGen.initialize(1024);
KeyPair keys = keyGen.generateKeyPair();
```

A KeyGenerator object is first created by calling the static getInstance() method, which takes a string argument identifying the algorithm used by the key generator. DSA is the signature algorithm provided by the default SUN security provider. Before a KeyGenerator object can be used to create keys, it must be initialized with the initialize() method. The initialize() method takes one argument specifying the strength of the keys to be created (this argument is in fact the length of the keys in bits). The value 1024 provides sufficient strength for most keys. Another initialize() method defined in the KeyGenerator class allows you to specify the source of randomness for the key generation. After initializing the key generator, a key pair is created simply by calling generateKeyPair().

The last two classes specifically relevant to keys are Identity and IdentityScope. The Identity class represents real-world entities such as people and organizations and is used to identify the owner of a key pair. An Identity object has a name, a public key, and a set of certificates certifying the public key. This is sufficient information to model a real-world entity for security purposes. The IdentityScope class represents a group of identities and is implemented as a repository of Identity objects. The IdentityScope class introduces the notion of *identity scope* (that is, no two Identity objects in the same scope can have the same public key).

Digital Signatures

The Signature class is an engine class that provides the functionality of a digital signature algorithm. A digital signature algorithm takes arbitrary-sized input and a private key and generates a fixed-size signature validating the source of the data. A signature can easily be verified using the public key corresponding to the private key used to generate the signature. The Signature class is capable of performing two major functions:

☐ Signing data

☐ Verifying the signature of signed data

These two uses of the `Signature` class translate into two of the three states in which a `Signature` object can be found: UNINITIALIZED, SIGN, or VERIFY. A `Signature` object is always in one of these states and performs differently based on the state it is in. For example, the `update()` method is always used to supply data to a `Signature` object, but the operation performed on the data (signing or verifying) is determined by the state of the `Signature` object. To sign or verify the data once it has been supplied, you use the `sign()` and `verify()` methods, respectively.

There are three steps involved in using a `Signature` object to sign data or verify a signature:

1. Initializing with a public key for verifying or a private key for signing
2. Supplying data (updating)
3. Signing or verifying

Following is an example of using a `Signature` object to sign an array of bytes (`b`):

```
Signature signature = Signature.getInstance("SHA/DSA");
signature.initSign(keys.getPrivate());
for (int i = 0; i < b.length; i++)
  signature.update(b[i]);
byte[] signatureData = signature.sign();
```

A `Signature` object is first created using the static `getInstance()` method and specifying the "SHA/DSA" algorithm. The object is then initialized for signing using the `initSign()` method and passing in a private key. The `Signature` object is then supplied with data a byte at a time by calling the `update()` method repeatedly in a `for` loop. Finally, the data is signed and consequently a signature is generated with a call to `sign()`. This signature can be verified using a similar series of steps:

```
signature.initVerify(keys.getPublic());
for (int i = 0; i < b.length; i++)
  signature.update(b[i]);
boolean validSignature = signature.verify(signatureData);
```

Notice that the code is structured very much like the code for signing data, except that the `initVerify()` method is called with a public key. Furthermore, the `verify()` method is used to verify the signature, returning a Boolean result.

Listing 18.2 contains the source code for the `SignTest` application, which uses code similar to the two examples you just saw. The `SignTest` application is a little more interesting in that it signs the contents of a file you provide as a command-line argument. The application also verifies the newly created signature.

Listing 18.2. The source code for the SignTest application.

```
 1: public class SignTest {
 2:    public static void main(String[] args) {
 3:       if (args.length != 1) {
 4:          System.out.println("Usage: java SignTest FileName");
 5:          System.exit(0);
 6:       }
 7:       System.out.println("Initializing...");
 8:
 9:       try {
10:          // Generate a key pair
11:          KeyPairGenerator keyGenerator = KeyPairGenerator.getInstance("DSA");
12:          keyGenerator.initialize(1024);
13:          KeyPair keys = keyGenerator.generateKeyPair();
14:
15:          // Create and initialize a signature to use for signing and verifying
16:          Signature signature = Signature.getInstance("SHA/DSA");
17:
18:          // Read data from the file and sign it
19:          signature.initSign(keys.getPrivate());
20:          FileInputStream inStream = new FileInputStream(args[0]);
21:          while (inStream.available() != 0)
22:             signature.update((byte) inStream.read());
23:          inStream.close();
24:          System.out.println("Signing    " + args[0] + "...");
25:          byte[] signatureData = signature.sign();
26:
27:          // Verify the signed data
28:          signature.initVerify(keys.getPublic());
29:          inStream = new FileInputStream(args[0]);
30:          while (inStream.available() != 0)
31:             signature.update((byte) inStream.read());
32:          inStream.close();
33:          System.out.println("Verifying signature for " + args[0] + "...");
34:          if (signature.verify(signatureData))
35:             System.out.println(args[0] + " successfully signed and verified.");
36:          else
37:             System.out.println("Verification failure signing " + args[0] + ".");
38:       }
39:       catch (Exception e) {
40:          System.err.println(e);
41:       }
42:    }
43: }
```

18

NOTE

The source code and executable for the SignTest application are available from the companion Web site for this book (http://www.mcp.com/info/1-57521/1-57521-347-8), along with the other programs developed throughout this lesson and the rest of the book.

The application begins by generating a key pair using the `KeyPairGenerator` class (Lines 11 through 13) and creating a `Signature` object (Line 16). The `Signature` object is initialized for signing with a private key and is supplied with data from the file provided as a command-line argument (Lines 19 through 23). The file data is signed with a call to the `sign()` method (Line 25).

The verification process begins with a call to `initVerify()`, which initializes the `Signature` object with a public key (Line 28). File data is again supplied using the `update()` method (Lines 29 through 32). The signature is verified with a call to `verify()` (Line 24), which returns a Boolean result indicating the validity of the signature.

Following is the command used to execute the `SignTest` application, providing a text file named `Test.txt` as the command-line argument:

```
java SignTest Test.txt
```

Here is the resulting output:

```
Initializing...
Signing Test.txt...
Verifying signature for Test.txt...
Test.txt successfully signed and verified.
```

Certificates

The Java Security API models certificates using the `Certificate` interface. It is worth pointing out that the `Certificate` interface doesn't provide any semantics of its own, meaning that it doesn't take on the responsibility of validating an identity. This validation must be taken care of by an application that implements the `Certificate` interface. The `Certificate` interface is provided primarily as an organizational structure to bring together relevant pieces of information involved in a certificate.

Message Digests

The `MessageDigest` class is an engine class that encapsulates the functionality of a message digest, which is used to create digital fingerprints of data. Recall from earlier in the lesson that a message digest takes arbitrary-sized input and generates a fixed-size output called a *digest hash code* that uniquely identifies the data.

There are three steps involved in using a `MessageDigest` object to create a digest hash code:

1. Creating the `MessageDigest` object
2. Supplying data (updating)
3. Generating the digest hash code

Listing 18.3 contains the source code for the `MessageDigestTest` application, which computes a digest hash code for a string supplied as a command-line argument.

18

Listing 18.3. The source code for the MessageDigestTest application.

```
1: public class MessageDigestTest {
2:   public static void main(String[] args) {
3:     if (args.length != 1) {
4:       System.out.println("Usage: java MessageDigestTest \"Message\"");
5:       System.exit(0);
6:     }
7:
8:     // Create the message digest
9:     MessageDigest msgDigest = null;
10:    try {
11:      msgDigest = MessageDigest.getInstance("SHA");
12:    }
13:    catch (NoSuchAlgorithmException e) {
14:      System.err.println(e);
15:    }
16:
17:    // Update the message digest and calculate the digest hash code
18:    msgDigest.update(args[0].getBytes());
19:    byte[] digest = msgDigest.digest();
20:    for (int i = 0; i < digest.length; i++)
21:      System.out.print(digest[i] + " ");
22:  }
20: }
```

The MessageDigestTest application first creates a MessageDigest object by using the getInstance() method and providing the name of the algorithm (Line 11). With the message digest created, data is supplied to it with a call to the update() method; notice that the string argument is converted to bytes using the getBytes() method (Line 18). The digest hash code is then generated with a simple call to the digest() method (Line 19). Finally, the digest hash code is output so that you can see the results. Of course, digest hash codes are binary numbers, so there's nothing meaningful to see except that a digest hash code is unique to a given string.

Following is the command needed to execute the MessageDigestTest application on the string Howdy!:

```
java MessageDigestTest Howdy!
```

Here are the results of this command:

```
119 -92 -64 81 -84 88 50 60 91 35 -13 -102 -110 -102 -25 80 -73 -111 -65 90
```

Just to make sure that digest hash codes are in fact unique to every string, take a look at the digest created by changing the string Howdy! to Howdy?:

```
40 70 83 101 -20 -71 57 -113 -44 16 -74 -121 75 -124 -99 -63 -80 45 -9 -29
```

Even though only one character of the string changed, the digest hash code came out entirely different. This simple test supports the concept that a digest is a digital fingerprint for data.

Access Control Lists

Access control lists form the last major part of the Java Security API. The package java.security.acl is devoted entirely to providing the interfaces and exceptions required for access control lists. The primary interface defined in this package is Acl, which represents an access control list. There is also an AclEntry interface, which (not surprisingly) represents an entry in an access control list. The java.security.acl package also defines the interfaces Group, Owner, and Permission, all of which play an important support role in regard to access control lists.

It's important to understand that the java.security.acl package consists solely of interfaces and exceptions and contains no instantiable, or concrete, classes. Specific implementations of the interfaces defined in the java.security.acl package are included in the default security provider (SUN) package, sun.security.acl. Of course, this package isn't part of the public Java Security API, but it does play an important role behind the scenes.

Summary

In this lesson, you learned all about the Java Security API and the various features it has to offer. You began the lesson with a conceptual look at cryptography because cryptography is at the core of the Security API. You learned about the differences between conventional and public-key encryption, along with the fundamental concepts surrounding public-key encryption. With cryptography theory fresh on your mind, you learned about the main purpose of the Java Security API, which is to provide a way of authenticating applets so that they can be trusted and given access to more system services.

The remainder of the lesson focused on the specifics of the Security API and the classes and interfaces that make it work. You learned how to create and manage keys, signatures, and message digests and saw plenty of sample source code along the way. You also got a glimpse at how security providers are supported in the API, as well as certificates and access control lists. It's certainly worth noting that the Java Security API is a complex topic that could warrant an entire book. Even so, this lesson gave you enough practical information to start being productive with Java security.

Q&A

Q What is the relationship between a public key and a private key?

A A public key and a private key together form a pair of mathematically related numbers; the specifics of the mathematical relationship is determined by the encryption algorithm employed. The functional relationship between the keys is that information encrypted with one key can only be decrypted with the other key.

So, to encrypt a message so that only one person can read (decrypt) it, you encrypt the message with that person's public key. The only way to decrypt the message is with that person's private key (which only that person has). The other use of key pairs is in validating the source of a piece of information. In this situation, you encrypt a message using your private key. This message can in turn be decrypted by anyone with your public key. Because your public key can decrypt only messages that have been encrypted with your private key, there is no doubt that the message came from you.

Q I'm still confused. How does a message digest relate to a signature?

A A message digest provides a shorthand way of uniquely identifying a piece of information, much like a fingerprint is a shorthand way of uniquely identifying a person. Similarly, a signature is a shorthand way of identifying a piece of information *and* the source of the information. Signatures combine a message digest hash code with a private key to bind a piece of information, or message, with the person or organization sending or publishing the information.

Q What exactly is an engine class?

A An engine class is a Java class that provides an interface to the functionality furnished by a certain type of security algorithm. For example, the Signature class is an engine class that provides an interface to a general signature algorithm. Likewise, the MessageDigest class provides an interface to a general message digest algorithm. Security providers such as the default SUN provider furnish specific instances of these algorithms such as DSA or SHA.

Q How do I generate my own personal key pair?

A You use the javakey tool that ships with the JDK 1.1. This tool is covered in detail in the next lesson.

18

Day 19

Creating Signed Java Objects

by Michael Morrison

In the previous lesson, you learned all about the Java Security API and the support it has for various cryptographic features. You also learned that the primary reason JavaSoft created the Security API was to facilitate the authentication of applets. The previous lesson addressed applet authentication in conceptual terms, but it never got around to explaining exactly how you sign an applet for authentication purposes. Today's lesson picks up where the previous lesson left off by showing you how to do these things:

- [ ] Use the javakey security tool
- [ ] Sign JAR files with javakey

This lesson begins with an overview of the javakey tool, including the capabilities it has as well as the different options it supports. The lesson then shows you exactly how to create signed Java objects using the javakey tool. You can think of this lesson as the practical counterpart to the previous lesson; you'll see much of the theory you learned yesterday in action today.

Using the javakey Security Tool

The javakey security tool is provided with the JDK 1.1 and allows you to generate and verify signatures for JAR files. You learned all about JAR files on Day 17, "Working with Java Archives." If you recall, JAR files are used as a way to compress and package Java classes and resources for better organization and more efficient distribution. JAR files also support the digital signing of files to facilitate trusted applets. You sign JAR files using the javakey tool.

Identities and Signers

The javakey tool revolves around the concepts of *identities* and *signers*, which are real-world entities such as people, companies, or organizations. The significance of identities and signers is that they both have a *public key* associated with them. The difference between the two is that signers also have a *private key* associated with them (identities have only a public key). Additionally, signers must have at least one *certificate* verifying their public key, but certificates are completely optional for identities. Not surprisingly, identities aren't capable of signing files; only signers can sign files.

> *identity:* An entity that has a public key associated with it.
>
> *signer:* An entity that has a key pair associated with it, along with at least one certificate verifying the public key.

You might be wondering why you should even bother with identities if they can't sign files. Identities are a general abstraction of an entity that is very useful because you don't have access to any entity's private key other than your own. In other words, javakey commands that require someone else's public key operate with respect to an identity rather than a signer. In reality, all entities are signers because it's impossible to create one key without the other. However, with respect to a local instance of javakey, most entities are identities.

The javakey tool is associated with a persistent database that stores information about entities and their respective keys and certificates—along with whether or not the entities are considered trusted. All entities in the database are associated with a username for identification purposes; this username is what you use with the javakey tool to identify entities for various operations. When an entity is added to the database, its trust can be specified using a simple Boolean argument. If no trust is explicitly declared, javakey assumes that the entity is not trusted. I suppose it's a rather jaded tool!

NOTE

> The javakey database is stored by default in a file named identitydb.obj, located in the JDK installation directory. You can change the filename and location of the database using the identity.database property found in the master security properties file, java.security. The java.security file is located in the lib\security directory under the main JDK installation directory.

You create an identity using the -c option with the javakey tool, like this:

```
javakey -c mike
```

This command results in the following output:

```
Created identity mike[identitydb.obj][not trusted]
```

The newly created identity named mike is untrusted by default. To create an initially trusted identity, you just tack on true to the command, like this:

```
javakey -c mike true
```

The output of this command follows:

```
Created identity mike[identitydb.obj][trusted]
```

Notice that this time the identity is listed as being trusted. Specifying false to javakey ensures that the identity isn't trusted (which is the same as the default trust). Creating a signer is not much different than creating an identity, except that you use the -cs options:

```
javakey -cs keith true
```

Following is the output of this command:

```
Created identity [Signer]keith[identitydb.obj][trusted]
```

Remember that signers require a private key as well as at least one certificate, so you must provide these items at some point. If you want to change the trust of an identity or signer once the identity or signer is in the database, you can do so using the -t option with javakey, like this:

```
javakey -t keith false
```

The resulting output of this command is as follows:

```
keith is trusted: false
```

19

In this example, keith became untrustworthy, so his trust was revoked using the -t option. You can check the trust of an entity using the -li option, which lists information about an entity:

```
javakey -li keith
```

Following is the output of this command:

```
Identity: keith
[Signer]keith[identitydb.obj][not trusted]
        no keys
        no certificates
        No further information available.
```

Similar to the -li option, the -ld option lists information about all the entities in the database. Because the -ld option lists information about all the entities in the javakey database, it doesn't require any additional arguments. Following is an example of using the -ld option:

```
javakey -ld
```

The output of this command follows:

```
Scope: sun.security.IdentityDatabase, source file:
➡C:\JDK1.1.3\BIN\..\identitydb.obj

[Signer]keith[identitydb.obj][not trusted]
        no keys
        no certificates
        No further information available.

mike[identitydb.obj][trusted]
        no public key
        no certificates
        No further information available.

[Signer]mmorrison[identitydb.obj][trusted]
        public and private keys initialized
        certificates:
        certificate 1   for  : CN=Michael Morrison, OU=Interactive Media Group,
        ➡O=The Tribe, C=USA
                        from : CN=Michael Morrison, OU=Interactive Media Group,
        ➡O=The Tribe, C=USA

        No further information available.
```

Keys

Identities and signers aren't very useful without keys. Fortunately, the javakey tool makes it easy to create a key pair for a signer; you just use the -gk option, like this:

```
javakey -gk keith DSA 1024
```

Following is the output of this command:

```
Generated DSA keys for keith (strength: 1024).
```

This command creates a key pair and automatically associates it with the specified signer in the javakey database. In this example, the signer's username is keith. The last two arguments to the -gk option are the *algorithm* and *key length* for the key pair. The DSA algorithm is the standard algorithm provided by the default SUN security provider. Another popular algorithm is MD5/RSA, which you must install separately if you want to use it. The key length is the number of bits used to represent each key. The key length directly determines the strength of the encryption used by the keys. A key length of 1024 provides a very strong level of security. In some cases, you may want to opt for less key strength to improve the efficiency of the encryption algorithm and therefore speed up the encryption process.

You can export the public and private keys for an entity to a file using the -ek option to javakey, like this:

```
javakey -ek keith keith_pub.key keith_priv.key
```

Following is the output of this command:

```
Public key exported to keith_pub.key.
Private key exported to keith_priv.key.
```

The -ek option takes a username, public key filename, and private key filename as its arguments. The *username* is the name of the entity whose keys you are exporting; the *public key filename* and *private key filename* are the files to which the keys are written. It's important to note that private keys can be exported only for signers; public keys can be exported for both signers and identities. To export just the public key for a signer or identity, just leave off the private key filename.

Why would you want to export keys? Well, anyone you send an encrypted file to must be capable of decrypting the file in order to use it. Decryption is accomplished via your public key, which you must somehow give to the person or organization. For example, you might give a friend your public key on a floppy disk so that they can decrypt e-mail messages you've encrytped with your private key. The file on the disk would be the exported key file generated by javakey with the -ek option. What about private keys? Because you have to keep your private key to yourself, the only reason you would export a private key is to back it up for safe keeping.

You can import keys for entities using the -ik and -ikp options. Importing a key is useful in situations where people provide you with their public keys, which you are going to use to decrypt files they have encrypted with their private keys. You use the -ik option to import public keys for identities; you use the -ikp option to import key pairs for signers. Following is an example of importing a public key for an identity:

```
javakey -ik josh josh_pub.key
```

Similarly, you can import a key pair for a signer using the `-ikp` option, like this:

```
javakey -ikp sarah sarah_pub.key sarah_priv.key
```

Certificates

If you recall from the previous lesson, a *certificate* is a digitally signed statement from one entity verifying the ownership of another entity's public key. The `javakey` tool allows you to create, import, display, and save certificates. Certificates are critical to the function of `javakey` because they validate the authenticity of an entity's public key.

Certificates are complex-enough structures that it isn't sufficient to define them solely with command-line arguments to `javakey`. Instead, you create what is known as a *directive file*, which is simply a file containing detailed information required for the creation of a certificate. More specifically, you must provide the following information in a directive file when creating a certificate:

☐ Information about the signer of the certificate

☐ Information about the entity whose public key is being authenticated

☐ Information about the certificate itself

☐ The name of the signature algorithm to be used, if other than the default DSA algorithm

☐ The name of a file in which to store a copy of the certificate

Listing 19.1 contains a directive file for an imaginary entity named Jack Walsh.

Listing 19.1. An example directive file for an imaginary entity named Jack Walsh.

```
# Information about the signer
issuer.name=mmorrison
issuer.cert=1

# Information about the entity whose public key is being authenticated
subject.name=jwalsh
subject.real.name=Jack Walsh
subject.org.unit=Organized Crime Division
subject.org=Chicago Police Department
subject.country=USA

# Information about the certificate
start.date=1 Oct 1997
end.date=1 Oct 1998
serial.number=1001

# Name of the file to which to save a copy of the certificate
out.file=jwalsh_cert.cer
```

19

As you can see, a directive file contains a list of arguments and associated values that are used to create a certificate. Most of the directive file arguments are required; a few are optional. The following chart lists the directive file arguments used in the example in Listing 19.1, along with whether they are optional or required.

Argument Name	Optional/Required	Description
issuer.name	Required	User name of the signer signing and issuing the certificate
issuer.cert	Required only if the certificate being generated is not self-signed	The issuer's certificate to be used to sign the certificate file; this is the number that javakey previously assigned to the issuer's certificate when it generated or imported it
subject.name	Required	Username of the entity (identity or signer) whose public key is being authenticated
subject.real.name	Required	Entity's common name
subject.org.unit	Required	Entity's organizational unit
subject.org	Required	Entity's organization
subject.country	Required	Entity's country
start.date	Required	Certificate's valid start date
end.date	Required	Certificate's expiration date
serial.number	Required	Unique number used to distinguish this certificate from other certificates signed by this signer
out.file	Optional	Name of a file to which the certificate is saved

19

NOTE

The javakey tool defaults to using the DSA algorithm to generate a certificate using a directive file. You can specify a different algorithm by setting the security.algorithm argument in the directive file to the name of the algorithm. Keep in mind that a security provider for the algorithm must be available and that the keys for each entity must use the algorithm.

There is no standard file extension for directive files, so they are typically named without an extension. For example, the directive file shown in Listing 19.1 might be called `jwalsh_certdir`. Assuming that this is the case, following is an example of using the `javakey` tool to create a certificate based on the `jwalsh_certdir` certification directive file:

```
javakey -gc jwalsh_certdir
```

The certificate created by this command is automatically added to the database under Jack Walsh's username, `jwalsh`. You can export a certificate from an entity in the database to a file using the `-ec` option to `javakey`, like this:

```
javakey -ec jwalsh 1 jwalsh_jwalsh_cert.cer
```

The `-ec` option takes a username, certificate identifier, and filename as its arguments. The *username* is the name of the entity whose certificate you are exporting; the *certificate identifier* is the unique identifier assigned to the certificate. You can find this identifier by using the `-li` option with `javakey`, which lists information about an entity including its certificates and their identifiers. The *filename* argument used with the `-ec` option specifies the file to which a certificate is exported. You can display an exported certificate using the `-dc` option, like this:

```
javakey -dc jwalsh_ jwalsh_cert.cer
```

You can also import certificates using the `-ic` option, like this:

```
javakey -ic jwalsh somecert.cer
```

This sample command imports the certificate located in the file `somecert.cer` into the javakey database and associates it with the entity named `jwalsh`.

Options

You've seen most of the options supported by the `javakey` tool throughout the lesson. Because it can be helpful to see the syntax of the various `javakey` options, Table 19.1 lists them all, including their arguments and a brief description of how they are used.

Table 19.1. Options supported by the `javakey` security tool.

Option	Description
`-c` *identity* {true¦false}	Creates a new identity with the specified *identity* name; the optional Boolean value specifies whether the identity is to be considered trusted (`false` by default)
`-cs` *signer* {true¦false}	Creates a new signer with the specified *signer* name; the optional Boolean value specifies whether the identity is to be considered trusted (`false` by default)

19

Option	Description
-dc *certfile*	Displays the certificate stored in the file *certfile*
-ec *entity certnum certfile*	Exports the certificate identified by *certnum* from the specified *entity* to the file *certfile*
-ek *entity pubkeyfile {privkeyfile}*	Exports the public key for the specified *entity*, and optionally the private key (for a signer), to the specified files *pubkeyfile* and *privkeyfile*
-gc *directivefile*	Generates a certificate based on the specified *directivefile*
-gk *signer algorithm keysize {pubkeyfile} {privkeyfile}*	Generates a key pair for the specified *signer* using the specified *algorithm* and *keysize* key length; optionally, the keys are written to the files *pubkeyfile* and *privkeyfile*
-g *signer algorithm keysize {pubkeyfile} {privkeyfile}*	Shortcut for the -gk command to generate a key pair for the specified *signer*
-gs *directivefile jarfile*	Signs the specified JAR file, *jarfile*, according to the supplied *directivefile*
-ic *entity certfile*	Imports the public key certificate from the file *certfile*, associating it with the specified *entity*
-ii *entity*	Sets information for the specified *entity*; after executing this command, javakey prompts you to type in text information that is associated with the entity
-ik *identity pubkeyfile*	Imports the public key from the file *pubkeyfile*, associating it with the specified *identity*
-ikp *signer pubkeyfile privkeyfile*	Imports the key pair from the files *pubkeyfile* and *privkeyfile*, associating them with the specified *signer*

continues

19

Table 19.1. continued

Option	Description
-l	Lists the usernames of all entities in the javakey database
-ld	Lists detailed information about all entities in the javakey database
-li *entity*	Displays detailed information about the specified *entity*
-r *entity*	Removes the specified *entity* from the javakey database
-t *entity* {true¦false}	Sets the trust for the specified *entity*

A lot of the functionality of these options may seem familiar from the preceding lesson, when you performed some of the same functions directly in Java code. The reason for this is that the javakey tool is written using the same Java Security API you learned about yesterday; there is nothing magical about javakey. Technically, you could write your own javakey tool using the standard Security API classes and interfaces. There's no reason for you to do that, however, because javakey provides everything you need in terms of security management. It may be comforting to know that you have the power at your fingertips to directly harness Java security functionality.

Signing JAR Files with javakey

The main premise of the Java Security API and the javakey tool is to allow you to digitally sign JAR files. The rest of this lesson is devoted to showing you step-by-step how to sign a JAR file. The process of signing a JAR file can be broken into four distinct steps:

- ☐ Becoming a signer
- ☐ Generating a key pair
- ☐ Generating a certificate
- ☐ Signing the JAR file

In actuality, the first three steps are required only the first time you sign a JAR file, but they are still very important because you must perform them the first time through.

Becoming a Signer

Before you can do anything in terms of using javakey to sign files, you must become a signer. Signers can sign files using their private key; other parties can verify the resulting signature by using the signer's public key. To become a signer, you must create a signer in the javakey database using the -cs option. Following is the command required to create a signer for myself (feel free to use your own username):

```
javakey -cs mmorrison true
```

The resulting output of this command follows:

```
Created identity [Signer]mmorrison[identitydb.obj][trusted]
```

The username mmorrison is a unique name identifying me in the local javakey database. Notice that I specified true in the command, which indicates that I am a trusted signer. If you can't trust yourself, who can you trust?

Generating a Key Pair

A signer can't do anything useful until it has a *key pair*—a public key and a private key that are mathematically related. You create a key pair using the javakey tool with the -gk option. Following is the command used to create a key pair for the signer I just created for myself:

```
javakey -gk mmorrison DSA 512 mmorrison_pub.key
```

The resulting output of this command follows:

```
Generated DSA keys for mmorrison (strength: 512).
Saved public key to mmorrison_pub.key.
```

This command creates a key pair for the signer mmorrison using the DSA algorithm and a key length of 512 bits. The newly created public key is also exported to the file mmorrison_pub.key so that it can be shared with others. Although the -gk option also supports the storing of the private key in a file (as the public key was in this example), it can be dangerous leaving your private key lying around. Remember that your private key must be carefully guarded so that it remains private.

19

NOTE

> The key pair generated in this example uses the DSA algorithm, which was designed specifically for signing files. Some algorithms such as RSA allow you to encrypt files in addition to signing them. To use the RSA algorithm to sign or encrypt files, the key pair must be generated to support the RSA algorithm. In other words, the key pair generated in this example wouldn't work for RSA encryption because it is designated to use DSA. The point is that the type of encryption algorithm specified for a key pair must match the encryption algorithm used to encrypt files.

Generating a Certificate

After generating a key pair, you are ready to generate a certificate verifying the public key. If you recall from earlier in the lesson, at least one certificate is required of a signer if the signer is to be able to sign files. To generate a certificate, you must use a directive file. You can easily create a certificate for yourself that is self-signed, meaning that the certificate is verified by yourself. Granted, self-signing doesn't have much leverage when it comes to others trusting your signature, but in this case, you're just generating a certificate for your own use. Listing 19.2 contains a certificate directive file named `mmorrison_certdir`.

Listing 19.2. The `mmorrison_certdir` directive file for a self-signed certificate.

```
# Information about the signer
issuer.name=mmorrison

# Information about the entity whose public key is being authenticated
subject.name=mmorrison
subject.real.name=Michael Morrison
subject.org.unit=Interactive Media Group
subject.org=The Tribe
subject.country=USA

# Information about the certificate
start.date=1 Oct 1997
end.date=1 Oct 1998
serial.number=1001

# Name of the file to which to save a copy of the certificate
out.file=mmorrison_cert.cer
```

The arguments used in this directive file were covered earlier in this lesson. The main thing to notice about the directive file is that the signer and the entity whose public is being authenticated are both the same person—me! This is proof that I am self-signing my own certificate. To generate a certificate based on this directive file, execute the following command:

```
javakey -gc mmorrison_certdir
```

Here is the resulting output of this command:

```
Generated certificate from directive file mmorrison_certdir.
```

With a certificate generated, it's a good time to check out the `javakey` database to see what information is maintained about the signer we've created. Issue the following command to find out detailed information about the `mmorrison` signer:

```
javakey -li mmorrison
```

19

The resulting output of this command follows:

```
Identity: mmorrison
[Signer]mmorrison[identitydb.obj][trusted]
        public and private keys initialized
        certificates:
        certificate 1    for  : CN=Michael Morrison, OU=Interactive Media Group,
                                O=The Tribe, C=USA
                         from : CN=Michael Morrison, OU=Interactive Media Group,
                                O=The Tribe, C=USA

        No further information available.
```

As you can see, the output of the -li javakey option contains a decent amount of information about the signer. First off, it indicates that the signer's public and private keys have been initialized, which should come as no surprise. The certificate for the signer is also listed, as is the information that the signer has validated the certificate. Of course, in this example, the signer is the same as the entity whose key is being validated.

Signing a JAR File

And now, the moment you've been waiting for! You've created a signer, a key pair for the signer, and a certificate authenticating the public key. You're now officially ready to sign a JAR file. Similar to the generation of certificates, the information required to sign JAR files must be provided in a directive file. This information follows:

- ☐ The name of the signer
- ☐ The unique identification number of a certificate for the signer
- ☐ The certificate chaining depth
- ☐ The base name of the files in which to store the signature

Listing 19.3 contains a directive file named mmorrison_signdir that uses the mmorrison signer to sign the BorderPanel.jar JAR file created in Day 5, "Introduction to JavaBeans."

Listing 19.3. The mmorrison_signdir directive file for signing the BorderPanel.jar JAR file.

```
# Username of the signer
signer=mmorrison

# Unique identifier for the signer's certificate
cert=1

# Chain depth of a chain of certificates to use
chain=0
```

continues

19

Listing 19.3. continued

```
# Base name for the signature files
signature.file=BPSIGN

# Name of the resulting JAR file
out.file=BorderPanel_s.jar
```

The following chart lists the directive-file arguments used in this directive file, along with whether they are optional or required.

Argument Name	Optional/Required	Description
signer	Required	Username of the signer
cert	Required	Unique identification number of a certificate for the signer
chain	Required	Certificate chaining depth
signature.file	Required	Base name of files in which to store the signature
out.file	Optional	Name of a file in which to store the resulting signed JAR file

Most of these arguments are pretty obvious except for the chain argument. The chain argument allows you to specify a chain of certificates to be used when authenticating the public key of the signer. The chain of certificates is determined by the cert argument in combination with the chain argument; the chain begins with the certificate identified by cert and continues through a number of certificates equal to the value of chain. The chain argument isn't supported in the JDK 1.1 version of javakey, but it is nonetheless required for future compatibility reasons. For now, you can just set chain to 0.

The signature.file argument specifies the base filename for the signature files generated by javakey. Signature creation results in the generation of two files named with .SF and .DSA extensions. The base filename specified in the signature.file argument is used with these extensions to generate the files containing signature information for the signing operation.

You may be wondering why the out.file argument is optional. It seems that you would always have to provide the name of the signed JAR file, right? Not exactly. If no signed JAR filename is supplied with the out.file argument, the JAR filename is used, but the .jar extension is replaced with .sig to indicate that the file is signed.

To sign the BorderPanel.jar JAR file using the mmorrison_signdir directive file, issue the following command:

```
javakey -gs mmorrison_signdir BorderPanel.jar
```

19

This command results in the following output:

```
Adding entry: META-INF/MANIFEST.MF
Creating entry: META-INF\BPSIGN.SF
Creating entry: META-INF\BPSIGN.DSA
Adding entry: BorderPanel.class
Adding entry: BorderStyle.class
Signed JAR file BorderPanel.jar using directive file mmorrison_signdir.
```

This output clearly shows what is happening as the new (signed) JAR file is being created. The files in the original JAR file are simply added to the new JAR file, while the two new signature files are first created and then added to the JAR file. To double-check the contents of the JAR file, issue the following command using the jar utility:

```
jar tf BorderPanel_s.jar
```

This command results in the following output:

```
META-INF/MANIFEST.MF
META-INF\BPSIGN.SF
META-INF\BPSIGN.DSA
BorderPanel.class
BorderStyle.class
```

Congratulations! You now have a signed JAR file that effectively gives all the files contained within it privileges not afforded to untrusted files. Your Java code can now run rampant with blatant disregard for the safety of others. Well, provided someone using the JAR file decides to accept you as a trusted entity. Remember that Java security is only as effective as you are willing to responsibly apply it.

Summary

In this lesson, you learned how to use the javakey security tool to sign JAR files so that they can be trusted. Trusted JAR files are important in that they allow trusted Java applets to bypass the stringent default security measures imposed on untrusted applets. This lesson began with an overview of the javakey tool, including how it manages identities, signers, keys, and certificates. You then learned about the various options available to the tool.

The second part of the lesson focused on signing JAR files using the javakey tool. You worked step-by-step through a complete example involving the signing of a JAR file you created earlier in this book. You learned how to create a signer, how to generate a key pair, and how to generate a certificate. You then used this information to sign a JAR file, thereby making its contents trusted.

19

Q&A

Q How can I remove an entity from the `javakey` database?

A Just use the `-r` option and specify the username of the entity to be removed.

Q Does signing a JAR file affect the original file?

A No. Signed JAR files are always created as new files, leaving the original JAR file untouched. The new (signed) JAR file is named based on the `out.file` argument specified in the directive file; if `out.file` isn't specified, the new file uses the name of the original JAR file with a `.sig` extension.

Q How do I apply for a certificate through a certification authority?

A There are a few different certification authorities on the Web that you can use to obtain certificates. Two notable authorities are Verisign and Entrust, whose Web sites can be found at `http://www.verisign.com` and `http://www.entrust.com`, respectively. Keep in mind that although you can generate a self-signed certificate for your own purposes, other users may not trust your applets unless you obtain a certificate through a reputable certification authority.

Q What is the Java Cryptography Extension and how does it apply to code signing?

A The Java Cryptography Extension (JCE) is an extension to the Java Security API that provides additional encryption algorithm implementations such as RSA and DES. The JCE impacts code signing in that it provides more flexibility in selecting an encryption algorithm.

Day 20

Things You Can't Do in Java: Using the Java Native Interface

by Michael Morrison

Although the Java programming language and runtime system offer everything you need to develop applets and applications, there are times when you may have to go beyond Java. For example, you may have legacy code written in another language such as C++ that you simply don't want to bother porting to Java. In this case, you ideally want to be able to call the code from Java and effectively take advantage of both Java code and natively compiled C++ code in the same application. Although this scenario may sound complicated, it's actually not too difficult to pull off with Java 1.1.

Java 1.1 includes an API known as the Java Native Interface (JNI). The JNI is an interface to a set of methods that can be called from native code. The methods provided by the JNI allow native code to interact with Java objects and methods. For example, you can use the JNI to manipulate the public fields of Java objects as well as to call public methods. From the Java side of things, a native method looks no different than a Java method. Using the JNI, you can even embed the Java virtual machine in a native application and use Java as a scripting language. This lesson explores the JNI and how it makes many of these features possible.

More specifically, in this lesson you learn:

- ☐ JNI Basics
- ☐ The importance of native code
- ☐ The drawbacks of native code
- ☐ How to generate native headers with `javah`
- ☐ How to map Java data types
- ☐ How to access Java information from native code

JNI Basics

The Java Native Interface (JNI) is exactly what its name implies: a Java interface for native code. The JNI provides a standardized, uniform approach to accessing Java objects and related information from native code. Based on this description, you may be wondering why the JNI is necessary. You may already know that Java code could interact with native code before Java 1.1, so the JNI technically isn't a necessity for working with native code. Or is it?

In Java 1.0, you could interact with native code from Java, but there was no consistent standard. This was because the native code integration in Java 1.0 depended on the Java virtual machine (VM) implementation. Sure, the Java VM is very standardized as far as what it must accomplish, but there are no rules regarding how a VM is implemented under the hood. Keep in mind that the Sun VM that ships with the JDK is a reference implementation of a Java VM, not the standard implementation. In fact, there is no standard implementation, just a standard set of requirements.

The point I'm trying to make is that every Java VM provides the same functionality, but each goes about it in a different way. Why does this matter? Well, when you accessed Java objects from native code in Java 1.0, you required an intimate knowledge of the VM because there was no defined interface. In the absence of an interface, developers wrote VM-dependent code to integrate Java with the native world. The JNI alleviates the problem of VM dependency by defining a standard set of methods, or functions, available to native code that can be used to access Java objects. Figures 20.1 and 20.2 show the difference between native code integration in Java 1.0 and that in Java 1.1 using the JNI.

Figure 20.1.

A native method call in Java 1.0.

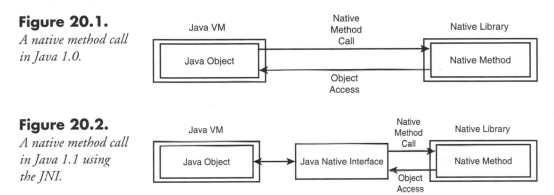

The first thing you may notice in the figures is that the native method is contained within a native library. This is required because Java code cannot statically link with native code; instead, a library is used that can be dynamically linked at runtime. In Windows, this type of library is called a dynamic link library (DLL); on Solaris, the library is called a shared object.

The main thing to point out about the figures is how the native library is completely shielded from the Java VM when the JNI is used. This is what eliminates the VM-specific dilemma present in Java 1.0 native code integration. When a native method is called from Java 1.1, it is passed a pointer to a JNI interface. That's right—a *pointer*! We're talking native code now, which means that you have to worry about things like pointers and memory allocation. The native method accesses object fields and methods solely through the JNI interface. The JNI is a rich-enough interface that you should never need (or want) to tangle with the VM directly.

The When and Why of Native Code

You understand the rationale behind the JNI, but you still may not fully understand the importance of native code and its relationship to Java. Or you may just be confused about when it's necessary to integrate native code into a Java project. I will attempt to clear up any confusion you have in these matters. You may be surprised to find out that I don't recommend using native code unless it's absolutely necessary.

The best way to get a handle on the importance of native code is to understand the scenarios in which native code is required of Java code. There are three main reasons for integrating native code with Java code:

- ☐ To access system functionality beyond the Java environment
- ☐ To improve performance
- ☐ To interface with legacy code

Reaching Beyond the Java Environment

The Java API provides a very rich set of features for doing all kinds of interesting things, but there are some specialized situations in which you need functionality not provided by the Java API. More specifically, you may have to access information specific to the underlying operating system. For example, if you have a Java application developed specifically to run on the Windows platform, you may have some reason to determine the version of Windows. The Java API doesn't provide any facility for determining such a platform-dependent piece of information, so you have to resort to the native Win32 API.

An even better example of why native code is important for reaching beyond the Java environment is the Java API itself. The Java API is riddled with native methods implemented in C. Although this may come as a shock to you, there is no reason for Java to reimplement the functionality provided by the underlying operating system. The usage of native code in the Java API also results in Java user interface elements blending in well with native elements.

Consider the drawing routines provided by an operating system such as Windows. The Win32 API defines a graphics interface known as the Graphics Device Interface (GDI), which is responsible for providing the bulk of the graphics features in Windows. Rather than reimplement all this functionality, the Java API uses GDI functions to implement its own AWT graphics features. Of course, this is carried out entirely in native code.

Improving Performance

Performance is another popular motive for using native code with Java. The reasoning is that Java code is sluggish because it has to interpret bytecodes, so native code must be faster. When you compare Java bytecode executables to native executables, this reasoning is certainly valid. However, native Java compilers are appearing, as are just-in-time compilers, which compile Java classes to native code on the fly when needed.

There is no reason why natively compiled Java code can't be just as fast as native code compiled from any other language. Likewise, Java compilers will continue to evolve and get better with optimizations, which will drastically improve performance. The point of this discussion is that performance isn't necessarily a valid excuse for using native code anymore. The main exception to this statement is the situation in which you are so bent on maximizing performance that you use a language-like assembler, which allows you to perform coding

20

optimizations that even a C or C++ compiler can't make. However, you would have to isolate this code into relatively small methods to justify the development effort because an assembler is considerably more difficult to use than Java or even C.

Interfacing to Legacy Code

The final motive for using native code is to interface Java code with an existing native application or library, also known as *legacy code*. You may have a native library you simply don't have the time, resources, or desire to rewrite in Java, in which case you would have to interface with the library using the JNI. Assuming, of course, that you are writing new code in Java that somehow needs the native library. With this approach, you can take an existing code base in C++, for example, and gradually port it to Java using the JNI along the way. Although the goal is to eventually move everything to Java, the JNI gives you the freedom to make it a smooth transition.

The Cost of Native Code

The use of native code sounds good enough, but there has to be a cost, right? Of course. It turns out that the cost of using native code is pretty high. Following are the three main drawbacks to using native code:

- ☐ Kills platform independence
- ☐ Raises serious security issues
- ☐ Imposes method call overhead

Platform Dependence

Think back to when you first learned Java; what was one of the big selling points of going with Java? Platform independence! Java is the first major programming language and runtime system to successfully make platform independence a reality. And unfortunately, native code destroys this reality. Native code is, by definition, native. So it only makes sense that a Java program that relies on native code depends on the target platform for the code. As an example, consider that memory management is drastically different between the Windows and Macintosh platforms. Likewise, the file systems vary between the Windows and UNIX platforms.

Security Woes

Another big drawback to using native code is the security threat inherent in its use. The Java programming language and runtime environment go to great lengths to keep you from being able to hurt anything, such as memory you aren't supposed to be tampering with. Contrast this with native code, which has free reign to manipulate memory however it sees fit.

20

Another way to envision the security scenario is to imagine the Java VM as a watchdog looking out for problems in executing Java code. If a piece of code tries something dangerous, the VM is there to stop it. However, the VM has no way of knowing how to watch over native code and therefore doesn't even try. The security measures so important to Java are effectively disabled when you use native code. This results in native code having a lot of power, including the power to corrupt the VM itself.

In case you're getting nervous about how other people are using native code, let me clarify that native code can be used only by applications and trusted applets; untrusted applets absolutely aren't allowed to access native code. So there is no risk of visiting a Web page and picking up an applet that uses native code to blow up your monitor. First, the applet isn't allowed access to native code. Second, it would be difficult to blow up a monitor using any code.

Method Call Overhead

The final drawback to using native code is the overhead involved in making calls to native methods. This may not seem like a big deal until you consider that performance is one of the motives for using native code. The reason there is overhead in calling native methods is because the Java VM must halt its normal bytecode interpretation and package method arguments for the native method being called. Granted, this is a pretty quick process, but you have to take it into account when you're trying to squeeze out every ounce of performance.

The way to strike a balance between using native methods to improve performance without negating it with call overhead is to make sure that you have enough code to justify the call. In other words, the improved performance of a piece of code provided by a native implementation must be significant enough to offset the loss in call overhead. Again, let me add that the validity of the whole performance issue surrounding Java will continue to diminish as Java compilers evolve.

Two Sides of the Fence

When dealing with native methods and Java, you always have to think in terms of which side of the fence you are on: the Java side or the native side. What I mean is that the integration of native code with Java involves some work in both Java code and in the native code implementation itself. This is necessary because your Java code must know about any native methods you plan to use, just as it must know about Java methods. Likewise, you have to consider the native code itself and how it will interact with Java objects, methods, and data.

The Java Side of the Fence

On the Java side of the fence, your only real interest is in defining any native methods you plan to use. Fortunately, this is a very simple task and involves merely providing a method definition in your Java class. The difference between a native method definition and a normal Java method definition is that the native definition uses the native modifier and doesn't provide an implementation. For example, check out the following Java method:

```
public int computeSquare(int x) {
  return x * x;
}
```

Notice that the method definition consists of a method signature followed by the method implementation enclosed in parentheses. Hopefully this structure is at least vaguely familiar to you! If for some reason you wanted to rewrite this method as a native method, you would change the definition to this:

```
public native int computeSquare(int x);
```

Notice that the native modifier is used to signify that this is a native method; the implementation for the method will be provided in an external native library. Additionally, because the implementation will be provided elsewhere, the method definition ends with a semicolon immediately following the signature.

I haven't mentioned anything about how a native method is associated with a native library. This is a very important part of using native methods because Java code knows nothing about how to find a native method when It comes across a method definition. There is no direct association in Java between a native method and the native library it is contained within. Instead, you just load the native library from Java code, and Java looks for any native methods in the library when it needs them.

The method responsible for loading native libraries from Java is loadLibrary(), which is provided in the java.lang.System class. The loadLibrary() method takes the filename of a native library as its only argument. For example, if the computeSquare() native method you just saw was located in a Windows (Win32) DLL named Goodies.dll, you would load the DLL like this:

```
loadLibrary("Goodies");
```

Notice that the file extension of the library isn't required. The loadLibrary() method operates this way so that libraries can be loaded in a platform-independent fashion. For example, if you also provided a Solaris version of the Goodies native library, the filename would more than likely be libGoodies.so. However, the same loadLibrary() call would still work fine with no modification; loadLibrary() takes care of determining a platform-specific library name based on the name you provide it.

OK, loadLibrary() sounds great, but when exactly do you load a native library? It seems that a native method could be called at any time, so how can you guarantee that the library has been loaded before a native method call? In a static initializer, of course! A *static initializer* is a block of static code executed the first time a class is loaded. By loading any and all native

20

libraries in a static initializer, you guarantee that any native methods called from the class will be successfully found in their respective libraries.

static initializer: A block of static code executed the first time a class is loaded.

Following is the `computeSquare()` native method example complete with a static initializer that loads the `Goodies` native library:

```
class CalculateSomeStuff {
  public native int computeSquare(int x);

  static {
    loadLibrary("Goodies");
  }
}
```

Notice that a static initializer is just a block of code defined at the class level with the `static` modifier. When the `CalculateSomeStuff` class is first loaded, the static code is executed and the `Goodies` native library is loaded. That wraps up your Java responsibilities for working with native code—pretty simple!

The Native Side of the Fence

This native code thing is looking pretty easy so far. Well, as soon as you jump over the fence to the native side of things, it gets much uglier. I'm not trying to scare you away from using native methods, I'm just giving you a little warning that the bulk of the work in using native methods is handled directly in native code using the JNI, which can sometimes get messy. Throughout this lesson, I'm going to demonstrate how to work with C++ as the native language. You can also use C, but I encourage the use of C++ because it provides a clean interface to the JNI thanks to its object-oriented nature.

The native side of the fence involves the actual creation of native methods, which includes the association of native method implementations with Java method signatures. The rest of this lesson is primarily devoted to handling the native side of native code integration. Rather than getting into all the gory details in this section, let me take a moment to summarize what is required to successfully create a native method in native code. Following are the main steps involved in native method creation:

1. Generate a native header file from a Java class file.
2. Implement native methods in native code.
3. Compile native code into a native library.

The first step involves the automatic creation of a native header using the javah tool that ships with the JDK. This tool examines a Java class and generates suitable method prototypes for native versions of all native methods. The second step is the development of the native methods, which is the actual programming involved in implementing the methods. This step is where you make calls to the JNI to access Java objects, fields, and methods. The final step involves compiling the methods into a native library that can be dynamically linked with Java code.

To get a better feel for what these steps mean, take a look at the following list of resulting files created after each step:

1. Header file (.h)
2. Source code files (.c, .cpp, and so on)
3. Native DLL or shared object library files (.DLL, .so)

That pretty well sums up the basic steps required to implement and use native methods. The remainder of the lesson covers this process in much greater detail.

Generating Native Headers with javah

The first step in writing a native implementation of a method is to generate a header file with the appropriate method prototype. The reason for this step is that there are special data types you must use in native code if you are to correctly access Java data. You learn more about this data mapping a little later in the lesson. The other reason you should opt for a generated header file instead of writing one yourself is that there are arguments to native methods that are passed in addition to the arguments defined in the Java method definition.

You generate a native header using the javah tool that ships with the JDK. The javah tool analyzes a Java class file and generates a header file suitable for C/C++. Following is the syntax of the javah tool:

```
javah Options ClassName
```

The *Options* argument specifies an option that determines how the tool operates. The javah tool provides a variety of options, but the one you're particularly interested in is -jni, which causes javah to generate a header file. The *ClassName* argument is the name of the Java class for which you want to generate a header. If the class is part of a package, you must provide the complete package name. For example, this is how you would use javah to generate a header file for the java.awt.Graphics class:

```
javah -jni java.awt.Graphics
```

20

The header file generated by javah has a .h extension with the same base name as the class; underscores are used in place of package delimiters. For example, the generated header file for the java.awt.Graphics class would be named java_awt_Graphics.h.

As an example of how the javah tool is used to generate headers, let's work through a complete sample application that uses a native method. Earlier in this lesson, I mentioned that a common use of native code is to access platform-specific information such as the version number of Windows. Listing 20.1 contains the source code for SysInfo, an application that has a native method named displaySystemInfo() that performs this very function (in addition to a few others).

Listing 20.1. The Java source code for the SysInfo application.

```
 1: public class SysInfo {
 2:   public static void main(String[] args) {
 3:     displaySystemInfo();
 4:   }
 5:
 6:   private static native void displaySystemInfo();
 7:
 8:   // Static startup code
 9:   static {
10:     System.loadLibrary("SysInfo");
11:   }
12: }
```

Notice that the displaySystemInfo() native method is defined using the native modifier and no method body (Line 6). Also notice that its native library, SysInfo, is loaded in a static initializer (Lines 9 through 11). This code follows exactly the procedure you learned earlier in the lesson. To generate a C/C++ header file for this class, compile the class and execute the javah tool like this:

javah -jni SysInfo

Because the SysInfo class is part of the default package, there is no need to specify a package name. This command results in the generation of the header file SysInfo.h (see Listing 20.2).

Listing 20.2. The C/C++ header file for the SysInfo DLL.

```
 1: /* DO NOT EDIT THIS FILE - it is machine generated */
 2: #include <jni.h>
 3: /* Header for class SysInfo */
 4:
 5: #ifndef _Included_SysInfo
 6: #define _Included_SysInfo
 7: #ifdef __cplusplus
 8: extern "C" {
```

20

```
 9: #endif
10: /*
11:  * Class:     SysInfo
12:  * Method:    displaySystemInfo
13:  * Signature: ()V
14:  */
15: JNIEXPORT void JNICALL Java_SysInfo_displaySystemInfo
16:   (JNIEnv *, jclass);
17:
18: #ifdef __cplusplus
19: }
20: #endif
21: #endif
```

Ouch, that looks a little messy! Granted, the header looks complicated at first, but it's really pretty simple. The main thing you're interested in is the Java_SysInfo_displaySystemInfo() method, which is the native version of the displaySystemInfo() method you defined in the SysInfo Java class (Lines 15 and 16). You may have noticed some strange identifiers being used with this method; these identifiers (JNIEXPORT, JNICALL, and so on) are used to facilitate the dynamic accessibility of the method. The most critical pieces of information in this header are the arguments to the method, which are of type JNIEnv* and jclass. These two arguments are a pointer to the Java Native Interface and a reference to the SysInfo class, respectively. You learn how to use the JNI pointer a little later in this lesson.

It's also important to note the name of the native method generated in the header, Java_SysInfo_displaySystemInfo() Native method names are generated based on the name of the Java package, class, and method name. Native method names consist of the word Java followed by the package name, class name, and method name of the method, all separated by underscores. In this case, there is no package name because the default package is being used.

To implement the native method in C++, you must copy the method prototype from the header into a source file named SysInfo.cpp. Listing 20.3 contains the source for this method.

Listing 20.3. The C++ source code for the SysInfo DLL.

```
 1: #include "SysInfo.h"
 2: #include <windows.h>
 3:
 4: void JNICALL Java_SysInfo_displaySystemInfo(JNIEnv* env, jclass thisClass) {
 5:   // Display Win32-specific system information
 6:   WORD majorVer = LOWORD(GetVersion());
 7:   WORD minorVer = HIWORD(GetVersion());
 8:   printf("Windows version  = %d.%d.%d.%d\n", LOBYTE(majorVer),
 9:     HIBYTE(majorVer), LOBYTE(minorVer), HIBYTE(minorVer));
10:   printf("Available memory = %.2f MB\n", GetFreeSpace(0) / 1024.0 / 1024.0);
```

continues

Day 20

Listing 20.3. continued

```
11:   printf("Screen size      = %dx%d\n", GetSystemMetrics(SM_CXSCREEN),
12:     GetSystemMetrics(SM_CYSCREEN));
13:   printf("Mouse present    = %s", GetSystemMetrics(SM_MOUSEPRESENT) == 0 ?
14:     "No\n":"Yes\n");
15: }
```

As you can see, the `Java_SysInfo_displaySystemInfo()` method calls native Win32 functions to get information about the native system such as the version number, the amount of available memory, the screen size, and whether the mouse is present. If you aren't using a Windows platform or you aren't familiar with the Win32 API, please bear with me through this example.

With the C++ code for the native method in place, you're ready to compile the code into a native library. For this example, I used Visual C++ 5.0, which is part of Microsoft's Visual Studio development environment. I used the visual development environment and created a project for the C++ code. You can also use the command-line compiler to compile the code if you don't want to fool with the visual environment. The project and workspace files, as well as all related source code, are available from the companion Web site for the book. If you opt to use the provided project file, just select Build from the Visual C++ Project menu; a DLL will be built from the compiled source code. If you want to build the DLL from a command line, do so with the following command:

```
cl -Ic:\jdk1.1.3\include -Ic:\jdk1.1.3\include\win32 -LD SysInfo.cpp -
FeSysInfo.dll
```

WARNING

If you have the JDK installed to a directory other than jdk1.1.3, be sure to alter the command accordingly.

This command launches the command-line Visual C++ compiler to compile the C++ code and generate a DLL named `SysInfo.dll`. With the DLL complete, you're ready to try out the example:

```
java SysInfo
```

WARNING

Make sure that the DLL is available to the `SysInfo` application. Do this either by copying the DLL to the same directory in which the application is located (assuming that you have . in your `CLASSPATH` statement) or by explicitly including the path for the DLL in `CLASSPATH`. If you

> receive a java.lang.UnsatisfiedLinkError error, you know the
> application is having trouble finding the DLL.

The resulting output of this command follows:

```
Windows version  = 4.10.0.192
Available memory = 1.00 MB
Screen size      = 1280x1024
Mouse present    = Yes
```

This output is generated entirely by the native Win32 code, which is being called by Java code in the SysInfo application. This obviously opens the door for a wide range of interesting development opportunities because you are effectively reaching beyond the Java environment to access native system features.

Mapping Java Data Types

The SysInfo example is interesting in that it demonstrates the integration of native code into a Java application. However, the example doesn't demonstrate how native code accesses Java objects, which is often a requirement when integrating native code with Java. Before getting into the details of how native code interacts with Java constructs, it's important to understand how Java data is modeled in the native environment. Because you clearly can't work directly with Java data types in native code, the JNI provides a mechanism for mapping Java data types to native data types. Table 20.1 shows the mapping of Java data types to native types.

Table 20.1. Java data types mapped to native data types.

Java Type	Native Type	Native Storage
Object	jobject	Object handle
Class	jclass	Class handle
String	jstring	String object handle
boolean	jboolean	8 bits
unsigned byte	jbyte	8 bits
unsigned short	jshort	16 bits
char	jchar	16 bits
int	jint	32 bits
long	jlong	64 bits

continues

Table 20.1. continued

Java Type	Native Type	Native Storage
float	jfloat	32 bits
double	jdouble	64 bits
void	void	N/A

You may be confused about the names of the native data types in Table 20.1. These types are defined in the jni.h header file, which is part of the JDK. Following are a few of the definitions in jni.h:

```
typedef unsigned char     jboolean;
typedef unsigned short    jchar;
typedef short             jshort;
typedef float             jfloat;
typedef double            jdouble;
typedef jint              jsize;
```

This list of definitions clearly shows the C/C++ representations of some of the Java data types listed in Table 20.1. For example, the Java boolean data type becomes an unsigned char in C/C++ because C/C++ don't directly support a boolean data type.

Accessing Java Information from Native Code

To access and manipulate Java information from a native method, you must use the JNI pointer passed into the method. Although you didn't use this pointer, you saw it earlier in the lesson in the SysInfo example as the env argument to the Java_SysInfo_displaySystemInfo() method:

```
void JNICALL Java_SysInfo_displaySystemInfo(JNIEnv* env, jclass thisClass)
```

The JNI pointer provides an interface to a set of methods that enable access to Java objects. These methods are what you use to access Java objects, fields, and methods from native code. The next few sections show you how to access various types of Java information using the JNI methods.

Identifying Java Information

Because native code is implemented separately from the Java class with which it is associated, there is no direct association between class information and native code. In other words, accessing an object field (member variable) from native code isn't as simple as this:

```
this.count = 50;
```

Technically, you do have access to the this pointer from native code, but you can't directly manipulate fields like this because of platform-dependency issues. Instead, you use a JNI method to find a field based on the field's signature. This method returns a unique identifier for the field, which you then use to get and set the field's value using other JNI methods. The idea is that you use JNI methods to do anything relating to Java information access. You use this approach to eliminate any platform-dependency problems.

Fields and methods are accessed using this identifier approach; the JNI provides methods for finding the identifiers for fields and methods, which can then be used in other JNI methods that allow you to get and set fields and call methods. Java objects and classes are a little different in that they are referenced using a jobject or jclass reference instead of an identifier. Even so, jobject and jclass are really just handles to the Java objects, and therefore can be thought of as a type of identifier.

Accessing Java Fields

To access a Java field from native code, you must first find the field's identifier and then use the identifier to get or set the field's value. To find a field's identifier, you use the GetFieldID() method defined in the JNI. The GetFieldID() method uses the field's signature to find the field's unique identifier. Field signatures are specified as symbolic strings that identify the data type of the field. Table 20.2 lists the field signature symbols supported by the JNI.

Table 20.2. The Java field signature symbols supported by the JNI.

Java Type	Signature Symbol
array	[
class	L
end of class	;
method	(
end of method	)
boolean	Z
byte	B
char	C
short	S
int	I
long	J
float	F
double	D
void	V

20

This whole signature idea may seem a little strange at first; just keep in mind that the whole point is to provide a way of representing Java field data types as strings. To understand how field signatures work, take a look at the following fields:

```
int       count;
boolean[] switches;
float     angle;
String    name;
String[]  messages;
```

Using the symbols listed in Table 20.2, you can generate string signatures for these field types. Following are the fields and their respective signatures:

Field	Signature
count	I
switches	[Z
angle	F
name	Ljava/lang/String;
messages	[Ljava/lang/String;

Notice that field signatures for a primitive data type are very simple. For example, the signature for the count integer field is simply I. Likewise, the signature for an array of a primitive type is just the type preceded by [. For example, the signature for the array of Booleans field, switches, is [Z.

Signatures for nonprimitive types are a little more complicated. Nonprimitive data types are actually classes, and therefore must be specified as such in a signature. The signature for class types involves symbols for the beginning of the class, the class name, and the end of the class. For example, the name field's signature is Ljava/lang/String;, which identifies the String class. The L preceding the class name marks the start of the class; the ; following the class name marks the end of the class. Arrays of classes are identified using the [symbol, just as in primitive arrays.

Once you know the signature for a field, you can get the field's identifier using the GetFieldID() method. Following is an example of using this method to get the count field's identifier:

```
jfieldID fCountID = env->GetFieldID(thisClass, "count", "I");
```

Notice that the env JNI pointer is used to call the GetFieldID() method, which takes the class containing the field, the name of the field, and the signature of the field as arguments. The thisClass jclass argument is passed into all static native methods, which is where you typically determine field identifiers.

Getter Methods

Once you have the identifier for a field, you can get a copy of the field by calling a getter method appropriate to the field type. Table 20.3 lists the field getter methods supported by the JNI.

Table 20.3. Field getter methods supported by the JNI.

Method	Field Type	Return Type
GetObjectField()	Object	jobject
GetBooleanField()	boolean	jboolean
GetByteField()	byte	jbyte
GetCharField()	char	jchar
GetShortField()	short	jshort
GetIntField()	int	jint
GetLongField()	long	jlong
GetFloatField()	float	jfloat
GetDoubleField()	double	jdouble

Going back to the count example, you can retrieve the value of the count field by calling GetIntField() and providing the field identifier, like this:

```
jint myCount = env->GetIntField(thisObject, fCountID);
```

The thisObject jobject argument to GetIntField() is passed into all nonstatic native methods, which is where you access any object instance information such as field values.

Setter Methods

Once you have a field value in a native data type such as jint, you are free to work with it in native code however you choose. If you decide to set the field value back on the Java side, you use a setter method appropriate to the field type. Table 20.4 lists the field setter methods supported by the JNI.

Table 20.4. Field setter methods supported by the JNI.

Method	Field Type	Value Type
SetObjectField()	Object	jobject
SetBooleanField()	boolean	jboolean
SetByteField()	byte	jbyte
SetCharField()	char	jchar

continues

20

Table 20.4. continued

Method	Field Type	Value Type
SetShortField()	short	jshort
SetIntField()	int	jint
SetLongField()	long	jlong
SetFloatField()	float	jfloat
SetDoubleField()	double	jdouble

Naturally, the setter methods complement the getter methods you just learned about. Following is an example of using a setter method to set the count field after modifying the native myCount variable:

```
myCount++;
env->GetIntField(thisObject, fCountID, myCount);
```

Pond: **A Field Access Example**

Now that you know how to access fields from native code, a complete example may help solidify your understanding. The example you work through in this section, Pond, uses a native method to calculate a value based on three Java fields. Before getting to the code, let's start with a little background information.

I'm in the process of building a pond in my backyard; to buy the right size pump and filter, I have to determine the volume of the pond in gallons. One way to accomplish this is to time how long it takes to fill a five-gallon bucket with a hose and then time how long it takes to fill the entire pond. This approach assumes, however, that my pond is already dug with the liner in place. What if you want to determine the volume beforehand so that you can buy a pump and filter before you start digging? You just use simple math!

To determine the volume of a pond in cubic feet, you just multiply the average width times the average length, and then multiply by the average depth. I refer to these dimensions as *average* because few ponds are rectangular and most have varying depths. Once you calculate the pond's volume in cubic feet, converting to gallons is as simple as multiplying by 7.5. This results in the following complete equation:

Volume (in gallons) = *Length* * *Width* * *Depth* * 7.5

I thought it would be interesting to place this equation in a native method as an exercise in accessing fields. You could try to make the argument that placing this calculation in a native method improves performance, but it wouldn't be a very good one. A piece of code this small wouldn't be improved enough to justify the overhead in calling the native method. Besides, simple multiplication is a very efficient operation to begin with. Listing 20.4 contains the source code for the Pond class used in this example.

20

Listing 20.4. The Java source code for the Pond class.

```
1: public class Pond implements Serializable {
2:    private float length, width, depth;
3:
4:    // Constructors
5:    public Pond() {
6:       this (0.0f, 0.0f, 0.0f);
7:    }
8:
9:    public Pond(float l, float w, float d) {
10:      length = l;
11:      width = w;
12:      depth = d;
13:   }
14:
15:   // Accessor methods
16:   public float getLength() {
17:      return length;
18:   }
19:
20:   public void setLength(float l) {
21:      length = l;
22:   }
23:
24:   public float getWidth() {
25:      return width;
26:   }
27:
28:   public void setWidth(float w) {
29:      width = w;
30:   }
31:
32:   public float getDepth() {
33:      return depth;
34:   }
35:
36:   public void setDepth(float d) {
37:      depth = d;
38:   }
39.
40:   // Natives
41:   private static native void initPond();
42:   public native float getVolume();
43:
44:   // Static startup code
45:   static {
46:      System.loadLibrary("Pond");
47:      initPond();
48:   }
49: }
```

20

The Pond class is a straightforward Java class with three fields: length, width, and depth (Line 2). These fields have corresponding accessor methods that provide an interface to the fields. More important to this discussion are the two native methods defined in the class, initPond() and getVolume() (Lines 41 and 42). The initPond() method is responsible for initializing the field identifiers; the getVolume() method actually calculates the pond volume. The Pond class uses static initializer code to load the Pond native library and call the initPond() native method (Lines 45 through 48).

The following command generates a C/C++ header for the Pond class:

javah -jni Pond

Listing 20.5 contains the code for the resulting header file, Pond.h.

Listing 20.5. The C/C++ header file for the Pond DLL.

```
 1: /* DO NOT EDIT THIS FILE - it is machine generated */
 2: #include <jni.h>
 3: /* Header for class Pond */
 4:
 5: #ifndef _Included_Pond
 6: #define _Included_Pond
 7: #ifdef __cplusplus
 8: extern "C" {
 9: #endif
10: /*
11:  * Class:     Pond
12:  * Method:    initPond
13:  * Signature: ()V
14:  */
15: JNIEXPORT void JNICALL Java_Pond_initPond
16:     (JNIEnv *, jclass);
17:
18: /*
19:  * Class:     Pond
20:  * Method:    getVolume
21:  * Signature: ()F
22:  */
23: JNIEXPORT jfloat JNICALL Java_Pond_getVolume
24:     (JNIEnv *, jobject);
25:
26: #ifdef __cplusplus
27: }
28: #endif
29: #endif
```

The Pond header file doesn't present any surprises. One important thing to note is the arguments to each method. Both take a JNIEnv* as their first argument, but the Java_Pond_initPond() method takes a jclass argument as its second argument (Line 16), and the Java_Pond_initPond() method takes a jobject argument (Line 24). These different argument types reflect the difference between static and nonstatic native methods.

The next step in the Pond example is the creation of the native method implementations. Listing 20.6 contains the source code for Pond.cpp.

Listing 20.6. The C++ source code for the Pond DLL.

```
 1: #include "Pond.h"
 2:
 3: // Global field IDs
 4: jfieldID fLengthID;
 5: jfieldID fWidthID;
 6: jfieldID fDepthID;
 7:
 8: void JNICALL Java_Pond_initPond(JNIEnv* env, jclass thisClass) {
 9:    // Find the fields
10:    fLengthID = env->GetFieldID(thisClass, "length", "F");
11:    fWidthID = env->GetFieldID(thisClass, "width", "F");
12:    fDepthID = env->GetFieldID(thisClass, "depth", "F");
13: }
14.
15: jfloat JNICALL Java_Pond_getVolume(JNIEnv* env, jobject thisObject) {
16:    // Get the field values
17:    jfloat length = env->GetFloatField(thisObject, fLengthID);
18:    jfloat width = env->GetFloatField(thisObject, fWidthID);
19:    jfloat depth = env->GetFloatField(thisObject, fDepthID);
20:
21:    // Calculate and return the volume
22:    return length * width * depth * 7.5f;
23: }
```

The field identifiers used to access the Pond fields are stored in global variables (Lines 4 through 6). These variables are initialized in the Java_Pond_initPond() method (Lines 10 through 12), which is called from the static initializer code in the Pond class. The field identifiers are used in the Java_Pond_getVolume() method to calculate the volume of the pond. The values of the fields are obtained using the GetFloatField() method and passing in the field identifiers (Lines 17 through 19). The pond volume is then calculated and returned using the pond volume equation presented earlier in the lesson (Line 22).

To build the Pond DLL, either use the Visual C++ project file available from the companion Web site and select Build from the Project menu in Visual C++ or execute the following command:

```
cl -Ic:\jdk1.1.3\include -Ic:\jdk1.1.3\include\win32 -LD Pond.cpp -FePond.dll
```

This command launches the command-line Visual C++ compiler to compile the C++ code and generate a DLL named Pond.dll. The DLL is ready to go, but you don't have a way of

20

testing any of the code. Listing 20.7 contains the source code for the PondTest application, which uses the Pond class to calculate the volume of a pond.

 NOTE

> If you're working through this example on a Solaris machine, you build
> a shared object with the following command:
>
> ```
> cc -G -I/usr/local/jdk1.1.3/include -I/usr/local/jdk1.1.3/
> ➥include/solaris Pond.cpp -o libPond.so
> ```

Listing 20.7. The Java source code for the PondTest application.

```
 1: public class PondTest {
 2:   public static void main(String[] args) {
 3:     // Make sure that we have the right number of args
 4:     if (args.length != 3) {
 5:       System.out.println("Usage: java PondTest Length Width Depth");
 6:       System.exit(0);
 7:     }
 8:
 9:     // Convert the args to floats
10:     float length = Float.valueOf(args[0]).floatValue();
11:     float width = Float.valueOf(args[1]).floatValue();
12:     float depth = Float.valueOf(args[2]).floatValue();
13:
14:     // Create the Pond object and display the volume in gallons
15:     Pond pond = new Pond(length, width, depth);
16:     System.out.println("Pond length = " + pond.getLength() + " feet");
17:     System.out.println("Pond width  = " + pond.getWidth() + " feet");
18:     System.out.println("Pond depth  = " + pond.getDepth() + " feet");
19:     System.out.println("Pond volume = " + pond.getVolume() + " gallons");
20:   }
21: }
```

The PondTest application takes three command-line arguments that specify the average length, width, and depth of the pond. It converts these argument strings to floating-point numbers (Lines 10 through 12) and then creates a Pond object with them. The pond dimensions are then output along with the volume, which is calculated with a call to the native getVolume() method. As you can see, the PondTest application doesn't have to do anything special to call the native method; it looks just like any other Java method.

To try out the PondTest application, execute the following command:

```
java PondTest 8 13 3
```

The resulting output of this command follows:

```
Pond length = 8.0 feet
Pond width  = 13.0 feet
Pond depth  = 3.0 feet
Pond volume = 2340.0 gallons
```

Calling Java Object Methods

Methods are called in a way very similar to the way in which fields are accessed: You obtain an identifier for a method and use it to call the method. Method identifiers are obtained using the GetMethodID() method, which works very much like the GetFieldID() method. As when determining field identifiers, you use the GetMethodID() method to find a method based on a method signature. Method signatures are constructed just like field signatures. For example, take a look at the following method definitions:

```
int getCount();
void setSwitches(boolean[] b);
void setAngle(float a);
String getName();
int processMessages(String[] m);
```

Applying the signature symbols from Table 20.2, you can easily obtain the signatures for each of these methods:

Method	Signature
getCount()	()I
setSwitches()	([Z)V
setAngle()	(F)V
getName()	()Ljava/lang/String;
processMessages()	([Ljava/lang/String;)I

The signatures look a little messy at first, but when you break down the symbols, they are very straightforward. Now that you have an understanding of how symbols work, I'll let you in on a little secret: You can use a tool to determine field and method signatures. The javap tool, which ships with the JDK and is used to disassemble Java classes, can determine signatures for the fields and methods in a class. To output signatures for the fields and methods in a class, use the -s and -p options to javap, like this:

```
javap -s -p Pond
```

The -s option tells javap to output signature information; the -p option tells it to include information about private members. Listing 20.8 contains the results of executing this command on the Pond class.

20

Listing 20.8. The results of using the `javap` tool to get the signatures for the Pond class.

```
 1: Compiled from Pond.java
 2: public synchronized class Pond extends java.lang.Object implements
    ➥java.io.Serializable
 3:     /* ACC_SUPER bit set */
 4: {
 5:     private float length;
 6:     /*   F   */
 7:     private float width;
 8:     /*   F   */
 9:     private float depth;
10:     /*   F   */
11:     public Pond();
12:     /*   ()V   */
13:     public Pond(float,float,float);
14:     /*   (FFF)V   */
15:     public float getLength();
16:     /*   ()F   */
17:     public void setLength(float);
18:     /*   (F)V   */
19:     public float getWidth();
20:     /*   ()F   */
21:     public void setWidth(float);
22:     /*   (F)V   */
23:     public float getDepth();
24:     /*   ()F   */
25:     public void setDepth(float);
26:     /*   (F)V   */
27:     private static native void initPond();
28:     /*   ()V   */
29:     public native float getVolume();
30:     /*   ()F   */
31:     static static {};
32:     /*   ()V   */
33: }
```

The field signatures are listed at the beginning of the class dissection (Lines 5 through 10). Because all the fields are simple `float` types, their signatures are all F. The next two signatures are the constructors of the class, which both return `void` types by definition. The second constructor takes three `float` arguments, which is evident by the signature (FFF)V. The signatures for the rest of the methods in the class are consistent with the signature symbols you've learned about, which only makes sense.

Getting back to accessing methods from native code, once you have a method identifier, you can easily call the method using one of the caller methods provided by the JNI. The JNI caller methods take a variable number of arguments, which is necessary because methods vary widely in their argument lists. There is a caller method specific to each type of data returned by the method called. Table 20.5 lists the caller methods supported by the JNI.

20

Table 20.5. Caller methods supported by the JNI.

Method	Return Type
CallObjectMethod()	jobject
CallBooleanMethod()	jboolean
CallByteMethod()	jbyte
CallCharMethod()	jchar
CallShortMethod()	jshort
CallIntMethod()	jint
CallLongMethod()	jlong
CallFloatMethod()	jfloat
CallDoubleMethod()	jdouble
CallVoidMethod()	jvoid

As an example of using a caller method, this is how you would call the getCount() method mentioned earlier in the lesson.

```
env->CallIntMethod(thisObject, "getCount", "()I");
```

If you want to call a static method, you have to do things a little differently. To find the method identifier for a static method, you must use the GetStaticMethodID() method. Similarly, there is a set of caller methods suited to static methods; these methods are named CallStaticObjectMethod(), CallStaticBooleanMethod(), and so on.

NOTE This discussion has focused on calling Java methods by passing a variable number arguments to the appropriate caller method. You can also call methods by passing a va_arg structure or jvalue array of arguments to a caller method, but the resulting code isn't as clean as the variable argument approach.

20

Accessing Java Objects

Strings and arrays are treated as first-class objects in Java, unlike C/C++ where they are given no special treatment. This presents an interesting situation for native code trying to access Java strings and arrays.

Arrays

The fact that arrays are objects in Java is a good reason for not allowing direct array access in native methods. Instead, you use JNI methods to access and manipulate arrays. This should come as no surprise because the JNI always shields you from directly accessing information in Java. To find out the length of an array, you use the JNI `GetArrayLength()` method:

```
jsize GetArrayLength(JNIEnv* env, jarray array);
```

As you can see, Java arrays are represented by the `jarray` data type in native code. When working with arrays using the JNI, it makes a big difference whether you are dealing with an array of scalar quantities (integers, floats, and so on) or an array of objects. The JNI provides two groups of methods for dealing with these two types of arrays. To access individual elements in an array of objects, you use the following getter and setter methods:

```
jobject GetObjectArrayElement(JNIEnv* env, jarray array, jsize index);
void SetObjectArrayElement(JNIEnv* env, jarray array, jsize index, jobject
value);
```

Both methods take a `JNIEnv*`, a `jarray`, and the index of the element to access. The `SetObjectArrayElement()` method also takes the value to which you want to set the array element, which is of type `jobject`.

This approach of accessing individual array elements is fine for objects, but it is inefficient for scalar types. Therefore, the JNI provides methods to get an entire array of scalars as opposed to individual elements. Table 20.6 contains a list of these methods.

Table 20.6. Scalar array getter methods supported by the JNI.

Method	Return Type	Java Type
GetBooleanArrayElements()	jboolean*	boolean[]
GetByteArrayElements()	jbyte*	byte[]
GetCharArrayElements()	jchar*	char[]
GetShortArrayElements()	jshort*	short[]
GetIntArrayElements()	jint*	int[]
GetLongArrayElements()	jlong*	long[]
GetFloatArrayElements()	jfloat*	float[]
GetDoubleArrayElements()	jdouble*	double[]

All these methods conform to the following general method definition:

```
NativeType GetArrayElements(JNIEnv* env, jarray array, jboolean* isCopy);
```

20

The first two arguments are pretty straightforward, but the third requires some explanation. The *isCopy* argument is a Boolean value set by the Java VM that indicates whether the array returned is the original array or a copy of it. If the array is the original, any changes you make to the array are permanent. On the other hand, if you are given a copy, you have the option of committing any changes or throwing them away. Arrays are released back to Java using one of a number of release methods provided by the JNI. Table 20.7 lists the supported release methods.

Table 20.7. Scalar array release methods supported by the JNI.

Method	Return Type	Java Type
ReleaseBooleanArrayElements()	jboolean*	boolean[]
ReleaseByteArrayElements()	jbyte*	byte[]
ReleaseCharArrayElements()	jchar*	char[]
ReleaseShortArrayElements()	jshort*	short[]
ReleaseIntArrayElements()	jint*	int[]
ReleaseLongArrayElements()	jlong*	long[]
ReleaseFloatArrayElements()	jfloat*	float[]
ReleaseDoubleArrayElements()	jdouble*	double[]

These release methods all conform to the following general method definition:

```
void ReleaseArrayElements(JNIEnv* env, jarray array, NativeType elements,
➥jint mode);
```

The first two arguments are pretty straightforward; the third refers to the native array of elements. The final element is an integer that can be one of the following constants:

Constant	Meaning
0	Copy array back and release local storage
JNI_COMMIT	Copy array back but don't release local storage
JNI_ABORT	Release local storage without copying array back

20

NOTE The JNI also supports the creation of arrays using the NewObjectArray() and NewScalarArray() methods.

Strings

Because strings are objects in Java, it should come as no surprise that they are treated as objects by the JNI. However, the JNI is a native interface, which means that it provides a C/C++ interface to Java information. Because C and C++ treat strings as arrays of characters instead of objects, the JNI functions must handle converting Java string objects to native character arrays. Furthermore, the JNI has to contend with the fact that there are two standards for representing textual information: Unicode and UTF-8. The Java VM uses UTF-8 internally, which is an 8-bit variation of the Unicode format.

WARNING

> You can't directly access a string passed into a native method as though it was an array of characters. You must always use a JNI method to gain access to a string. Manipulating a string argument directly as a char* can cause serious problems such as potentially crashing the Java VM!

The length of a string is often the first piece of string information you obtain before manipulating a string. To determine the length of a Java string in native code, you use the `GetStringLength()` method or the `GetUTFStringLength()` method, depending on whether the native platform supports Unicode or UTF-8. Following is an example of using `GetStringLength()` to determine the length of a Unicode string named `sentence`:

```
int len = env->GetStringLength(sentence);
```

To gain access to a string in a native method, you must use the `GetStringChars()` method or the `GetStringUTFChars()` method. These methods obtain a Java string as an array of characters; they both return a char*. Following is an example of obtaining a char* pointer to the `sentence` string:

```
char* mySentence = env->GetStringChars(sentence, 0);
```

The second argument to `GetStringChars()` is the index of the beginning of the string; 0 indicates that you want the entire string. When you are finished working with a string, you must release the pointer by calling the `ReleaseStringChars()` method or the `ReleaseStringUTFChars()` method, depending on whether the native string is a Unicode or a UTF-8 string. Here is how you release the `sentence` string:

```
env->ReleaseStringChars(sentence, mySentence);
```

Notice that the char* pointer is passed along as the second argument to the `ReleaseString()` method. This clarification is necessary because you can have multiple string pointers.

At this point, it's probably a good idea to take a look at an example that pulls together what you've learned about accessing arrays and strings. This stuff can get overwhelming at times,

20

and a straightforward example can often make it all clear. It can also add more confusion, but hopefully that won't be the case here! Listing 20.9 contains the source code for the Alphabetize application, an application that accepts a series of strings as command-line arguments and then sorts them alphabetically using a native method.

Listing 20.9. The Java source code for the Alphabetize application.

```
 1: public class Alphabetize {
 2:   public static void main(String[] args) {
 3:     // Make sure that we have at least two string args
 4:     if (args.length < 2) {
 5:       System.out.println("Usage: java Alphabetize String1 String2
          ➥<StringN>");
 6:       System.exit(0);
 7:     }
 8:
 9:     // Copy the arguments into a string array
10:     String[] strings = new String[args.length];
11:     for (int i = 0; i < strings.length; i++)
12:       strings[i] = args[i];
13:
14:     // Print the unalphabetized strings
15:     for (int i = 0; i < strings.length; i++)
16:       System.out.print(strings[i] + " ");
17:
18:     // Alphabetize the strings
19:     alphabetizeStrings(strings);
20:
21:     // Print the alphabetized strings
22:     System.out.println();
23:     for (int i = 0; i < strings.length; i++)
24:       System.out.print(strings[i] + " ");
25:   }
26:
27:   // Natives
28:   private static native void initAlphabetize();
29:   private static native void alphabetizeStrings(String[] strings);
30:
31:   // Static startup code
32:   static {
33:     System.loadLibrary("Alphabetize");
34:     initAlphabetize();
35:   }
36: }
```

20

The Alphabetize application begins by copying the command-line arguments into a string named strings (Lines 10 through 12). It then displays the strings just to clarify their original, unalphabetized order (Lines 15 and 16). The strings are sorted alphabetically with a call to alphabetizeStrings(), a native method (Line 19). Finally, the strings are displayed again so that you can see that they were successfully alphabetized (Lines 22 through 24).

The `Alphabetize` application relies on two native methods: `initAlphabetize()` and `alphabetizeStrings()` (Lines 28 and 29). This native method pair should be somewhat familiar to you from the `Pond` example earlier in the lesson, in which two methods were used in a similar fashion. The first method, `initAlphabetize()`, is a static method responsible for getting the method identifier for the `String.compareTo()` method, which is necessary to perform the string sorting. The `alphabetizeStrings()` method performs the string sort by using the `String.compareTo()` method to compare strings. Not surprisingly, the `Alphabetize` DLL is loaded in the static initializer for the class, which is also where the `initAlphabetize()` method is called (Lines 32 through 35).

The following command generates a C/C++ header file for the `Alphabetize` class:

```
javah -jni Alphabetize
```

Listing 20.10 contains the code for the generated `Alphabetize.h` header file.

Listing 20.10. The C/C++ header file for the `Alphabetize` DLL.

```
 1: /* DO NOT EDIT THIS FILE - it is machine generated */
 2: #include <jni.h>
 3: /* Header for class Alphabetize */
 4:
 5: #ifndef _Included_Alphabetize
 6: #define _Included_Alphabetize
 7: #ifdef __cplusplus
 8: extern "C" {
 9: #endif
10: /*
11:  * Class:     Alphabetize
12:  * Method:    initAlphabetize
13:  * Signature: ()V
14:  */
15: JNIEXPORT void JNICALL Java_Alphabetize_initAlphabetize
16:    (JNIEnv *, jclass);
17:
18: /*
19:  * Class:     Alphabetize
20:  * Method:    alphabetizeStrings
21:  * Signature: ([Ljava/lang/String;)V
22:  */
23: JNIEXPORT void JNICALL Java_Alphabetize_alphabetizeStrings
24:    (JNIEnv *, jclass, jobjectArray);
25:
26: #ifdef __cplusplus
27: }
28: #endif
29: #endif
```

Hopefully, this stuff is starting to look familiar to you. The main thing to notice about this header is that the string array passed into Java_Alphabetize_alphabetizeStrings() is passed as a jobjectArray (Line 24). This fact confirms that the JNI treats Java strings as objects. Let's move on to the source code that makes this example tick; Listing 20.11 contains the source code for Alphabetize.cpp.

Listing 20.11. The C++ source code for the Alphabetize DLL.

```
 1: #include "Alphabetize.h"
 2:
 3: // Global method ID
 4: jmethodID mCompareToID;
 5:
 6: void JNICALL Java_Alphabetize_initAlphabetize(JNIEnv* env,
    ➥jclass thisClass) {
 7:   // Find the String.compareTo() method
 8:   jclass stringClass = env->FindClass("java/lang/String");
 9:   mCompareToID = env->GetMethodID(stringClass, "compareTo",
10:     "(Ljava/lang/String;)I");
11: }
12:
13: void JNICALL Java_Alphabetize_alphabetizeStrings(JNIEnv* env,
14:   jclass thisClass, jobjectArray strings) {
15:
16:   // Sort the string array using a bubble sort
17:   int numStrings = env->GetArrayLength(strings);
18:   for (int i = 1; i < numStrings; i++) {
19:     for (int j = i - 1; j >= 0; j--) {
20:       jobject string1 = env->GetObjectArrayElement(strings, j);
21:       jobject string2 = env->GetObjectArrayElement(strings, j + 1);
22:       if (env->CallIntMethod(string1, mCompareToID, string2) > 0) {
23:         env->SetObjectArrayElement(strings, j, string2);
24:         env->SetObjectArrayElement(strings, j + 1, string1);
25:       }
26:     }
27:   }
28: }
```

The Java_Alphabetize_alphabetizeStrings() method requires the String.compareTo() method to pull off the string sort. Because this method is part of the Java API, you must obtain a method identifier for it to call it. This is accomplished in the Java_initAlphabetize() method, which finds the java.lang.String class and uses it to get the method identifier for the compareTo() method (Lines 8 through 10). Notice the signature string used to define the compareTo() method; you could have obtained this signature by using the javap tool and specifying the java.lang.String class.

20

With the `compareTo()` method identifier in hand, the `Java_Alphabetize_alphabetizeStrings()` method can get to work sorting the strings alphabetically. I'm not going to get into the details of the bubble-sort algorithm used to sort the strings, but I will direct your attention to the methods used to access the array of strings. The `GetObjectArrayElement()` method is used to retrieve an individual string from the array. Strings are compared using the `compareTo()` method through a call to `CallIntMethod()`. Finally, string elements in the array are set using the `SetObjectArrayElement()` method. Once you get comfortable with the idea of using the JNI as an interface, native code starts to look pretty clear.

Following is an example of executing the `Alphabetize` application with a list of strings:

```
java Alphabetize Red Green Blue Yellow Purple Orange Gold
```

The resulting output of this command follows:

```
Red Green Blue Yellow Purple Orange Gold
Blue Gold Green Orange Purple Red Yellow
```

As you can see, the strings are neatly sorted alphabetically, just as you expected. Who would think that it was C++ code doing all the work behind the scenes? You, of course!

Summary

This lesson took you on a whirlwind tour through the Java Native Method Interface (JNI), which allows native C/C++ code to interact with Java constructs in a platform-independent manner. You began the lesson by contemplating some scenarios in which native code is required, along with some reasons against using native code unless it is absolutely necessary. You then moved on to learning how there are two perspectives to using native code: the Java side and the native side. You learned that each side has its own responsibilities. The lesson then accelerated to showing you how to access Java objects, fields, and methods using the JNI. You worked through three different sample applications that demonstrated different ways to use the JNI.

Even though this lesson is one of the longer lessons you've encountered in this book, I'm not going to have you believe it has covered everything there is to know about native code integration with Java. In fact, I strongly encourage you to use what you've learned in this lesson to explore the JNI more thoroughly on your own. The goal of this lesson was to cover the most important features of the JNI and to demonstrate some practical ways in which to use them.

Q&A

Q Can native methods override normal Java methods?

A Yes, provided that the method being overridden is not declared as `final`.

Q How does the C approach to using the JNI differ from the C++ approach used in this lesson?

A Because C doesn't involve objects in any way, there is no concept of calling a JNI method using a JNI pointer (`JNIEnv*`). Instead, you must call the JNI methods as normal C functions and pass the `JNIEnv*` pointer as the first parameter. This approach is functionally equivalent to the C++ approach, but it isn't nearly as clean.

Q Can you handle Java exceptions in native code?

A Yes, but there is no `try/catch` facility. Instead, you must call the JNI `ExceptionOccurred()` method to explicitly check for the occurrence of an exception.

Q Does Java's automatic garbage collection still work properly in native code?

A Yes. The JNI introduces the concepts of local references and global references to distinguish between data that is automatically garbage collected and data that has to hang around. Local references are created when an object is passed into a native method. They are automatically garbage collected when the method exits. You can have them explicitly garbage collected before exiting the method by releasing them with a call to the JNI `DeleteLocalRef()` method. Conversely, you can turn a local reference into a global reference with a call to `NewGlobalRef()`. Global references must always be explicitly released using the `DeleteLocalRef()` method, or memory leaks will occur.

20

Day **21**

Things to Come in Java 1.2

by Michael Morrison

As you are no doubt aware, Java has evolved a great deal in a relatively short period of time. The release of Java 1.1 marked a significant step in this evolution, with many new features being added to the language. However, as feature-rich as Java 1.1 is, there are still plenty of areas where Java can stand improvement. JavaSoft is keenly aware of this situation and is working on even more new features for a future version of Java, perhaps Java 1.2. This lesson takes you on a tour of the new features slated for Java 1.2, as well as some additional APIs and tools that will be released as separate extensions to Java. Specifically, this lesson covers the following topics:

☐ Java core enhancements, including Java Foundation Classes (JFC), Java Commerce, Java Interface Description Language (IDL), and JavaBeans Glasgow

☐ Standard Java extensions, including Java Naming and Directory Interface (JNDI), Java Media, and Java Management

☐ Other Java technologies, such as PersonalJava, EmbeddedJava, and JavaBeans migration tools

The information you learn in this lesson is geared toward helping you understand the future of Java and what to expect in terms of new functionality. For this reason, the lesson is more conceptual than previous lessons in the book. Nevertheless, I think you'll find the information presented in this lesson useful as you chart your own future as a Java developer and user.

The Future of Java

To me, one of the most exciting things about Java is JavaSoft's relentless pursuit for new functionality. Java contains built-in support for far more features than any other language or computing platform has ever attempted to support. For example, in C++, you have to resort to proprietary third-party libraries for networking, compression, or encryption. Not so with Java. Granted, an argument could be made that a specialized type of service such as encryption should be provided by third-party companies. However, Java is designed to be totally extensible, meaning that although JavaSoft provides default implementations for many of Java's features, the door is wide open for third-party implementations. In fact, Java's support for a wide range of features is what allows third-party implementations to be integrated seamlessly with the Java environment.

Java's extensibility has a great deal to do with its future, because no one company can be expected to provide the answers to every software development need (contrary to some marketing campaigns). For this reason, the future of Java is largely dependent on the types of things developed by companies other than JavaSoft. However, the rich feature set and extensible nature of Java is what allows developers to do truly interesting things with Java. The future of Java is therefore affected both by JavaSoft's commitment to improve the language and runtime environment and third-party companies who build applications and reusable components based on the Java core.

The half of this equation that you learn about in this lesson is JavaSoft's role in the future of Java. More specifically, you learn about the new APIs and tools that are currently under development for a future release of Java. It's important to understand that the Java API is broken up into a core API and a set of standard extension APIs. The core API is what is typically referred to as the Java API and is shipped with the JDK. The standard extension APIs are a set of individual APIs available separately from the JDK.

21

Java Core Enhancements

The core Java API defines a minimal set of functionality a Java implementation must support in order to be considered Java-compliant. For example, when a Web browser claims to support Java, it must fully support the core API. This guaranteed support for the core API is what allows Java developers the luxury of being able to write Java programs once and have them run on any Java-compliant platform. The latest core API as of this writing is Java 1.1, which ships with the JDK 1.1.

Although the core API defines a minimal set of functionality for Java platforms, it is quite comprehensive, as you've no doubt seen throughout this book. Nevertheless, some enhancements to the core API are in the works and will more than likely appear in the next major release of Java, version 1.2. Following are four of the most significant enhancements to the core Java API:

- [ ] Java Foundation Classes (JFC)
- [ ] Java Commerce
- [ ] Java Interface Description Language (IDL)
- [ ] JavaBeans Glasgow

Java Foundation Classes (JFC)

The Java Foundation Classes (JFC) are a group of graphical user interface classes that allow you to build powerful user interfaces for applets or applications. The JFC is similar to the AWT, but the JFC includes more applied user interface elements such as image buttons, tables, gauges, and tree views. The JFC also includes a 2-D graphics API that provides advanced two-dimensional graphics capabilities. Similar to the JFC's user interface classes, the 2-D graphics support in the JFC builds upon the existing support in the AWT.

The JFC is largely based on Netscape's Internet Foundation Classes (IFC) and will eventually be provided as additions to the java.awt and java.awt.image packages that are part of the core Java API. Because you already learned a great deal about the JFC on Day 4, "Foundation Classes and Java Frameworks," I won't go into any more detail here.

Java Commerce

As the Internet continues to move toward becoming a viable marketplace, the need for a secure commercial transaction protocol becomes more critical. Because Java is fast becoming the programming platform of choice for the Internet, it stands to reason that Java needs to provide support for handling secure commercial transactions. Java Commerce is a new API that provides a solution to the problem of dealing with commercial transactions on the

21

Internet. The goal of Java Commerce is to establish an open, extensible environment for financial management across distributed networks such as the Internet. Java Commerce is slated to become a part of the core Java API.

Java Commerce consists of the following major components:

- ☐ An infrastructure
- ☐ A database
- ☐ Payment cassettes
- ☐ Service cassettes
- ☐ Administration user interfaces

The infrastructure of the Java Commerce API is the architectural framework through which the rest of the API operates. The infrastructure is critical because it gives the Commerce API its extensibility. This extensibility in turn allows the Commerce API to grow and expand to face the inevitable new challenges that will arise when dealing with financial transactions on the Internet.

The database portion of the API serves as a repository for user information, such as payment methods and the user's shipping address. The database part of the API relies on encryption to ensure that user information is kept secure. Encryption is very important because the database contains highly sensitive information such as a user's credit card number—definitely something you don't want someone to be able to access without authorization.

To facilitate financial transactions, the Commerce API uses *cassettes*, which are software modules that implement specific financial protocols. The two different types of cassettes supported are payment cassettes and service cassettes. A *payment cassette* defines the protocol for making electronic payments. There is a different type of payment cassette for each type of payment. For example, there are payment cassettes for credit cards, debit cards, and eventually electronic cash. Using Java Commerce, a user could have different payment cassettes, much like people carry different payment instruments in their wallets (credit cards, debit cards, cash, and so on). Interestingly enough, Java Commerce uses the notion of a wallet to organize and manage payment cassettes.

NEW TERM

cassettes: Software modules used by Java Commerce that implement specific financial protocols.

payment cassette: A cassette that defines the protocol for making electronic payments.

Service cassettes are more general purpose than payment cassettes and model any type of value-added financial service, such as financial analysis or tax preparation. For example, you might purchase a service cassette to help balance your electronic checkbook or determine your net worth. The significance of service cassettes is that they define protocols through which specific financial services can take place.

NEW TERM   *service cassette:* A cassette that defines a protocol for performing applied, value-added financial transactions.

The last part of the Java Commerce API is the administrative user interfaces, which are a comprehensive set of user interfaces that facilitate the management of commerce-related information. For example, user information and commerce system options are maintained through these user interfaces. For more information on Java Commerce, check out the Java Commerce Web pages at `http://www.javasoft.com/products/commerce/index.html`.

Java Interface Description Language (IDL)

Java Interface Description Language (IDL) is an API aimed at providing a means of connecting Java client programs to network servers running on other computing platforms. IDL is an industry standard protocol for performing client/server communications across different platforms. One of the major uses of Java IDL is to transparently connect Java client programs to *legacy systems* via CORBA objects.

CORBA (Common Object Request Broker Architecture) is the open industry standard for dealing with the complexities associated with distributed, heterogeneous networks. As its name implies, IDL defines the interface for CORBA objects, which outlines the services an object can request and provide, along with the kinds of data the object can interact with. Java IDL will become a part of the core Java API, most likely in the next release. Day 14, "Java and CORBA," took a close look at CORBA and how it applies to Java.

NEW TERM   *legacy system:* An outdated computer system that hasn't been updated for compatibility with current technologies. Most mainframes qualify as legacy systems.

Following are the major parts of Java IDL:

☐ A client framework that allows Java IDL clients to be designed as either applets or stand-alone applications

21

- ☐ A server framework that allows Java applications to act as network servers for IDL clients
- ☐ A development tool that automatically generates stub code for specific remote object interfaces

For more information on Java IDL, take a look at the Java IDL Web pages at `http://www.javasoft.com/products/jdk/idl/index.html`.

JavaBeans Glasgow

JavaBeans, the software component model for Java you learned about on Days 5 and 6, is proving to be one of the most significant parts of the Java API. For this reason, JavaSoft has taken a hard look at JavaBeans and assessed its weaknesses in hopes of making it a more useful technology for the future of Java. The results of this assessment come in the form of Glasgow, which is the code name of the next release of JavaBeans. Glasgow provides a wealth of new functionality for JavaBeans and will be included in the next major release of the core Java API. Following are the four major enhancements to JavaBeans as defined in the Glasgow specification:

- ☐ A runtime containment and services protocol
- ☐ An object aggregation and delegation model
- ☐ An object activation framework
- ☐ Native drag-and-drop service

The runtime containment and services protocol is aimed at providing Beans a means of interacting with their container, be it a Web browser, applet, or application. This protocol allows a Bean to query its container to find out about any available functionality it can access and use.

The object aggregation and delegation model focuses on the problem of multiple inheritance and the fact that Java doesn't support it. For example, Beans can't derive from multiple classes to inherit two different types of functionality, which would be beneficial in some cases. The aggregation and delegation model suggests using aggregate objects to handle certain types of tasks not specifically suited to the Bean. A Bean might therefore contain objects as member variables that are responsible for performing certain tasks, as opposed to performing the tasks directly.

The object activation framework defines an architecture for establishing typed data, determining supported data types of a Bean, and binding typed data to a Bean. When I say "typed data," I mean data that has an associated viewer or editor that is used to manipulate the data. For example, image data is typed in a sense that you must use an image editing application to edit it, as opposed to a text editor. By providing a typing mechanism, the JavaBeans architecture becomes more "intelligent" because data types can be linked with Beans that perform a function specific to the data type.

The last major enhancement to JavaBeans offered by Glasgow is a native drag-and-drop service. This service is designed to be platform-independent from a programming perspective, meaning that it will result in API additions to the core AWT. However, the implementation of the drag and drop service is designed to be platform-dependent so that Beans can interact with native applications via drag-and-drop. To find out the latest information on JavaBeans Glasgow, take a stroll through the Java Glasgow Web pages at `http://splash.javasoft.com/beans/glasgow.html`.

Standard Java Extensions

Beyond the core Java API, JavaSoft has plans for API extensions that will ship as separate products. These API extensions address specialized applications of Java, which is why they aren't part of the core API. Nevertheless, they are still developed entirely in Java and will be available for use by developers. Following are the main Java extensions planned for the near future:

- Java Naming and Directory Interface (JNDI)
- Java Media
- Java Management

Java Naming and Directory Interface (JNDI)

Naming and directory services are important to enterprise networks because they provide a means of sharing a variety of information about network users, services, and applications, among other things. Java Naming and Directory Interface (JNDI) is a standard Java extension API that provides a unified interface to enterprise naming and directory services. Because JNDI is based on Java's standard object model, applications can operate on naming and directory information as standard Java objects. Additionally, JNDI is itself platform-independent, meaning that applications don't have to deal with a specific naming or directory service implementation if they adhere to the JNDI API. To find out more information about JNDI, check out the JNDI Web pages at `http://www.javasoft.com/products/jndi/index.html`.

Java Media

Another standard Java extension is Java Media, which is a set of multimedia APIs that aims to add a significant level of multimedia support to Java. In some ways, Java Media is the most

21

ambitious of the standard extensions because of how much functionality it encompasses. The following are the major components of Java Media:

- Java Media Framework (JMF)
- Java Collaboration
- Java Telephony
- Java Speech
- Java Animation
- Java 3D

The heart of the Java Media API is the Java Media Framework (JMF), which defines the overall architecture and protocols used by the other media APIs. JMF itself consists of three parts: Java Media Player, Java Media Capture, and Java Media Conference. Together, these three APIs encompass the low-level facilities necessary for much of the other media APIs to function. For example, the Java Media Player includes support for the synchronization, control, processing, and presentation of compressed, streamed, and timed media such as video and audio. In other words, it handles all the low-level details involved with managing timed media.

Java Collaboration is an API geared toward multiparty communication over networks. Online games may require this type of communication, for example. Java Collaboration will address the complexities involved with the management of two-way multiparty communication, such as registering parties and marshalling the flow of information between parties. It isn't clear yet whether Java Collaboration will tackle the inherent problem of synchronization in its approach to multiparty communication.

Not surprisingly, Java Telephony tackles the issue of integrating telephones with computers. With Java Telephony, you can exercise a great deal of control over telephone calls; you'll be able to throw your answering machine away and write a software version in Java!

Java Speech marks Java's entry into speech recognition and synthesis. This API will open the door for interactive Java applications involving features such as text-to-speech. I'm personally waiting for a talking Web browser!

The Java Animation API works in concert with the core Java 2D API in providing animation support for 2-D objects. Predictably enough, Java Animation will use the Java Media Framework heavily for all the timing aspects of animation.

The last area of Java Media is Java 3D, which is an API supplying 3-D graphics capabilities. Java 3D provides support for the creation, manipulation, and graphical rendering of geometric 3-D objects. Java 3D is expected to rely on native services whenever possible in order to speed up the computationally heavy task of rendering 3-D objects. This reliance could involve hardware acceleration if 3-D rendering hardware is available. For more information on Java Media, visit the Java Media Web pages at `http://www.javasoft.com/products/java-media/index.html`.

Java Management

Java Management is slated to answer the needs of integrated network management systems. It includes a wide range of interfaces, classes, and applets to facilitate the development of integrated management solutions. The primary goal of the Java Management API is to provide a unified approach to handling the complexities involved in developing and maintaining resources and services on a heterogeneous network. Using the Java Management API, developers will be able to rapidly develop network management applications supporting a wide range of systems on large and often complex networks. To find out more about Java Management, stop by the Java Management Web pages at `http://www.javasoft.com/products/JavaManagement/index.html`.

Other Java Technologies

All of the new Java technologies you've learned about in this lesson thus far are planned for inclusion in a future release of the core Java API or as a standard Java extension. A few Java technologies don't fit in either of these categories. I'm referring to APIs that aren't going to be part of the core API and that don't qualify as standard extensions. I'm also referring to technologies that aren't APIs at all, such as tools that are used to enhance the Java platform in some way. The following are two APIs and a set of tools that fall into this category of "other" Java technologies:

- PersonalJava
- EmbeddedJava
- JavaBeans migration tools

PersonalJava

PersonalJava is an API designed for use in networked hardware products, such as "Internet in a box"-type electronic devices. Any electronic device that requires an Internet connection could benefit from having the compact operating environment provided by PersonalJava. Examples of such products include handheld computers and video games. The Personal-Java API is a subset of the core API, because it is designed to be very compact. The PersonalJava API does add some functionality not found in the core API that is applicable

21

only to embedded network applications. For the most part, however, PersonalJava is a scaled-down version of the core Java API. Following are the core API packages included in the Personal Java API:

```
java.applet
java.awt
java.awt.datatransfer
java.awt.event
java.awt.image
java.awt.peer
java.beans
java.io
java.lang
java.lang.reflect
java.net
java.util
java.util.zip
```

PersonalJava doesn't provide all of the functionality available in these packages. For example, the `java.awt` package includes some functionality that isn't necessary in embedded network applications. Therefore, the `java.awt` package is partially implemented in PersonalJava. The same situation applies to the `java.io` and `java.util` packages. For more information about PersonalJava, check out the PersonalJava Web pages at `http://www.javasoft.com/products/personaljava/`.

EmbeddedJava

Similar to PersonalJava, EmbeddedJava is an API designed as a subset of the core Java API. Unlike PersonalJava, the EmbeddedJava API is designed specifically for electronic devices requiring highly compact embedded applications. Examples of such products include pagers, office peripherals, network routers, and electronic switches. The primary difference between EmbeddedJava and PersonalJava is that EmbeddedJava is designed for severely resource-constrained environments such as those with little memory, whereas PersonalJava is designed for compact networked environments. The difference is clear when you consider that EmbeddedJava is a subset of PersonalJava. To find out more about EmbeddedJava, check out the EmbeddedJava Web pages at `http://www.javasoft.com/products/embeddedjava/`.

JavaBeans Migration Tools

Although JavaBeans is showing strong signs of becoming a major player on the component software scene, JavaSoft has valid concerns over its relationship with other component models. More specifically, JavaSoft didn't want to leave developers having to make a judgement call between using JavaBeans or Microsoft's ActiveX. The reality is that a great deal of ActiveX controls are already available, and even more applications exist that are dependent on ActiveX. Therefore, ActiveX is a technology that isn't going anywhere soon. JavaSoft reasoned that it would be strategically smart to allow JavaBeans to peacefully coexist with ActiveX. They developed two tools to accomplish this goal:

- ☐ JavaBeans Bridge for ActiveX
- ☐ JavaBeans Migration Assistant for ActiveX

The JavaBeans Bridge for ActiveX enables you to use Beans as ActiveX components in ActiveX environments such as Microsoft Visual Basic. This capability is significant because it alleviates the problems concerning moving component development to JavaBeans while maintaining an ActiveX-based application. The JavaBeans Bridge basically creates an ActiveX wrapper to house a Bean so that it appears to be an ActiveX component. For more information on the ActiveX Bridge, check out the ActiveX Bridge Web site at `http://java.sun.com/beans/bridge`.

Another tool useful in moving from ActiveX to JavaBeans is the JavaBeans Migration Assistant for ActiveX, which generates skeletal JavaBeans code from ActiveX components. The Migration Assistant analyzes ActiveX components and creates the source code for a Bean with a similar structure and feature set. Of course, there is no way for the Migration Assistant to generate code for JavaBeans method implementations. In other words, you'll still have to develop code for the methods in a converted Bean, but the Migration Assistant will automatically create the data structures and method definitions. To find out more about the JavaBeans Migration Assistant for ActiveX, check out the Migration Assistant Web page at `http://java.sun.com/beans/assistant`.

Summary

This lesson took you on a tour through many of the future enhancements to Java. Many of these enhancements are slated to be included in the next major release of Java, Java 1.2, and others will be part of the standard Java extensions. Still other Java-related technologies are going to be available as subsets of existing APIs, and a pair of tools is being released to help improve the integration of JavaBeans components into ActiveX-based environments. All of these Java technologies will improve the viability of the Java platform as a whole and are therefore important to at least understand at a conceptual level. This lesson gave you a solid enough introduction to these technologies that you can go learn more about them on your own.

21

Q&A

Q Why are the standard extension APIs provided separately from the core Java API?

A Because the core Java API is designed to be as compact as possible; any functionality not applicable to a wide range of applications doesn't merit inclusion in it. This restriction keeps the core API from becoming bloated with functionality that only applies to a specialized minority of applications. For example, the Java Management API is only useful to a small set of applications and would therefore be unnecessary overhead for the core API.

Q When are all these neat technologies going to be available?

A They all vary in their release dates, but as of this writing some are available in beta form, some are at the specification stage, and some are still on the drawing board. To find out the current status of all Java-related technologies, check out the Java API Overview and Schedule Web page at `http://www.javasoft.com/products/api-overview/index.html`.

Q Are there any changes planned for the Java language itself?

A No, the Java language was frozen as of version 1.0. However, Java 1.1 introduced inner classes to the language, which technically violated the 1.0 freeze. Because the change didn't impact the Java virtual machine, the folks at JavaSoft figured it wasn't too harmful of a change. Besides, inner classes were practically a necessity in order for the delegation event model to be possible. Looking beyond the exception made for inner classes, I wouldn't expect to see any other changes to the Java language in the future.

Q How do PersonalJava and EmbeddedJava relate to JavaOS and JavaChips?

A JavaOS is an operating system based on the Java virtual machine that is expected to be used with the JavaChip family of Java-based microprocessors. When JavaOS runs on a JavaChip, the Java virtual machine is physically implemented in silicon on the microprocessor. JavaOS and JavaChips provide an ideal platform for PersonalJava and EmbeddedJava applications.

INDEX

Symbols

2-D graphics (JFC), 78
3-D borders, 42
  drawing, 49-53
  grooved, 43-44
  lowered, 42
  raised, 43
  ridged, 44
3D API (future of Java), 448

A

access control lists, 380
  Security API, 388
accessibility features (JFC), 78-79

accessing
  arrays with native code, 432-433
  databases, 172-173
    native drivers, 173
    ODBC drivers, 173-174
    with SQL, 174-178
  fields from native code, 421-422
    getter methods, 423
    Pond sample application, 424-429
    setter methods, 423-424
  operating system information, 410
  strings with native code, 434-438

accessor methods, 45-46
  Beans design patterns, 114
acknowledgement from server, waiting for, 152-153
Acl interface, 388
AclEntry interface, 388
ActionEvent class, 26
actionPerformed( ) method
  ActionEvent class, 26
  WorldExplorer applet (listing 10.6), 234
ActiveX, JavaBeans migration tools, 450-451
ActiveX Bridge (Beans), 140-141
  events, 142
  methods, 141

properties, 141
Web site, 451
adapter classes, 11
adapters (event), 30-31
inner classes, 31-33
**address book sample program
(JDBC), 198**
clearing the screen, 205-206
database fields, 199
deleting records, 209-210
displayResults( ) method,
204-205
event handlers, 200-201
execute( ) method, 203-204
executeQuery( )
method, 204
finding records, 206-208
initializeDatabase( )
method, 202-203
placeholders, 205
saving records, 208-209
user interface, 199-200
**AddressBook class construc-
tor (listing 9.7), 200**
AdjustmentEvent class, 26
**adjustmentValueChanged( )
method (AdjustmentEvent
class), 26**
**administration of Java Web
Server, 324-326**
**AFC (Application Founda-
tion Classes), 100**
CAB files, 102
components, 100-101
graphics features, 102
Win32 resource
support, 102
**algorithms, creating key
pairs, 395**
Alphabetize application
C++ source code for
(listing 20.11), 437
header file for
(listing 20.10), 436
listing 20.9, 435

**Animation API (future of
Java), 448**
anonymous local classes, 201
**APIs (Application Program-
ming Interfaces)**
Commerce (future of Java),
443-445
EmbeddedJava, 450
extension
JNDI (Java Naming
and Directory
Interface), 447
Management, 449
Media, 447-449
Internationalization
BreakIterator class, 228
Calendar class, 226
ChoiceFormat class, 228
Collator class, 228
DateFormat class, 227
Format class, 225
MessageFormat class,
227-228
NumberFormat
class, 225
ResourceBundle
class, 224
TimeZone class, 226
JavaBeans, 106
application builder tool
support, 108
event handling, 108
Glasgow (future release),
446-447
introspection, 107
JAR files, 370-371
migration tools, 450-451
persistence, 108
property management,
106-107
reflection, role of,
241-242
source code, 123
see also Beans; JAR files

PersonalJava, 449-450
Reflection, 243-244
Array class, 247
Class class, 244
Constructor class, 247
Field class, 245
Member interface, 245
Method class, 246
Modifier class, 247-248
Security, 380-381
access control lists, 388
certificates, 386
digital signatures,
383-386
keys, 382-383
message digests, 386-387
providers, 381-382
Servlet, 330
classes, 331-332
HelloWorldServlet
sample servlet,
334-336
Servlet interface,
332-334
Applet class, 7
<APPLET> tag, 8
archive attribute, 370
"appletcations"
creating, 13-15
listing 1.4, 13-14
overview, 16-17
security, 16
testing, 15-16
applets
CapitalQuery sample
application as, 310-313
compared to applications,
4-5
frame windows, 5-6
main( ) method, 5
security, 6
creating, 7
listing 1.1, 7
embedding in Web pages, 8

execution, 7-8
JAR files, using, 370
merging with applications,
   13-15
   overview, 16-17
   security, 16
   testing, 15-16
testing, 9-10
trusted, 6, 379
unsigned, 5
**appletviewer, testing applets,
9-10**
application builder tools
Beans, using with, 109-110
JavaBeans API support
   for, 108
**Application Foundation
Classes,** *see* **AFC**
application frameworks, 72
AFC (Application Founda-
   tion Classes), 100
   CAB files, 102
   components, 100-101
   graphics features, 102
   Win32 resource
      support, 102
IFC (Internet Foundation
   Classes), 86-88
   choosers, 90-91
   drawing methods, 91-92
   sample applet, 92-100
   views and components,
      88-90
   windows, 91
JFC (Java Foundation
   Classes), 72-73
   2-D graphics, 78
   accessibility features,
      78-79
   clipboard operations
      support, 75
   delegation event
      model, 75
   desktop colors, 75

drag-and-drop
   support, 78
graphics and image
   handling, 76
keyboard navigation
   support, 75-76
lightweight component
   model, 74, 77
pluggable look and
   feel, 77
popup menus, 76
printing support, 75
scrolling support, 76
Swing (JFC beta release),
   79-86
**application-level
protocols, 146**
applications
Beans
   connecting with
      events, 137
   creating, 135-136
   customizing, 136-137
   testing, 137-140
compared to applets, 4-5
   frame windows, 5-6
   main( ) method, 5
   security, 6
complete member access,
   role of reflection, 241
creating, 10-12
   listing 1.3, 10-11
execution, 12
handwritten, using with
   Beans, 110-111
merging with applets, 13-15
   overview, 16-17
   security, 16
   testing, 15-16
public member access, role
   of reflection, 240-241
RMI (Remote Method
   Invocation)
   compiling, 280

designing, 277-280
sample application,
   280-285
rmiregistry, 272
testing, 12
**archive attribute (<APPLET>
tag), 370**
archives (JAR files)
advantages of, 362
   backward-compatibility,
      363
   cross-platform, 363
   extensibility, 363
   fewer HTTP transac-
      tions, 362
   file storage
      efficiency, 362
   security, 362
creating, 368-369
   for Beans, 118
examining, 366-368
extracting files from, 369
JavaBeans, relationship
   with, 371
manifest files, 363-365
signing, 403-405
   listing 19.3, 403-404
using, 370
Array class, 247
**arrays, accessing with native
code, 432-433**
**attributes, archive
(<APPLET> tag), 370**
authentication information
sending to servers, 152
trusted applets, 379
AWT components
as Beans, 115
see also components
AWTEvent class, 22

B

backward-compatibility, advantages of JAR files, 363
Basic Object Adapter (BOA), 293
BDK (JavaBeans Development Kit), 122
    BeanBox test container, 122-123
        connecting Beans with events, 129-130
        editing Beans, 127-128
        overview, 123-126
        runtime mode, 130
        saving Beans, 130, 134
        testing Beans, 131-134
    JavaBeans API source code, 123
    sample Beans, 123
    tutorial, 123
BeanBox test container, 122-123
    connecting Beans with events, 129-130
    editing Beans, 127-128
    execution, 124
    overview, 123-126
    runtime mode, 130
    saving Beans, 130, 134
    testing Beans, 131
        BorderPanel Bean, 131-133
        ImagePanel Bean, 133-134
BeanBox window, 125
Beans
    application builder tools, using with, 109-110
    AWT components as, 115
    bridges, 140-141
        events, 142
        methods, 141

properties, 141
    using with, 111
connecting with events, 129-130
converting components to, 115-116
    JAR files, 118
    serialization, 116-117
customizers, 126
editing in BeanBox, 127-128
handwritten code, using with, 110-111
high-level API services, 107
interfaces, 112
JAR files, relationship with, 371
low-level API services, 107
methods, 111-113
moving, 128
property management, 106-107
requirements of, 113
    default constructors, 113
    delegation event model, 115
    design patterns, 114
    instantiable, 113
    serializable, 114
resizing, 128
saving in BeanBox test container, 130, 134
source code, 134-135
    connecting with events, 137
    creating with, 135-136
    customizing in, 136-137
    testing in, 137-140
structure of, 111-113
testing in BeanBox test container, 131
    BorderPanel Bean, 131-133

ImagePanel Bean, 133-134
    see also JavaBeans API
binding objects, 271
BOA (Basic Object Adapter), 293
BorderPanel Bean, testing in BeanBox test container, 131-133
BorderPanel class
    constructors, 49
    creating, 46-48
    drawing 3-D borders, 49-53
    listing 3.1, 46-48
    testing, 53-54
borders (3-D), 42
    drawing, 49-53
    grooved, 43-44
    lowered, 42
    raised, 43
    ridged, 44
BorderStyle interface, creating custom components, 45
BorderTest applet (listing 3.2), 53-54
boundaries (text), formatting for internationalization, 228-229
BreakIterator class, 228
bridges (Beans), 140-141
    events, 142
    methods, 141
    properties, 141
    using with, 111
browsers, CORBA support, 298
btnNewClicked( ) method, clearing the screen with (listing 9.11), 206
buffered drawing (IFC views), 89

builder tools
Beans, using with, 109-110
JavaBeans API support
for, 108
**business logic
(databases), 171**

C

C++ source code
Alphabetize application
(listing 20.11), 437
Pond sample application
(listing 20.6), 427
SysInfo DLL (listing 20.3),
417-418
**CAB files, AFC support
for, 102**
**Caffeine technology
(Visigenic), 300**
Calendar class, 226
callbacks
CORBA, 292
designing RMI
applications, 279
**caller methods (JNI),
430-431**
**calling methods in native
code, 429-431**
**Capital.java file
(listing 14.5), 305**
**CapitalQuery class
(listing 14.8), 308**
**CapitalQuery sample
application (CORBA), 303**
building with VisiBroker,
303-306
client application creation,
306-307
execution, 308-309
as Java applet, 310-313

network communications,
310
server application creation,
307-308
**CardLayout layout
manager, 60**
**cassettes (Commerce
API), 444**
Certificate class, 386
**certificates (security),
377-378**
creating, 402-403
javakey tool, 396-398
Security API, 386
self-signed (listing 19.2), 402
certification authorities, 378
**CGI (Common Gateway
Interface),
HttpServletRequest
methods, 349**
chaining (servlets), 329
**CharacterIterator
interface, 228**
**chat servers (RMI sample
application), 280-285**
**ChatServer.java (server class),
listing 13.3, 283-284**
ChoiceFormat class, 228
choosers (IFC), 90-91
Class class, 244
**ClassDissector sample
application (reflection),
249-251**
listing 11.1, 250-251
classes
ActionEvent, 26
adapter, 11
AdjustmentEvent, 26
anonymous local, 201
Applet, 7
Array, 247
AWTEvent, 22

Beans, requirements of,
113-115
BorderPanel
constructors, 49
creating, 46-48
drawing 3-D borders,
49-53
testing, 53-54
BreakIterator, 228
Calendar, 226
CardLayout layout
manager, 60
Certificate, 386
ChoiceFormat, 228
Class, 244
Client (listing 14.6), 306
ClientApplet (listing 14.9),
311-312
Collator, 228
ComponentEvent, 23
Connection, 181-183
Constructor, 247
ContainerEvent, 23
creating in JDBC, 193
Date, 227
DateFormat, 227
DBConnector, 193
connect( ) method,
194-195
connected( )
method, 196
disconnect( ) method,
196-197
instance variables,
193-194
DecimalFormat, 225
Driver, 179-181
DriverManager, 179
engine, 381
event adapters, 30-31
inner classes, 31-33
Field, 245

FocusEvent, 23
Format, 225
foundation
    AFC (Application
        Foundation Classes),
        100-102
    IFC (Internet Founda-
        tion Classes), 86-100
    JFC (Java Foundation
        Classes), 72-86
GenericServlet, 333, 347
HttpServlet, 333-334,
    347-348
Identity, 383
IdentityScope, 383
ImagePanel
    constructors, 54-58
    testing, 58-59
InputStream, 256-257
ItemEvent, 26-27
KeyEvent, 24
KeyPair, 383
KeyPairGenerator, 383
ListResourceBundle, 224
Locale, 217-221
    methods, 222-223
MessageDigest, 386-387
MessageFormat, 227-228
Method, 246
MinApplet (listing 1.1), 7
MinAppletcation
    (listing 1.4), 13-14
MinApplication
    (listing 1.3), 10-11
Modifier, 247-248
MouseEvent, 24
NumberFormat, 225
ObjectInputStream,
    258-259
ObjectOutputstream, 258
ODBCConnector, 197-198
OracleConnector
    (listing 9.6), 198
OutputStream, 257

Panel, 46
POP3Reader
    creating, 149-151
    testing, 156-157
PrivateKey, 383
PropertyResourceBundle,
    224
Provider, 382
PublicKey, 383
Reader, 151-152
ResourceBundle, 223-224
ResultSet, 184-185
RuleBasedCollator, 228
Security, 382
serialization
    Externalizable
        interface, 261
    protecting data
        from, 262
    Serializable interface,
        259-261
    versioning objects,
        263-265
in Servlet API, 331-332
ServletConfig, 342-345
Signature, 383-386
SimpleTimeZone, 226
SMTPSender
    creating, 158-159
    testing, 162-163
Statement, 183
stubs/skeletons, writing,
    275-276
TabPanel, 66-67
    creating, 60-61
    designing, 61
    drawing tabs, 63-66
    pane management,
        61-62
    tab management, 62-63
    testing, 67-69
TabPanePanel
    (listing 3.5), 62
TextEvent, 27

Timer (listing 2.2), 33-35
TimerEvent (listing 2.3), 36
TimerEventMulticaster
    (listing 2.4), 37
TimeZone, 226
UnicastRemoteObject, 273
WindowEvent, 25
Writer, 151-152
see also components;
    interfaces
clauses (SQL), WHERE,
175-176
clearing the screen, address
    book sample program
    (JDBC), 205-206
ClickMe applet (inner
    classes), listing 2.1, 32
client applications
    (CaptialQuery sample
    application), creating,
    306-307
Client class (listing 14.6), 306
client-server (databases), 169
Client.java (remote object),
    listing 13.2, 281-282
ClientApplet class
    (listing 14.9), 311-312
clipboard operations support
    (JFC), 75
cloning objects with serializa-
    tion, 254-255
code, see listings; source code
Collaboration API (future of
    Java), 448
collation, 228
Collator class, 228
Color Chooser (IFC), 90
colors (JFC), 75
ColorTextView component
    (listing 4.2), 98-99
columns (databases), 169
    accessing, 184-185
command-line options
    (javakey tool), 398-400

commands
HTTP (Hypertext Transfer
Protocol), 348
GET, 333, 358
POST, 333, 353-357
POP3 (Post Office
Protocol 3), 148
SMTP (Simple Mail
Transfer Protocol), 157
SQL (Structured Query
Language)
COMMIT, 175
DELETE, 174, 177
INSERT, 174-177
ROLLBACK, 175
SELECT, 174, 177
UPDATE, 174, 178
**Commerce API (future of
Java), 443-445**
**COMMIT statement
(SQL), 175**
**Common Object Request
Broker Architecture, *see*
CORBA**
compiling
native code, 418-419
RMI applications, 280
**complete member access
applications, role of
reflection, 241**
**component bridges (Beans),
140-141**
events, 142
methods, 141
properties, 141
using with, 111
**componentAdded( ) method
(ContainerEvent class), 23**
ComponentEvent class, 23
**componentHidden( ) method
(ComponentEvent class), 23**
**componentMoved( ) method
(ComponentEvent class), 23**

**componentRemoved( )
method (ContainerEvent
class), 23**
**componentResized( ) method
(ComponentEvent class), 23**
components
3-D borders, 42
drawing, 49-53
grooved, 43-44
lowered, 42
raised, 43
ridged, 44
AFC (Application Founda-
tion Classes), 100-101
converting to Beans,
115-116
JAR files, 118
serialization, 116-117
custom
access methods, 45-46
BorderPanel class,
46-49, 53-54
constants, 45
creating, 44-45
drawing 3-D borders,
49-53
ImagePanel class, 54-59
TabPanel class, 60-69
IFC (Internet Foundation
Classes), 88-90
standard AWT components
as Beans, 115
Swing (JFC beta release),
81-82
see also Beans; classes
**componentShown( ) method
(ComponentEvent class), 23**
compression
advantages of, 362
Beans into JAR files, 118
**configuring servlets
(ServletConfig class),
342-345**

connect( ) method
Connector interface, 191
DBConnector class,
194-195
listing 9.2, 194-195
connected( ) method
Connector interface, 191
DBConnector class, 196
listing 9.3, 196
connecting
Beans with events,
129-130, 137
to servers, 151-152, 159
Connection class, 181-183
Connector interface, 190-192
listing 9.1, 192
constants
BorderStyle interface,
creating custom compo-
nents, 45
Locale class, 220-221
Constructor class, 247
constructors
AddressBook class
(listing 9.7), 200
BorderPanel class, 49
default for Beans, 113
ImagePanel class, 54-58
Locale class, 217
ContainerEvent class, 23
**containsHeader( ) method
(HttpServletResponse
interface), 350**
**controller (MVC architec-
ture), 80**
conventional encryption, 375
**converting components to
Beans, 115-116**
JAR files, 118
serialization, 116-117

CORBA (Common Object Request Broker Architecture), 287-289, 445
CapitalQuery sample application, 303
  building with VisiBroker, 303-306
  client application creation, 306-307
  execution, 308-309
  as Java applet, 310-313
  network communications, 310
  server application creation, 307-308
comparisons
  to DCOM (Distributed Component Object Model), 314-315
  to RMI (Remote Method Invocation), 269, 315-316
CORBAServices, 296-297
  OrbixWeb support for, 302
  Visigenic support for, 300-301
IDL (Interface Definition Language), 294-296
IIOP, 293
with Java, advantages of, 297
OMG (Object Management Group), 290
ORBs (Object Request Brokers), 291-293
  OrbixWeb, 301-302
  selecting, 298
  VisiBroker for Java, 299-301
overview, 290-291
server callbacks, 292
Web browser support for, 298

CORBAServices, 296-297
OrbixWeb support for, 302
Visigenic support for, 300-301
cross-platform, advantages of JAR files, 363
cryptography, 374-375
  see also encryption
custom components
accessor methods, 45-46
BorderPanel class
  constructors, 49
  creating, 46-48
  drawing 3-D borders, 49-53
  testing, 53-54
constants, 45
converting to Beans, 115-116
  JAR files, 118
  serialization, 116-117
creating, 44-45
ImagePanel class
  constructors, 54-58
  testing, 58-59
TabPanel class, 66-67
  creating, 60-61
  designing, 61
  drawing tabs, 63-66
  pane management, 61-62
  tab management, 62-63
  testing, 67-69
custom events, creating, 33-39
customizing Beans, 126
in source code, 136-137

D

data types, mapping
to IDL types, 295
to native data types, 419-420

database management system (DBMS), 168
databases, 168
business logic, 171
client-server, 169
columns, 169
  accessing, 184-185
instances, 169
JDBC (Java Database Connectivity), 178, 190
  address book sample program, 198-210
  Connection class, 181-183
  Connector interface, 190-192
  creating classes, 193
  DBConnector class, 193-197
  Driver class, 179-181
  DriverManager class, 179
  future of, 187
  ODBCConnector class, 197-198
  ResultSet class, 184-185
  sample program, 185-186
  Statement class, 183
local compared to remote, 170
native drivers, 173
ODBC drivers, 173-174
rows, 169
  accessing, 185
schemas, 169
single-tiered architecture, 171
SQL (Structured Query Language), 174-175
  DELETE statement, 177
  INSERT statement, 176-177

SELECT statement, 177
UPDATE statement, 178
WHERE clause,
    175-176
tables, 169
three-tiered architecture, 172
transactions, 175
two-tiered architecture,
    171-172
user interface, 171
Web sites for
    information, 170
Date class, 227
DateFormat class, 227
dates and times, formatting
for internationalization,
226-227
DBConnector class, 193
connect( ) method, 194-195
connected( ) method, 196
disconnect( ) method,
    196-197
instance variables, 193-194
DBMS (database manage-
ment system), 168
DCOM (Distributed
Component Object Model),
compared to CORBA,
314-315
DecimalFormat class, 225
decryption, 374-375
default constructors
(Beans), 113
defaultReadObject( ) method
(Serializable interface),
260-261
defaultWriteObject( ) method
(Serializable interface),
260-261
defining native methods,
412-414
delegate (MVC
architecture), 81

delegation event model,
20-21, 75
custom events, creating,
    33-39
event adapters, 30-31
    inner classes, 31-33
event delivery, 27
    problems with, 29
    unicast compared to
        multicast, 27-29
low-level events, 21-22
    ComponentEvent
        class, 23
    ContainerEvent class, 23
    FocusEvent class, 23
    KeyEvent class, 24
    MouseEvent class, 24
    WindowEvent class, 25
requirements of Beans, 115
semantic events, 25
    ActionEvent class, 26
    AdjustmentEvent
        class, 26
    ItemEvent class, 26-27
    TextEvent class, 27
DELETE statement (SQL),
174, 177
deleteRecord( ) method
(listing 9.14), 210
deleting records, address
book sample program
(JDBC), 209-210
deserialization, 258
design patterns of Beans, 114
design time, 122
designing
RMI applications, 277
    callbacks, 279
    minimizing object
        lookups, 277-279
    security, 279-280
servlets, 352-353
TabPanel class, 61

desktop colors (JFC), 75
destroy( ) method
applets, 8
Servlet interface, 332
servlets, 347
digital signatures, 5, 376-377
JAR files, advantages of, 362
message digests, 378
Security API, 383-386
trusted applets, 6
DII (Dynamic Invocation
Interface), 293
directive files
creating certificates,
    396-397, 402-403
listing 19.1, 396
signing JAR files, 403-405
disconnect( ) method
Connector interface, 191
DBConnector class,
    196-197
listing 9.4, 196
displayResults( ) method
address book sample
    program (JDBC),
    204-205
listing 9.10, 204
Distributed Component
Object Model (DCOM),
compared to CORBA,
314-315
distributed computing,
268-269
objects
    locating with RMI
        (Remote Method
        Invocation), 270-272
    placement on
        network, 270
    RMI (Remote Method
        Invocation), compared to
        CORBA, 269
doGet( ) method
(servlets), 358

doPost( ) method (servlets), 353-357

drag-and-drop support (JFC), 78

draw( ) method (IFC), 91-92

drawing
3-D borders (BorderPanel class), 49-53
tabs (TabPanel class), 63-66

drawing methods (IFC), 91-92

drawView( ) method (IFC), 91-92

Driver class, 179-181

DriverManager class, 179

DSI (Dynamic Skeleton Interface), 302

Dynamic Invocation Interface (DII), 293

E

e-mail
application-level protocols, 146
authentication information, sending to servers, 152
connecting to servers, 151-152, 159
headers, 146-147
MIME encoding, 146
POP (Post Office Protocol), 147
POP3Reader class
creating, 149-151
testing, 156-157
querying servers for, 153-154
reading from servers, 147-149
retrieving from servers, 154-156
sending to servers, 158-162

SMTP (Simple Mail Transfer Protocol), 157-158
SMTPSender class
creating, 158-159
testing, 162-163
waiting for acknowledgement from server, 152-153

editing Beans in BeanBox, 127-128

EmbeddedJava API (future of Java), 450

embedding applets in Web pages, 8

encryption, 374-375
certificates, 377-378
conventional, 375
digital signatures, 376-377
message digests, 378
public-key, 375-376
see also Security API

engine classes, 381

English InfoBundle class (listing 10.9), 236

errors, see exceptions

event adapters, 30-31
inner classes, 31-33

event delivery, 27
problems with, 29
unicast compared to multicast, 27-29

event handlers
address book sample program (JDBC), 200-201
JavaBeans API, 108

event listeners, 20
event delivery, 27-29

event response methods, 21

event sources, 20
event delivery, 27-29

event state objects, 20

events
ActiveX Bridge (Beans), 142
connecting Beans with, 129-130, 137
creating custom, 33-39
delegation event model, 20-21, 75
low-level, 21-22
ComponentEvent class, 23
ContainerEvent class, 23
FocusEvent class, 23
KeyEvent class, 24
MouseEvent class, 24
WindowEvent class, 25
registration methods, 21
semantic, 21, 25
ActionEvent class, 26
AdjustmentEvent class, 26
ItemEvent class, 26-27
TextEvent class, 27

exceptions
RemoteException, 273-274
UnavailableException (servlets), 341-342

execute( ) method
address book sample program (JDBC), 203-204
Statement class, 183

executeQuery( ) method
address book sample program (JDBC), 204
Statement class, 183

executeUpdate( ) method (Statement class), 183

execution
applets, 7-8
applications, 12
BeanBox test container, 124
CaptialQuery sample application (CORBA), 308-309

export( ) method
(UnicastRemoteObject
class), 273
exporting keys, 395
extensibility, advantages of
JAR files, 363
extension APIs
JNDI (Java Naming and
Directory Interface), 447
Management, 449
Media, 447-449
external windows (IFC), 91
Externalizable interface, 261

F

Field class, 245
fields
accessing from native code,
421-422
getter methods, 423
Pond sample application,
424-429
setter methods, 423-424
identifiers (JNI), 420-421
signatures, 421-422
File Chooser (IFC), 91
file storage, advantages of
JAR files, 362
files, extracting from JAR
files, 369
finding records, address book
sample program (JDBC),
206-208
findRecord( ) method
(listing 9.12), 207
FocusEvent class, 23
focusGained( ) method
(FocusEvent class), 23
focusLost( ) method
(FocusEvent class), 23
Font Chooser (IFC), 90
Format class, 225

formatting international data,
224-225
dates and times, 226-227
numbers, 225
sorting text, 228
text boundaries, 228-229
text messages, 227-228
foundation classes, 72
AFC (Application Founda-
tion Classes), 100
CAB files, 102
components, 100-101
graphics features, 102
Win32 resource
support, 102
IFC (Internet Foundation
Classes), 86-88
choosers, 90-91
drawing methods, 91-92
sample applet, 92-100
views and components,
88-90
windows, 91
JFC (Java Foundation
Classes), 72-73
2-D graphics, 78
accessibility features,
78-79
clipboard operations
support, 75
delegation event
model, 75
desktop colors, 75
drag and drop
support, 78
graphics and image
handling, 76
keyboard navigation
support, 75-76
lightweight component
model, 74, 77
pluggable look and
feel, 77
popup menus, 76

printing support, 75
scrolling support, 76
Swing (JFC beta release),
79-86
frame windows, applications
compared to applets, 5-6
French InfoBundle class
(listing 10.10), 236
French LabelsBundle class
(listing 10.8), 235
future of Java, 442-443
Commerce API, 443-445
EmbeddedJava API, 450
IDL (Interface Description
Language), 445-446
JavaBeans
Glasgow, 446-447
migration tools, 450-451
JDBC (Java Database
Connectivity), 187
JFC (Java Foundation
Classes), 443
JNDI (Java Naming and
Directory Interface), 447
Management API, 449
Media API, 447-449
PersonalJava API, 449-450

G

GenericServlet class, 333, 347
GET method (HTTP), 333
writing servlets, 358
getConnection( )
method, 195
getConnectionURL( )
method
Connector interface,
191-192
ODBCConnector class, 197
GetFieldID( ) method, 421
getInitParameter( ) method
(ServletConfig class), 342

getInitParameterNames( ) method (ServletConfig class), 342
getMessageFromServer( ) method (listing 7.2), 155-156
GetMethodID( ) method, 429
getMoreResult( ) method (Statement class), 183
getMoreResults( ) method (Statement class), 183
getParameter( ) method (HttpServletRequest class), 349-350
getServletConfig( ) method (Servlet interface), 332
getServletContext( ) method (ServletConfig class), 342
getServletInfo( ) method (Servlet interface), 332
getter methods (JNI), 423
getUpdateCount( ) method (Statement class), 183
Glasgow (JavaBeans future release), 446-447
global programming, 214-215
   formatting data, 224-225
     dates and times, 226-227
     numbers, 225
     sorting text, 228
     text boundaries, 228-229
     text messages, 227-228
   internationalization, 215-216
   locales, 214-217
     creating, 221
     Locale class, 217-221
     retrieving information about, 222-223
   localization, 215-216
   program data, 217

   resource bundles, 223-224
   system data, 217
   user data, 217
   WorldExplorer sample applet, 229-237
graphical applications, *see* **applications**
graphics
   2-D (JFC), 78
   AFC (Application Foundation Classes), 102
   handling (JFC), 76
grooved borders, 43-44
GUIs (graphical user interfaces), *see* **application frameworks**

H

handwritten code, *see* **source code**
header files
   Alphabetize application (listing 20.10), 436
   generating for native methods, 415-419
   Pond sample application (listing 20.5), 426
   SysInfo DLL (listing 20.2), 416-417
headers (e-mail), 146-147
heavyweight components, 74
HelloWorldServlet sample servlet, 334-336
   listing 15.1, 334-335
high-level API services (Beans), 107
HTML (Hypertext Markup Language)
   Minimal Applet Web page (listing 1.2), 8
   tags, <APPLET>, 8, 370

HTTP (Hypertext Transfer Protocol)
   request methods, 348
     GET, 333, 358
     POST, 333, 353-357
   transactions, advantages of JAR files, 362
HttpServlet class, 333-334, 347-348
HttpServletRequest interface, 349-350
HttpServletResponse interface, 350-351

I

identifiers (JNI), 420-421
identities (javakey tool), 392-394
Identity class, 383
IdentityScope class, 383
IDL (Interface Definition Language), 294-296, 445-446
   CapitalQuery sample application, 304
   mapping data types to, 295
IFC (Internet Foundation Classes), 86-88
   choosers, 90-91
   drawing methods, 91-92
   sample applet, 92-100
   views and components, 88-90
   windows, 91
IFCDemo applet
   HTML code (listing 4.3), 99
   listing 4.1, 95-96
IIOP (CORBA), 293
IIOP Gatekeeper, 300
image handling (JFC), 76

ImagePanel Bean, testing in BeanBox test container, 133-134
ImagePanel class
  constructors, 54-58
  listing 3.3, 55-58
  testing, 58-59
ImageTest applet (listing 3.4), 59
importing keys, 395
InfoBundle class
  French (listing 10.10), 236
  U.S. (listing 10.9), 236
init( ) method
  applets, 7-8
  Servlet interface, 332
  servlets, 341
  WorldExplorer applet (listing 10.3), 231
initializeButtons( ) method (listing 9.8), 201
initializeDatabase( ) method
  address book sample program (JDBC), 202-203
  listing 9.9, 202-203
inner classes
  ClickMe applet (listing 2.1), 32
  event adapters, 31-33
input streams, 256
InputStream class, 256-257
INSERT statement (SQL), 174-177
installing Java Web Server, 323-324
instance variables (DBConnector class), 193-194
instances (databases), 169
instantiability of Beans, 113
instantiate( ) method, creating Beans, 136

Interface Definition Language, *see* **IDL**
Interface Repository (ORBs), 293
interfaces
  Acl, 388
  AclEntry, 388
  Beans, 112
  CharacterIterator, 228
  Connector, 190-192
    listing 9.1, 192
  custom components
    accessor methods, 45-46
    BorderStyle, 45
    creating, 44-45
  Externalizable, 261
  HttpServletRequest, 349-350
  HttpServletResponse, 350-351
  Key, 383
  Member, 245
  Remote, 272
  Serializable, 116, 243, 259-261
  Servlet, 332
    GenericServlet class, 333
    HttpServlet class, 333-334
  see also classes; event listeners
internal windows (IFC), 91
internationalization, 215-216
  formatting data, 224-225
    dates and times, 226-227
    numbers, 225
    sorting text, 228
    text boundaries, 228-229
    text messages, 227-228
  WorldExplorer sample applet, 229-237
  see also global programming
Internationalization API
  BreakIterator class, 228
  Calendar class, 226

  ChoiceFormat class, 228
  Collator class, 228
  DateFormat class, 227
  Format class, 225
  MessageFormat class, 227-228
  NumberFormat class, 225
  ResourceBundle class, 224
  TimeZone class, 226
Internet Foundation Classes, *see* **IFC**
Internet Text Messages, 146-147
interpreter, testing applications, 12
introspection (JavaBeans API), 107
  role of reflection, 241-242
Iona Technologies' OrbixWeb (ORB), 301-302
Iona Web site, 302
ISO language codes, Web site for, 218
ItemEvent class, 26-27
itemStateChanged( ) method
  ItemEvent class, 27
  WorldExplorer applet (listing 10.4), 232

J

JAR (Java Archive) files
  advantages of, 362
    backward-compatibility, 363
    cross-platform, 363
    extensibility, 363
    fewer HTTP transactions, 362
    file storage efficiency, 362
    security, 362
  creating, 368-369
    for Beans, 118

examining, 366-368
extracting files from, 369
JavaBeans, relationship
    with, 371
manifest files, 363-365
signing, 403-405
    listing 19.3, 403-404
using, 370
**JAR (Java Archive) utility,
365-366**
creating JAR files, 368-369
examining JAR files,
    366-368
extracting files from JAR
    files, 369
options, 365-366
Java
with CORBA, advantages
    of, 297
data types, mapping to IDL
    (Interface Definition
    Language), 295
future of, 442-443
    Commerce API,
        443-445
    EmbeddedJava API, 450
    IDL (Interface Defini-
        tion Language),
        445-446
    JavaBeans Glasgow,
        446-447
    JavaBeans migration
        tools, 450-451
    JFC (Java Foundation
        Classes), 443
    JNDI (Java Naming
        and Directory
        Interface), 447
    Management API, 449
    Media API, 447-449
    PersonalJava API,
        449-450
IDL module equivalent
    (listing 14.2), 295

ORBs (Object Request
    Brokers)
    OrbixWeb, 301-302
    selecting, 298
    VisiBroker for Java,
        299-301
Java Database Connectivity,
    see **JDBC**
Java Developer Connection
    Web site, 83
Java Foundation Classes,
    see **JFC**
Java Media Framework,
    see **JMF**
Java Naming and Directory
    Interface, *see* **JNDI**
Java Native Interface, *see* **JNI**
Java Servlet Development
    Kit, *see* **JSDK**
Java Web Server, 322
    administration, 324-326
    installing, 323-324
    Web site, 322
JavaBeans API, 106
    application builder tool
        support, 108
    event handling, 108
    Glasgow (future release),
        446-447
    introspection, 107
    JAR files
        relationship with, 371
        using, 370
    migration tools, 450-451
    persistence, 108
    property management,
        106-107
    reflection, role of, 241-242
    source code, 123
    see also Beans; JAR files
JavaBeans Bridge for
    ActiveX, 451

JavaBeans Development Kit
    (BDK), 122
    BeanBox test container,
        122-123
        connecting Beans with
            events, 129-130
        editing Beans, 127-128
        overview, 123-126
        runtime mode, 130
        saving Beans, 130, 134
        testing Beans, 131-134
    JavaBeans API source
        code, 123
    sample Beans, 123
    tutorial, 123
JavaBeans Migration
    Assistant for ActiveX, 451
javah tool, 415
    generating header files,
        415-419
javakey tool, 392
    certificates, 396-398
        generating, 402-403
    command-line options,
        398-400
    creating signers, 400-401
    identities, 392-394
    key pair generation, 401
    keys, 394-396
    signers, 392-394
    signing JAR files, 403-405
javap tool, 429
    listing 20.8, 430
javax.servlet package, 331
javax.servlet.http
    package, 331
JDBC (Java Database
    Connectivity), 178, 190
    address book sample
        program, 198
        clearing the screen,
            205-206
        database fields, 199

deleting records,
   209-210
displayResults( )
   method, 204-205
event handlers, 200-201
execute( ) method,
   203-204
executeQuery( )
   method, 204
finding records, 206-208
initializeDatabase( )
   method, 202-203
placeholders, 205
saving records, 208-209
user interface, 199-200
Connection class, 181-183
Connector interface,
   190-192
creating classes, 193
DBConnector class, 193
   connect( ) method,
      194-195
   connected( )
      method, 196
   disconnect( )
      method, 196-197
   instance variables,
      193-194
Driver class, 179-181
DriverManager class, 179
future of, 187
ODBCConnector class,
   197-198
ResultSet class, 184-185
sample program, 185-186
Statement class, 183
JDBC-ODBC bridge, 182
**JFC (Java Foundation
Classes), 72-73**
   2-D graphics, 78
   accessibility features, 78-79
   clipboard operations
      support, 75
   delegation event model, 75

desktop colors, 75
drag-and-drop support, 78
future of Java, 443
graphics and image
   handling, 76
keyboard navigation
   support, 75-76
lightweight component
   model, 74, 77
pluggable look and feel, 77
popup menus, 76
printing support, 75
scrolling support, 76
Swing (JFC beta release), 79
   component suite, 81-82
   MVC architecture,
      80-81
   pluggable look and feel,
      79-80
   SwingSet sample
      application, 82-86
**JMF (Java Media Frame-
work), 448**
**JNDI (Java Naming and
Directory Interface), 447**
**JNI (Java Native
Interface), 408**
   GetFieldID( ) method, 421
   GetMethodID( )
      method, 429
   identifying Java fields,
      420-421
   overview, 408-409
   pointers, 420
   see also native code
**JSDK (Java Servlet Develop-
ment Kit), 330**
   classes, 331-332
   HelloWorldServlet sample
      servlet, 334-336
   Servlet interface, 332
      GenericServlet class, 333
      HttpServlet class,
         333-334

K

Key interface, 383
key pairs
   creating, 401
   public-key encryption, 375
**keyboard navigation support
(JFC), 75-76**
KeyEvent class, 24
KeyPair class, 383
KeyPairGenerator class, 383
**keyPressed( ) method
(KeyEvent class), 24**
**keyReleased( ) method
(KeyEvent class), 24**
keys
   exporting, 395
   importing, 395
   javakey tool, 394-396
   Security API, 382-383
**keyTyped( ) method
(KeyEvent class), 24**
keywords
   static, 262
   transient, 262

L

LabelsBundle class
   French (listing 10.8), 235
   U.S. (listing 10.7), 234
**language support, see global
programming**
**layout managers,
CardLayout, 60**
legacy systems, 445
   interfacing with Java, 411
**libraries (native), loading,
413-414**
lightweight components, 74
   JFC, 77
listeners (event), 20
   event delivery, 27-29

listings
AddressBook class constructor, 200
Alphabetize application, 435
  C++ source code, 437
  header file, 436
BorderPanel class, 46-48
BorderTest applet, 53-54
Capital.java file, 305
CapitalQuery class, 308
ChatServer.java (server class), 283-284
ClassDissector application (reflection), 250-251
clearing the screen with btnNewClicked( ) method, 206
ClickMe applet (inner classes), 32
Client class, 306
Client.java (remote object), 281-282
ClientApplet class, 311-312
ColorTextView component, 98-99
connect( ) method, 194-195
connected( ) method, 196
Connector interface, 192
deleteRecord( ) method, 210
directive files, 396
disconnect( ) method, 196
displayResults( ) method, 204
findRecord( ) method, 207
getMessageFromServer( ) method, 155-156
HelloWorldServlet sample servlet, 334-335
IDL methods, 296
IFCDemo applet, 95-96
  HTML code, 99
ImagePanel class, 55-58
ImageTest applet, 59

InfoBundle class
  French, 236
  U.S., 236
initializeButtons( ) method, 201
initializeDatabase( ) method, 202-203
Java equivalent of IDL modules, 295
javap tool, 430
JDBC sample program, 185-186
LabelsBundle class
  French, 235
  U.S., 234
LocaleInfo application, 222-223
manifest file for Juggler Bean, 368
MessageDigestTest application, 387
MinApplet class source code, 7
MinAppletcation class, 13-14
MinApplication class, 10-11
Minimal Applet Web page (HTML source code), 8
modules (IDL), 294
ObjServer.java, 278
ODBCConnector class, 197
OracleConnector class, 198
PanelTest applet, 138
Pond application
  C++ source code, 427
  header file, 426
  Java source code, 425
PondTest application, 428
POPChecker servlet, 353-357
POPTest program, 156-157
ProviderInfo application, 382

Query.IDL (CaptialQuery sample application), 304
saveRecord( ) method, 208-209
self-signed certificates, 402
sendMail( ) method, 160-161
Server class, 307
service( ) method (servlets), 346-347
ServletConfig class, 343-344
signing JAR files, 403-404
SignTest application, 385
SMTPTest application, 163
SysInfo application, 416
  C++ source code, 417-418
  header file, 416-417
TabPanel class, 66-67
TabPanePanel class, 62
TabTest applet, 67-68
Timer class, 33-35
TimerEvent class, 36
TimerEventMulticaster class, 37
TimerTest applet, 38
waitForMessage( ) method, 152-153
WorldExplorer applet
  actionPerformed( ) method, 234
  init( ) method, 231
  itemStateChanged( ) method, 232
  localizeUI( ) method, 233
  member variables, 230
ListResourceBundle class, 224
loading
  native libraries, 413-414
  servlets, 340-341
local classes, anonymous, 201

local databases, compared to
remote, 170
Locale class, 217-221
  methods, 222-223
LocaleInfo application
  (listing 10.1), 222-223
locales, 214-217
  creating, 221
  Locale class, 217-221
  resource bundles, 223-224
  retrieving information
    about, 222-223
localization, 215-216
  WorldExplorer sample
    applet, 229-237
  see also global programming
localizeUI( ) method
  (WorldExplorer applet),
  listing 10.5, 233
locating objects with RMI
  (Remote Method Invoca-
  tion), 270-272
logical database models
  single-tiered, 171
  three-tiered, 172
  two-tiered, 171-172
low-level API services
  (Beans), 107
low-level events, 21-22
  ComponentEvent class, 23
  ContainerEvent class, 23
  FocusEvent class, 23
  KeyEvent class, 24
  MouseEvent class, 24
  WindowEvent class, 25
lowered borders, 42

M

mail
  application-level
    protocols, 146
  authentication information,
    sending to servers, 152

connecting to servers,
  151-152, 159
headers, 146-147
MIME encoding, 146
POP (Post Office
  Protocol), 147
POP3Reader class
  creating, 149-151
  testing, 156-157
querying servers for,
  153-154
reading from servers,
  147-149
retrieving from servers,
  154-156
sending to servers, 158-162
SMTP (Simple Mail
  Transfer Protocol),
  157-158
SMTPSender class
  creating, 158-159
  testing, 162-163
waiting for
  acknowledgement from
  server, 152-153
main( ) method, applications
  compared to applets, 5
Management API (future of
  Java), 449
manifest files, 118, 363-365
  for Juggler Bean
    (listing 17.1), 368
mapping data types
  to IDL types, 295
  to native data types,
    419-420
Media API (future of Java),
  447-449
Member interface, 245
member variables
  (WorldExplorer applet),
  listing 10.2, 230

merging applets with
  applications, 13-15
  overview, 16-17
  security, 16
  testing, 15-16
message digests, 378
  Security API, 386-387
MessageDigest class, 386-387
MessageDigestTest application (listing 18.3), 387
MessageFormat class,
  227-228
messages, formatting for
  internationalization,
  227-228
Method class, 246
methods
  accessor, 45-46
  actionPerformed( ),
    ActionEvent class, 26
  ActiveX Bridge (Beans), 141
  adjustmentValueChanged( ),
    AdjustmentEvent class, 26
  Beans, 111-113
  caller (JNI), 430-431
  calling in native code,
    429-431
  componentAdded( ),
    ContainerEvent class, 23
  componentHidden( ),
    ComponentEvent class, 23
  componentMoved( ),
    ComponentEvent class, 23
  componentRemoved( ),
    ContainerEvent class, 23
  componentResized( ),
    ComponentEvent class, 23
  componentShown( ),
    ComponentEvent class, 23
  connect( )
    Connector interface, 191
    DBConnector class,
      194-195

connected( )
  Connector interface, 191
  DBConnector class, 196
containsHeader( ),
  HttpServletResponse
  interface, 350
defaultReadObject( ),
  Serializable interface,
  260-261
defaultWriteObject( ),
  Serializable interface,
  260-261
deleteRecord( ),
  listing 9.14, 210
destroy( )
  applets, 8
  Servlet interface, 332
  servlets, 347
disconnect( )
  Connector interface, 191
  DBConnector class,
  196-197
displayResults( ), address
  book sample program
  (JDBC), 204-205
doGet( ), servlets, 358
doPost( ), servlets, 353-357
draw( ), IFC, 91-92
drawView( ), IFC, 91-92
event response, 21
execute( )
  address book sample
    program (JDBC),
    203-204
  Statement class, 183
executeQuery( )
  address book sample
    program (JDBC), 204
  Statement class, 183
executeUpdate( ), Statement
  class, 183
export( ),
  UnicastRemoteObject
  class, 273

findRecord( ),
  listing 9.12, 207
focusGained( ), FocusEvent
  class, 23
focusLost( ), FocusEvent
  class, 23
getConnection( ), 195
getConnectionURL( )
  Connector interface,
    191-192
  ODBCConnector
    class, 197
GetFieldID( ), 421
getInitParameter( ),
  ServletConfig class, 342
getInitParameterNames( ),
  ServletConfig class, 342
getMessageFromServer( ),
  listing 7.2, 155-156
GetMethodID( ), 429
getMoreResult( ), Statement
  class, 183
getMoreResults( ), State-
  ment class, 183
getParameter( ),
  HttpServletRequest class,
  349-350
getServletConfig( ), Servlet
  interface, 332
getServletContext( ),
  ServletConfig class, 342
getServletInfo( ), Servlet
  interface, 332
getter (JNI), 423
getUpdateCount( ),
  Statement class, 183
HTTP (Hypertext Transfer
  Protocol), 348
  GET, 333, 358
  POST, 333, 353-357
identifiers (JNI), 420-421
  in IDL (Interface Definition
  Language), 295
    listing 14.3, 296

init( )
  applets, 7-8
  Servlet interface, 332
  servlets, 341
initializeButtons( ),
  listing 9.8, 201
initializeDatabase( ), address
  book sample program
  (JDBC), 202-203
instantiate( ), creating
  Beans, 136
itemStateChanged( ),
  ItemEvent class, 27
keyPressed( ), KeyEvent
  class, 24
keyReleased( ), KeyEvent
  class, 24
keyTyped( ), KeyEvent
  class, 24
Locale class, 222-223
main( ), applications
  compared to applets, 5
mouseClicked( ),
  MouseEvent class, 24
mouseDragged( ),
  MouseEvent class, 24
mouseEntered( ),
  MouseEvent class, 24
mouseExited( ),
  MouseEvent class, 24
mouseMoved( ),
  MouseEvent class, 24
mousePressed( ),
  MouseEvent class, 24
mouseReleased( ),
  MouseEvent class, 24
native
  accessing Java informa-
    tion, 420
  creating, 414-415
  defining, 412-414
  generating header files
    for, 415-419
  performance disadvan-
    tages, 412

next( ), ResultSet class, 185
paint( ), drawing 3-D
  borders, 49
read( ), InputStream
  class, 257
readExternal( ),
  Externalizable
  interface, 261
registration, 21
saveRecord( ), listing 9.13,
  208-209
sendError( ),
  HttpServletResponse
  interface, 350
sendMail( ), listing 7.4,
  160-161
sendRedirect( ),
  HttpServletResponse
  interface, 350
service( )
  Servlet interface, 332
  servlets, 345-347
setDateHeader( ),
  HttpServletResponse
  interface, 350
setHeader( ),
  HttpServletResponse
  interface, 350
setIntHeader( ),
  HttpServletResponse
  interface, 350
setStatus( ),
  HttpServletResponse
  interface, 350
setter (JNI), 423-424
signatures, 429-431
size of, 195
start( ), applets, 7-8
stop( ), applets, 8
textValueChanged( ),
  TextEvent class, 27
waitForMessage( ),
  listing 7.1, 152-153
windowActivated( ),
  WindowEvent class, 25

windowClosed( ),
  WindowEvent class, 25
windowClosing( ),
  WindowEvent class, 25
windowDeactivated( ),
  WindowEvent class, 25
windowDeiconified( ),
  WindowEvent class, 25
windowIconified( ),
  WindowEvent class, 25
windowOpened( ),
  WindowEvent class, 25
write( ), OutputStream
  class, 257
writeExternal( ),
  Externalizable
  interface, 261
**Microsoft Application
  Foundation Classes,**
  see **AFC**
**Migration Assistant Web
  site, 451**
**migration tools (JavaBeans),
  450-451**
**MIME (Multipurpose
  Internet Mail
  Extensions), 146**
**MinApplet class
  (listing 1.1), 7**
**MinAppletcation class
  (listing 1.4), 13-14**
**MinApplication class
  (listing 1.3), 10-11**
**Minimal Applet Web page
  (listing 1.2), 8**
**minimizing object lookups
  (RMI), 277-279**
model (MVC architecture), 80
Modifier class, 247-248
modular programming, 327
modules (IDL), 294
  Java equivalent
    (listing 14.2), 295
  listing 14.1, 294

mouseClicked( ) method
  (MouseEvent class), 24
**mouseDragged( ) method
  (MouseEvent class), 24**
**mouseEntered( ) method
  (MouseEvent class), 24**
MouseEvent class, 24
**mouseExited( ) method
  (MouseEvent class), 24**
**mouseless operation support
  (JFC), 75-76**
**mouseMoved( ) method
  (MouseEvent class), 24**
**mousePressed( ) method
  (MouseEvent class), 24**
**mouseReleased( ) method
  (MouseEvent class), 24**
moving Beans, 128
**multicast event delivery,
  compared to unicast, 27-29**
**multimedia (Media API),
  447-449**
multiple language support,
  see global programming
**Multipurpose Internet Mail
  Extensions (MIME), 146**
**MVC (model-view-controller)
  architecture, 80-81**

N

naming service
  (CORBA), 300
native code
  accessing arrays with,
    432-433
  accessing Java fields,
    421-422
    getter methods, 423
    Pond sample application,
      424-429
    setter methods, 423-424
  accessing strings with,
    434-438

calling object methods,
    429-431
compiling, 418-419
disadvantages of, 411
    performance, 412
    platform dependence, 411
    security, 411-412
mapping data types to,
    419-420
when to use, 409
    accessing operating system
        information, 410
    improving performance,
        410-411
    interfacing to legacy
        code, 411
    see also JNI (Java Native
        Interface)
native drivers, accessing
    databases, 173
native libraries, loading,
    413-414
native methods
    accessing Java
        information, 420
    creating, 414-415
    defining, 412-414
    header files, generating for,
        415-419
Netscape Internet Founda-
    tion Classes, see IFC
network communications,
    CaptialQuery sample
    application (CORBA), 310
networks
    placement of objects
        on, 270
    RMI (Remote Method
        Invocation), 268
        callbacks, 279
        compared to
            CORBA, 269
        compiling
            applications, 280

designing applications,
    277-280
locating objects,
    270-272
minimizing object
    lookups, 277-279
remote objects, 272-274
sample application,
    280-285
security, 279-280
serialization, 276-277
skeletons, 275
stubs, 274-275
writing stubs/skeletons,
    275-276
socket programming, 268
next( ) method (ResultSet
    class), 185
NULL values (database
    columns), 184
NumberFormat class, 225
numbers, formatting for
    internationalization, 225

O

Object Management Group,
    see OMG
object persistence, 255-256
    JavaBeans API, 108
    transient keyword, 262
object references (serializa-
    tion), 117
Object Request Brokers, see
    ORBs
object serialization, 254
    of Beans, 114
    cloning objects, 254-255
    converting components to
        Beans, 116-117
    Externalizable interface, 261
    InputStream class, 256-257

ObjectInputStream class,
    258-259
ObjectOutputStream
    class, 258
OutputStream class, 257
persistence, 255-256
protecting data from, 262
reflection, role of, 242-243
RMI (Remote Method
    Invocation), 276-277
Serializable interface,
    259-261
streams, 256
versioning objects, 263-265
ObjectInputStream class,
    258-259
ObjectOutputStream
    class, 258
objects
    binding, 271
    CORBA, 289
        compared to DCOM
            (Distributed Compo-
            nent Object Model),
            314-315
        compared to RMI
            (Remote Method
            Invocation), 315-316
        CORBAServices,
            296-297
        IDL (Interface Defini-
            tion Language),
            294-296
        IIOP, 293
        with Java, advantages
            of, 297
        OMG (Object Manage-
            ment Group), 290
        ORBs (Object Request
            Brokers), 291-293
        overview, 290-291
        server callbacks, 292
        Web browser support
            for, 298

distributed computing, 269
   locating with RMI
      (Remote Method
      Invocation), 270-272
   placement on
      network, 270
   minimizing lookups (RMI),
      277-279
   remote, 272-274
      passing, 276-277
   World Wide Web support
      for, 289
ObjServer.java
   (listing 13.1), 278
ODBC (Open Database
   Connectivity) drivers,
   accessing databases,
   173-174
ODBCConnector class,
   197-198
   listing 9.5, 197
OMG (Object Management
   Group), 290
   Web site, 294
operating systems
   accessing information
      from, 410
   disadvantages of native
      code, 411
operators, WHERE clause
   (SQL), 176
OracleConnector class
   (listing 9.6), 198
OrbixWeb (ORB), 301-302
   CORBAServices
      support, 302
ORBs (Object Request
   Brokers), 291-293
   OrbixWeb, 301-302
   selecting, 298
   VisiBroker for Java,
      299-301
      building CaptialQuery
      sample application,
      303-306

output streams, 256
OutputStream class, 257

P

packages
   javax.servlet, 331
   javax.servlet.http, 331
   see also APIs
paint( ) method
   3-D borders, 49
   tabs, 63
pane management (TabPanel
   class), 61-62
Panel class, 46
PanelTest applet
   (listing 6.1), 138
passing remote objects,
   276-277
payment cassettes
   (Commerce API), 444
peerless components, 74
peers, 74
performance
   disadvantages of native
      code, 412
   improving with native code,
      410-411
permanent unavailability
   (servlets), 342
persistence, 255-256
   JavaBeans API, 108
   transient keyword, 262
PersonalJava API (future of
   Java), 449-450
physically handicapped,
   accessibility features in JFC,
   78-79
placeholders, address
   book sample program
   (JDBC), 205
platform dependence,
   disadvantages of native
   code, 411

pluggable look and feel
   JFC (Java Foundation
      Classes), 77
   Swing (JFC beta release),
      79-80
pointers (JNI), 420
Pond sample application
   (field access from native
   code), 424-429
   C++ source code for
      (listing 20.6), 427
   header file for
      (listing 20.5), 426
   Java source code for
      (listing 20.4), 425
PondTest application
   (listing 20.7), 428
POP (Post Office
   Protocol), 147
POP3Reader class
   creating, 149-151
   testing, 156-157
POPChecker servlet
   (listing 16.3), 353-357
POPTest program
   (listing 7.3), 156-157
popup menus (JFC), 76
POST method (HTTP), 333
   writing servlets, 353-357
printing support (JFC), 75
private keys, 376
PrivateKey class, 383
program data (global
   programming), 217
programming code, see
   source code
properties
   ActiveX Bridge (Beans), 141
   management (JavaBeans
      API), 106-107
Properties window
   (BeanBox), 125-126
PropertyResourceBundle
   class, 224

protecting data from serialization, 262
protocols
    application-level, 146
    HTTP (Hypertext Transfer Protocol)
        GET method, 333, 348, 358
        POST method, 333, 348, 353-357
        transactions, advantages of JAR files, 362
    POP (Post Office Protocol), 147
    SMTP (Simple Mail Transfer Protocol), 157-158
Provider class, 382
ProviderInfo application (listing 18.1), 382
providers (Security API), 381-382
public keys, 376
public member access applications, role of reflection, 240-241
public-key encryption, 375-376
    certificates, 377-378
    digital signatures, 376-377
    message digests, 378
PublicKey class, 383

Q-R

query strings (URLs), 349
Query.IDL (CaptialQuery sample application), listing 14.4, 304
querying servers for e-mail, 153-154

raised borders, 43
RDBMS (relational database management system), 168
read( ) method (InputStream class), 257
Reader class, 151-152
readExternal( ) method (Externalizable interface), 261
reading e-mail from servers, 147-149
records, address book sample program (JDBC)
    deleting, 209-210
    finding, 206-208
    saving, 208-209
reflection, 240
    ClassDissector sample application, 249-251
    complete member access applications, 241
    JavaBeans, 241-242
    public member access applications, 240-241
    security, 248-249
    serialization, 242-243
Reflection API, 243-244
    Array class, 247
    Class class, 244
    Constructor class, 247
    Field class, 245
    Member interface, 245
    Method class, 246
    Modifier class, 247-248
registration methods, 21
relational database management system (RDBMS), 168
remote databases, compared to local, 170
Remote interface, 272
Remote Method Invocation, see RMI

remote objects, 272-274
    Client.java (listing 13.2), 281-282
    passing, 276-277
RemoteException, 273-274
removing, see deleting
request methods (HTTP), 348
    GET, 333
        writing servlets, 358
    POST, 333
        writing servlets, 353-357
requirements of Beans, 113
    default constructors, 113
    delegation event model, 115
    design patterns, 114
    instantiable, 113
    serializable, 114
resizing Beans, 128
resource bundles, 223-224
    WorldExplorer sample applet, 234-237
ResourceBundle class, 223-224
response methods, 21
result sets
    displaying, address book sample program (JDBC), 204-205
    Statement class, 183
ResultSet class, 184-185
retrieving
    data, address book sample program (JDBC), 198
    clearing the screen, 205-206
    database fields, 199
    deleting records, 209-210
    displayResults( ) method, 204-205
    event handlers, 200-201

execute() method,
    203-204
executeQuery()
    method, 204
finding records, 206-208
initializeDatabase()
    method, 202-203
placeholders, 205
saving records, 208-209
user interface, 199-200
e-mail from servers,
    154-156
ridged borders, 44
RMI (Remote Method
Invocation), 268
callbacks, 279
compared to CORBA, 269,
    315-316
compiling applications, 280
designing applications, 277
locating objects, 270-272
minimizing object lookups,
    277-279
remote objects, 272-274
sample application, 280-285
security, 279-280
serialization, 276-277
skeletons, 275
    writing, 275-276
stubs, 274-275
    writing, 275-276
URLs, 271
rmic utility, 275-276
rmiregistry application, 272
ROLLBACK statement
(SQL), 175
rows (databases), 169
accessing, 185
RuleBasedCollator class, 228
running
applets, 7-8
applications, 12
BeanBox test container, 124

CaptialQuery sample
    application (CORBA),
    308-309
runtime mode, 123
BeanBox test container, 130

S

saveRecord() method
(listing 9.13), 208-209
saving
Beans in BeanBox test
    container, 130, 134
records, address book
    sample program (JDBC),
    208-209
schemas (databases), 169
screen, clearing (address book
sample program), 205-206
scrolling support (JFC), 76
searching records, address
book sample program
(JDBC), 206-208
security
access control lists, 380
"appletcations", 16
applications compared to
    applets, 6
certificates, 377-378
designing RMI applications,
    279-280
digital signatures, 5,
    376-377
disadvantages of native
    code, 411-412
encryption, 374-375
    conventional, 375
    public-key, 375-376
JAR files, advantages of, 362
javakey tool, 392
    certificate generation,
    402-403
    certificates, 396-398

command-line options,
    398-400
creating signers, 400-401
identities, 392-394
key pair generation, 401
keys, 394-396
signers, 392-394
signing JAR files,
    403-405
message digests, 378
reflection, 248-249
servlets, 329-330
trusted applets, 6, 379
Security API, 380-381
access control lists, 388
certificates, 386
digital signatures, 383-386
keys, 382-383
message digests, 386-387
providers, 381-382
Security class, 382
security context, 179
SELECT statement (SQL),
174, 177
selecting ORBs (Object
Request Brokers), 298
self-signed certificates
(listing 19.2), 402
semantic events, 21, 25
ActionEvent class, 26
AdjustmentEvent class, 26
ItemEvent class, 26-27
TextEvent class, 27
sendError() method
(HttpServletResponse
interface), 350
sending
authentication information
    to servers, 152
e-mail to servers, 158-162
sendMail() method
(listing 7.4), 160-161

sendRedirect( ) method
(HttpServletResponse
interface), 350
Serializable interface, 116,
243, 259-261
serialization, 254
of Beans, 114
cloning objects, 254-255
converting components to
Beans, 116-117
Externalizable interface, 261
InputStream class, 256-257
ObjectInputStream class,
258-259
ObjectOutputStream
class, 258
OutputStream class, 257
persistence, 255-256
protecting data from, 262
reflection, role of, 242-243
RMI (Remote Method
Invocation), 276-277
Serializable interface,
259-261
streams, 256
versioning objects, 263-265
serialver utility, generating
version numbers, 264-265
server applications
(CaptialQuery sample
application), creating,
307-308
server callbacks
(CORBA), 292
Server class (listing 14.7), 307
servers
ChatServer.java
(listing 13.3), 283-284
connecting to,
151-152, 159
Java Web Server, 322
administration, 324-326
installing, 323-324
Web site, 322

querying for e-mail,
153-154
reading e-mail from,
147-149
retrieving e-mail from,
154-156
sending
authentication informa-
tion to, 152
e-mail to, 158-162
waiting for
acknowledgement from,
152-153
service cassettes
(Commerce API), 445
service( ) method
Servlet interface, 332
servlets, 345-347
listing 16.2, 346-347
services, 328
Servlet API, 330
classes, 331-332
HelloWorldServlet sample
servlet, 334-336
Servlet interface, 332
GenericServlet class, 333
HttpServlet class,
333-334
Servlet interface, 332
GenericServlet class, 333
HttpServlet class, 333-334
ServletConfig class, 342-345
listing 16.1, 343-344
servlets, 322
advantages of, 328
chaining, 329
designing, 352-353
destroy( ) method, 347
GenericServlet class, 347
HelloWorldServlet sample
servlet, 334-336
HttpServlet class, 347-348
HttpServletRequest
interface, 349-350

HttpServletResponse
interface, 350-351
init( ) method, 341
loading, 340-341
modular programming, 327
overview, 327-329
POPChecker (listing 16.3),
353-357
security, 329-330
service( ) method, 345-347
ServletConfig class,
342-345
trusted, 329
UnavailableException,
341-342
untrusted, 329
writing, 351-352
GET method
(HTTP), 358
POST method (HTTP),
353-357
setDateHeader( ) method
(HttpServletResponse
interface), 350
setHeader( ) method
(HttpServletResponse
interface), 350
setIntHeader( ) method
(HttpServletResponse
interface), 350
setStatus( ) method
(HttpServletResponse
interface), 350
setter methods (JNI),
423-424
Signature class, 383-386
signatures
fields, 421-422
methods, 429-431
see also digital signatures
signers
creating, 400-401
javakey tool, 392-394

signing JAR files, 403-405
    listing 19.3, 403-404
SignTest application
    (listing 18.2), 385
SimpleTimeZone class, 226
single-tiered architecture
    (databases), 171
skeletons, 275
    writing, 275-276
SmartAgent technology, 299
SMTP (Simple Mail Transfer
    Protocol), 157-158
SMTPSender class
    creating, 158-159
    testing, 162-163
SMTPTest application
    (listing 7.5), 163
socket programming, 268
sorting text, formatting for
    internationalization, 228
source code (Beans), 134-135
    connecting with events, 137
    creating, 135-136
    customizing, 136-137
    testing, 137-140
    using with, 110-111
    see also listings
sources (event), 20
    event delivery, 27-29
Speech API (future of
    Java), 448
SQL (Structured Query
    Language), 174-175
    COMMIT statement, 175
    DELETE statement,
        174, 177
    INSERT statement,
        174-177
    ROLLBACK statement, 175
    SELECT statement,
        174, 177
    UPDATE statement,
        174, 178
    WHERE clause, 175-176

Star Trek analogy, 254
start( ) method (applets), 7-8
stateless Web connections,
    288-289
Statement class, 183
statements (SQL)
    COMMIT, 175
    DELETE, 174, 177
    INSERT, 174-177
    ROLLBACK, 175
    SELECT, 174, 177
    UPDATE, 174, 178
static initializers, 413
static keyword, 262
status codes
    (HttpServletResponse
    interface), 351
stop( ) method (applets), 8
streams, 256
    InputStream class, 236-237
    ObjectInputStream class,
        258-259
    ObjectOutputStream
        class, 258
    OutputStream class, 257
strings, accessing with native
    code, 434-438
Structured Query Language,
    see SQL
stubs, 274-275
    writing, 275-276
Swing (JFC beta release), 79
    component suite, 81-82
    MVC architecture, 80-81
    pluggable look and feel,
        79-80
    SwingSet sample applica-
        tion, 82-86
SwingSet sample application,
    Swing (JFC beta release),
    82-86
Symantec Web site, 199
symmetric encryption, 375

SysInfo application
    C++ source code for
        (listing 20.3), 417-418
    header file for (listing 20.2),
        416-417
    listing 20.1, 416
system colors (JFC), 75
system data (global program-
    ming), 217

T

tab management (TabPanel
    class), 62-63
tables (databases), 169
TabPanel class, 66-67
    creating, 60-61
    designing, 61
    drawing tabs, 63-66
    listing 3.6, 66-67
    pane management, 61-62
    tab management, 62-63
    testing, 67-69
TabPanePanel class
    (listing 3.5), 62
tabs, drawing (TabPanel
    class), 63-66
TabTest applet (listing 3.7),
    67-68
tags, <APPLET>, 8
    archive attribute, 370
Telephony API (future of
    Java), 448
temporary unavailability
    (servlets), 342
testing
    "appletcations", 15-16
    applets, 9-10
    applications, 12
    Beans in BeanBox test
        container, 131
        BorderPanel Bean,
            131-133
        ImagePanel Bean,
            133-134

Beans in source code, 137-140
BorderPanel class, 53-54
ImagePanel class, 58-59
POP3Reader class, 156-157
SMTPSender class, 162-163
TabPanel class, 67-69
text, formatting for interna-tionalization
boundaries, 228-229
messages, 227-228
sorting, 228
TextEvent class, 27
textValueChanged( ) method (TextEvent class), 27
three-tiered architecture (databases), 172
Timer class (listing 2.2), 33-35
TimerEvent class (listing 2.3), 36
TimerEventMulticaster class (listing 2.4), 37
TimerTest applet (listing 2.5), 38
times and dates, formatting for internationalization, 226-227
TimeZone class, 226
Toolbox window (BeanBox), 125
transactions (databases), 175
transient keyword, 262
transient member variables, 117
transparency (IFC views), 89
transporter beam analogy, 254
trusted applets, 6, 379
trusted code, 249
trusted servlets, 329
two-tiered architecture (databases), 171-172
type libraries, 141

U

U.S. InfoBundle class (listing 10.9), 236
U.S. LabelsBundle class (listing 10.7), 234
UnavailableException (servlets), 341-342
unicast event delivery, compared to multicast, 27-29
UnicastRemoteObject class, 273
unsigned applets, 5
untrusted code, 249
untrusted servlets, 329
UPDATE statement (SQL), 174, 178
URLs (uniform resource locators), 181-183
query strings, 349
RMI (Remote Method Invocation), 271
user data (global program-ming), 217
user interface
address book sample program (JDBC), 199-200
databases, 171
see also application frame-works
utilities
JAR (Java Archive), 365-366
creating JAR files, 368-369
examining JAR files, 366-368
extracting files from JAR files, 369
options, 365-366
rmic, 275-276
serialver, generating version numbers, 264-265

V

variables
instance variables (DBConnector class), 193-194
transient member variables, 117
version numbers, generating, 264-265
versioning serialized objects, 263-265
views
IFC (Internet Foundation Classes), 88-90
MVC architecture, 80
VisiBroker for Java (ORB), 299-301
building CaptialQuery sample application, 303-306
network communications, 310
Visigenic Web site, 302
visual application builder tools
Beans, using with, 109-110
JavaBeans API support for, 108

W-Z

waitForMessage( ) method (listing 7.1), 152-153
Web browsers, CORBA support, 298
Web pages, embedding applets in, 8
Web sites
ActiveX Bridge, 451
Commerce API informa-tion, 445
for database information, 170

EmbeddedJava API
  information, 450
IDL information, 446
Iona Technologies, 302
ISO language codes, 218
Java Developer
  Connection, 83
Java Web Server, 322
JavaBeans Glasgow
  information, 447
JDBC information, 187
JDBC-ODBC bridge
  information, 182
JNDI information, 447
Management API informa-
  tion, 449
Media API
  information, 449
Migration Assistant, 451
ODBC information, 174
OMG (Object Management
  Group), 294
PersonalJava API informa-
  tion, 450
SQL information, 175
Symantec, 199
Visigenic, 302
**WHERE clause (SQL),
  175-176**

**Win32 resource support
  (AFC), 102**
**windowActivated( ) method
  (WindowEvent class), 25**
**windowClosed( ) method
  (WindowEvent class), 25**
**windowClosing( ) method
  (WindowEvent class), 25**
**windowDeactivated( )
  method (WindowEvent
  class), 25**
**windowDeiconified( )
  method (WindowEvent
  class), 25**
WindowEvent class, 25
**windowIconified( ) method
  (WindowEvent class), 25**
**windowOpened( ) method
  (WindowEvent class), 25**
windows
  frame, applications
    compared to applets, 5-6
  IFC (Internet Foundation
    Classes), 91
World Wide Web (WWW)
  object support in, 289
  stateless connections,
    288-289

**WorldExplorer sample
  applet, 229-237**
  actionPerformed( ) method
    (listing 10.6), 234
  init( ) method
    (listing 10.3), 231
  itemStateChanged( )
    method (listing 10.4), 232
  localizeUI( ) method
    (listing 10.5), 233
  member variables
    (listing 10.2), 230
**write( ) method
  (OutputStream class), 257**
**writeExternal( )
  method (Externalizable
  interface), 261**
Writer class, 151-152
writing
  servlets, 351-352
    design, 352-353
    with GET method
      (HTTP), 358
    with POST method
      (HTTP), 353-357
  stubs/skeletons, 275-276

MACMILLAN COMPUTER PUBLISHING USA

A VIACOM COMPANY

Support:

If you need assistance with the information in this book or with a CD/Disk accompanying the book, please access the Knowledge Base on our Web site at **http://www.superlibrary.com/general/support**. Our most Frequently Asked Questions are answered there. If you do not find the answer to your questions on our Web site, you may contact Macmillan Technical Support **(317) 581-3833** or e-mail us at **support@mcp.com**.

Maximum Java 1.1

Glenn Vanderburg, et al.

This fast-paced, expert-level programming guide is the ultimate book for programmers who want to take Java to the next level. Written by Java experts, this must-have resource explores the Java 1.1 language, tools, and core Java API without reviewing fundamentals or basic techniques. It's loaded with in-depth coverage of the most advanced topics.

Maximum Java 1.1 explores advanced applet programming, animation, writing 2-D games, JavaBeans, security, VRML applets, GridBagLayout, and Advanced Event Handling in detail. It also shows how new Java class libraries and frameworks make Java work with client/server systems, relational databases, and persistent object databases. The CD-ROM is packed with source code from the book, Sun's JDK, and a collection of the best Java development tools.

$49.99 USA, $70.95 CAN
ISBN: 1-57521-290-0, 900 pages

Teach Yourself to Create a Home Page in 24 Hours

Rogers Cadenhead

This book is a carefully organized tutorial that is divided into 24 short, one-hour chapters that teach the beginning Web page author what he or she needs to know to make a Web page operational in the shortest time possible.

The quickest and easiest way to learn how to create your own Web pages is with a WYSIWYG editor. No HTML is required! The book steps you through the process using Claris Home Page, a leading Web page editor for novices. The Windows and Macintosh CD-ROM includes a full working copy of Claris Home Page Lite and a collection of examples from the author.

$24.99 USA, $35.95 CAN
ISBN: 1-57521-325-7, 336 pages

Java 1.1 Developer's Guide, Second Edition

Jamie Jaworski

Written by a highly technical and experienced Web programmer, this detailed guide uses many illustrations and examples to show users how to exploit Java to develop real-world applications. It's a must-have resource for experienced Web developers. In this book, you will explore the Java interface, Java in client/server environments, debugging, VRML extensions, network programming, protocol handlers, Java and the World Wide Web, and more!

$49.99 USA, $70.95 CDN
ISBN: 1-57521-283-8, 800 pages

Teach Yourself Netscape 4 Web Publishing in a Week, Second Edition

Wes Tatters and Rafe Coburn

Designed for anyone interested in learning Web publishing, *Teach Yourself Netscape 4 Web Publishing in a Week, Second Edition* is the easiest way to learn how to produce attention-getting, well-designed Web pages for the Netscape 4 environment. This book completely covers new Netscape development features such as JavaScript style sheets, frames, plug-ins, Java 1.1 applets, and JavaScript 1.2. It also teaches how to use the Netscape Composer editor to easily create all kinds of Web pages.

The CD-ROM includes a fully licensed version of Netscape Communicator for Windows 95, Windows 3.1, and Macintosh, plus a variety of additional HTML editing tools, templates, source code, templates, icons, and graphics.

$29.99 USA, $42.95 CDN
ISBN: 1-57521-165-3, 600 pages

Add to Your Sams.net Library Today
with the Best Books for Internet Technologies

ISBN	Quantity	Description of Item	Unit Cost	Total Cost
1-57521-290-0		Maximum Java 1.1 (Book/CD-ROM)	$49.99	
1-57521-325-7		Teach Yourself to Create a Home Page in 24 Hours (Book/CD-ROM)	$24.99	
1-57521-283-8		Java 1.1 Developer's Guide, 2E (Book/CD-ROM)	$49.99	
1-57521-165-3		Teach Yourself Netscape 4 Web Publishing in a Week, 2E (Book/CD-ROM)	$29.99	
		Shipping and Handling: See information below.		
		TOTAL		

Shipping and Handling: $4.00 for the first book, and $1.75 for each additional book. If you need to have it NOW, we can ship product to you in 24 hours for an additional charge of approximately $18.00, and you will receive your item overnight or in two days. Overseas shipping and handling adds $2.00. Prices subject to change. Call between 9:00 a.m. and 5:00 p.m. EST for availability and pricing information on latest editions.

201 W. 103rd Street, Indianapolis, Indiana 46290

1-800-428-5331 — Orders   1-800-835-3202 — FAX   1-800-858-7674 — Customer Service

Book ISBN 1-57521-347-8